Cancelled Earlier

MORMONS AT THE MISSOURI, 1846–1852

MORMONS AT THE MISSOURI, 1846–1852
"AND SHOULD WE DIE . . ."

By Richard E. Bennett

University of Oklahoma Press : Norman and London

F
598
.B46
1987

Publication of this book has been made possible in part by a grant from the Andrew W. Mellon Foundation.

16129488

Library of Congress Cataloging-in-Publication Data

Bennett, Richard Edmond, 1946–
    Mormons at the Missouri, 1846–1852.

    Bibliography: p.   7-18-90
    Includes index.
    1. Mormons—Missouri River Valley—History—19th century. 2. Missouri River Valley—History. I. Title.
F598.B46 1987   977'.02   87-40208
ISBN 0-8061-2086-x (alk. paper)

The paper in this book meets the guidelines for permanence and durability of the Committee on Production Guidelines for Book Longevity of the Council on Library Resources, Inc.

CONTENTS

ILLUSTRATIONS

FIGURE

MAPS

TABLES

ACKNOWLEDGMENTS

This work would not have been possible without the assistance of very supportive and encouraging men and women. To Philip P. Mason, of Wayne State University, and Leonard J. Arrington, of Brigham Young University, I owe a special debt. Professor Mason encouraged me to tackle a demanding subject in the history of the development of the American West. Professor Arrington, the outstanding scholar of Mormon history, has provided me with several research opportunities through the years and provoked my dream of writing on Winter Quarters into reality.

I wish also to pay special thanks to the staff of the Historical Department of The Church of Jesus Christ of Latter-day Saints in Salt Lake City for their valuable, unending assistance and cooperation in making available every published and unpublished source required to do justice to the topic. In particular, I wish to thank search-room supervisor James L. Kimball Jr., for his assistance and kindness. His scholarly insights and archival sense have helped me immeasurably, and his friendship is prized. I also thank the staff in the Archives and Library of the Reorganized Church of Jesus Christ of Latter Day Saints in Independence, Missouri, for their valuable assistance. My sister-in-law, Colinda Dyer Elieson, deserves commendation for her expertise in typing from the beginning drafts through the finished product.

I owe a special debt of gratitude to the University of Manitoba for providing me with the necessary paid study leave and to my colleagues at the Elizabeth Dafoe Library of that university who were kind enough to accommodate my time away.

Finally, and above all, I thank my loyal wife, Patricia, for her joyous companionship, her undeviating support and encouragement, and her own recurring sacrifice of time and talents on my behalf. I freely dedicate this work to her and to our five children, the youngest of whom—David—was born while this work was in labor during our own "winter quarters" in Salt Lake City.

While so many have assisted me, I nevertheless am solely responsible for the contents and the interpretations that characterize this work. I trust it will be a lasting credit to them all.

Winnipeg, Manitoba   RICHARD EDMOND BENNETT

MORMONS AT THE MISSOURI, 1846–1852

And should we die before our journey's through,
Happy day! all is well!
We then are free from toil and sorrow too;
With the just we shall dwell!

—From "Come, Come Ye Saints," by William Clayton

INTRODUCTION

Joseph Smith Jr., the Mormon prophet, and his brother, Hyrum, had been dead scarcely a year when the Latter-day Saints decided to leave their beloved city of Nauvoo, Illinois, and risk their future in the isolated Rocky Mountain West. Joseph Smith's image and impact on the now prophetless church loomed as large in death as it had in life. As one disciple, William W. Phelps, proclaimed, the prophet's murder would preserve the church at America's expense. God would "vex this nation, and all nations, that have rejected and slain his prophets and apostles: Then comes the day of calamity: then passes this bitter cup: then, brethren and sisters, we can laugh at distress and their trouble."

Brigham Young, who assumed leadership over the church as the highest-ranking ecclesiastical figure, reinforced Phelps's tone of urgency and anticipation:

> It is the mind of the Spirit to the Saints scattered abroad throughout this Continent to gather Westward, to the place appointed, for a hiding place to Jacob, yea a home to Israel, while the desolation and wickedness maketh desolate the lands and cities where the voice of prophets have been heard unheeded.

Even if pressure from opponents had never reached intolerable levels, the Mormons would have left Nauvoo eventually. Like mariners fleeing the vortex of a sinking ship, they felt the need to come out of "Babylon" and to put a safe distance between them and God's imminent scourging of America. They sought only time for an orderly departure and to find a hiding place where the church in isolation could catch its breath and become there what every other location had prevented it from being.

It was this spirit of immediacy and escape, born of repeated persecution and opposition, this belief in divine retribution and premillennial expectations that largely colored the tenor of their time and faith. The story of the Latter-day Saints at the Missouri takes place against an ever-changing backdrop of scenery and attitudes in a period of unmatched agitation and disruption. Everything was in transition. Their society, economy, leadership councils, even their doctrines, patterns of worship, and religious practices, were uprooted and distended, transported and reevaluated. And in the process they left a permanent impression on the history of Mormonism and of America.

What had brought them to this impasse? The Church of Jesus Christ of Latter-day Saints, organized in Fayette, New York, on 6 April 1830, sprang into being from the proclaimed visions, revelations, and teachings of Joseph Smith Jr. Based on such religious tenets as Christian primitivism and premillennialism, restoration of divine truths and priesthoods, the Book of Mormon as an ancient American book of scripture, and modern revelation, the church attracted a coterie of enthusiastic followers and flourished for much of the 1830s in Kirtland, Ohio, near present-day Cleveland. An ever-expanding missionary force proselyted along the eastern seaboard, north into Upper Canada, and before the end of the decade in the British Isles, with encouraging success. While at Kirtland they built a temple, refined their organization, and added to their canon of scripture.

At the same time they made repeated unsuccessful efforts to establish the "New Jerusalem" in the "center stake of Zion" proclaimed as Independence, Missouri, which at that time was but a fledgling outfitting town on the Missouri River. Their attempts to headquarter at Independence failed in a climate of overzealousness, misunderstanding, suspicion, and eventual persecution. Missouri refused to accept Mormonism and all that went with it, a rejection most cruelly evident in Governor Lilburn W. Boggs's now-infamous executive order of 1838 to "exterminate" the Mormons (as they were then pejoratively called) and to drive them from the state.

Forced out of Missouri at gunpoint, the Latter-day Saints eventually found a friendly refuge in western Illinois, on the banks of the Mississippi River north of Quincy. Joseph Smith soon called the settlement Nauvoo, "the city beautiful." Founded in 1839, the little river town rapidly became the Mormon capital, home to thousands of converts, and by 1845, it was the largest city in the state. Here another temple, larger and more impressive than the earlier Kirtland edifice, was constructed to accommodate the constantly developing patterns of worship and religious ordinances.

By the time of Joseph Smith's death in June 1844, the practice of plural marriage had established itself amid a handpicked quorum of believers. This, in conjunction with the economic and political jealousies of surrounding Illinois communities, the ongoing bitterness between the Missourians and the Mormons, the Mormon habit of block voting, their clannishness, and their religious fervor, contributed to an atmosphere of mounting tension and instability. Eventually it was determined that the Mormons must be dislodged whatever the cost. Many expected, somewhat naïvely, that the elimination of Joseph and Hyrum Smith would ruin the young church. On the contrary, their deaths seemed to fire the flames of faith. Nevertheless, the "martyrdom" was an unmistakable signal to Mormon leaders that they either leave voluntarily or face an inevitable civil war.

At this juncture, on the eve of a dramatic forced exodus to someplace—anyplace where this peculiar people could practice their religion—this book begins. Though much has been written about the route followed and the leading personalities involved, surprisingly little attention has been paid to the central issues at hand. Largely overlooked in the hurry to get the story to Utah have been such matters as the development of plans, economics, theological and ecclesiastical adaptations and implementations, dealings with the federal government and the Indians, and a host of other bread-and-butter issues. Specific to the present book, the history of Winter Quarters, the interim headquarters of the Mormons from 1846 to 1848 while they were in transit from Illinois to the mountains, has been sadly neglected. Far more attention, for instance, has been devoted to the march of the five-hundred-man Mormon battalion from the Missouri River to California than to the more than ten thousand people left behind at Winter Quarters and in nearby settlements.

What accounts for this omission? Is it because Winter Quarters was, after all, only temporary, a dreary, death-ridden layover on the way to a far more glorious climax "far away in the West"? Or is it because it was an interregnum period, occurring as it did after the death of Joseph Smith and before Brigham Young's ordination as president? The fact that no temple was ever built at Winter Quarters or that few, if any, physical landmarks other than a cemetery now remain may have deterred some inquirers.

Whatever the reasons, scholars are guilty of an incredible disinterest in and an appalling ignorance of the history of the Mormons at Winter Quarters (now Florence, Nebraska) and the events in Iowa leading up to its establishment. Palmyra, New

York, cradle of Mormonism, is revered in song and pageant; Kirtland, Ohio, is ever remembered; Nauvoo is now a restorationist's delight. But Winter Quarters, and its successor, Kanesville (Council Bluffs), Iowa, headquarters of the church for over two years and home to thousands for as long as Nauvoo ever was, have been inexcusably slighted. Far too much happened in the Missouri Valley to be ignored any longer. Here revelations were proclaimed, apostolic supremacy and succession pronounced and made firm, and a battalion raised amid formidable obstacles and opposing attitudes. At Winter Quarters women exercised the priesthood, new patterns of worship were implemented, and plans for the great trek west were solidified. Polygamy and the law of adoption and other new and barely tested doctrines were practiced in the open. And here faith deepened while apostasy flourished. Whatever the causes for this unfortunate oversight, this book is written to fill that void.

The Latter-day Saints were not alone, of course, in looking west for solutions to their problems, for the rest of the country was stirring to the strains of a similar impulse, which a New York City editor first phrased in 1845 as "manifest destiny." It was time again for Americans to expand westward; time to flee the East for the wilds and opportunities of Oregon, California, and Texas; time to prevent any further intrusions on what surely was American soil on the west coast; and time to establish greater trade with the Far East. Florida had just entered the Union (as the twenty-seventh state) in March 1845, and Texas, the "Lone Star Republic," had done the same shortly afterward. James K. Polk had been elected president in 1844 over Henry Clay in large measure because of his commitments to territorial expansion in the West. By 1845 five thousand people were already settled in Oregon. Consciously or unconsciously, and for whatever other reasons, Brigham Young and his band of followers were participating in part of a much larger and relentless American westward movement.

By 1846, America's population, doubling every decade, stood at 20,794,000. That same year foreign immigration reached a new all-time high with 154,000 new arrivals, mostly from Great Britain, a foreshadowing of the millions to come. The United States was experiencing a mild economic recovery from the depression between 1838 and 1843, and would not experience another "boom" until the discovery of gold in California in 1848.

The Nauvoo Temple. Photo no. P 570, reproduced with the permission of the Church Archives, The Church of Jesus Christ of Latter-day Saints.

New advances were being made in science, industry, and agriculture. It was the era of rapid expansion of the nation's railroads, the advent of the telegraph in 1844, and the imminent invention of the sewing machine. America was alive to the notion of discovery and expansion, of overcoming and civilizing the West.

But if territorial expansions were manifest, it was ever a point of debate whether that "peculiar institution" of slavery should be permitted to expand west with the rest of the country. This was also the time of abolitionists and slavery defenders, the Federal Fugitive Slave Law and the Underground Railroad, that tenuous interim between the 1820 Missouri Compromise and the Dred Scott case of 1857, which denied blacks citizenship even in the North and ruled Clay's compromises unconstitutional. Significantly, the same year the Mormons were fleeing Nauvoo for freedom in the West, the U.S. House of Representatives passed the Wilmot Proviso forbidding slavery in any new territories acquired from Mexico during the upcoming campaign against that nation. The slavery issue would fester into civil war just fifteen years later. Whether for rejecting Joseph Smith (as his followers believed) or slavery, the nation would indeed suffer the "calamity" and "distress" that William Phelps and scores of astute statesmen and politicians across the land had been predicting. In 1846, that "year of decision," the country's mood was expansionist, the times unsettling, and the future uncertain.

Having provided this short review, let me add this very personal note with respect to my outlook and interpretation. Though a Latter-day Saint and an avid student of Mormon manuscripts and history, I have tried hard not to be a slave to prejudice or to prate a certain religious interpretation; rather, I have endeavored to be fair. I have tried to tell a true story without consciously making an argument, presenting a case, or establishing a faith.

Since almost every writer of Mormon history has had a difficult time remaining neutral, I have relied very heavily on primary documentation and unpublished manuscripts and have followed those sources wherever they have taken me. They are admittedly primarily Mormon-oriented, since the historical experience described here is overwhelmingly a Mormon one; consequently, my perspective in part reflects that conscious reliance.

As far as possible I have retained original spellings and sentence structure, with only minimal and essential corrections and alterations. Photographs, illustrations, maps, and drawings were selected on the basis of their relevance, authenticity, and interest, some having never before been published.

Finally, let it be clearly understood at the outset that what follows is a story of a religious people in an American wilderness. These people, like many before and after, believed in their faith and in what they were doing. That made all the difference then, and that is what really matters now.

PART ONE

"IT IS NO PLACE FOR THE SAINTS":
THE MORMONS BEGIN LEAVING NAUVOO

> I feel as though Nauvoo will be filled with all manner of abominations. It is no place for the Saints; and the Spirit whispers to me that the brethren had better get away as fast as they can. . . . I hope the brethren will not have trouble there, but the dark clouds of sorrow are gathering fast over that place.[1]

So confided Brigham Young, the Mormon leader, just three weeks after he and his closest advisors secretly abandoned the Mormon capital on the Mississippi River. "Nauvoo—the Beautiful," the "City of Joseph," the "center stake of Zion," and onetime haven for the Latter-day Saints, by the fall of 1845 had become their "prison," a place of persecution fraught with physical danger and increasing apostasy, no longer suitable for whatever future designs Young had in mind for saving the Church of Jesus Christ of Latter-day Saints.

As early as April 1845, Illinois Governor Thomas Ford had advised Mormon leaders to leave the state. Claiming that Joseph Smith prior to his death had told him the Mormons were contemplating moving west, Ford advised Young that "it would be good policy for your people to move to some far distant country. Your religion is new and it surprises the people as any great novelty in religion generally does. I do not foresee the time when you will be permitted to enjoy quiet."[2] Ford merely advised the painfully obvious: leave or be destroyed.

While the summer of 1845 passed fairly harmlessly, September saw the beginning of serious troubles as enemies of the church began setting fires in small settlements outside Nauvoo. In early October these "anti-Mormons" held a series of meetings in Carthage and Quincy, Illinois, and adopted the "Quincy Convention," demanding the removal of the Mormons by May 1846.[3] Later that same month, Governor Ford, fearful of an all-out civil war in Hancock County, ordered a peacekeeping army to the Nauvoo area to at best postpone what he foresaw as inevitable widescale violence.

But Young, the forty-four-year-old interim head of the church by right of his position as senior member of the Quorum of the Twelve Apostles, did not need Governor Ford or anyone else to convince him of the gravity of the situation. He feared the impending catastrophe and had concluded early on that the "Saints" must seek a new refuge in total isolation. In an October 1845 letter to Wilford Woodruff, then in England, Young had confided that "they have told us plainly that the prejudice of the people are such that the state cannot posably protect us and that it is therefore advisable for us to remove as the only conditions of peace. We have determined," he concluded, "to do so in the Spring,"[4]

Irene Hascall, a young woman living in Nauvoo, reported on the worsening situation. "The [T]welve have issued a proclamation that if they will let them alone this winter . . . and do what they can to prepare us for journeying, all that follow the [T]welve will go where they will not trouble [the] United States with Mormon religion. . . . I think probably they will cross the Rocky Mountains to a healthier climate."[5]

A spring 1846 exodus had been determined at least as early as 28 August 1845 when authorities decided "that 3,000 able-bodied men should be selected to prepare themselves to start in the spring to Upper California, taking their families with them."[6] By 9 September, that number had been cut in half.[7] At the October conference of the church, which convened in the completed portions of the Nauvoo Temple, some five thousand of the faithful listened to detailed plans and timetables for the spring evacuation. William Huntington, a member of the Nauvoo High Council, recorded that "the Church resolved to leave Nauvoo and seek a resting place westward wherever God would lead them."[8] Abiding by the wishes of church leaders, many heads of household promised to consecrate their properties, possessions, and energies to the church, not only to leave with their own families but also to assist in every way the exodus of the many widowed, infirm, and destitute among them. This "Nauvoo Covenant," as it was called, was prerequisite to the successful completion of their departure plans, and Young would hold them to it.[9]

Further evidence of their determination to leave was the formation of four companies of one hundred families each, the first being "the Twelve's company" to consist of the twelve apostles, other lower-level church leaders, and their families.[10] In turn, twenty-one more companies were established with captains assigned to organize, outfit, and supervise all departure preparations for his particular company.[11] With each family averaging better than five people, this October scheme would have accommodated 12,500 souls—roughly two-thirds of Nauvoo's estimated population of 17,000.[12]

Through the fall of 1845, Nauvoo was alive with preparations. "Nearly every man was some kind of a mechanic to build wagons," one woman remembered, "and the whole mind of the people was engaged in the great work of emigrating west in the Spring."[13] "Nearly every work-shop in the city has been converted into a wagon maker's shop," another reporter observed. "Even an unfinished portion of the Temple is thus used, and every machine appears to be employed in making, repairing, or finishing wagons, or other articles necessary for the trips." By the end of the year three thousand families had been organized, with two thousand wagons either completed or in the late stages of construction.[14] And by January the Nauvoo High Council could state unequivocally that at least church leaders would begin leaving "some time in March."[15] Most others anticipated leaving shortly after the completion of the temple scheduled for April or May, also in time to meet the Quincy Convention deadline.[16]

But if their timetable was clear, their intended place of refuge was not. The matter was addressed in such vague, ambivalent, even contradictory terms that the church leadership seemed not to have made a definite decision before leaving Nauvoo. Before his death, Joseph Smith had anticipated impending persecutions and had predicted a westward migration for the church—or at least for some of it. Anson Call, as early as 1842, reported that Joseph Smith had said "the Saints would continue to suffer much affliction and would be driven to the Rocky Mountains" and that some then in Nauvoo would "go and assist in making settlements and build cities and see the saints become a mighty people in the midst of the Rocky Mountains."[17] Orson Pratt and Heber C. Kimball, when halfway across Iowa, remembered that "the Prophet had this mission in contemplation, viz., to find a location west of the Rocky Mountains," and that "whenever Joseph spoke on that subject, he proposed to send a company of young men as pioneers to seek a location."[18] As late as February 1844, Joseph

Smith had instructed the apostles "to send out a delegation and investigate the location of California and Oregon, and hunt out a good location, where we can remove to after the temple is completed and where we can build a city in a day, and have a government of our own, [and] get up into the mountains, where the devil cannot dig us out."[19] Although many men volunteered for the expedition, Nauvoo's worsening social and political climate throttled the plan.[20]

Even if Governor Ford had overheard Joseph Smith projecting a move west,[21] the fact remains that if he ever did anticipate it, he referred to it only in vague, obscure generalities without ever specifying a timetable or particular place of settlement.[22] And while some contend that Young had decided on the valley of the Great Salt Lake before leaving Nauvoo, the fact is that he spoke only vaguely about it, and oftentimes in the most misleading of terms, perhaps deliberately so as to confuse and bewilder his enemies. For several months, Mormon leaders had been studying John C. Frémont's trans-Missouri maps and expeditionary reports of 1842 and 1843 as well as other works on the Rocky Mountain region, which may have led them to consider seriously the Great Salt Lake Valley but not necessarily to decide on it.[23] In letters to Wilford Woodruff, Young indicated they would head west of the Rocky Mountains to the area of the "Bay of St. Francisquo" and of Vancouver Island, or, in other words, somewhere in the vast area of "Upper California" covering almost all of the west coast.[24] And in a letter to another apostle, Orson Hyde, Young merely said, "it will be over the Mountains, but to define the spot we cannot at present."[25]

Yet regardless of where they would eventually locate "Zion," and whether his plan owed anything to Joseph Smith, Young was determined to leave Nauvoo as quickly as possible. They would leave to find a new home "in some good valley in the neighborhood of the Rocky Mountains" where they could worship without persecution and where they would "infringe upon no one, and not be likely to be infringed upon."[26] Only as the Saints moved westward and gleaned more solid, on-site information from fur traders, mountain men, and Jesuit fathers, did the answers crystallize. And even after later conferences with these knowledgeable men, the most specific Young could be was "to go to the Bear River Valley, Great Basin, or Salt Lake."[27] For the present, the exodus and their preservation as a church and as a people were their primary concerns.

Wagon building, however, was not the only matter that preoccupied Nauvoo's citizenry during the turbulent fall of 1845, for it also marked a time of intense religious activity and a flowering of some of Mormonism's most unique theology and practice. For almost five years the Mormons had been constructing the majestic Nauvoo Temple on the crown of the hill overlooking the Mississippi. Made of white limestone and erected at what was then an enormous cost of several hundred thousand dollars, it measured 128 feet east and west, 80 feet north and south, and 60 feet high, with the tower and spire rising an additional 98 ½ feet.[28] At the time of its completion in May 1846 (although many of the interior rooms were never completely finished), it was the largest structure north of St. Louis and west of Chicago. Tragically, they were now about to leave it. But before doing so, many longed to participate in what they believed to be sacred saving ordinances both for themselves and their kindred dead, ordinances such as celestial marriage, baptisms for the dead, family sealings and adoptions, and other ceremonies that could be performed only in the "House of the Lord."[29] Though this work took precious time, they would not be denied what they had prepared for and anticipated so long.

Consequently, temple work began in Nauvoo on 10 December 1845 and continued night and day until late January. Many worked in the temple in one capacity or another from early in the morning until past ten at night, since it was intended that "every worthy man" and woman should receive his or her endowment. The endowment, then, was to the believing and worthy Latter-day Saints, a spiritual climax, a reward for their labors, a commitment to church leadership, and a prerequisite spiritual preparation for the impending struggles ahead.

Had the temple been completed sooner, the exodus would have begun that much earlier. "The main and only cause of our tarrying so long," admitted Young, "was to give the brethren those blessings in the Temple, for which they have labored so diligently and faithfully to build, and as soon as it was prepared, we labored incessantly almost night and day to wait on them until a few days prior to our departure."[30]

Temple work was also an opportunity for Young to demonstrate that what Joseph Smith had begun, he would fulfill, a point of rich significance in the heated and on-going debate over succession and the future of the movement. He knew, as did most other thinking people, that until a new headquarters was established, the church itself was in a vulnerable position. Instability and uncertainty would breed insecurity among members, especially new converts, and missionary work invariably must be postponed. It was, as he said, "the salvation of the Church," somewhere in the West where a standard could be raised, another temple reared, and a firm, conspicuous gathering place organized, that motivated their plans. Until these goals were attained, the church was in an exposed and precarious position. And the tragic spectacle of groping in the wilderness would prove good ammunition for opposing sects and contenders for the leadership of the church.[31]

Clearly Mormonism was in a crisis and had been so since Joseph Smith's death. While most of the membership accepted the Quorum of the Twelve Apostles as the interim leadership of the church with Young as its head, just which man should eventually obtain the presidency was to many unclear.[32] Several claimed Smith's mantle. Sidney Rigdon, first counselor in the First Presidency from 1833 to 1844, had returned to Nauvoo in August 1844 and presented his credentials to be "guardian" of the church, but attracted the allegiance of only a mere handful of followers.[33] William Parker was using peepstones and impersonating religious leaders to induce belief in his claims.[34] Several, including Lyman Wight, who in March 1845 had led a company of some one hundred fifty to southern Texas on a mission he claimed had been commissioned by Smith, maintained that the rightful heir to the presidency was Joseph Smith III, oldest son of Joseph, who was then only thirteen years old.[35]

But by early 1846 these claims were minor threats compared to that of James J. Strang and his advocates. Strang, baptized by Smith just months before his death, had persuaded many that he was the legitimate successor, and to prove it, publicly proclaimed a vision in which Smith supposedly ordained him to establish the church in Wisconsin. Strang soon published revelations, claimed the discovery of another book of ancient scripture (The Book of the Law of the Lord), established a church in Voree, Wisconsin, and later fled to Beaver Island in northern Lake Michigan.[36]

Strang's excesses eventually led to his murder in 1856 and the subsequent loss of most of his followers, but in late 1845 "Strangism" was a strong contender and a very real threat to Young's efforts to move the church west. Several outstanding leaders and personalities were going with Strang, including William Marks, former president of the Nauvoo stake, John E. Page, an apostle until his excommunication in February 1846, William Smith, Joseph's younger brother and former member of the Quorum of the Twelve, Lucy Mack Smith, Joseph's aging mother, Judge George H. Adams, and William McLellen.

Why Strang was making serious inroads is not difficult to understand. Contrasting dramatically with Young's pragmatism and deliberateness was Strang's charismatic personality reminding many of Joseph Smith. Many took comfort in his allegiance to the Book of Mormon and several early Mormon doctrines, and unlike the empty claim of Sidney Rigdon, Strang had established a formally organized church with an accelerating, far-reaching missionary effort directly aimed at Mormon branches in America and England.[37] Contributing even more to its initial popularity was its antipolygamy stance. Polygamy, though practiced on a small scale by many in the church hierarchy since 1843, had been publicly denied mainly out of fear of inciting public hostility.[38] While some were opposed to polygamy on theological and moral grounds, others found it hard to reconcile private performance with its public denial.[39] Gilbert Watson, for one, observed that polygamy "was taught confidentially to strangers by brethren and sisters who had remained long enough in the city to become indoctrinated therein. Yet this system was publicly proclaimed against on the stand by the authorities."[40] Lastly, some like the former mayor of Nauvoo and counselor in the First Presidency, John C. Bennett, were still smarting from public rebuke, chastisement, and excommunication on the grounds of immorality and other alleged moral infractions and may have joined Strang to get back at the Twelve. Until Strang himself was found secretly practicing and condoning polygamy some years later, his antipolygamist disciples formed the backbone of his society.

Strangite missionaries unquestionably enjoyed considerable success at Young's expense. Writing in January 1846, Isaac Paden, president of a small Mormon congregation in Knoxville, Illinois, northeast of Nauvoo, told of how "the principle part" of his branch had recently become disaffected. "Many of them are filled with the notion that J. Strang is the man to lead the Church. . . . I am convinced that Strang under the present situation of the Church will cause the greatest split that ever has been made."[41] Soon afterwards, fulfilling his own prediction, Paden himself become disillusioned and left the church.[42]

On 8 February, William Huntington in describing the last days of Nauvoo, said it was "a *solemn* time . . . ever to be remembered. Many were backing out, leaving the Church and following a false prophet by the name of *Strang*."[43] When Wilford Woodruff returned to Nauvoo in April from his mission to England, he was appalled at the success Strangism was having in the former Mormon capital.[44] Little wonder Orson Hyde, the apostle charged with overseeing the church in Nauvoo during Young's absence complained, "It is no very desirable job to stay where hell boils over every breeze that blows."[45]

Despite Young's efforts to defuse and minimize Strang's inroads (at one point he told Hyde to "let Strangism alone it is not worth the skin of a flea"), Strang converted some three to four thousand people before he was through, and Young could not overlook the impact.[46] In fact, some of his own leaders and most effective trailblazers would soon be casting their lot with Strang. As long as the church had no resting place, it was in an exposed and dangerous situation, a transient flock in search of higher ground.[47]

Thus despite the importance of temple work, a lengthy postponement of departure was out of the question. Other compelling matters, bred out of fear, rumor, and suspicion, were also at work. For one, there was the almost universal fear in Mormon circles that a U.S. army would suddenly appear on their doorsteps to interrupt their intended march, a fear not entirely without justification. Certainly many migrants then moving west or shortly about to do so suspected the Mormon cause.[48] Between 1843 and 1846 traffic over the Oregon and California trails mushroomed from an estimated 1,100 travellers to 8,000. Fifteen thousand were preparing to leave in 1847, and 1848 would see another 19,000 out on the trail.[49] Many of these overlanders were from Missouri and Illinois and were antagonistic towards everything the Latter-day Saints represented. No one more perfectly personified that hostility than former Missouri Governor Lilburn W. Boggs, who himself would be California-bound in April 1846. The Mormons despised and condemned Boggs for his 1838 "extermination" order to expel them from Missouri, while in return Boggs blamed the Mormons for an unsuccessful attempt on his life in 1842.[50]

As early as the spring of 1846, some Oregon trains were avoiding travel altogether on the north side of the Platte River because of rumors that five thousand heavily armed Mormons were marching westward intent on murdering emigrants and confiscating property.[51] And for various reasons, not the least of which were prior discussions between Latter-day Saints and disgruntled Indians,[52] rumor had it that the Mormons would incite Indians against the migrating parties.[53]

Francis Parkman, who in 1846 was on the plains to describe firsthand Indian life-styles and traditions, captured the intense anti-Mormon feelings of many on the trails. "No one could predict what would be the result when large armed bodies of these fanatics should encounter the most impetuous and reckless of their old enemies on the prairie."[54] Such animosities would harden as the Mormons made their way west, but by February 1846 there were already enough complaints against them that the War Department and Office of Indian Affairs were genuinely concerned.

To complicate matters further, the Oregon question was not yet settled with Britain, nor would it be until June 1846 when negotiations finally guaranteed modern Oregon for the American republic. In the meantime, war with Britain was a very real possibility.[55] Similarly, California, New Mexico, and most of the continent west and south of the Missouri River were under Mexican control, and armed conflict with Mexico was imminent.

Add to this mix Young's unclear intentions and vague statements of a final destination and it is little wonder Washington was concerned.[56] As already noted, Young seemed publicly ambivalent on the issue: In one letter it was Vancouver Island, in another San Francisco, and in a third the Great Basin. And it was public knowledge that Samuel Brannan, acting under Young's instructions, had earlier departed New York with a shipload of 235 Mormons bound for Yerba Buena (San Francisco).[57] Whether practicing deliberate evasiveness or trying to keep open his options for as long as he could, Young did succeed in raising official concern.

Nonetheless, it would be a mistake to conclude that he wanted to breed excessive fear and suspicion. Quite the contrary, for he was seeking government support of his endeavors, not its intervention. It was a perilously fine line which only the shrewdest could walk. Indeed, in late January 1846, just days before the exodus began, Young dispatched his personal emissary, Jesse C. Little, to court President Polk's favor and to attract lucrative government contracts by offering to build forts and bridges and to serve in the army against either Great Britain or Mexico, if necessary. Little's instructions were that "if our government shall offer any facilities for emigrating to the Western coast, embrace those facilities, if possible."[58]

But until Young was satisfied that Polk would sympathize with his offer and believe his intentions, he could not be entirely confident that his political enemies (especially those from Missouri) were not outmaneuvering him and planning some sort of disturbance or impediment, either at the Mississippi or some remote place along the western trek. As late as December 1845, Governor Ford had been hinting that "it is very likely that the Government at Washington will interfere to prevent the Mormons from going west of the rocky mountains," concluding that "many intelligent persons sincerely believe that they [the Mormons] will join the British if they go there, and be more trouble than ever."[59] Nor was Ford the only bearer of bad news, for Sam Brannan himself hurriedly dispatched the following warning in early January from New York harbor:

> I have received positive information that it is the intention of the Government, to disarm you, after you have taken up your line of march in the spring, on the ground of the law of nations or the treaty existing between the United States and Mexico, "that an armed force of men shall not be allowed to invade the territory of a foreign nation."[60]

Just how much Brannan's informants really knew and what measure of credence Mormon leaders put in his warnings may never be known. But upon receiving Brannan's communication just three days after dispatching Little to Washington, a worried Young confided, "We ask God our Heavenly Father to exert his power in our deliverance that we may be preserved to establish truth upon all the face of the earth."[61]

Accelerating matters even further were more immediate threats of arrest and assassination. Church leaders were constantly sought after on one charge or another during the fall of 1845.[62] Most writs were for the arrest of Young and other of Joseph Smith's accomplices in connection with the destruction of the *Nauvoo Expositor* newspaper just prior to the murders of Joseph and Hyrum Smith.

At a secret meeting held in the attic of the temple on 10 January, members of the Council of Fifty, an advisory body Smith established to give counsel on political and civic affairs, discussed

Brigham Young when he was about forty-eight years of age. Reproduced with permission from the Church Archives, The Church of Jesus Christ of Latter-day Saints.

"the subject of leaving this place . . . the time, when, etc. Trouble was near at hand, was the decided opinion of the Council." [63] "If you should tarry," Joseph L. Heywood advised, "your safety would be greatly endangered." He recommended a speedy departure "with a cavalcade of one thousand armed men" to discourage obstructions, for "the enemy knows the only way in which they can get up a row, and that is by attempting arrest." [64]

Nor was anyone dismissing lightly the fear of assassinations, especially in light of Edmund Durphy's murder the preceding

The Exodus from Nauvoo. First printed in T. B. H. Stenhouse, *The Rocky Mountain Saints: A Full and Complete History of the Mormons.*

month.[65] There were enough anti-Mormons, disaffected members, and apostates around to take every rumor seriously. Confided Young in a diary note of 18 January:

> A meeting of the Captains of emigrating companies was held in the attic atory of the Temple, to ascertain the number ready and willing to start should necessity compel our instant removal, being aware that evil is intended towards us, and that our safety alone will depend upon our departure from this place, before our enemies shall intercept and prevent our going.[66]

Mormon leaders further believed that their earlier-than-anticipated departure would go far to prove their genuine intent and possibly free the rest of their Nauvoo followers from harassment, pillaging, crop burnings, and other problems.[67] By easing tensions, the temple could be finished, properties sold at better prices, and travel preparations completed.[68] Young felt compelled to buy time and forbearance, for he must have known that many of the poor and those just then arriving from distant branches of the church could not possibly be prepared and out of the city by the Quincy Convention's May deadline.

Faced then with the prospects of imminent arrest, assassina-

tion attempts, possible federal intervention, and an increasing
tempo of defection and apostasy, the "Company of the Twelve"
decided once and for all to terminate temple work and depart
quickly and quietly weeks before their March departure date.
On 26 January 1846, three days after Hosea Stout's assassination
warnings, another council was held, and the captains of companies "were ordered to warn all who had voluntered to stand as
minute-men to be in readiness." The next day all temple work
ceased, and by Friday "all was in suspense expecting every moment to have a start."[69]

On Sunday, 2 February, the Twelve Apostles, the recently
appointed trustees (John S. Fullmer, Joseph L. Heywood, and
Almon W. Babbitt) charged with the unenviable task of remaining behind to sell off all church and some private properties, and
a few select others met in private and decided to be ready to depart within four hours' notice and "let everything for the journey be in readiness," for, as Young noted, "if we are here many
days our way will be hedged up."[70] Two days later, Tuesday, 9
February 1846, the first of the advance company began quietly
crossing the frozen Mississippi, settling temporarily at Sugar
Creek, Iowa Territory, some nine miles away.

This, then, approximates the confused state of affairs in February 1846, when Mormon leaders stood poised, ready to move, if
necessary, with all requisite haste to escape whatever the church's
enemies might send against it. Uppermost in Young's mind was
a quick passage to the mountains. What he and those around
him underestimated, however, were the trials of the ensuing
march and the desire of his followers not to be left behind but to
go west with the Twelve, escape the persecutions, and assist
in securing a new mountain home. Young may have been able
to flee from his enemies, but he would never get away from his
own people.

2

THE MORMON TREK ACROSS IOWA

The desperate situation the departing Mormons faced at Sugar Creek, Iowa Territory, cannot be underestimated, for now there was absolutely no turning back. Though they would rather die in the wilderness than be killed in the streets of Nauvoo, unanswered questions taxed the faith and imagination of most everyone. *Where* were they going? *What* route would they take to get there? *How* would so large a population move within such time constraints over vast distances and in unfavorable winter weather?[1]

Plans were as desperate as circumstances and not at all certain to succeed. They depended on total sacrifice, compliance, good weather, noninterference by either friend or foe, and effective organization. As soon as the advanced company could assemble on the Iowa side of the Mississippi, it would be divided "so that a part of it might cross the mountains to the Great Basin soon enough to plant in the spring." An "express" of some three hundred able-bodied men would be selected to "go forward from the camp, leaving their families somewhere on the road, so as to travel with all speed."[2] Once a new home was established and life-sustaining crops planted, teams would return to bring on the families left in the wilderness. Meanwhile the thousands left in Nauvoo could set out directly and in better weather for their new home late in the spring.

A quick getaway from Nauvoo was doomed from the beginning. Just getting out of the city proved much more difficult than anyone had anticipated, and then assembling eighteen hundred people in some four hundred wagons in the dead of winter was no easy task.[3] The bitterly cold subzero temperatures in early February froze many in their tracks and discouraged all but the most hardy.[4] Invariably there were postponements, arguments over who should go in this first company, personal effects that had to be retrieved, broken and frozen equipment, sicknesses, last-minute unattended details, and a seemingly never-ending string of unsolved problems and concerns. Some were in camp by 4 February; others could not possibly make it for another three weeks. The press of private and church business prevented even Young's departure until 15 February and required his return to Nauvoo at least once within the month.[5]

Uncooperative and unpredictable weather further delayed them. Earlier in the month, the Mississippi River had completely frozen over, providing a quick and easy crossing for heavily loaded wagons, cattle, sheep, and other animals.[6]

Many took advantage of the circumstances, interpreting it as a divine favor. Yet by the end of the month, moderate temperatures had caused the river ice to break up and flow in large, dangerous chunks where before a solid sheet had formed a highway. Amasa Lyman, who departed Nauvoo on 23 February, "Found the ice running the river so it was impossible to cross that night except in a skiff which [he] succeeded in doing with great difficulty."[7] Orson Pratt said that many were detained on the Illinois side because of the ice flows on the Mississippi.[8] To transport large numbers of wagons, provisions, livestock, and other necessities by ferry across the Mississippi under the best of conditions was both time consuming and dangerous; to do so amid jagged, fast-moving ice flows, proved a formidable challenge.

Contributing to an extended stay at Sugar Creek were lengthy deliberations over which route to follow across Iowa Territory to the Missouri River. With one eye on Nauvoo and the other on the Far West, authorities underestimated the difficulties in the Iowa crossing. Evidence suggests they had only the fuzziest idea of what route to follow across Iowa.[9] Ezra T. Benson observed, "We crossed the Mississippi River leaving our beautiful city and Temple, not knowing where we should go."[10] Clara Decker Young said that theirs was an "uncertain pilgrimage" and that they "didn't know where they were going, only that it was across the plains."[11] Brigham Young later admitted that at the time of crossing the Mississippi, he did not know "whither they were going."[12]

Not surprising then, the last week to ten days at Sugar Creek were largely dominated by discussion of travel plans.[13] Several men in camp possessed considerable knowledge of Iowa: Bishop George Miller, in company with John A. Mikesell, had scouted ninety miles up the Des Moines River in the summer of 1840 on assignment from Joseph Smith to find a suitable place "for establishing and building up a stake or branch of the church."[14] In

Handwritten entry from the Horace K. Whitney Journal, 15–18 February 1846. At the time, Whitney was twenty-two years old. Reproduced with permission from the Church Archives, The Church of Jesus Christ of Latter-day Saints, Horace K. Whitney Collection.

Sugar Creek

From an oil-on-canvas painting of the Sugar Creek encampment about 1885 by C. C. A. Christensen. By permission of Ethel T. Christensen and with the assistance of the Museum of Church History and Art, The Church of Jesus Christ of Latter-day Saints.

July and August 1843, Jonathan Dunham had travelled all across Iowa as far west as the Missouri River, preaching to various Indian tribes along the way.[15] And in 1845, Henry G. Sherwood, former Nauvoo city marshall, and Joseph L. Heywood had travelled by horseback northwest across Iowa to visit James Emmett's settlement, at that time camped in the Vermillion River country.[16]

Three of these men, Miller, Dunham, and Sherwood, were at Sugar Creek, and at least two, Miller and Sherwood, actively participated in making travel plans. Several councils were convened, apparently without agreement. Bishop Miller grew frustrated with the delays and changes in plans and found himself increasingly critical of Young's style of leadership and personality. "While we were camped on Sugar Creek" he complained, "there was hardly a night without a council, and quite as many changes of plans as councils. . . . We had repeated delays, from causes that I could not understand."[17]

But understanding Iowa was precisely the difficulty, since the Iowa of 1846 posed a formidable challenge to any would-be overlander. Ever since the Black Hawk Indian War of 1830–32, eastern Iowa had been open to settlement. In 1838, it separated from Wisconsin and became a relatively small territory. From 1838 to 1846, its population had tripled from 30,000 to 96,000, most of whom were settlers clustered in the eastern counties along the Mississippi and Des Moines rivers. Although the lines of settlement were advancing inexorably westward onto newly acquired parcels of land the federal government purchased from retreating Indians, the population remained sparse.[18] Even the border with Missouri was ill defined.

Consequently roads leading westward in 1846 were few and of poor quality. In 1839 a federal highway or "agency road" opened from the Mississippi northwestward to the Sac and Fox Indian agency near Ottumwa on the Des Moines River. Along this route sprang a number of river communities the Mormons would pass through. But beyond these frontier settlements, in southeast and southcentral Iowa as far as the Knoxville meridian, or Red Rock line, in central Iowa, farms and fledgling, intermittent settlements were connected by the poorest of roads, more aptly described as surveyed trails. Travel was best either in the coldest parts of the winter by sled or in the dry summer after the spring rains. Beyond Appanoose and Wayne counties in southcentral Iowa and sprawling west to the Missouri River stretched a vast, unsurveyed, trackless wilderness.[19]

Understandably, then, the Mormons deliberated at length on the matter. Finally on 23 February 1846, the Twelve Apostles and captains of hundreds, tentatively agreed "to pass up the divide between the waters of the Des Moines and Missouri rivers."[20] This initial plan called for moving northwest along the so-called Farmington road to Bonaparte, where they planned to cross the Des Moines River "before the ice brakes up."[21] This had the dual advantage of an easy crossing of the Des Moines River and of remaining close to settled communities and farm lands which, as John D. Lee recorded, "would afford us opportunity of purchasing feed for both ourselves and teams."[22] At the same time scouts, such as Stephen Markham and George Miller, were "to go ahead and learn the best routes," and in this way, mile by mile and by trial and error, they would follow the river road through Farmington, Bonaparte, Bentonsport, and Keosauqua before striking more due westerly.[23] If all went according to plan, they would reach the Missouri River by mid-April, plant small acreages along the way for those coming behind, establish a portion of the camps somewhere west of the Missouri as a farm or way station for later traders, and "dispatch a swift company across the mountains with seeds for a spring crop."[24]

Knowing precisely what their travel plans were and where eventually they would cross the Missouri River was also important to those left behind in Nauvoo, where many were exploring the feasibility of chartering a steamboat for Council Bluffs or some other rendezvous spot on the Missouri River. Orson Hyde believed that many of the sick and infirm would be better served by water transport than overland travel. Hyde told the Nauvoo faithful to wait until an April conference "when we shall probably hear something more definite in regards to the matter."[25] Near the end of March, Hyde, anxious for clarification, asked Young, "Tell me where the first settlement will be made, if you can, and at what place property and people shall land on the Missouri River.'[26] Clearly, then, while at Sugar Creek, authorities had chosen neither a Missouri River crossing point nor the precise overland route to get there.

Finally, in addition to the weather, logistical difficulties, and sketchy travel plans, disorganization left much of the carefully orchestrated plan of departure from Nauvoo in tatters. Scores of company captains were opting to go with the advanced company, swelling it far beyond expectations. The originally conceived "Company of the Twelve" was now an overgrown amalgam of winter refugees. Desperately needed were new appointments, a redistribution of manpower, and an immediate census to determine just who was there, the availability of provisions, and the number and nature of livestock in camp.

Young, by now sustained as "President of the Camp of Israel," assembled the camp together on 17 February and organized it along military lines with captains over companies of tens, fifties, and hundreds.[27] "It will not do to start off helter-skelter without order and decorum," he said, calling for patience, obedience, and cooperation.[28] Each company was to have a clerk, an historian, and two commissaries. The latter were assigned to contact settlers and negotiate for food and provender and to distribute provisions fairly among the company. At least four companies, each approximating one hundred families, were organized: Brigham Young's, Heber C. Kimball's, George A. Smith's, and Amasa Lyman's.[29] Families assigned to one company were expected to remain in and report to that subdivision.

So it was that the Mormon pioneers, numbering over two

thousand by the end of February, waited and shivered in the snows of Sugar Creek.[30] On the eve of their departure, Young wrote James Clark, territorial governor of Iowa, announcing their intentions and seeking his sympathetic understanding of their plight. Young was particularly anxious for permission to make temporary farms in Iowa, if necessary, "in the settled or unsettled parts," in order to facilitate the exile.[31]

On 1 March 1846, over three weeks after the first crossing of the Mississippi, the "Camp of Israel" began moving west. Their objective was to reach the Missouri by mid-April. However, a few days of hard travel demolished the best laid plans, uncovering the harsh reality that most were more enthused than prepared for such an arduous journey. Everyone in the advanced company had been expected to come prepared with a year's provisions and all the necessities for extended travel. The well advised came with a solidly built wagon, a harness, a dependable team of horses or oxen, some cows, a thousand pounds of flour, a hundred pounds of sugar, farming and mechanical tools, cooking utensils, seeds, clothing, a musket, and other necessities.[32] But Young later lamented that "eight hundred men had reported themselves without a fortnight's provisions" and because of it were feeding off the supplies of the Twelve and others in the camp.[33] Consequently, they were soon interrupting the journey by seeking work on farms along the route, splitting rails, building barns and bridges, clearing acreages, and "whatever else offered itself" to pay for food and provisions.[34]

Helen Mar Kimball Whitney, daughter of Heber C. Kimball, noted that, "In that first exodus" there was such a determination to migrate with the first company that "hundreds started without the necessary outfit. They could neither procure sufficient teams nor provisions, which retarded our progress, and was the cause of a greater amount of suffering than there would otherwise have been. And my father," she recalled, "in speaking of it said, under the circumstances it would take years to reach the mountains."[35]

In defense of the unprepared, many were victims of circumstances beyond their control. Some had been requested to leave before sufficiently ready, while others were property rich but provision poor, having been unsuccessful in selling their Nauvoo holdings. For many the only way open lay in consigning their lands to the church—specifically the trustees left behind—and on such credit borrowing a "Church team" until their properties were sold. An estimated half of the 400 teams in camp were public property, i.e., church owned.[36]

In contrast, a few found themselves overly prepared and far too heavily loaded, a common problem with emigrants unfamiliar with the rigors of extended wagon travel in the West. Wrote Willard Richards after only nine days on the trail, "Do not take a 1,000 useless things when you start, to overload your teams. 1,000–1,200 [lb] is a good load for one team on a long journey. I gave away 4 or 500 lbs of flour to lighten my loads."[37]

While some were either over or under prepared, others came without the correct provisions. Flour, in its unprocessed state, was not as durable a food as parched corn, biscuits, crackers, and other breadstuffs, and was too susceptible to rapid spoilage and loss, especially in wet weather. Ironically, by the end of March, camp leaders were counseling those coming behind to bring more cash, household wares, and less bulky provisions. "Crockery, iron ware, light chairs, light stands, clocks, not forgetting all such kind of light valuable articles . . . about their houses" were recommended for bartering purposes.[38]

With men on the job instead of in the wagons, progress was painfully slow, which largely explains why most of the camp tarried another three weeks at Richardson's Point (near present-day Bloomfield) only fifty-six miles from Nauvoo. With many opting to stay behind, the main camp inched ahead along the north bank of the Fox River before veering to the southwest, stopping temporarily at the Chariton River and Shoal and Locust creeks in disputed borderlands between Iowa and Missouri.[39]

As the Mormons advanced beyond the more settled areas, detours for food and labor became more difficult and time-consuming. Several commissaries and traders travelled incognito far into northern Missouri to seek provisions from anti-Mormon farmers and settlers, some of whom had participated in driving the Latter-day Saints from the state just eight years before. Not surprisingly, the cost of provisions increased the further west they travelled. Corn that had sold for 12 to 15 cents per bushel along the Des Moines doubled in cost beyond the Chariton River.

The task of controlling so many people in such unfavorable circumstances was almost overwhelming. On leaving Sugar Creek, Young indicated that when he intended to call together the entire camp, he would raise a white flag, and when only the captains of companies, a blue one. But blue and white flags notwithstanding, by late March it had become obvious that camp or-

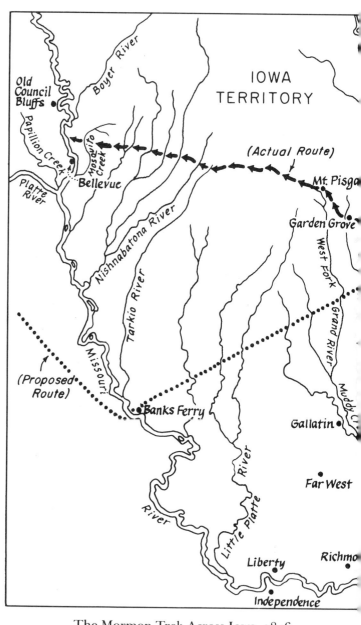

The Mormon Trek Across Iowa, 1846

SOURCE: J. N. Nicollet's *Report Intended to Illustrate a Map of the Hydrographical Basin of the Upper Mississippi River*, 28th

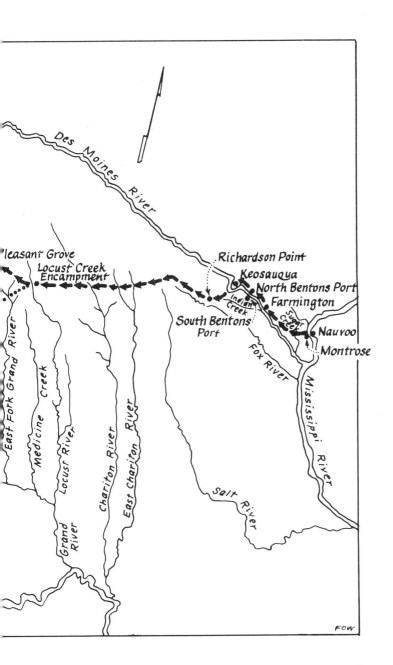

Cong., 2d sess., H. Doc. 52. The route markings superimposed, actual and proposed, are derived from manuscript sources.

ganization and manner of travel were too loose and unmanageable and were impeding rather than contributing to progress. Instead of rolling out in single file and staying in close proximity to one another, wagons often scattered fan-like for miles across the Iowa landscape, particularly west of the Des Moines River. Some were off exploring with Miller and the Pratt brothers while others were busy in some settlement or farm. Men on horseback were kept busy just carrying dispatches between separated companies. The entire camp never once reassembled for Sunday worship for over eight weeks.

Driven to exasperation by these setbacks and by the adventurous, independent, and competitive spirit of Bishop Miller and others like him, Young demanded stricter obedience and cooperation. His pent-up frustration finally vented itself in a dispatch written on 26 March from the Chariton River to Bishop Miller, Parley Pratt, and Orson Pratt:

> We have found to our entire satisfaction that the course taken by Brother Miller from the commencement of this campaign, and the course you are now pursuing has already . . . cost us sorrow and trouble. . . . You must know that this large body of people cannot be transplanted in a distant country without order in our travels. . . . It will not do for the camp to divide off in parties and each take their own course. . . . We have labored diligently to overtake your division of the camp so as to organize, but just so sure as we come within a few miles of you we find you off again seemingly determined to keep out of our reach. . . . Now this confused state of things cannot be borne any longer.[40]

Consequently the following day at an encampment somewhere between the Chariton River and Shoal Creek in southern Appanoose County, the camp was once again thoroughly reorganized. New captains and leaders were chosen where necessary, much stricter laws were adopted that required the companies to stay closer together, and several other changes were made to expedite travelling, or as the humbled Orson Pratt said, "for the convenience of journeying and to preserve good order."[41] Young was unanimously reelected president of the whole camp. And once again, Sherwood, Miller, and a few select others were dispatched to go ahead to learn the best route and to go on to the Platte country in western Iowa and arrange for more work projects.[42]

With all the captains reassembled, Young also announced a change of course that had been decided upon some ten days before at Richardson's Point. Because of diminishing supplies, rather than proceed in the original northwest direction toward Council Bluffs, they now decided to bear southwest, keeping closer to Missouri border settlements for trading purposes.[43] The decision, recommended by Henry G. Sherwood, called for the camp to travel through the northwest corner of Missouri among more settled areas and to cross the Missouri River at Banks Ferry just north of St. Joseph.[44] Once across, they would select "a fleet division" to cross over the mountains in time for a late planting while the rest would "pass on more leisurely perhaps one or two hundred miles and open a field."[45] Young was still clinging tenaciously to his scheme of getting as much of the camp as far west as possible in 1846, perhaps to Fort Laramie or beyond.[46]

But as much as inadequate provisions, unworkable organizations, and route changes impeded their movements, the most persistent problem was the incessantly cold and wet weather. Spring was so late in arriving that prairie pasture did not appear until mid-April, much later than anticipated. "We were traveling in the season significantly termed 'between hay and grass,'" wrote Eliza R. Snow, "and the teams feeding mostly on browse, wasted in flesh and had but little strength; and it was painful at times, to see the poor creatures straining every joint and ligature, doing their utmost, and looking the very picture of discouragement."[47]

As they suffered and slid across what Young called "a great mud hole" from Nauvoo to Grand River, time became a factor. The almost constant rain, sudden melting snows, swollen creeks, and mud were their constant companions. And as bad as things were in March, they deteriorated in April. "We were strung along clear across Iowa," wrote one journalist, "and such roads, from one rod to a mile in width on those bottomless prairies. When the turf would hold the wagons up, it was ok, but there might be a dozen or more all sunk in the mud at once, a short distance apart."[48]

Between mid-March and mid-April, the rains fell almost continually and with such intensity that progress was restricted to less than a half-mile per day.[49] Such agonizing delays, the sufferings of the travellers, the dangerously weakened condition of the draft animals, the unaffordably high prices for feed grain (up to

37 ½ cents per bushel of corn), wagons and equipment in constant disrepair,[50] rapidly depleting food supplies, and no prospects for better weather in the near future—all this demanded a reevaluation of their course and conduct. The dream of reaching the Rockies later that season was drowning in the mud flats of Iowa, and Young was growing increasingly worried and impatient. Something had to be done to save the lives of his followers, the livestock, and his great enterprise.

The revised plan desperately, prayerfully forged on the banks of swollen Locust Creek, had to solve several pressing problems. The camp itself, both man and beast, needed rest and refreshment. Crops needed planting and a way station needed to be established for the large emigrant trains about to depart Nauvoo. Money somehow had to be raised to finance their protracted journey. Finally, the proposed express company must be supplied and dispatched over the mountains immediately in time to plant late crops.

The scheme agreed upon was, consequently, multifaceted. To meet the needs of rest and a continuing food supply, large relief farms or way stations were proposed, the first to be located east rather than west of the Missouri River (as originally planned) at or near "the head" or source of Grand River some sixty to seventy miles northwest of their present position, the second at the Missouri, and possibly one or more further west.[51]

To take advantage of such open lands, the Mormons changed directions once again, reverting back to the original plan of moving northwest along Iowa Indian trails to Council Bluffs, thereby avoiding the Missouri settlements and Banks Ferry altogether.[52] "We consider it wisdom to avoid the settlements as much as possible," said Young, "for their seems to be only one disposition which is universal amongst the inhabitants in this region, and that is to speculate out of us as much as possible, and we mean to defeat them."[53]

The revised plan also called for sending fifty men ahead to the source of the Grand River to "build some huts [and] plant some grain and garden seeds." After that, the main body would travel northwest to the head of the Grand River, on to Council Bluffs on the Missouri River, and then over the mountains leaving behind at their new settlement, as Young put it, "those that have not the means to prosecute the journey—thereby furnishing a sojourning place for those that may here after come from the States."[54] Others would retrace their steps and pilot oncoming caravans along a better, more direct route avoiding creeks, bad roads, and high prices.[55]

But instead of one Iowa farm, as originally planned, the Mormons built two. While waiting near Locust Creek at a site named Pleasant Grove, the main camp received word that those trailblazers ahead had taken on a job "of building a jail and storehouse worth $250" for some settlers on the east fork of Grand River (Weldon Creek) only thirty miles ahead.[56]

By 25 April, Young caught up with the forward party. There he decided to establish a farm sooner than anticipated and "lay out a town plat" at Weldon Creek, partly because of unexpected employment opportunities in the area and the need for rest.[57] Furthermore, the site was closer to Missouri settlements where they could exchange unneeded articles for extensive provisions to outfit the mountain company.

Work began on the new farmsite on 27 April 1846 with one hundred men splitting rails, another forty-eight building log houses, others digging wells, and virtually everyone else involved in some fashion.[58] Meanwhile, Jedediah M. Grant, David Yearsley, John Davenport, and Francis Whitney were dispatched some forty or fifty miles down the Grand River to Missouri to barter not only for cows but also for badly needed bacon, flour, meal, and corn.[59]

Most of the camp remained at the site, eventually named Garden Grove, for over three weeks, building several log houses, cultivating the land, and, in typical Mormon style, establishing a local ecclesiastical government, or High Council, with Samuel Bent as presiding elder. Some two hundred people, by their own choice or by assignment, would remain to oversee and improve this first way station.

Not as well timbered or watered as they had hoped, Garden Grove was far too small to accommodate the oncoming companies.[60] Indeed, it had not been intended to fulfill that assignment. Besides, the place was infested with rattlesnakes. Some men killed eight or more per day despite instructions to destroy them only if they threatened human life.[61] Consequently scouts were soon exploring the headwaters region of the Grand River, twenty-seven miles northwest, to stake out the bigger farm originally proposed, one closer to the direct line of march many were then following from Nauvoo. Parley Pratt, apparently responsible for locating the site, gave it the Old Testament name of Mt. Pisgah.[62] There the scenes of Garden Grove were reenacted on a larger scale, and "a farm of several thousand acres was enclosed and planted."[63] As at Garden Grove, the land was divided into five-, ten-, and twenty-acre plots distributed, by lot, among individual families. Though the land was privately farmed, the effort was clearly a cooperative enterprise.[64] On 18 May 1846, Young and the Twelve arrived at Mt. Pisgah, where four days later they organized another High Council to regulate both church and civic matters.[65] Most who stayed at Mt. Pisgah, however briefly, found it beautiful and inviting, free from reptiles, and a welcome respite from the dreariness of the immediate past. Wrote Ezra T. Benson, "This was the first place where I felt willing in my heart to stay at, since I left Nauvoo."[66]

But more than farms and way stations, the Locust Creek plan had called for an immediate infusion of funds to supply the express mountain company. Yet where could they get monies in such an isolated wilderness? One solution lay in selling properties back in Nauvoo, but since sales were not going well, other measures were required.[67] Consequently it was decided at Garden Grove to instruct the trustees to enter into confidential negotiations to sell the recently completed Nauvoo Temple, then scheduled for dedication in just two weeks time. At the same time they agreed to try to sell the Kirtland Temple in Ohio and all other church properties in that area. Apostle Orson Pratt, who participated in these deliberations, explained their rationale: "Inasmuch as we were driven from our inheritances and homes and from the Temple," all future property sales "were but forced sales done for the purpose of keeping a poor people from perishing and that we would be justified by our Heavenly Father in so doing."[68]

These decisions were kept confidential for several months so as not to shock the religious sensitivities of many followers. But faced with a worsening economic situation, and endeavoring once and for all to sever all ties with Nauvoo in order to risk everything in a western wilderness, Young convinced his colleagues that they really had no other choice. Besides, it was far better to sell these structures to the "Gentiles" (a term frequently used to describe the non-Mormons) than to have them fall into the hands of the Strangites or other factions who were simultaneously maneuvering for possession of the Nauvoo Temple.[69] On 29 April the Quorum of the Twelve Apostles unanimously sustained Young's decision to sell the Nauvoo Temple for $200,000.[70] Without such funds, outfitting an express mountain company was almost impossible.

Original sketches in the Heber C. Kimball Journals of the wagon train in central Iowa on the morning (above) and the afternoon (below) of 18 May 1846, by a member of the Kimball family (possibly Peter Hansen). Reproduced with permission from the Church Archives, The Church of Jesus Christ of Latter-day Saints. Heber C. Kimball Collection.

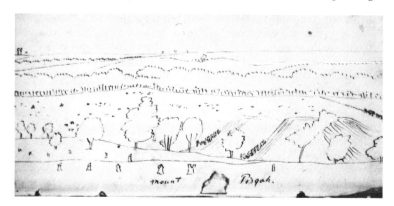

Original sketch in the Heber C. Kimball Journals of 1846 of the
Mt. Pisgah farm site's way station drawn by a member of the
Kimball family (possibly Peter Hansen). Reproduced with permission from the Church Archives, The Church of Jesus Christ
of Latter-day Saints. Heber C. Kimball Collection.

At a conference of the assembled camp at Garden Grove,
Young referred to his plan of encamping most in western Iowa
territory "while we go a little farther and lengthen out the cords
and build a few more stakes, and so continue until we can gather
all the saints . . . in the tops of the mountains."[71] Four days later,
in a confidential letter to Hyde and Woodruff, he said that "after feeding and nourishing and nursing them [the Saints] as a
mother does her infant till the last breast is sucked dry, we will
give them a good farm, send their teams back to Nauvoo, bless
them, and leave them."[72]

But as the weeks dragged on and the possibility of temple sales
waned, Young grew increasingly frustrated, becoming ever more
critical of what he perceived as an unwillingness on the part
of those who had covenanted to bring out the poor and save
the church. Too many, he thought, were unwilling to give up
their church teams to the advance company or to use them to
go back and bring out the destitute in Nauvoo, but were desperately holding onto them to retain their families. Said Young in
conference,

> The Saints have crowded on us all the while, and have com-
> pletely tied our hands by importuning and saying: Do not leave
> us behind. Wherever you go, we want to go, be with you, and

thus our hands and feet have been bound which has caused our delay to the present time, and now hundreds at Nauvoo are continually praying . . . that they may overtake us and be with us. . . . They are afraid to let us go on and leave them behind, forgetting that they have covenanted to help the poor away at the sacrifice of all their property.[73]

To prevent further delays, those having church teams were told either to surrender them immediately to the advance company and stay and build the farms or return to Nauvoo and fetch their families. After this painful decree many in camp, if they did not openly object, quietly returned to their wagons disillusioned and discouraged. To give up their only means of travel after giving all they had in return for a wagon or some other conveyance, only to be left in the wilds of Iowa, was asking almost too much. Said a dejected William Huntington:

> There I had one of the most severe trials I ever had—expecting that on Monday morning my goods and family to be left on the ground and by the charity of others to be helped up to the farm [Garden Grove], as I had no team of my own, having in Nauvoo, according to council given my house and lot into the hands of the Trustees in Trust by Deed, according to covenant of the whole Church at October [1845] conference that we would do all we could to help the Church away.[74]

The following Monday, 20 April, wagons and provisions were pooled together. But with the scarcity of food and other necessities, the leaders decided to send traders once again southward into the Missouri settlements along the Grand River to exchange watches, horses, feather-beds, and other prized personal possessions for oxen, cows, and foodstuffs.[75] Until they returned in mid-May, the camp was stalled.

The express scheme could have worked only if daily rations had been reduced to a scant one-half pound or less of bread stuff per person in the proposed mountain company. Though Young was unflinching, others began to counsel otherwise. Lorenzo Young, Brigham's older brother, speaking at a Sunday meeting on 18 April, called for calm reconsideration and common sense. "I speak not because I am aposed to the instruction that has been given but I do it merely to impress upon the minds of this camp the reality of being reduced to this scanty allowance." He then advised, "don't let the bump of ideality get so high and be carried away in anticipation to that extent that you will venture to take a journey of 12 months upon the scanty allowance of four ounces per day."[76]

Even Heber Kimball and Willard Richards, Young's closest advisors, began to differ publicly with him by urging a less demanding course, to accept the inevitability of their situation, and forget what was becoming madness—to send a large company over the mountains in 1846. Instead, they suggested the Twelve remain at Mt. Pisgah or one of their new settlements, send a small advance party westward, and winter at the main camps in western Iowa.[77]

But Young still resisted. If the Twelve were not going ahead, no one else would either. He again proposed that "the Twelve and such others as they might select should go."[78] He had little confidence that others, such as Bishop Miller, could be entrusted to find a suitable place and do the work he viewed as a responsibility of the Twelve.

Young's final harangue on the topic was perhaps the most biting, reflecting his frustration and apprehensions.

> We will not cross the Mountains as soon as we anticipated but I will not find fault I will let God do that. . . . I can tell the brethren what they are doing . . . they have hedged up their own way by praying continually saying I am poor I have done all I could for the church . . . and all the devils between this and the Nethermost part of Hell are acting in concert with your prayers.

He predicted they would not cross the mountains that season, which "is just what the Brethren want[,] they would rather go to Hell than to be left behind."[79]

On 2 June 1846, the camp, now numbering over five hundred wagons despite leaving several hundred people behind at Garden Grove and Mt. Pisgah, rolled out in the direction of Council Bluffs and beyond. Four days later they found the Indian trail to the Bluffs and pursued their journey westward, crossing the middle Noddaway River in the southwestern corner of present Adair County, the Nishnabotna River in western Cass County, and finally the west Nishnabotona and Keg Creek in Pottawattamie County before arriving at Indian and Mosquito creeks on 13 June.[80] It required only fourteen days to cover the last remaining one hundred miles to the Missouri River, during which the travellers enjoyed the unfamiliar luxury of dry, dusty trails. On their way they also passed by various Pottawattamie Indian

villages. Eventually, on 14 June 1846, two months behind sched-
ule, the main camp reached the Missouri, "sprawled like a silver
serpent in the sun of a mid-June morning," characteristically a
day or two after Bishop Miller.[81]

After 130 days and 327 miles, the trek across Iowa at long last
was over. While no one had anticipated an easy journey, few if
any had forseen such extreme difficulties, nor the interminable
delays. The crucible of Iowa would serve them well in times
to come.

"THE ADVANTAGES ARE MORE
THAN THE DISADVANTAGES":
THE DECISION TO WINTER AT THE MISSOURI

The problems facing the Latter-day Saints in the wilderness, estimated by late June 1846 at between three and six thousand, were serious and complex. Iowa had delayed and exhausted them beyond all expectation. Had they reached the Missouri River in April, as planned, or even in May, chances for sending the "Camp of Israel" over the mountains would have been more promising, but now the season was too late to embark upon such a hazardous journey into an unknown wilderness. Just to ferry their almost two thousand wagons across the river would take weeks.[1] And even if a small pioneer party could get away to reach wherever it was they were going—and no one yet seemed positively sure where that was—finding a suitable winter location in time to plant crops, cut hay for their herds, and prepare adequate shelter for the winter would tax their industry and ingenuity.[2]

Greatly complicating matters was their physically exhausted and economically depressed condition. Sickness and depleting food supplies—both danger signs—were already appearing. And how would the local Indians react to this intrusion? What of Indian agents and their attitudes? And what of the hated Missourians?

While assembling on the east bank of the Missouri River, the Mormons evaluated their alternatives.[3] George Miller had already reached the Missouri a day ahead of the main camp and had conferred with Peter Sarpy of the American Fur Company at his station at Trader's Point (Pointe-aux-Poules) concerning the Pottawattami Indians, ferry crossings, and overland trails westward.[4] The following day, as the lead wagons were struggling over the two branches of Mosquito Creek to take up positions south of the Blockhouse "above the trading houses"[5] (i.e. near Trader's Point), Miller reported on his talks with Sarpy and company.[6]

The first order of business was to construct a ferry.[7] Although

Sarpy owned and operated a small dinghy some nine miles down river connecting Pointe-aux-Poules with the Indian agency at Bellevue on the west, Young determined the Mormons should build a ferry of their own, one large enough for present and future purposes, thereby saving the high ferriage costs in moving so numerous a company. Furthermore, it would allow them to follow their own timetable.[8] Young appointed George Miller, Newel K. Whitney, and Albert P. Rockwood to present the matter to Sarpy and his colleagues and to offer them, in return for spikes, pitch, and other building materials, free use of the "skow" for their own needs whenever the Mormons would not require it. Sarpy agreed.[9]

Until the ferry was operable, the main camp retreated to higher ground on "Redemption Hill," as they termed it, up Mosquito Creek some nine miles from Trader's Point, to escape the bad water and thieving Omaha Indians who lived on the river's west side.[10]

Since the Mormon encampments sprawled over high bluffs and open prairie in sight of the Pottawattami Indian villages, Young forged a policy of establishing good relations with the Indians, of courting the favor and goodwill of government agents, and of developing a dialogue with Sarpy and his colleagues. As wanderers in a strange land, they had much to gain from cooperation and everything to lose without it.

Regarding the Indians, Young charged his people to "have nothing to do with the Pottawattamies, no trading or intercourse of any kind."[11] He was determined to avoid dangerous entanglements and the risk of offending the Indians in any way and gave strict orders that no one should trade or barter with them. Whatever trading was required would be done collectively and then only by camp leaders.

Actually the Mormons had little to fear from the Pottawattami. The two peoples had known each other for some time, and communication between Pottawattami chiefs and Mormon spokesmen had been ongoing for at least five years.[12]

No less important was the need to incur the favor of the Indian agents, who were in a position to report on Mormon plans, attitudes, and movements, and who had ready access, when required, to Colonel Stephen Watts Kearny and his U.S. Army of the West stationed only 200 miles south at Fort Leavenworth. If there was any truth to the rumors of Mormon collusion with the Indians, the agents would see it firsthand.

More difficult to control than any fear or distrust of the In-

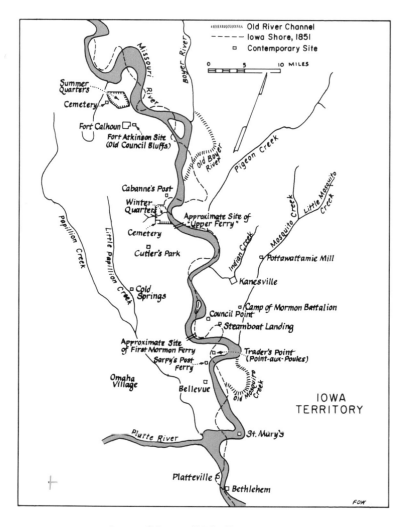

Area of Council Bluffs, 1846–50

SOURCES: Charles H. Babbitt, *The Early Days at Council Bluffs* (Washington, D.C.: Byron S. Adams, 1916), p. 7; Charles Kelly, ed., *Journals of John D. Lee 1846–47*, p. 160; Lynn Robert Webb, "The Contributions of the Temporary Settlements Garden Grove, Mount Pisgah and Kanesville, Iowa, to Mormon Emigration, 1846–52" (master's thesis, Brigham Young University, 1954), p. 110; Lawrence D. Clark, Scrapbook, LDS Church Archives; Gail George Holmes, "Winter Quarters Revisited—Untold Stories of the Seven-Year Stay of Mormons in the Missouri Valley 1846–53" (Omaha, n. d.), pp. 19–20.

dians or any other outsiders were the strong anti-American sentiments then shared by many inside the camp, a distrust borne from years of persecution in a land proclaiming religious liberty. But expressing such animosity in hearing range of federal Indian agents would not be in their best interests, and Young made sure that everyone understood. His concerns extended further than preventing military intervention, for he also courted the favor of the agents and sought their permission for winter camps on Indian lands. In a public meeting on 15 June, just a day after reaching the Missouri, he counseled the camp "to be wise and prudent, to hold their tongues and say nothing [against] this government, the war with Texas and Mexico etc. lest you subject ourselves to trouble and difficulties." The policy would be official silence— "say nothing about the government or about our organization or church rules; let them find these things out by their learning." [13]

Young's instructions apparently paid off, at least initially. Agent R. B. Mitchell reported a positive first impression. In a letter to his supervisor, Superintendent T. H. Harvey in St. Louis, Mitchell said he was "gratified to say that since their arrival," he had "seen nothing to which exception can be taken. The principal men seem determined to hold themselves aloof from the Indians." As to their attitude towards the United States, "they complain that they have been badly treated but declare their intentions to bear the American flag, to whatever country they may cast their lot." [14] Mitchell later described Mormon-Indian relations as "greatly more circumspect and unexceptionable than is usually found to be the case with emigrant bodies passing through this region of country." [15] He, nevertheless, stopped short of permitting the Mormons from wintering on Pottawattami lands. So long as they were only passing through on their way west, he would pose no objections. [16]

Young also established a positive relationship with the traders. Besides agreeing on ferry building, the Mormons and Peter Sarpy and company also discussed "the road, country, and climate to and about the Rocky Mountains," especially "about the great Bear river valley," covering such matters as living with the Indians, the feasibility of sending out an advanced party to the mountains, and possible sites for wintering the camp. [17]

Convinced of their intention to move further west and aware that sizable shipments of furs from the Indian winter hunts were likely detained up the Platte River among the Pawnees, Sarpy inquired whether the Mormons, while waiting at the Missouri, would be willing to contract out some forty teams "to bring 90,000 of furs and peltry from the head of Grand Island." The pay would be "$1,000 plus some fifteen or twenty barrels of pork, bread, etc."[18] Sensing "an opening for bigger jobs," Young quickly agreed and assigned a more than willing Bishop Miller and James Emmett to take forty wagons to Grand Island and bring back the shipment.[19]

Thus Young gladly dispatched Miller and Emmett, via Sarpy's ferry and the Papillion Creek to the Elkhorn River and up the Platte to rendezvous with the Pawnees. Under strict orders to keep their mission a secret from Indian agents, not in any way to offend the Indians, and to wait for the Twelve to catch up with them later, the Miller-Emmett expedition headed west in late June.

Meanwhile Sarpy reported that an army of U.S. dragoons was advancing north to intercept the Mormons and to "prevent their uniting with the Indians to fight the United States."[20] Sarpy reported that Mitchell had written to Colonel Kearny "for troops to take the Mormon leaders and drive off the Indians," who were making "depredations at Pottawattamie town."[21]

To dispel these falsehoods, Young commissioned Orson Hyde and Newel K. Whitney to meet with Mitchell and review their purpose and policy respecting the Indians. After conferring with Mitchell, Hyde and Whitney learned that he had not instigated any such call to the army, but had written a letter some weeks previously "because of his bad impressions of the Emmett Company" formerly stationed at the Vermillion.[22] Mitchell assured the Mormon delegation he was convinced of the law-abiding nature and good behavior of the Mormons now arriving at the Missouri.[23]

Though these rumors were false, when coupled with an awareness that many Missourians vehemently opposed even a temporary Mormon presence on their western borders, they created an uneasy climate. The result was a frenzied revival of the earlier plan to send a pioneer company to the mountains.[24] On 28 June, after saying, "all that men and hell could invent to hedge up the way of the camp would be hatched up," Young demanded that an express company go "to Bear River Valley in the Great Basin, without families, forthwith," to prevent the church from being "blown to the four winds and never gathered again."[25] "A company of some 2–3 or 500 able and effective men" without families were to head for "the Bear River Valley, Great Basin or Salt Lake, with the least delay possible." Their wives and children would be accommodated somewhere along the way—probably at Grand Island.[26] The Twelve Apostles would go with the pioneers "over the mountains to set up the Kingdom of God or its Standard yet this year."[27]

Parley Pratt and Solomon Hancock were immediately assigned to head to the farms and recruit for the company. Upon meeting any of the Saints along the way, they were to explain their threatened situation and call for volunteers "to try and forward the expedition." Hosea Stout, who met Pratt just east of the Bluffs, said of his mission, "he instructed us to push on with all possible speed that if we did not get to the Bluffs by the time that he returned [from Garden Grove and Mount Pisgah] it would be needful for us to go on and leave our families such was the necessity to push forward the expedition."[28]

U.S. Army officers were indeed in the area, though not to attack but to recruit. And instead of running away from the U.S. Army, the Mormons were on the verge of becoming a part of it. On 26 June 1846, Captain James Allen and three other officers of the Army of the West arrived at Mt. Pisgah to meet with Mormon leaders.[29] A gracious Captain Allen gained William Huntington's permission to mount the stand and on behalf of the president of the United States invited the Mormons to enlist in the army to fight in the recently declared war against Mexico.

Shocked by his audacity to ask them to assist a government they popularly distrusted, and blinded to the possible advantages, Huntington recorded that he "followed him with an address, as the old saying is 'by answering a fool according to his folly.'"[30] Nonetheless Huntington provided Allen with a letter of introduction to the authorities at the Bluffs and sent him on his way.

Within hours Pratt arrived in camp with orders to recruit up to five hundred men for the pioneer company. Pratt apparently passed by Captain Allen unaware and when told of the officer's request was considerably excited, though undeterred from enlisting pioneers to head west.[31]

Wilford Woodruff, then passing through Mt. Pisgah, shared Huntington's doubts. "I had some reason to believe them to be spies and that the president had no hand in it."[32] Thus he sent Thomas Grover ahead at full gallop to conceal all cannons and artillery from Allen's view and to reach the Bluffs with the news before Allen's arrival. Grover arrived at headquarters only a few

hours ahead of Allen.[33] Whether he was the first to inform
Young and the Twelve of the Battalion request or whether they
had heard it earlier from Missouri traders is unimportant. What
is significant is that even before conferring with Captain Allen,
Young, Heber Kimball, and Willard Richards "decided to raise
the men wanted."

Young had been hoping for this or some similar good news
ever since sending Jesse Little back to Washington the previous
January to "embrace" whatever facilities for emigrating to the
western coast the government might offer.[34] After leaving Nauvoo, Little had travelled to his native New Hampshire to confer
with his friend, Governor John H. Steele, who in turn wrote him
several letters of introduction to senior officials in President
Polk's cabinet.[35]

On his way to Washington, Little had stopped in Philadelphia
and preached at a special conference of the church. Ironically,
this was 13 May—the day the United States declared war on
Mexico. In attendance was a young, non-Mormon lawyer destined to play a leading role in Mormon relations with Washington for years to come—Colonel Thomas L. Kane. Son of John
Kintzing Kane, attorney general of Pennsylvania and close friend
of President Polk, young Kane had been following newspaper
reports of Mormon persecutions with genuine sympathy. Kane
introduced himself to Little after the meeting and the two spent
the rest of the day in earnest conversation.[36] That evening Kane
obtained from Little a letter of introduction to Brigham Young,
since he had decided to go to the Missouri and travel to California with the Mormons. In exchange, Little obtained letters of introduction to Vice-President George M. Dallas and to other
highly placed officials.[37] Without Kane's input and connections, it
is doubtful Little would have gotten very far.

Little's arrival in Washington was superbly well timed. In the
latter part of May, President Polk and his cabinet were absorbed
with wartime planning and political maneuvering. Whether Polk
had been angling for the war, he and the nation were totally unprepared for it. Recently appointed commander of the armed
forces, General Winfield Scott had just called for a volunteer
army of 50,000 men in addition to the standing army, and it was
agreed that 20,000 would be called up from western and southwestern states, including Missouri.[38]

With his cabinet and trusted Democratic senators such as
Senator Thomas H. Benton of Missouri (a bitter enemy of the

Mormons), Polk formulated a blueprint that involved at first a three-pronged attack: (1) General Taylor to cross the Rio Grande with a much enlarged volunteer army to invade northern Mexico and capture Monterrey and other cities; (2) Commodore David Conner to blockade the Mexican ports on the Gulf of Mexico; and (3) Commodore John D. Sloat to seize San Francisco and blockade other California ports. After further discussion and revision, the president decided to involve the Army of the West by sending Colonel Kearny to occupy Santa Fe and if at all possible to reach California, overpower its Mexican garrisons, and secure the region for the United States.[39] Kearny, in Polk's words, was "to acquire for the United States, California, New Mexico, and perhaps some others of the Northern Provinces of Mexico" as ransom when negotiating a peace with Mexico.[40]

Polk's plan called for Kearny to take 1,000 Missouri mounted volunteers west plus "another 1,000 mounted men" to support his positions and guard supply lines. His most serious doubt, despite Senator Benton's assurances to the contrary, was whether it was too late in the season "to collect a force on the Western frontier of Missouri in time to reach the Sacramento River in California."[41]

Against this backdrop of fast-moving events, Little arrived in Washington on 21 May. He met the president informally the next day at a social gathering, but had little chance to discuss his request seriously. The following day he met with Amos Kendall, former postmaster general, who "thought arrangements could be made" to assist the Mormon emigration "by enlisting 1000 of our men, arming, equipping and establishing them in California to defend the country."[42] Kendall was likely speaking with inside knowledge of the administration's evolving intentions.[43]

Little did not see Polk again for another eleven days. Anxious to speed matters along and to reemphasize the desperate straits of the Latter-day Saints, he sent a letter to the president on 1 June. Acting under Kane's advice, Little threatened that if the Mormons were unsuccessful in getting support from Washington, they might seek it from another source.

> [We] are true hearted Americans . . . and have a desire to go under the outstretched wings of the American Eagle. We would disdain to receive assistance from a foreign power, although it should be proffered, unless our government shall turn us to

be foreigners. Means for the gathering of poor we must obtain. . . . and if I cannot get it in the land of my fathers, I will cross the trackless ocean where I trust I shall find some friends to help.[44]

What Polk would have done had the Mormons joined hands with the British can only be speculated, but clearly it was a possibility not to be taken lightly.

It is in the Mormon overtures to England that much of Kane's true motivation may be seen. As interested as he may have been in the humanitarian aspects of Mormonism, his first loyalty was clearly to the United States. Contrary to most historical assumptions, long before ever meeting Little, Kane had privately decided to visit the Mormons, for he believed they were too susceptible to British overtures and might seriously complicate the Oregon Treaty negotiations then in progress. In a revealing letter dated 29 May 1846 to his brother Elisha, Kane admitted "that it has weighed upon my mind for months past whether it was not my duty to go with the Mormons." He continued:

this increased as I began to see signs of something which even to my eyes looked like English tampering with their leaders. I became oppressed the more . . . when two days ago I saw a letter which disclosed kind assistance to the emigrant parties from the Hudson's Bay Company, found I could not rest without consulting somebody whose opinion to me would be of more weight than Papa's ridicule.[45]

On 28 May, Kane met privately with Polk and "told him all" he knew of the Mormons and their leaders and what he "knew of H.B. Majesty's interference." As a result of that meeting, Polk encouraged Kane to travel to the Bluffs and secure Mormon loyalty, considering his offer of "the highest and most praiseworthy patriotism."[46]

On 2 June, the cabinet approved Polk's plan and authorized Kearny "to receive into service as volunteers a few hundred of the Mormons who are now on their way to California." Fully aware of the exodus then underway, yet wary of Mormon intentions and attitudes, Polk's invitation was "to conciliate them, attach them to our country, and prevent them from taking part against us."[47] Furthermore, the Mormons just happened to be in a most strategic position at the time and, if persuaded, could expedite Kearny's march to California in time to participate in that season's campaign.

Despite the potential advantages and the cabinet's approval, Polk proved hesitant. The following day, in company with Amos Kendall, Polk conferred for three hours with Little, who offered the immediate services of the Mormon people. Altering the cabinet's plan somewhat, Polk inquired whether "500 or more" Mormons would be willing to volunteer to serve in the U.S. Army, but only after they reached California and then only to help defend that territory.[48] Little, unimpressed with having to wait until they reached the coast, tried unsuccessfully to dissuade Polk at a follow-up meeting the next day. Perhaps unknown to Little were Polk's sensitivities to key Democratic senators opposed to the arrival in California of thousands of Latter-day Saints. To send Mormons to California as part of the army at public expense might exasperate an already alarmed, anti-Mormon citizenry. Hence Polk's revised plan to trim the number to 500 and then not to enlist them until Kearny's army had taken possession of California.[49] Despite his concerns, Little penned a letter accepting the president's offer on the evening of 5 June 1846.

Kane met with Polk and Secretary of War W. L. Marcy on 8 June, possibly to review the Mormon Battalion matter, offer to carry dispatches to Colonel Kearny, and in other ways prepare for his journey west.[50] On 9 June, Kane and Little left Washington and traveled together as far as St. Louis. From there Little went north to Nauvoo and eventually across Iowa, arriving among his people on 6 July, while Kane headed toward Fort Leavenworth arriving there in late June.

Why did the Mormons enlist at the Missouri River and not, as Polk indicated, in California? W. Ray Luce maintains that Marcy's orders of 3 June were written ambiguously and were "misinterpreted" by Kearny. Thus, Luce argues, "a vaguely worded letter rather than a presidential plan led to the march of the Mormon Battalion."[51]

There are problems with this argument, however. It is true that Polk indicated a California enlistment; Kendall believed the same thing. But for reasons not entirely known, Marcy's orders, which both he and Polk carefully drafted, say nothing about recruiting Mormons in California. Rather, a careful reading, the kind that Kearny must have given it, leaves little doubt that the Polk administration had a last-minute change of mind and ordered Kearny to call the Mormons immediately. More worried about securing California that season than offending it, Marcy likely persuaded Polk to change his thinking. Marcy's official order read as follows:

It is known that a large body of Mormon emigrants are en route to California for the purpose of settling in that country. You are desired to use all proper means to have a good understanding with them, to the end that the U.S. may have their cooperation in taking possession of, and holding that country. It has been suggested here, that many of these Mormons would willingly enter into the service of the United States, and aid us in our expedition against California. You are hereby authorized to muster into service such as can be induced to volunteer; not, however, to a number exceeding one-third of your entire force.[52]

How could the Mormons have assisted in taking "possession" of California if not already enlisted? And how could they participate in the "expedition" unless a part of it?

Marcy further instructed Kearny that upon arriving in California, "you are authorized to organize and receive into the service citizens of 'Nueva Helvetica' on the Sacramento river, such portion of these citizens as you may think useful to aid you to hold the possession of the country." Had this meant the Mormons, surely Marcy would have said so. He concluded by investing "a large discretionary power" in Kearny with respect to all these matters.[53]

Kearny did not misinterpret Marcy's orders. Rather he read between the lines and used common sense. Considering Polk's desire to strengthen Kearny's army, get it off to California at all speed, and aware that Missouri might be unable to raise a second company of a thousand infantry, Kearny followed Marcy's orders.[54] On 19 June, well before Kane's arrival, he ordered Captain James Allen to "endeavor to raise from among them [the Mormons] four or five companies of volunteers to join me in my expedition to that country [California]."[55]

Meanwhile, at Mosquito Creek on the morning of 1 July 1846, Captain Allen presented his credentials to Young and other leaders and asked for an immediate twelve-month enlistment of 500 healthy volunteers between the ages of eighteen and forty-five. Enlistees in each of the proposed five companies would be free to choose their own officers and march to California in the rear of the First Missouri militia via Santa Fe. They would receive pay and allowances from the moment of joining and when discharged would be allowed to retain their guns and accoutrements furnished them along the way.[56] Allen stressed that if they could not raise 500 men, "they did not want any,"[57] and that

Council Bluffs Ferry and a group of cottonwood trees. From a sketch by Frederick Piercy first printed in James Linforth, *Route from Liverpool to Great Salt Lake Valley.*

From an oil-on-canvas painting, by C. C. A. Christensen, of *B*[rig-ham] *Y*[oung] *Calling Volunteers for the Mormon-Battalion*, June–July 1846. Reproduced with permission from the Museum of Church History and Art, The Church of Jesus Christ of Latter-day Saints.

owing to the lateness of the season, the organization must be completed in six days.[58] Young quickly agreed.

But why did he consent to the plan when most in camp opposed it? The reasons are multiple. First, the scheme answered their immediate problem of where they could legally winter. Seeing his opportunity, Young drove a hard bargain by extracting Allen's permission to locate on Indian lands on both sides of the river without government interference.[59] Second, military service meant badly needed income that had not been obtained from temple sales. Each recruit would be paid $42 in advance for clothing as well as periodic payments along the way. If the men were to forgo uniforms and turn their clothing allotments over to the camp, it could mean $21,000. Add to this a sizable portion of their year's wages, and church leaders were thinking in terms over $50,000.[60] A third factor weighing upon Young's mind was California—not necessarily Upper California or the Great Basin area, but lower or southern California along the coast. "Let the Mormons be the first men to set their feet on the soil of California," he said.[61] By obtaining and improving lands now and selling them later they could realize handsome profits.[62]

There were, of course, other reasons. It was an excellent publicity gesture. Public opinion of the Latter-day Saints was extremely prejudiced, and a Mormon effort to support the war might go far to lessen negative attitudes. Enlistment might also enhance the possibility of obtaining future lucrative government contracts. Cooperation now could mean greater benefits later. And by complying with Allen's request, any possibility of government intervention in their westward march would be obviated. Better a beholden government than a belligerent one.

Last of all, the Mormon Battalion call provided Young with the ideal excuse for not reaching the mountains, as predicted, in 1846. If the government could be blamed for their own frustrating failures and delays crossing Iowa and made the whipping boy for whatever else might occur the coming winter, so much the better.[63]

It was a sacrifice, yes, but well enough worth it. And one volunteer, reflecting on it later said,

> it was like a ram caught in a thicket and that it would be better to sacrifice the ram than to have Isaac die. Reflecting upon the subject, it came to my mind that Isaac, in the figure, represented the church . . . and for the saving of its life I was willing to go on this expedition.[64]

But recruiting the required number of men proved formidable. Wilford Woodruff, writing more enthusiastically than accurately (something he was often prone to do), recorded that "when 500 men were called for, they steped forth instantly at the call of the President . . . and went away with cheerful hearts . . . preparing the way for the building of Zion."[65] In fact, it just wasn't so, for Young and the Twelve had a very difficult time convincing their people of the rightness of the decision.

Whereas the governor of Missouri raised the first company of 1,000 mounted volunteers in only a few days, it took Allen almost a month to organize his Mormon battalion of only half that size.[66] Why the hesitations and objections? First of all, a large number genuinely distrusted the U.S. government and desired to leave the United States altogether, regarding any overtures to support it with suspicion. Memories remained of persecutions suffered in Missouri in the 1830s and Washington's refusal to counter Governor Lilburn W. Boggs's extermination order.[67]

Though they continued to revere the Constitution and its protection of religious freedom, many had lost confidence in the government to guarantee such rights. Evidence seems to exist that some sort of covenant was made in the Nauvoo Temple—perhaps a sequel to the endowment—"to avenge the blood of the Prophets, Joseph and Hyrum Smith, on the United States and to overthrow her power, beginning first with Illinois and Missouri."[68] Whether the faithful made such a vengeful oath is hard to prove since this is the claim of a bitter apostate, but it is probable that several renounced their American citizenship. "As our father and mother or the nation that has born us has rejected us and driven us out," declared Wilford Woodruff on the eve of his departure from Nauvoo, "I feel to resign my citizenship because I cannot enjoy it. I would advise all the Saints that they cast not another vote . . . but resign all offices."[69]

Such sentiments did not reflect a fanatic fringe. Lucius M. Scovil, who came on with the later Nauvoo wagon trains, yearned to get his family "out of this boasted Republic, where they will suffer men to be butchered in cold blood and the guilty go unpunished." Said he, "I disdain this government as I do the gates of hell although my forefathers have fought and bled to obtain their freedom. . . . I desire to see this government go to the shades of oblivion."[70]

Hosea Stout, on first hearing Allen's request, was indignant and looked upon it "as a plot laid to bring trouble" on the Mormons. "For in the event that we did not comply with the requisition," said Stout, "we supposed they would now make a protest to denounce us as enemies to our country and if we did comply that they would then have 500 of our men in their power to be destroyed as they had done our leaders at Carthage. I confess that my feeling was uncommonly wrought up against them."[71] Stout was convinced that Allen wanted nothing more than to ascertain the true strength and size of the Mormon encampment.

Many in camp were probably less politically agitated than those quoted above; nevertheless, most held ill will toward Washington, a negative attitude that was the most powerful obstacle to the call of the Battalion.[72] If not everyone agreed with Stout, Scovil, and Taylor, it appears that the general intention was to flee to the Rockies and the safety of those western valleys, and escape the "overflowing scourge" that many believed God would pour out upon America for rejecting His prophets.

Besides, enlisting as infantry and marching two thousand

miles was no more appealing to them than it was to the Missourians, who, while rallying to serve in a mounted regiment, declined to do so in an infantry battalion. And enlisting in an army already largely made up of Missouri volunteers was similarly repulsive.

Another formidable roadblock was concern for the welfare of abandoned families. With so many away, who would be left to guard against Indian and other Missouri-inspired depredations? Where would their families winter? Who would build shelters and homes? [73]

Little wonder, then, that faced as he was with such opposition Young offered a multitude of safeguards and comforting proposals. "Every man that enlists," he said during a massive recruiting meeting at Mosquito Creek on 13 July, "will have his name, and the names of his wife and children inserted in a book, and what directions you have to give in relation to them; and if we find that we have more families than we can take forward, we will take them to Grand Island and leave men to take care of them till we go and return to fetch them." He then promised the recruits "if God spares my life, that your families shall be taken care of, and shall fare as ours do." [74] A final assurance was the planned appointment of ninety bishops from among trusted men in camp to meet the special needs of the Battalion families. [75] And to the women, he felt compelled to promise that none of their menfolk would be killed in battle.

Leaders urged the volunteers to turn over their wages to the church as one sum to be administered by the proposed bishops, who would "keep a correct account of all moneys and other property received by them, and how disposed of at the risk of being brought before the council and reproved." [76] In response, as early as 21 July, Captain Jefferson Hunt, on behalf of the members of Company "A," authorized church agent and presiding bishop, Newel Whitney, "to receive the payment of the cheques returned by members of said company, and apply them to such uses as may be specified thereon." Similar letters were soon received from the other commandants and officers of the various companies. [77]

Despite these several objections, the Battalion fell in line in large measure due to Young's leadership. It is doubtful, however, if he could have succeeded without the help of either Captain Allen or Colonel Kane. Allen's courteous manner and respectful attitude were strong mitigating factors. Said Stout, "He was a

plain non assuming man without that proud overbearing strut
and self conceited dignaty which some call an officer-like appearance." During their short conversation, Allen, on Stout's request, told of the progress of the war. "I was much pleased with
his manner as a gentleman," he confessed, "notwithstanding my
prejudice against not only him but also the government which
he was sent here to represent."[78]

Colonel Kane (a title given more out of respect and mission
than commission) had arrived from Fort Leavenworth on 11 July.
Though slight of build and sickly in nature (Stout called him "uncommonly small and feminine"), he had courage, common sense,
and genuine sympathy for the Mormons.[79] He brought firsthand
information and, as a friend of the president, convinced many
that Allen was on a bona fide mission, acting without ambiguity
or deceit. Wilford Woodruff, initially suspicious of Allen's request, credited his change of attitude directly to Kane, who,
he recorded, "manifested the spirit of a gentleman and much
interest in our welfare," and from the information provided,
he concluded "that God had begun to move upon the heart of
the President and others in this Nation to begin to act for our
interest."[80]

The first four companies of the "Mormon Battalion" were
mustered in by 16 July. Straining hard to complete the final company the following day, Young proposed three choices: enlist, return to Nauvoo several times and "bring on the poor," or go immediately with the volunteers at great personal cost and sacrifice
over the mountains. Whichever way, few would be permitted to
stay with their families. By sunset on 17 July, Allen had his battalion complete, with more than enough laundresses and more
women and children than expected.[81]

On Saturday evening, 19 July, at a recently constructed bowery close to Mormon ferry and the "Liberty Pole,"[82] a farewell
ball was held with William Pitt's band furnishing the music. "A
more merry dancing soul I have never seen, though the company went without refreshments," wrote Kane. "Dancing continued until the sun dipped below the Omaha Hills," at which
time, according to Kane,

> Silence was called, and a well cultivated mezzo-soprano voice,
> belonging to a young lady with fair face and dark eyes, gave
> with quartette accompaniment a little song, . . . touching to all
> earthly wanderers:
> "By the rivers of Babylon we sat down and wept. We wept
> when we remembered Zion."

There was danger of some expression of feeling when the song was over, for it had begun to draw tears! but breaking the quiet with his hard voice, an Elder asked the blessing of heaven on all who "with purity of heart and brotherhood of spirit" had mingled in that society, and then all dispersed, hastening to cover from the falling dews.[83]

On 21 July 1846, the Mormon Battalion marched out of camp, forty days after the first detachment of dragoons had left Fort Leavenworth, thirty-five after the departure of the first Missouri companies under Colonel Alexander W. Doniphan, and twenty-one days behind Kearny.[84] Whether the Battalion proved valuable to the U.S. Army, it facilitated the Mormon stay at the Bluffs. Recalled Young, "though looked upon by many with astonishment and some with fear, [it] has proved a great blessing to this community. It was indeed the temporal salvation of our camp."[85]

With the battalion gone, energies were directed toward finding a suitable winter way station. Before Captain Allen departed, Young extracted from him, on behalf of the president of the United States, from agent R. B. Mitchell, and from the several Pottawattami chiefs, permission to settle on Pottawattami lands.[86] Sensing Mitchell's hesitancy to speak on Indian matters beyond his jurisdiction and realizing that the newly appointed Council Bluffs agent, John Miller, had not yet assumed his post, Young was determined to use the battalion to bargain for permission to settle on either side of the river. Had Miller been present, Young would have sought his permission too, since he would have held authority over Mitchell and over Indian land west of the Missouri. In the meantime, if it meant positing the authority of U.S. military officers against the jurisdiction of local Indian agents, so be it.[87]

Even prior to the call of the battalion, Young had concluded that most of the Saints must settle at Grand Island on the Platte River. From their studies of Frémont's recent expeditions to the Rocky Mountains, Mormon leaders knew it was "the longest fresh water river island perhaps in America," with rich soil, abundant timber, and sufficient elevation to secure it from the annual spring floods. Frémont had recommended it "as the best point for a military position on the Lower Platte."[88] Sarpy supported their tentative plan, and Captain Allen recommended it as the best place for wintering between the Missouri River and Fort Laramie. Both indicated that the island was large enough for grazing their numerous cattle, sufficiently well timbered, had a good salt spring, and was home to countless buffalo.[89] Only Mitchell, the Council Bluffs subagent, was critical of the Grand Island plan, wondering aloud how so large a group could comfortably winter there among less-than-friendly Pawnee.[90]

Mitchell's comments apparently went unheeded, for by the second week of July Young had determined to settle at Grand Island. "Thither we want to go without delay," he wrote in a letter to the Saints at Garden Grove, "with all the teams of the camp, unload from five hundred to one thousand of the wagons and return immediately to Nauvoo, Garden Grove, etc. and before spring carry to the Platte every poor but honest soul that has not the means to go."[91] Demanding "no deafness" on the matter, Young believed the plan providentially provided. "If everyone is diligent, we expect the whole Church will be together, at that point before winter closes upon us. That is the Gospel." George Miller would scout out the location while retrieving Sarpy's furs and confirm the propriety of their deliberations.

Had the Grand Island scheme materialized, Garden Grove would have been sold off to the highest bidder,[92] Mt. Pisgah, if not a victim of the same fate, would have been but meagerly maintained, and a few would have wintered cattle along the east banks of the Missouri River. Most, however, would have assembled on the island away from possible Missouri depredations and fortified against any Indian or government attacks. With the Grand Island camp underway, a very small party might yet head over the mountains, put in spring crops, and fulfill Young's long-held dream of an 1846 toehold in the Great Basin.

But the arrival in camp of Thomas L. Kane and Wilford Woodruff in mid-July was the beginning of the end of the Grand Island plan. As indicated, Kane convinced Mormon leaders that Washington would not interfere militarily against the Mormons. Secondly, he strongly advised against Grand Island on political grounds and suggested a Missouri River encampment, convincing Young that he stood a better chance of persuading the Office of Indian Affairs not to interfere with Mormon settlements at the Missouri than at locations further west.[93]

Fresh from a mission to England, Woodruff reported to the Twelve that church affairs were in desperate straits. Reuben Hedlock, presiding authority there, was channeling money for emigration purposes into schemes for his own personal enrichment.[94] Furthermore, James J. Strang had sent Martin Harris, one of the original "Three Witnesses" to the gold plates, and

other missionaries to England to work among the Mormon con-
gregations. Unless something was done immediately, the church
stood to lose everything in the British Isles, possibly its richest
source of converts. The Twelve hastily decided to send three
apostles—John Taylor, Orson Hyde, and Parley Pratt—to England with travel funds largely supplied from Battalion contributions. With such key leaders required elsewhere, moving the
main camps 200 miles further west, cutting hay, and completing
all preparations in time for winter would be that much more
difficult.

Woodruff also brought firsthand information on the deteriorating situation in Nauvoo. Though the city was being rapidly
evacuated, the most destitute, unless removed systematically,
would require desperate rescue later. All through summer, reports had pointed to a worsening condition that culminated in
September's "Battle of Nauvoo." Rather than sell off the Iowa
farms and move the Camp to Grand Island with all the attendant complications and sufferings, would it not be wiser to remain near the Bluffs and provide a closer winter quarters for the
inevitable Nauvoo exiles?

There were other contributing factors. To ferry across the
Missouri the entire population, now taking up encampments on
the east side, would be a terribly time-consuming task. Furthermore, another complicated ferriage would be required to cross
the Elkhorn River only thirty miles west. To move a small company of two thousand or less may have been manageable, but to
transport the entire church was now nearly impossible given
time constraints. Finally, the delays encountered in raising the
Battalion added to the demise of the Grand Island scheme. It
had taken weeks to explain, convince, and recruit.

So it was that by 17 July 1846, scarcely ten days after Young's
proclaimed "gospel" of wintering at Grand Island, plans were
drastically revised, once again evidence of the spontaneity and
changeability in Mormon decision-making. Immediate needs
overrode any master plan that may have existed either in heaven
or on earth. Hundreds of wagons were already on the west side
of the river while perhaps two or three times as many were awaiting their turn to cross. Despite the almost nonstop operation of
their ferry, improvements on its west bank landing, and the
probable use by some of Sarpy's "old Gentile ferry," long delays
were inevitable.[95] Wrote Parley Pratt, "The ferry ran night and
day for a long time, and still could not complete the crossing of

the camps till late in the season."[96] Several hundred on the Iowa side were following the lead of Henry W. Miller and others whom Young had assigned to remain on Pottawattami land, assist in cattle grazing efforts, and help bring on Nauvoo refugees.

While organizing east-bank settlers, Young received discouraging news from fur-laden teamsters returning from Grand Island and the Pawnee Indian villages. The island was not nearly as habitable as previously reported, travel getting there was difficult along the Platte River bottoms, and the area seemed to be a center of warfare between the Pawnee and the Sioux.[97] Even government farmers and Presbyterian missionaries were fleeing the area "through fear of the [Sioux] Indians."[98]

Such news spelled the end of whatever remained of the Grand Island scheme, so that by the end of July, even the idea of sending the Twelve and other leaders first to Grand Island and possibly further west, was once and for all abandoned.[99] Some consideration was given to establishing headquarters at the Elkhorn River twenty-five miles north in order to stay clear of the Omaha and Oto Indians and to be that much farther west come spring, but after due consideration even that idea was abandoned.[100] Young and the Twelve finally concluded by late July that while Bishop Miller might spend the winter among the Pawnee, the main camp would winter on the west bank of the Missouri, despite the fact the Pottawattami would have welcomed and the government allowed them to stay on the east side.[101]

The reasons for choosing to winter at the Missouri River were compelling and increasingly obvious. Their great herds of cattle could graze on either side of the river on the peavines and rush bottoms that provided excellent feed even during winter months; they were relatively close to the Missouri settlements of St. Joseph, Linden, and Savannah, where they could carry on trade for desperately needed grain and other materials; the area was well watered; transporting large machinery and components for mills and other operations to a river site would be easier and cheaper; the many valleys on both sides of the river offered needed shelter from summer sun and winter winds; proximity to the Saints on the Iowa side was important for fast communication, easier trade, and church unity; and finally, by staying they could get right to work preparing for the coming winter. Young decided to stay "notwithstanding" the fact that the land was hotly disputed by both Oto and Omaha Indians. "I am willing," he said, "because the advantages are more than the disadvantages."[102] In retrospect, one wonders where else they could have gone without moving everyone back across the river, necessitating, in turn, a time-consuming recrossing in the spring.

The decision to winter at the Missouri was probably the only choice, given the delays, broken plans, and frustrated schedules. The Iowa trek had exhausted and detained them beyond expectation. The absence of a sufficient ferry had necessitated building their own, which was not completed until almost the first of July. Establishing good relations with Sarpy and other traders as well as with the local Indian agents had required careful consideration. News from Nauvoo and England demanded immediate attention. Even before Allen's call for the Battalion, it had become obvious they could not proceed much further. The Battalion, however, provided them temporary permission to winter in the vicinity, and by the time they learned the Grand Island scheme was unfavorable, thousands were already across the river. Hence, with many taking advantage of the season when the river was low and crossing over to the west side, and others taking up winter residences across the river on the Iowa side, Young and the Twelve decided that the headquarters of the camp for the upcoming winter should be on the west bank of the Missouri River. It was not the Rockies, but for a season "Zion" would rest in the "borders of the wilderness."

SETTLING IN AT WINTER QUARTERS
AND ENVIRONS:
SEPTEMBER–DECEMBER 1846

While awaiting final word on the Grand Island plan, those pioneers already on the west side of the Missouri River stopped at a temporary resting place, recommended by George Miller, on the Petit Papillion Creek, which they called Cold Springs or Butterfly Bluff. Situated four miles northwest of the ferry landing and fifteen miles above Bellevue, Cold Springs served as camp headquarters and provided a much needed rest for most of a hot, sweltering July.[1]

Once the Mormons decided to winter at the Missouri, several parties explored northwestward along its banks as far as the old Missouri Encampment and old Fort Calhoun and as far west as the Elkhorn, in hopes of finding a larger, more suitable winter campsite.[2] But they could find "no place better" than the relatively well-timbered, well-watered area about Cold Springs.[3] However, as an increasing number of wagons rolled into an already overcrowded campground, a more commodious, more defensible location was required.

Consequently, explorations intensified in early August along "the divide" between the Missouri and the Elkhorn rivers, resulting in the discovery of a more acceptable campsite on higher ground fourteen miles north of Cold Springs and three miles west of the Missouri River.[4] Called "Cutler's Park" after Alpheus Cutler, its discoverer, the site was situated on a raised prairie between two ridges or bluffs among the gently rolling steppe lands two and one-half miles west of the Missouri River.[5]

The sheltered hollow soon filled with wagons, which were separated into two divisions—Young's camp on the south and Heber Kimball's on the north. Both in turn were organized into two large squares. Plenty of water was available, and everything seemed ready for the building of Nebraska's first city.

Colonel Thomas Kane, who mingled with the Latter-day Saints

for two months before returning to Washington, vividly described Cutler's Park in its formative days.

It was situated . . . upon some finely rounded hills that encircle a favorite cool spring. On each of these a square was marked out and the wagons as they arrived took their positions along its four sides in double rows, so as to leave a roomy street or passage way between them. The tents were disposed also in rows, at intervals between the wagons. The cattle were folded in high-fenced yards outside. The quadrangle inside was left vacant for the sake of ventilation, and the streets, covered with leafy arbor work, and kept scrupulously clean, formed a shaded cloister walk. This was the place of exercise for slowly recovering invalids, the day-home of the infants, and the evening promenade of all.[6]

At a general meeting on 9 August in a shaded grove north of camp, Young and the Twelve gave their official approval of the site despite the relative lack of timber, announced an organizational blueprint, and indicated their intentions to establish government and maintain order. The first priority was to reorder the camp from a travelling into a resident organization of two or three standing divisions or companies with a local government or Municipal High Council.[7] Alpheus Cutler, appointed president of the Winter Quarters High Council and sustained by the uplifted hands of over three hundred people in attendance, was responsible not only for his council but also, indirectly, for the one across the river.[8] As their first item of business the new High Council appointed a standing guard, or a police force, to act under the jurisdiction of the newly appointed marshal, Horace S. Eldridge.[9] Young then gave several instructions respecting camp cleanliness, trespassing on nearby Indian cornfields, and other immediate concerns.[10]

Drawing upon their Iowa experiences, Young partitioned the two companies into smaller subdivisions of hundreds and tens with a foreman over each "to have the charge of all the men and boys in his subdivision." All were to work under him and be subject to the council.[11] Leaders with stewardship over smaller, well-defined units, so it was argued, could more effectively manage the labors of the camp and more adequately fulfil the needs of those in their jurisdictions. By 12 August the first division and its twelve subdivisions numbered 324 men over ten years of age, with another 800-plus women and children.[12] Kimball's division

Crossing the Missouri River. From an oil-on-canvas painting by
C. C. A. Christensen. Reproduced with permission from the
Museum of Church History and Art, The Church of Jesus
Christ of Latter-day Saints.

consisted of only five subdivisions of 228 men and boys, 230
wagons, and comparatively fewer animals.[13]

During the weeks that followed they worked at cutting hay,
fencing in herds, erecting a meeting place, digging wells, and
draining mires. Until sufficient hay had been cut and stacked as
winter feed for cattle—and by early September they had cut
from 1,500 to 2,000 tons from the prairie wild grass—cabin
building would have to wait.[14]

Aware they were on disputed territory between contending
bands of Indians, camp authorities arranged to meet first with
the Omaha and later with the Oto after they had returned from
their biannual buffalo hunts. Albert P. Rockwood, Jedediah M.
Grant, and Charles Bird were directed to arrange a council with
the Omaha in late August. Going into the Cutler's Park powwow
of 28 August 1846, both sides knew what they wanted from the
other. The Mormons sought permission to settle in the area for
at least two years, use a reasonable amount of timber, cut grass,

City of the Saints at Cutler's Park, 1846. Original sketch in the Heber C. Kimball Journals of 1846, drawn by a member of the Kimball family (possibly Peter Hansen). The sketch is really one long horizontal with the bottom half carrying on to the right of the top half. The small size of the journal did not permit a fold-out. Reproduced with permission from the Church Archives, The Church of Jesus Christ of Latter-day Saints, Heber C. Kimball Collection.

and make improvements. In addition they wanted good relations with the Indians and a positive reception to deflect simmering criticisms from the Office of Indian Affairs. For their part, the Omaha saw the opportunity as a way to protect themselves from their enemy the Sioux. And in return for their concessions, they were determined to seek assistance and favors of every kind.

Big Elk, principal chief of the Omaha nation, Standing Elk, his son, Logan Fontenelle, their interpreter, a half breed and an experienced trader in his own right, and seventy other lesser chiefs and braves represented the Omaha claim while Young, the rest of the Twelve, and the High Council spoke for the Latter-day Saints. The large double tent used for the occasion was soon so crowded that camp historian Willard Richards had to listen and take notes from outside the canvas wall. After shaking hands and smoking the traditional pipe of peace, Young presented his case. He reviewed the call of the Battalion and their decision to stop at the Missouri for the winter and offered the Omaha assistance in planting their crops, learning mechanical trades and blacksmithing, and transporting corn from Trader's Point, but stressed their determination not to participate in any conflicts with warring tribes. "We wish to do you good," he concluded.[15] Big Elk, through Fontenelle, got right to the point.

I am an old man and will have to call you all my sons. I am willing you should stop in my country but I am afraid of my great father at Washington. . . . We have been oppressed by other tribes because we were weak. We have been like the hungry dog which runs through camp in search of something to eat and meets with enemies on every side. We have been oppressed for ten years; many times we could have defended ourselves, but our great Father told us not to fight. . . . We heard you were a good people, we are glad to have you come.[16]

In agreeing to offer use of timber and water, Big Elk extracted a promise for agricultural and mechanical assistance, gun repair, and a pledge not to kill much game in the area. Knowing the Oto would want a share in the treaty provisions, he advised the Mormons to move their encampment several miles northward to undisputed Omaha land "so that we may have the benefit of your improvements after you leave." Agreeing to a Mormon stay for up to two years, Big Elk concluded, "While you are among us as brethren, we will be brethren to you. I like, my son, what you have said very well."[17] His only provision was that their negotiations be approved by the Indian agents. Three days later their agreement was put into writing.[18]

Meanwhile Orson Pratt was heading a delegation to the Oto Indians to arrive at a similar understanding and "to know definitely whether we might stay in peace."[19] The Oto were anxious that the Mormons "should not close with the offer of the Omahas and go up the river," since they might not share in whatever improvements were made.[20] Like the Omaha, the Oto also promised noninterference.

Conspicuously absent from these councils was John Miller, the newly appointed Council Bluffs Indian agent. Whether en route to his new post or simply uninvited, Miller did not look kindly on these proceedings and eventually contested the treaties despite Captain Allen's permission and Kane's assurances. In time it would spell trouble, but for the present, Young got what he needed and the Indians capitalized on their opportunity.

Though the Mormons did not accept Big Elk's offer to move to his undisputed land (likely because they did not want to be any further away from Missouri trading centers or any closer to the Sioux), they did explore further north near the end of August, discovering a better camping area nearer the river and closer to their newly proposed ferry site.[21]

The favored spot, eighteen miles north of Bellevue on a bench of land above the river, was drained on the north and south by two creeks and bounded on the north and west with high bluffs naturally suited for defensive purposes.[22] Favoring the change to the new site were its natural defenses, seclusion from strong prairie winds, and proximity to good streams that would permit the construction of a water-powered flour mill.[23]

On Friday, 11 September, the Twelve officially selected the new site.[24] Surveying began under Young's personal direction in the late afternoon and continued for several days until, on the morning of 23 September, the first parties began selecting their lots on the new site.[25]

Winter Quarters was situated on a level flat on the second bluff from the river with brooks on the north and south end. Running roughly parallel to the bend of the river, the town plat extended southeast from a relatively high bluff on the north, where they placed several pieces of brass cannon.[26]

Major Thomas H. Harvey, who visited Winter Quarters in late fall, offered this description:

> [It] is situated on the South bank of the Missouri river 18 miles above Bellevue in the Omaha country, upon a beautiful table land, rising I would judge about fifty feet above common water, running back about 600 yards to the Bluffs, and extending down the river . . . about 1 ½ miles; the Bluff or rather the high land rises beautifully above the table land. The camp is a regularly laid out town embracing the width of the table land and extending along the river a mile or more.[27]

Covering some six to eight hundred acres gently sloping towards the Missouri, the site was closer to the river than many preferred. At least three men, Jedediah M. Grant, Samuel Russell, and Lorenzo Young, objected to extending the city boundaries so close to the river bottoms, believing higher land to be much healthier.[28] At a mid-September meeting of the Twelve, the High Council, and other leaders, half voted for locating a little higher and little further to the west and over a broader area,[29] but in the end were reluctantly persuaded by Young, Orson Pratt, and Heber Kimball that the more compact site near the river was preferable. In answer to the persistent objection of unhealthy, poisonous gases rising from vegetable decompositions along the river, Kimball assured them they would rise and be blown away by the prevailing winds without injuring the settlement.[30]

Soon Nebraska's first city was divided into five-acre blocks measuring 20 by 40 rods (380 by 660 feet) each with twenty lots per block.[31] In turn, each lot measured 4 by 10 rods (72 by 165 feet). Sufficiently wide streets were laid out, two of which, First and Second Main, ran southeast to northwest at an angle of 22½ degrees west of north parallel to the river, with another fourteen streets intersecting at right angles to the two main streets. The city plat initially called for forty-one blocks, sixteen named streets, and 594 lots.[32] All houses were to be built on the outside of each block near the streets with yards running inward up against those of the homes behind them so as to form, as at Cutler's Park, a ventilated, protected garden area. Such an arrangement, it was thought, would also create more community camaraderie. Five wells per block (none on the streets) were the maximum permissible.[33] Outhouses were to be placed at the rear of every lot and dug at least 8 feet deep.[34] Thus a full-sized block could accommodate twenty houses and a population of from 150 to 300 people.[35] South of the city, a large stockyard was sectioned off for the cattle.

Bridges were soon built across the creek on the south leading to the cattle yards and across Turkey Creek (formerly Willow Creek and later Mill Creek) on the north adjoining the city with the military installations above the northern bluff. Contracts were also let out to build a large water mill on Turkey Creek west of the bridge.[36]

As at Cutler's Park, Winter Quarters was apportioned out along family divisional lines with Young's division occupying most of the center of the city, Heber Kimball's company in the more southerly neighborhoods, Wilford Woodruff and his forty families occupying one entire block, presumably along Woodruff Street, and Cutler's clan along the riverbanks, where most of the sheep were stockaded and haying operations conducted.[37]

Later, in November, because of Indian pillagings, most lots

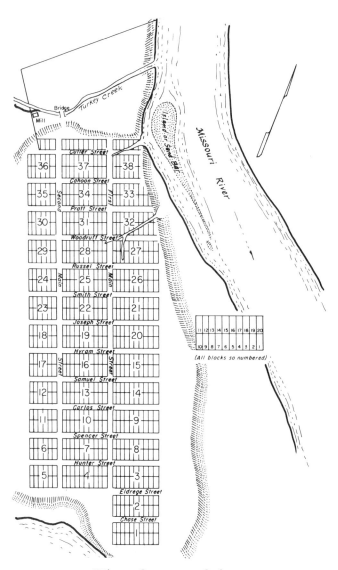

Winter Quarters, 1846–47

An educated guess would place the Council House in block 22 not far from Brigham Young's home, which probably was on a corner lot in block 25. Other public buildings included a store, a carding-machine house, a hostel for visitors, and possibly a few small schoolhouses. SOURCE: Thomas L. Kane Collection, Brigham Young University Library.

south of Hyrum Street were evacuated "to form a line of defense against the Indians on the south." At the same time, lots were extended up to and including Turkey Creek and its outlet, so that the city was moved northward and considerably compacted. Most houses from below Hyrum Street were repositioned into a line along the north side of Hyrum Street to form a solid wall of buildings. A tall picket fence was eventually constructed running from this line to the bluffs and to the river's edge.[38] The removal itself was not difficult, since most cabins had not yet been constructed.

As if on cue, on the very first day of moving onto the site, yet another rumor reached camp that a U.S. Army of dragoons was approaching.[39] Though again a false alarm, it proved the catalyst for reorganizing the Nauvoo Legion (that city's militia) into twelve companies of twenty-five men each and an artillery company of sixty-three men under John Scott. Winter Quarters' Nauvoo Legion was a volunteer standing militia on call anytime.[40]

Once ground breaking for spring crops, fencing of fields, hay-cutting and stacking, and some preliminary sowing were completed, all hands turned to building suitable shelter. Up until mid-October, virtually every man, woman, and child had been living in tents, makeshift hovels, and wagons now practically waterlogged and canvas-torn. With the lateness of the season upon them, the situation was fast becoming critical with a rapidly increasing number suffering from exposure and sickness. Complicating matters was the relative lack of timber in the area,[41] and both Indian and government restrictions on its use.[42] Hence timber parties began travelling upstream in October to cut cottonwood, lynnwood, and willows and then raft the wood down the river, though not without mishaps caused by strong currents and frequent sandbars.[43] Most gathered firewood from a small island across from camp that possessed an abundance of driftwood at the time.[44]

The quality of the homes varied widely from large, sturdy, two-story affairs with solid floors throughout to inadequate cabin shanties without doors or floors and only partial roofs. Some were not cabins at all but mere dugouts in a nearby bluff. Many families, particularly those of absent Mormon Battalion soldiers, were totally dependent on the skills and schedules of those appointed to assist them.

Some of the leaders had the most substantial homes largely because many more people lived in their homes than elsewhere.

For instance, Heber Kimball's house—not completed until late December—was a story and a half high, built of logs hewed on the inside, and it contained two small rooms on each floor. Like most of the larger, better built houses in Winter Quarters, it was covered with oak shingles, boasted a brick chimney (from brick gathered at the old abandoned garrison sites fourteen miles away), puncheon floors (logs split three inches thick and hewed on one side), and, peculiar to Kimball's home, a six-paned window in each room.[45] For extra protection against wind and rain, two tents were spread on the roof, not an uncommon practice. Residing here were no less than eighteen people—Heber Kimball, a wife, and four little boys in one room, William Kimball's young family in another room, six people in another, and two of Heber's other wives in the fourth room.[46] His six other homes, built for family members and plural wives, stood adjacent to the larger homestead described above. Kimball and his family went on to build another twenty-five cabins, most of which were for the poor in his division.[47]

Surely the most singular-looking edifice in town was Dr. Willard Richards's home. Called "the Octagon," potato heap, coal pit, roundhouse, or doctor's den, depending on the mood of the observer, it functioned as a private residence, an office for the Twelve and High Council, a make-shift hospital, and a post office. As the sketch illustrates, it was a true octagon with a sloping roof of puncheon logs that reached to a window at the center of the raised ceiling providing daylight. The roof was covered with straw and forty-five loads of earth.[48]

Near Brigham Young's large home on Main Street,[49] the bishops constructed a one-and-one-half-story Council House, a sort of community center, town hall, and gathering place all in one. Twenty-two by thirty-two feet in size, it had hewn log floors, fireplaces, and windows. Because of its size, most social events and indoor religious gatherings were held there.[50] A bowery was erected nearby to serve as an outdoor center for public meetings, conferences, and other large assemblies.

While some homes were large and adequately built, most others were considerably smaller, single-room structures twelve by eighteen feet or twelve by twelve feet, possibly 7 feet high, and made of lynnwood or cottonwood logs. Most had dirt floors. Most roofs were made by splitting oak timbers into boards or "shakes" (six inches wide by three feet long and one-half inch thick) kept in place by weight poles, while others were made

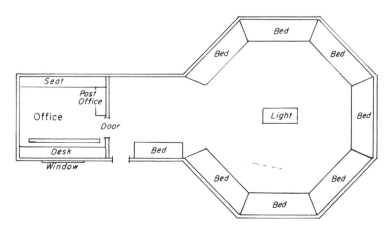

The plan of Willard Richards's Octagon and office, Winter Quarters, 1847. Source: Journal History of the Church, 31 December 1846.

of willows, straw, and earth about a foot thick. Chimneys were made of either prairie sod or brick, and doors were made of shakes pinned together and finished with a string latch. Inside, log houses were daubed with clay and other makeshift caulking. A very few had the luxury of fireplaces made of either brick or pounded clay.[51]

With winter coming on, many people were forced to move into only partially completed cabins and were glad even of that. Hosea Stout, on 24 November, celebrating the day his family moved into their "little shanty," wrote, "this day was the first day that my only living child [he had lost several by this time] now seven months and two days old ever was in a house, being born in the wild, rude and uninhabited prairies and remained so till now, a perfect child of nature."[52] Said Eliza R. Snow of her humble cabin:

> The log house we moved into was partly chinked and mudded, leaving large crevices for the wind—then cold and blustering. This hastily erected hut was roofed on one side, with a tent-cloth thrown over the other, and withal was minus a chimney. A fire, which was built on one side, filled the house with smoke until it became unendurable. . . . Our cooking was

done out of doors until after the middle of November, when a chimney was made.[53]

The city's location on sloping land caused serious problems, particularly during thunderstorms. Since gutters were unknown, scenes like the following were common.

> In the evening the wind came from the North accompanied by torrents of rain which ran like rivulets down the streets. It bursted into my house in torrents, and filled it up in a few moments untill I had to throw the watter out by the bucket full untill we were all completely drenched.[54]

Furnishings were meager, even crude. Fireplaces were rare and stoves even more so. Most furniture either had been left behind in Nauvoo or long since discarded or traded away. A typical household contained barrels, chests for tables, the occasional wooden chair or two, trunks, and homemade bedsteads.[55] One new bride, with more to be thankful for than most, provided this helpful description.

> We made curtains serve as partitions to divide the bedroom, repositories, etc. from the kitchen. Most of our furniture we had made to order—such as cupboards and bedsteads—they being attached to the house, also tables and chairs, and stools, and an occasional rocking chair, relics of other days, graced our ingleside. I was fortunate in having one of the latter, which I had brought with me. And here I received my "setting out" in crockery ware, etc. which, though not very extensive, was deemed quite immense for these times.[56]

Although bare, drafty, and unpretentious, the cabins were more comfortable than the dugouts or caves some were living in near the riverbanks and bluffs. These "sod caves," looking like outdoor potato cellers, had fireplaces at the upper end and were supported by ridgepoles and two center uprights. The ceilings were reinforced with willow and straw to minimize seepage, and blankets improvised for doors. A few had window panes positioned right into the dirt walls. Margaret Phelps, whose husband had recently died while marching with the Battalion, and who was herself deathly sick with fever, described her dwelling in less than glowing terms.

> Winter found me bed-ridden, destitute, in a wretched hovel which was built upon a hillside; the season was one of constant rain; the situation of the hovel and its openness, gave free ac-

cess to piercing winds and water flowed over the dirt floor, converting it into mud two or three inches deep; no wood but what
my little ones picked up around the fences, so green it filled the
room with smoke; the rain dropping and wetting the bed
which I was powerless to leave.[57]

Realizing how unhealthy such sod houses and caves were, and
fearful of cave-ins from heavy spring rains and runoffs, city authorities constantly encouraged those living in cabins, who had
room, to give shelter to others less fortunate than they. Come
spring Young instructed the sod dwellers to leave "and go into
their tents and waggons and live in them and they will do well."
Most incredibly, some families were forced to pass the winter
barely surviving in snow-covered tents and poorly heated covered wagons.[58]

It was a time of make-do or do without. Some women, like
Eliza Lyman, were not content to live in mere hovels or to wait
forever for their husbands or bishops to build them a home. "My
sister Caroline and I," she wrote,

> have been trying to build a log house for ourselves as we do not
> feel comfortable where we are. We first got possession of an old
> house which we pulled down and had the logs moved to a spot
> where we wanted it put up again. As we could not get anyone to
> lay it up for us, we went at it ourselves and laid it up the rest of
> the way and put dirt soot on it. There I built a fire place and
> chimney till it was about as high as my head and some brother
> stopped it for me. We had one window of three panes of glass.
> We divided the room with a wagon cover and let D. R. Clark
> and wife have one part as he had helped to build it. We had
> each room enough to put our bed by having the foot of the
> bedsteads come together and about six foot square from there
> to the fire.[59]

Owing to their industry and spirit of mutual cooperation and
support that characterized their endeavors, the "Camp of Israel"
transformed itself into a prairie city in barely two months. For-
tunately, they were blessed with a long, mild fall.[60] Thomas Bullock, recently arrived from Nauvoo, made this observation of the
city in late November.

> [I] went through the City—where, nine weeks ago there was
> not a foot path, or a Cow track, now may be seen hundreds of
> houses, and hundreds in different stages of completion—im-
> possible to distinguish the rich from the poor. The Streets are

wide and regular and every prospect of a large City being
raised up here.[61]

By 30 December 1846, Winter Quarters consisted of 538 log cabins, 83 sod houses, and a population of 3,483. Eventually "about
800" cabins, huts, caves, and hovels were built and occupied.[62]
As the cold, dark winter began to set in, little wonder that
Young could indulge in some self-satisfaction.

I feel like a father with a great family of children around me,
in a winter storm, and I am looking with calmness, confidence
and patience for the clouds to break, and the sun to shine,
so that I can run out and plant and sow and gather in the
corn and wheat and say, "Children, come home, winter is approaching again, and I have homes, and wood, and flour, and
meal . . . and I am ready to kill the fatted calf and make a joyful
feast to all who will come and partake."[63]

But if conditions were stabilizing at the Missouri in late 1846,
they were rapidly deteriorating for those left back at the Mississippi. Most had fled Nauvoo by the summer. Over two thousand
had come on in February's advanced camp, and hundreds followed intermittently throughout March and April. At least three
thousand left in May, so that by mid-August, according to one
informal census, only "250 males old and young" or an estimated population of 1,000 to 1,500 remained.[64] Many of those
who had departed found employment along the Mississippi
River at Galena, Burlington, St. Louis, or elsewhere in hopes of
outfitting themselves and families and of joining the main camp
later in the year. Those remaining could not afford to leave and
were dependent on absent sons and husbands at the Bluffs, in
the Battalion, or elsewhere. Their reliance on others is aptly por-
trayed in an imploring letter to Brigham Young from Elizabeth
Gilbert, a widow who was left behind by those she believed had
promised to take her to the Bluffs.

It [Nauvoo] is truly a lonesome and dismal place . . . I want
to know what I shall do[.] Is it best for me to remain among the
gentiles? . . . my body is almost worn out a struggling to get a
shelter for my head. . . . tell all my friends that I yet live and
my faith in the gospel is as firm as the everlasting hills and
strangism has no effect on my mind . . . if you think it wisdom
for me to come out this fall how shall I gather[?] Council me as
though I was your child or Sister and whatever you say that I
will do.[65]

It had always been the plan to send teams and wagons back to Nauvoo as soon as circumstances at the Missouri permitted. As shown, the need to bring out the poor was a contributing factor to the demise of the Grand Island plan. While appointing the High Council for the Pottawattami land settlements on 21 July, the Twelve gave it the charge, among other duties, to bring "all the poor saints brought from Nauvoo and locate them here for the winter." Much consideration had also been given to selling the temples, with most of the funds to go to the outfitting of latecomers or, preferably, to pay river passage for the entire lot to within a few miles of the Bluffs.[66]

Sometime in September, Newel Whitney, whose duties as presiding bishop were directed toward the temporal welfare of the entire church membership, returned to Nauvoo to purchase much-needed flour and other provisions for those left behind.[67] By 9 September, while almost every other hand at Cutler's Park was preparing for winter, a dozen or more men whose families were still back at Nauvoo, eagerly volunteered to join Orville M. Allen's relief company and return with extra teams to help out.[68] More were to come.

But the matter took on greater urgency only a few days after Allen's departure. On 24 September, Daniel H. Wells and William Cutler arrived in haste from the Mississippi with news of the late Battle of Nauvoo. Feared and rumored since even before the February exodus, armed conflict had begun on 12 September. A handful of town defenders, perhaps a hundred, had fought against a vastly superior force.[69] Despite the obvious departure of so many city residents and the promise of the rest to leave as soon as possible, Mormon opponents determined to force the expulsion of the remnant population.

Fearing the inevitable crisis, everyone who could possibly afford it got out of town. but those too poor to leave had no other choice but to turn to the church for assistance. On 31 August 1846, the Nauvoo trustees reported that 750 people were calling on them daily for aid to leave and "to procure food to subsist on; they are also very destitute of clothing."[70] A series of lynchings broke out on farms near Nauvoo just prior to the attacks on the city itself. The Battle of Nauvoo, or "Nauvoo War" as some termed it, lasted five days, during which time several were killed on both sides before the defenders prudently surrendered on 17 September.[71]

The end of the battle was effectively the beginning of the so-called "poor camp." Scores of families with the barest of provisions crossed the river into Iowa to flee hostilities, only to face intense suffering. Thomas Kane, while returning to Washington after his successful efforts at raising the Mormon Battalion, stumbled on the scene, and though given to a crusading pen, his description of the impoverished refugees was likely not far from the mark.

> Dreadful indeed, was the suffering of these forsaken beings. Cowed and cramped by cold and sunburn, alternating as each weary day and night dragged on, they were, almost all of them, the crippled victims of disease. They were there because they had no homes, nor hospital nor poor-house nor friends to offer them any. They could not satisfy the feeble cravings of their sick: they had not bread to quiet the fractious hunger cries of their children. Mothers and babes, daughters and grandparents, all of them alike, were bivouacked in tatters, wanting even covering to comfort those whom the sick shiver of fever was searching to the marrow.[72]

Such was the report of Wells and Cutler, with the further sad news that the sale of the temple and other properties was virtually impossible, given the disruptive social climate.

Later word trickling back from Nauvoo substantiated their worst fears. Orville M. Allen reported that the poor camp was very sick and subsisting on boiled or parched corn for days at a time.[73] "I wod rather die chewg a root, than lie bleaching on the banks of this river," reported Thomas Bullock.[74] Such tidings naturally aroused the sympathies of almost everyone at the Bluffs, themselves still without shelter. Many of them had relatives in the poor camps. At a special meeting on Sunday, 27 September, on the west side of Main Street in Winter Quarters, Young described the sufferings and called for immediate relief teams and donations.[75]

Since the decision had only recently been made to vacate Cutler's Park for Winter Quarters, causing further hay-cutting and house-building delays, and since those over in Iowa were better prepared, with supposedly more time to prepare for the coming winter, the Twelve instructed the east side settlements to carry the burden of rescuing the poor camp. "Let the fire of the covenant which you made in the House of the Lord burn in your hearts" counseled Young.[76]

The specifics of the plan as presented to the Pottawattamie

High Council were to send back one or two other rescue companies led by James Murdock and Allen Taylor, with some twenty-five more teams, and to assist Captain Allen in his relief efforts.[77] While returning to Nauvoo, they were to cut and stack all the hay they could "in some bye place each day" to guarantee feed during their return journey in the colder weather. The poor camps were then to be located at Garden Grove, Mt. Pisgah, and other Iowa farms to minimize travel and to prevent a further burden on the already hard-pressed settlements at the Bluffs.[78] However, not everyone on the east side agreed with Young's assessment that they were better prepared than their counterparts at Winter Quarters. They were already carrying the brunt of providing for Mormon Battalion families and felt that this was another heavy burden. Yet most responded favorably.[79] Murdock and Taylor and company were on their way not long before Allen arrived at Montrose, Iowa, attempting the first rescue.[80]

By 9 October, the Allen company was on its way west with the first company of 157 souls in twenty-eight wagons. The Taylor and Murdock camps rounded up the rest by early November.[81] The return journey, over what Bullock referred to "as the most damnable road I ever travelled," was relatively uneventful, though, because of constant sickness, exhaustion, prairie fires, and not a little squabbling, the Allen company took fifty days to make the trip of 335 miles, far longer, apparently, than Taylor's[82] Surprisingly only one or two perished during the entire episode.

Many now worn out, tired, and disillusioned, decided to take their chances wintering at either the east or west forks of the Nishnabotona River or at other small, prairie shantyville settlements that had been popping up all along the Mormon trail in western Iowa ever since the previous summer. Almost all of them depended on trade with Missouri farmers and settlements for survival.[83] The rest were likely absorbed into any one of scores of encampments on the immediate east bank of the Missouri, which were forming on almost every spring or creek boasting a grove of timber. By year's end the east-side Mormons were scattered over 10,000 square miles and as far east as Bentonsport and Farmington.[84] Only a handful of the poor camp, including Thomas Bullock, made it all the way to the Missouri, arriving, finally, at Winter Quarters on 28 November 1846.

While the main body of the church was settling in at Winter Quarters and in western Iowa, one other satellite settlement was making camp on the Niobrara (L'Eau Qui Court, or Running

Winter Quarters on the Missouri River, 1846. From a canvas painting by C. C. A. Christensen. Courtesy of the Brigham Young
University Fine Arts Collection, all rights reserved.

Water) River some one hundred fifty miles north of the Bluffs.
Led by the independent and increasingly disenchanted George
Miller, the so-called Ponca settlement resulted from a combina-
tion of broken plans and differing objectives.

George Miller and James Emmett, be it remembered, Brigham Young had dispatched to Grand Island in late June to explore Grand Island and beyond for a winter-quarters site and to
bring back a possible fur shipment for Peter Sarpy. Miller had
also been ordered to await the Twelve for a possible trek to the
mountains that year. Miller's company of fifty-two wagons arrived at the Pawnee Loup Indian village in mid-July only to discover that the Sioux had recently destroyed the place while the
Pawnee were away on a buffalo hunt. Only the quick thinking of
government farmers and Presbyterian missionaries had saved
the Pawnee women and children from certain death, and they
were leaving the camp as Miller arrived.[85] Miller agreed to send
some men to protect the missionaries and families on their way
back to the Indian agency at Bellevue and to carry Sarpy's furs.

Catching Quails. From a canvas painting by C. C. A. Christensen. Courtesy of the Brigham Young University Fine Arts Collection, all rights reserved.

Having heard of the Sioux attacks, Young sent out another company of twenty-five men and their families on 22 July, under the direction of John Mikesell, Newel Knight, and Joseph Holbrook, to reinforce the Grand Island encampment and to wait for further instructions. Mikesell and his company of seventy-two wagons reached the Pawnee Village on 1 or 2 August, at which time Miller was exploring the area, repairing damage, restoring the Pawnee corn crops, and awaiting further word.[86]

But between 22 July and early August, the Twelve had definitely abandoned all plans for a mountain trek and a major Grand Island encampment that season, and an express was sent to Miller and his enlarged company either to winter alone at Grand Island or, preferably, to return to the Missouri. Miller received word of the new plans on 7 August along with Young's directions that, if he opted to remain at the south side of the Loup Fork or at Grand Island on the South Platte and wait for the Twelve in the spring, he was authorized to organize a High Council and to serve as senior president over the camp.[87]

When Young's communication reached Miller, he was in conference with eight Ponca Indian chiefs, who had arrived in the village to make a defense pact with the Pawnee against the Sioux, their mutual enemy. Though disappointed at not finding the Pawnee at home, the Ponca did meet with Miller and, anxious for allies, invited his company to winter with them on the Niobrara River. Miller and Emmett, his chief counselor and part-time interpreter, despite serious reservations from many in the High Council and objections from several in camp, and before waiting for any possible counsel from the Missouri, agreed to the Ponca invitation. Miller spelled out some of his reasons in a letter to Young, including his belief that the Pawnee station was too dangerous. He went on to say that the Ponca promised them protection against the Sioux, the use of their timber and land for sowing grain and corn, and a pledge of noninterference, all in return for blacksmithing and farming assistance. Since the Ponca were supposedly "not more than fifty miles" north and "on our direct course to fort Larimie," Miller thought the plan a good one.[88]

The truth of the matter is that Miller and Emmett had designs of their own to set up a community similar to what Emmett had previously established on the Vermillion River, based upon "common stock principles" with all private property surrendered into their hands.[89] It was much the same economic order that Lyman Wight was creating in Texas, a system many opposed.

Fourteen families refused to follow Miller and stayed back at Grand Island.[90] Led by Jacob Gates, this small contingent soon hosted the return of the Pawnee, who "appeared friendly" and "expressed a willingness that the brethren should stay and promised to use them well."[91]

On hearing of the Grand Island split, Young concluded that Miller "was deceived in reference to the locality of Puncha and that he was running wild through the counsel of James Emmett."[92] They also considered Gates and his few followers in "rather precarious" circumstances and sent Jackson Redding to direct them to return to the Bluffs. The Gates camp subsequently arrived back at Winter Quarters on 10 October.[93]

Young's objections to Miller's course were both political and religious. They were well aware of Emmett's sordid track record among the Indians and the unkind attitude both the Sioux and Indian agents harbored against him. They also feared that an isolated Mormon encampment on the southern borders of Sioux territory was an open invitation to serious trouble, a move that might endanger the entire Mormon settlements at the Missouri. Emmett was a maverick, a wild-eyed dreamer in Young's mind. On the other hand, Miller greatly esteemed Emmett. "The excellencies of this man Emmit as a skilful hunter and pioneer cannot be too highly spoken of," said Miller. "He was perhaps never excelled, even by the renowned Daniel Boone." [94] But Young was convinced Miller and Emmett had been too easily persuaded to winter with the Ponca and might well become unwilling instigators of Sioux attacks.

By now Young had good reason to believe that Miller, if not in open competition, was determined to build a camp as equally successful as Winter Quarters. He further believed Miller might openly vie for leadership of the church, certainly for some gathering place other than the Great Basin. As renegade members of the Council of Fifty, Miller and Emmett were not taking lightly Young's tightening grip on the reins of church leadership. Consciously pursuing an inevitable clash, they were stayed only by their increasingly suspicious and defiant High Council. [95]

Young would have ordered their return, but perhaps sensed his instructions would not be followed. Besides, Winter Quarters was already so hard-pressed for provisions and pasture that Miller and Emmett might just as well stay where they were, but under strict guidelines to fulfill all promises with the Ponca, maintain strict neutrality between tribes, and "cultivate the spirit of perfect peace." [96]

The journey from the Pawnee to the Ponca village took eleven days and was three times further than anticipated, a fact Emmett likely knew but took careful pains to conceal. Travelling in three companies (Miller's, Emmett's and Holbrook's), they finally arrived at the Niobrara on 24 August. [97] Although the Ponca settlement was surprised at this unexpected arrival of 178 wagons and almost four hundred white settlers, they accepted them without serious incident. However, after Chief Tea-Nuga-Numpa (Buffalo-Bulls-Two) died just two days after rejoining his people, his successors had to quell suspicion that the whites were somehow responsible. For safety's sake, Miller was advised to move further east and settle on the north side of the Niobrara. On 8 September they laid out a site for their winter quarters about two miles from the confluence of the Missouri and Niobrara rivers near rushes and fine fishing holes. After cutting several tons of hay they erected a picket fort 106 feet wide with a gate at each end and large enough to accommodate 110 lots. [98]

Meanwhile several families led by Asahel Lathrop had become so disenchanted with Miller that they abandoned the Ponca settlement to follow the Missouri south until they arrived at Winter Quarters or until they found a suitable site for their own winter encampment.[99] In a letter of 20 September, Young counseled Miller to abandon the settlement and move down to the Bluffs. "If you want to locate your families here you have only to build a boat and drop them down to this place where you can become partakers of such like blessings as we enjoy."[100] Not surprisingly, Miller did not budge. As it turned out, Miller's maverick settlement was never threatened by the Sioux, although a frightening fire on 26 December, which "spread over the prairie as fast as a horse could run," burned most of their hay, several of their wagons, and so consumed their energies that several died, including Newel Knight.[101]

The end of 1846 is an ideal time to calculate the number of trekkers, since everyone had settled in for the winter and the large migrations from Great Britain were yet to arrive.[102] Without question the largest concentration of the Latter-day Saints was at Winter Quarters, but at no time did its population exceed 4,000. At the conclusion of a ward-by-ward census of the city in December, conducted by the several bishops, the exact population stood at 3,483, of which 757 were men, leaving a balance of 2,736 women and children.[103] Even by June 1847, Young did not estimate a Winter Quarters population in excess of 4,000.[104]

Across the river exact figures are harder to come by. It is known that at the end of 1846, 210 people lived in Bishop Joseph Knight's ward, and 319 in the nearby Blockhouse Branch.[105] A conservative estimate of the numbers in surrounding groves and settlements at Trader's Point, on the Boyer River, and in the immediate vicinity would be 2,500.[106] Almost 400 people spent the winter with George Miller at the Niobrara, while Asahel Lathrop's grazing center 100 miles south of Miller comprised some 50 people. Thus almost 7,000 Latter-day Saints spent the winter near Council Bluffs.

Add to this number the almost 1,500 in St. Louis,[107] the estimated 500 east of Garden Grove at Chariton Point, Burlington, Farmington, Iowa City, and other points (Kane estimates 1,325, likely an exaggeration), another 500 between Mosquito Creek and the Nishnabotona River, the 500 in the Battalion, 700 at Mt. Pisgah, 600 at Garden Grove,[108] 50 in Nauvoo, 300 in Burlington, Galena, and Alton on the Mississippi, and 200 at St. Joseph and

Table 1. *Mormon Population, 31 December 1846*

Location	Population
Winter Quarters	4,000
East Bank Missouri River	2,500 (est.)
Miller's Ponca Settlement	400
Lathrop Settlement	50
Total at the Missouri River	6,950
St. Louis	1,500
Between the Mississippi River and Garden Grove	500 (est.)
Between the Nishnabotona River and East Fork Mosquito Creek	500 (est.)
Mormon Battalion	500
Mt. Pisgah	700
Garden Grove	600
Nauvoo	50 (est.)
Burlington, Galena, Alton, etc.	300 (est.)
St. Joseph, Savannah, and other northwest Missouri towns	200 (est.)
Total in Iowa and Missouri	4,850
Grand total	11,800

Savannah, Missouri, and one arrives at the combined figure of approximately 11,800.[109] (See table 1.)

If 17,000 had lived in and about Nauvoo in December 1846, almost 70 percent of them were accountable among various Mormon clusters and encampments a year later.[110] Of the remaining 5,000, several hundred had converted to Strang, while others had returned to their homes disillusioned and disaffected. A small number were never Mormons to begin with.

Thus by the end of 1846 the Church of Jesus Christ of Latter-day Saints lay uprooted and strewn over a vast terrain stretching from Nauvoo to Winter Quarters, awaiting the wintry blast.

MORMONS, INDIANS, AND INDIAN AGENTS

Planting a large white community, no matter how temporary, in Indian territory among a destitute and suspicious native population was hazardous enough; to do so on disputed lands between two jealous tribes and within easy striking range of the Sioux was to risk potentially disastrous consequences. Even though treaties had been signed between the Latter-day Saints and the Omaha and Oto, the Mormon people rightly suspected difficulties. Their precarious situation demanded artful negotiations, incredible patience, and unending restraint to preserve harmony. In a very short time they found themselves on the receiving end of repeated Indian depredations and in the middle of intensifying and bloody intertribal conflicts. In large measure they were the architects of their own unenviable situation and eventually paid a high price for deciding to stay on Indian lands. Nevertheless, despite the trials, Mormon relations with the Indians remained uncommonly and surprisingly peaceful.

If patience and diplomacy characterized Mormon relations with the Indians, a spirit of suspicion dominated negotiations with representatives of the Office of Indian Affairs. A positive dialogue that commenced in mutual respect and understanding deteriorated into unfortunate acrimony and accusation. At issue were a host of factors: the obscurity of Mormon intentions, recurring changes and delays in their departure dates, alleged prejudice of Indian agents and subagents, Mormon negotiating tactics, and, at base, the very legality of building a sizable, seemingly permanent community on Indian lands.

Young's single objective was to live in peace among the Indians. He did not want and could not afford war and would sacrifice much to insure that end. The Saints had no conflict with the Indians and wished to live in harmony while regrouping and preparing for the trek further west.

Much in their theology prepared them to relate positively with the Indians. While other faiths believed in Christianizing them and had established schools, churches, and missions among numerous tribes—for example, the Catholics among the Pottawattami and the Presbyterians among the Pawnee—the Mormons believed they owned a special commission. A central doctrine of the Book of Mormon indicated that the American Indians, anciently called "Lamanites," were descendants of Jacob of the Old Testament, a remnant of the tribe of Joseph through Manasseh and consequently part of the ancient House of Israel, God's "chosen people." The Book of Mormon stated that though a fallen and cursed people because of transgression, "there are many promises which are extended to the Lamanites" and "at some period of time they will be brought to believe in his [Christ's] word."[1] According to the revelations given to Joseph Smith, "Jacob shall flourish in the wilderness, and the Lamanites shall blossom as the rose."[2] Although some of the early missions of the church to the Indians had proven unsuccessful, it was believed that the Lord's special promises were about to be fulfilled. Mormons felt they had a particular gospel to preach to the Indian and that God would preserve and support them in their efforts.

Wilford Woodruff, writing on New Year's eve, expressed a wish "that 1847 may not pass away until the Lamanites with their chiefs may begin to receive the gospel which the gentiles have rejected and cast out of their midst."[3] The expulsion of the Mormon people from their homes in Missouri and most recently in Nauvoo was perhaps a sign that God was removing His gospel from the "Gentiles" and was about to remember his ancient covenant people, the Lamanites.

These beliefs were held not only by camp leaders but pervaded the attitudes of the commoner as well. Fanny Murray, a sister of Brigham Young, writing to a friend back east said, "We do not suffer anything from fear of the Indians, for we know that for their sakes we are suffering all these things, and we are sure that the Lord Our God will not suffer them to destroy us."[4] Though many in camp did not share this absence of fear and prejudice, their religion demanded a genuine interest in the Indian's temporal and spiritual welfare. Much of the blame for the pitiable condition of the Indians, common sufferers in exile, the Mormons placed upon the same governments that had driven them out.

Regardless of their religious convictions, Young made it clear that this was neither the time nor the place for spreading the word. While at Winter Quarters they made few, if any, attempts to proselyte among their Indian neighbors and refrained from manning missions and schoolhouses among any of the tribes. The converting process would have to wait for a more propitious time.

To make war upon the Indians, then, was not only politically foolish and inexpedient, but patently offensive to Mormon beliefs. With so many men away in the army it was questionable whether the Mormons could have sustained any sort of extended armed conflict. Besides, the Indians might be valuable allies in warding off any attacking Missouri mobs or federal soldiers.

Aware of the potential danger, Young took every precaution. The linchpin in his peace policy was to display, but never use, armed force unless required in self-defense. This accounts, in part, for his determination to keep the settlements close together and for his scarcely concealed opposition to George Miller's establishment among the Ponca. Safety lay in convincingly large numbers and a strong, well-armed defense.

In January 1847 a company of Sioux with Chief Eagle at its head made a surprise visit to Asahel Lathrop's small encampment several miles north of Winter Quarters. Attracted, no doubt, by the immense number of cattle under Lathrop's jurisdiction, this band of over three hundred warriors clearly posed a serious threat to Lathrop's small contingent. While in the vicinity they killed thirty of Lathrop's herd and appeared poised for more. Lathrop invited Eagle and thirty of his braves to a feast, presented them gifts, and endeavored to make peace. Eagle responded that their purpose was to kill the Omaha and not the white man but that he sometimes had difficulty restraining his warriors.[5]

On hearing of this first serious encounter with the dreaded Sioux, Young immediately sent twenty-three extra armed men to bolster Lathrop's defenses and prevent further outbreaks. His instructions to Lathrop were clear and underlined his policy of dealing from strength.

> Let the loss be what it may, but you must be diligent and sleep with one eye open, and never again let the Indians or any other enemy within your fort. To do this is to throw yourself in the power of your enemy, as it gives him an advantage you cannot recall, until it is too late . . . keep them at respectful distance with the power always in your hands. . . .

Now, Brother Lathrop, you must watch as well as pray, and let the Indians get no advantage of you, or learn your numerical strength again, but do the best you can to give them such an opinion of your resources as to put them in awe . . . and at the same time inspire them with confidence in your good intentions [and] promote peace.[6]

The Sioux never again returned and never constituted a serious threat to the Mormons, even though opportunities to do so were many.

At Winter Quarters, meanwhile, it became standard policy to station armed guards near the cattle herds and around the perimeters of the city and in other conspicuous places to discourage Indian prowlers. Occasional cannon firing, military drills, and other conspicuous shows of force were all organized for defense and self-preservation.

A second and related policy was not to take sides with one tribe against the other. As much as the Omaha and Oto maneuvered for protection and favoritism, for the Latter-day Saints to incline to one or the other was extremely dangerous. Call for peace among them, but let the Indians fight their own battles—that was Mormon policy. In early negotiations with the Omaha, Young agreed to assist in their agricultural endeavors "but would not interfere in any of their difficulties with other tribes."[7] Such a course would surely have embroiled them in a savage cross fire and would have drawn the objections of the Indian agents, who were already concerned that just such an impasse might develop. Strict neutrality must govern all Mormon dealings.

A third principle was to leave the Indian alone, not to engage in any social or economic intercourse whatever, especially on an individual basis. In reality this was virtually impossible, given the Omaha's natural curiosity and constant visits to the camp and the documented sympathy many Mormons had for the begging and forlorn among the Omaha, especially the women and children. This policy coincided with federal regulations, and Young preferred not to contravene such laws and thereby give cause for investigation by Indian agents.

When in August several Oto brought roasting ears into camp to sell, Young, supposing they had been stolen from Omaha cornfields, warned his people not to buy them.[8] Trading must be left strictly to camp leaders and only on a collective basis. Liquor ("ardent spirits"), available in camp, was not to be traded to the Indians, though they often sought it. Those found guilty of sell-

MORMONS, INDIANS, AND INDIAN AGENTS

ing or distributing it among them were punished by the whip-
lash. Feeding the Indians, out of sympathy or for any other
cause, was likewise prohibited. Furthermore, the Saints were
constantly reminded to prevent their cattle from ranging on Indian cornfields and to be extra diligent not to disturb their
graves and unexpected burial places. Children especially, who
playfully roamed over the hills and surrounding graves, must be
particularly careful and "should be taught to let them alone."[9]

It was a strict rule that under no circumstances would sexual
relations between races be permitted. Such a practice had already caused difficulties and would not be countenanced.[10] All
forms of friendly camaraderie must be guarded against.[11] Shooting back, stealing, and every other form of vengeful activity were
likewise prohibited. "It was wrong to indulge in feelings of hostility and bloodshed toward the Indian, who might kill a cow, an
ox or even a horse," Young counseled. "To them the deer, the
buffalo, the cherry and plum tree or strawberry bed were free. It
was their mode of living to kill and eat." But if they persist in
robbing and stealing, "after being warned not to do so, whip
them."[12] Trespassers were best handled by the whip and not by
the gun. The Saints must refrain from shooting Indians even "if
they did catch them skinning their oxen."[13] At all costs bloodshed must be avoided. If anyone killed an Omaha for stealing,
he was guilty of murder and would be delivered to the appropriate Indian chief "to be dealt with as the Indians shall decide,
as that was the only way to save the lives of the women and
children."[14]

Despite these policies of nonalignment and noninvolvement,
occasional exchanges between people were inevitable. In December 1846 an unsuspecting party of Omaha were attacked by
a band either of Sioux or of Iowa within gunshot range of
Winter Quarters. The wounded Omaha, including Chief Big
Head, were brought into camp, where their wounds were immediately dressed.[15] For a time many of the Omaha, fearing further
attack, were allowed to pitch their tents next to Young's home.[16]
"They would weep and howl, cry, writhe and twist and make
every gesture that could be imagined," recalled Hosea Stout, and
"they made such a noise that President Young had them stopt."[17]
Big Elk's statement that "we have been like the hungry dog which
runs through camp in search of something to eat and meets with
enemies on every side" stood fulfilled.[18]

Accounting for their outburst was the even worse news that
sixty miles north the Sioux had attacked and killed seventy-three

Omaha.[19] Appleton Milo Harmon recorded that most of the victims had been shot through the head or heart while still asleep. "The Soux then cut off the noses of the dead as a token of spite and contempt which they held towards them and retreated."[20] When the survivors passed through town, they took with them Big Head's party and encamped a little north of Sarpy's ferry. Having pity on the Omaha, the High Council decided "to build them a house" at a spot naturally well fortified and from which they could detect the approach of an enemy at a distance.[21] Eventually many Omaha crossed the river to seek safety among the Pottawattami. Of all the tribes, the Mormons sympathized most with the Omaha. "The sufferings of these poor miserable beings," Harmon noted, "was immence and excited the sumpathey of our people who gave them several beef cattle and a great amount of bread."[22]

But as time passed, interracial problems became ever more disruptive and exasperating. Unsuccessful in recent buffalo hunts and unproductive in growing corn and other crops, the Omaha either stole or starved. Said Whitney, "They have had for some time in contemplation a grand buffalo hunt, which they have abandoned in expectation of living and sustaining themselves by the killing of our cattle instead."[23] Often they would kill camp beef and then try to sell it back. The increased tempo of Indian difficulties persuaded the High Council to fence in the city's southern perimeter and to picket most of the rest of town. Despite their labors, by mid-October the Indians "were killing two or three oxen per day."[24] Young counseled his listeners "not to let them into their tents for they would steal with one hand while you give them a loaf of bread in the other."[25]

Though concerned with their economic losses, Young worried more about restraining his people from overreacting. Believing dialogue the better alternative to confrontation, he called for a series of meetings. "We want such an understanding with the Omaha," he wrote, "as to prevent any collision or trouble for our feelings are kind toward them and all men."[26]

In response, Chief Big Elk admitted, "I can not guide all of my people; they are wild; they are just like the wolves of the prairie for when they are hungry they don't know better than to take what is handist."[27] He confessed that his tribe called him a liar when he told them the Mormons would help them. As a partial solution, he and Logan Fontenelle recommended they build fences around every cattle herd, large or small, in or out of the city, and that they whip any stealing Indian.[28] They further advised that they neither socialize nor befriend loiterers nor sell their dogs to the Indians. The Indians would kill them "so that they could more easily pilfer from us."[29] On repeated occasions Big Elk returned many stolen items in an effort to preserve peace and harmony.[30] Nevertheless, the stealing of cattle increased, straining relations almost to the breaking point. By late October at least fifty oxen and many sheep had been killed.[31] By April 1847, Stout said, "The amount of cattle killed by them the past winter and spring is incredible."[32] Incredible meant "from 3 to 5,000 dollars worth of cattle" as Young estimated, enough to cast serious doubt on any chance of moving the camp en masse to the mountains come spring.[33] To make matters worse, the Indians, so the Mormons claimed, were stealing not just because of hunger, but also out of spite and maliciousness. And not only the Omaha and the Oto were involved. By the spring of 1847, Ponca and Pawnee Indians also "were in the neighborhood stealing horses and cattle."[34] Apparently the Mormon cattle herds had become a popular attraction.

What had soured the soup? It would be easy to say the Omaha were running scared. Their numbers had been decimated, they felt themselves the victims of both Sioux and Oto depredations, and they were taking out their frustrations on peaceful neighbors. Without a supply of buffalo meat, beef would do just as well.

The Mormons had been guilty of some indiscretions of their own. After the Sioux slaughtered more than seventy Omaha, Henry W. Miller and Arza Adams, while leading a cattle-grazing company, had inadvertently stumbled onto the massacre site some days after the tragedy. The Sioux had stripped most of the dead of buffalo robes, moccasins, and leggings, while tents and lodges had also been carried off. But Miller, after nursing the wounds of one dying squaw, inappropriately took some tattered robes and forty beef hides he thought were stolen from the Mormons, as well as two stray Indian horses. Hearing of it, an anxious Young bolted off a letter saying, "if you have committed any such overt act in any degree, give not sleep to your eyes . . . till you have replaced every article which has been removed." He urged them "to appease the wrath of an ignorant but insulted people and therefore, if possible, save your lives."[35] Though the goods were all returned, an insult had been carelessly made.

While the Mormons cut down little of the scarce surrounding timber, what small amounts were used provoked the Omaha. As well, they were jealous of their visitors' many guns and their marksmanship in shooting wild turkey and other small animals. Because of their sheer numbers, the Mormons probably shot more game than the Indians preferred. And efforts at keeping the Indians out of the camp and preventing them from enjoying their fires and shelter during the winter were other contentious points.

In an April conference of all interested parties, Chief Big Elk gave his side of the matter as reported by W. W. Phelps.

> Said we were not wise in complaining so 'You cut hay but people must buy it if one wants to warm can't do it but you can take our wood and it won't grow up tomorrow—our fa[ther] will not buy our lands so good. . . . your head men said you would shelter us, but you come among us and first we know up rises a city eat up our grass kill our game scare it away come to live where we used to hunt and find pea vines and plenty of cattle must not kill your Cattle but our game all scared away— vines all trodden down—You were here to protect us, but down comes the Sioux and murderers us that your fault. . . . You can't raise up our timber can't raise up our dead men so you are the aggressors.'[36]

By the time Young had departed in April 1847 on his long-postponed journey to the Rockies, relations between Mormons and Indians had rapidly worsened. With Young gone, leadership eventually fell to Orson Hyde, the only apostle left at Winter Quarters after John Taylor and Parley Pratt led out a second large company in June. Hyde, only recently returned from Britain, relied heavily on Hosea Stout, leader of the town police and a somewhat impetuous hothead.

After meeting with Stout and Cornelius Lott in an acrimonious confrontation in late May, Big Elk wished that the "Big Red headed chief" [Young] were back, "for he would treat them better."[37] Ten days later, eighty Omaha came to town to negotiate peace and better understanding, but Stout met them on horseback and in armed fashion "according to the Danite system of horsemanship."[38] Young's dialogue was being replaced with Stout's intransigence and Hyde's ambivalence.

Matters came to a dangerous climax in June when word arrived at Winter Quarters that Omaha Indians had killed teamster Jacob Weatherby, unarmed, a few miles east of the Elkhorn River, the first apparent case of bloodshed between Mormons and Indians at the Missouri. The Omaha were also charged with allegedly killing four or five other whites sent out from the Indian agencies.[39] With Weatherby's death still fresh on his mind, Stout set out to round up an army to seek revenge upon the guilty Omaha. On 22 June, Stout rode out at the head of a slightly smaller than anticipated posse of fifty-three men "with the intention of making war on the Omahas in case they did [not] give up the murder[er]."[40] Speaking to the same matter, Orson Hyde indicated they intended to demand of R. B. Mitchell that he get the Omaha to turn over the offender.[41]

But upon arriving at Bellevue, Mitchell informed Hyde and Stout that being only the subagent, and with responsibilities for only the Pottawattami, he had no authority to act in behalf of the absent senior agent, Major John Miller. Stout, considering Mitchell a prejudiced, spineless "inveterate enemy to us" and "a most infamous rascal," suddenly saw what he considered a conspiratorial pretext to justify federal interposition.

> It would have therefore been very easy for him to played the game to engage us in a war with the Omahas and leave us in the difficulty . . . in case he led us into an engagement and did not mention his position or attempt to desert or betray us we would have put him to death.[42]

John D. Lee, who went along for the ride to Bellevue, recalled that Mitchell warned against any armed foray against the Indians and told them to beg off their hunt for the murderer. "Jesus Christ," he said, "could not hinder them from killing the cattle." Lee, like Stout, concluded that Mitchell was deliberately uncooperative and was cleverly trying to goad them onto armed conflict "to justify them in calling the militia on us."[43] Frustrated by Mitchell's determination not to pursue the criminals, Stout's posse returned home and "the whole expedition came to naught."[44]

Such mounting friction underlined the faltering relationship between the Mormons and the Office of Indian Affairs. The meeting at Bellevue was but a dramatic expression of mutual distrust that had been developing for several months. The heart of the Mormon complaint was the widespread conviction that Council Bluffs Indian agents were stooping to unethical tactics to guarantee their early removal from Indian lands. Inspired by religious prejudices, these agents, so it was believed, were poisoning the sentiments of the Omaha and the Oto and deliberately agitating them against the Mormons.

Young was even convinced that Mitchell, "from what he could learn," had been part of the Davies County, Missouri, mob that had put Joseph Smith in Liberty Jail in 1838.[45] How could justice be served by such a supposed Mormon-hater? Willard Richards noted Miller's refusal to reappoint one Mr. Case, a former government farmer among the Oto and Pawnee for twenty years and now a recent convert to Mormonism, as further proof of prejudice against them.[46] They also charged Superintendent Harvey with partiality for not paying any Pottawattami tribute money to G. Herring, Joseph Herring, and Lewis Dana, native Indian converts to Mormonism who had been adopted into the Pottawattami nation.[47]

These were, however, comparatively minor issues. Far more inflammatory were Mitchell's and Miller's alleged covert tactics at inciting the Omaha and the Oto against the Saints, for the Mormons believed that all of the complaints Chief Big Elk levelled at them—that they had demanded timberland, scared off game, and, worst of all, had caused the Sioux to attack—were phony objections planted in their minds by agents who were pressured to insure that the Mormon stay would, indeed, be only temporary.

Although such a charge is hard to prove, it does appear that the two agents were very busy reminding the tribes of their rights. Chief Young Elk admitted that, "Everything we [the Mormons] were doing was a great hinderment in selling [our] land etc. Agent had taken some considerable pains to learn them all their rights if they killed our cattle."[48] The Indians were also told, charged Young, that the Saints were not intending to abide by the original agreements and were planning to stay several more years than agreed. And though Young had not stipulated in writing that improvements made upon their lands would eventually belong to the Indians, Miller had been particularly vigilant in reminding them of their rights of possession. In short, the Mormons blamed the agents for prejudicing the previously friendly Indians against them to effect their earliest departure. Perhaps Kane said it best. As irritating as economic matters were,

> The real question to be considered is whether the women and children left behind in the Omaha town [Winter Quarters after the pioneers' departure] . . . are to be satisfied of their

own safety; or whether they shall remain as they have been prey to constant anxiety and believing themselves at the mercy of every petty official whose indiscreet impertinence may indulge itself in such remarks as reported.[49]

Clearly the Mormons believed that "petty officers" were "carrying sail in the West."

However, from the perspective of the Office of Indian Affairs, charged by Congress to enforce the June 1834 Indian Intercourse Act to prevent white intrusion and permanent settlement on Indian lands, the Mormons were, at least, borderline trespassers and potential troublemakers. Among the law's several provisions it prohibited whites from hunting or trapping in Indian country; it prevented settlement or inhabitation of any and all lands guaranteed the Indians; it prescribed penalties for anyone selling liquor or defrauding the Indians; and it called for the forcible eviction of anyone violating its provisions.[50] Its entire purpose, while not to discourage westward expansion, was designed to protect the Indian at least so long as he occupied his own territory. And in simple terms the Office of Indian Affairs never was convinced that the Mormon encampments at the Missouri, particularly on the west bank, were in the best interests of the Indians and the United States.

Although agents could point to various Mormon infractions of the law such as unauthorized liquor sales and timber cutting, two other issues created the most serious problems and eventually resulted in a serious rupture.[51] First of all, because the Mormons remained deliberately evasive and ambiguous in their settlement and departure plans, a climate of misunderstanding, suspicion, and distrust developed. Their intentions were all too vague and ill defined to be acceptable. Second, and ultimately most damaging, Mormon negotiating tactics and political maneuvering became increasingly disturbing and unacceptable.

From the very beginning Indian agents were aware of oft-quoted criticisms that the Mormons intended to ally themselves with the Indians to disturb America's frontier borders and overland trails. The public mind was abused with such a possibility. Warren Foote, a Mormon who left Nauvoo in May, provided this insight into a popular attitude of homesteaders on the frontier, in this case near Garden Grove, Iowa Territory.

The inhabitants here are very much scared. They are afraid that the "Mormons" will soon be upon them and slay men, women and children. I called into a house to see if I could sell anything. The man was not at home. As I turned to go out the woman said, "You are a Mormon[?]" . . . "Yes," I replied. She said, "There is a great many Indians up there where you are camped. . . . we hear that you are building forts and your women are marrying in with the Indians and that you are combining together and are coming down here to kill us all off." I told her that these stories were false. . . . She then said, "There are a great many women here that are almost scared to death, they are just ready to run." [52]

Missouri Governor John C. Edwards, writing to Secretary of War William L. Marcy, strongly suspected a Mormon-inspired insurrection:

They are a bad and deluded sect, and they have been harshly treated; but I suppose very correctly; yet they do not believe so, and under the treatment which they have received, if they are not enemies, both of our people and our government then they are better Christians and purer patriots than other denominations, a thing which no body in the west can believe.[53]

Many in Congress were convinced that the Saints intended "to loiter near the Bluffs and not go over the Mountains at all." From their Missouri River encampment they were in a better position to pay with vengeance some overdue accounts.[54] "We have long feared the consequences of their settlement on Indian lands," reported the *St. Joseph Gazette,* "and would that they were all safely landed in California." [55]

The following excerpt from a letter of some Missourians in Putnam County to President Polk in early July reflected the popular distrust.

There is a set of men denominating themselves Mormons hovering on our frontier, well armed, justly considered, as depredating on our property, and in our opinion, British emissaries, intending by insiduous means to accomplish diabolical purposes, [I]f circumstances favor, we consider it the duty of our common American father, to assume the responsibility, in defence of the "brave and hardy men of the frontier" to take the necessary measures to disarm and expel them from our border.[56]

Young well understood the popular concern over possible Mormon-Indian collusion, and although he never seriously entertained such action, he knew it was an ace in his hand when negotiating for government cooperation and understanding. As he had done before with talk of settling in British Canada and thereby courting favor in Washington, so he would do again with regards to the Indians. If the government "would treat us as they ought to," he said, "the saints would fight for them, and do them good, but they never would consent to be governed again by unjust judges or governors, let the consequence be what they might." And as to the Lamanites, "We have more influence with the Indians than all other nations on the earth and if we are compelled to, we will use it."[57] If an advantageous political situation presented itself, Young would not shy away from it.

Young's stance in this matter paralleled his tactics with the Indians: bargain from a position of power, threaten to use it in self-defense if necessary, but never really employ force. He could not seriously think of war with 500 men away, with little money, with so much sickness, with such great dreams. As it had always been, the Mormon plan was to escape and not engage their enemies.[58]

While fears of a Mormon-inspired Indian insurrection declined the longer the Saints stayed at the Bluffs, the growing concern of Indian agents was twofold: (1) the location of the Mormons' several encampments, and (2) the length of time they intended to stay. It had been initially understood from permission granted by Captain James Allen that the Mormons intended to stay only in Iowa Territory. To this plan Subagent Mitchell had given his permission, subject to that of his supervisors, believing it would be "for the apparent good of both parties."[59] In response to a 13 July 1846 letter from Superintendent Thomas H. Harvey detailing the Mormon arrival in the Council Bluffs subagency, William Medill, commissioner of the Office of Indian Affairs in Washington, manifested an understanding and conciliatory posture in offering tentative, conditional permission.

> Your direction to Mr. Mitchell that "so long as they (the Mormons) conduct themselves with propriety, and are only in the country on their passage west, he would not embarrass their movements" was correct and judicious, and they should also be distinctly informed that they cannot be permitted to make any permanent location there [east banks], or any longer stay than is actually necessary, and that it is expected that they will abstain from all interference with the Indians and move onwards as soon as possible.[60]

Unknown artist's conception of the city layout of Winter Quarters, 1846–47. Courtesy Winter Quarters Visitor Center, Omaha, Nebraska, The Church of Jesus Christ of Latter-day Saints.

Thus even before Kane had presented to President Polk Young's request to winter on Pottawattami lands, Medill had given all the necessary permission needed. But after Kane's presentation and after Judge J. K. Kane's special appeal to Polk in support of his son's efforts,[61] Medill winced at having been out-flanked. Furthermore, from what Kane apparently implied, the Mormons might want to stay longer. In a letter to Harvey six weeks later, Medill argued, "The object and intention of the Mormons in desiring to locate upon the lands in question, [Pottawattami] are not very satisfactorily put forth. If their continuance is really to be temporary for such length of time only as will enable them to supply their wants and procure the necessary means for proceeding on their journey, the Government will interpose no objection."

Fearful that an extended stay might "jeopardize" the survey and sales of newly acquired territorial land "and bring about a difficulty between Iowa . . . and the General Government," Medill instructed Harvey to visit the Mormons personally and "ascertain, if possible, the real intentions of these people in de-

An early Kane family engravure dating from approximately 1840. Thomas L. Kane is in the center. His brother Elisha Kent Kane is on the left. His father, John K. Kane, is on the right. Reproduced with the permission of the Church Archives, The Church of Jesus Christ of Latter-day Saints.

siring to remain."[62] Medill, while consenting to a temporary stay on the grounds of humanity and hospitality, was becoming increasingly uneasy.

Following instructions, Superintendent Harvey, in company with his subordinates, John Miller and R. B. Mitchell, visited the Mormon camps in early November 1846. "Their stay was too brief to call a council," recalled Willard Richards. "Indeed, I know not that any member knew of their presence until they were absent, except General Young."[63] Meeting the three officials "by the roadside" near his home at Winter Quarters quite by accident, Young was as surprised at their visit as they were at the size of Winter Quarters, at its signs of permanency, and at the industry of its people. Harvey was baffled at this large community on the west bank where permission had only been granted to stay on the Iowa side—and that, too, for only the season. Here was a city going up on Indian land without authority or permission!

During their "long chat," Harvey indicated that while he knew the Mormons had clearance to stay on the Iowa side, he "was not aware that they had authority from the Government to stop on Omaha lands, but they might have authority that I knew nothing of."[64] He expressed a desire that they had built their city on the Iowa side. Young responded that Captain Allen, before leaving with the Battalion, had proferred permission for settlements on Indian land if necessary.[65] Harvey knew nothing of such a document, nor did Medill, since it was never transmitted to Washington, likely because of Allen's untimely death.[66] Nor did he admit to any authority Allen had to make such a statement. Young went on to say they could not be moved until the Mormon Battalion returned. "I asked him," Harvey recalled, "how long they expected to remain where they were. He replied until they got ready to go. I required how long it would take them to get ready." Young, not one to be pushed, replied "it might be two, three, or four years."[67]

Without question Young believed he had good grounds for camping among the Omaha. Captain Allen had given authorization, the Omaha had consented in writing for at least a two-year stay, and the government should not now be so surprised at the sight of Winter Quarters when agents Mitchell and Miller had had ample time to report on the matter earlier. Young, aware that about that time Kane was presenting the matter to the Polk administration and seeking more official written, permission, put up a stiff front and gave Harvey to understand "that we would not be neither drove or pushed."[68] In a letter to Charles C. Rich, he concluded, "Major Harvey visited us and seemed pretty much disposed to move us to the east side of the river, but acknowledged we were too strong for him. We apprehend no difficulty from anything he can say or do having our confidence in a higher power."[69]

Many other points were discussed including a strong reminder not to cut Indian timber and not to infringe on Indian rights of any kind. Harvey concluded his report by saying,

> I am at a loss in forming an opinion in relation to the future movements of this . . . deluded people, they say their intentions [are] to cross the Mountains, if so, I cannot see any satisfactory reason for their making on the Missouri such substantial improvements. It may be that their object is to establish a chain of improvements to the Mountains, commencing on the Missouri.[70]

Back in Washington, Kane, armed with letters and documents from Willard Richards, endeavored to clarify the ambiguity and misunderstandings while trying to nail down official permission for an extended stay, but this time on the west rather than on the east bank. Though his efforts were tireless, they eventually failed.

Sensing that Allen's permission for west bank Indian land settlements might be legally insufficient, Young and the Twelve as early as 9 August 1846 had drafted a letter to President Polk reiterating Allen's assurances and requesting the president's views "of Allen's permit for us to stop on Indian lands, as soon as your convenience will permit."[71] Another letter was drafted three weeks later explaining the desire of the Indians to receive instruction in education, mechanic arts, and agriculture "and our facilities for giving them the desired information."[72] Young had made these overtures to the Omaha not only to gain their cooperation but also to court the favor of the president.

Apparently both letters were sent to Jesse Little in Philadelphia, since Kane did not leave the Mormon encampments until 7 September and did not get back to Washington until early November.[73] Little called upon Polk early in October and discussed "lands we might settle on provided California is retained," that is, somewhere in the mountain valleys, and the Mormons' desire to stay on Indian lands among the Omaha. He reported the same request to Commissioner Medill shortly afterwards, apparently the first time either Polk or Medill had heard of a west-bank encampment. According to Little, their response was positive and "everything will be right."[74] "There will be less difficulty with regard to the Omaha lease," said Kane, "than my Father had with regard to that of the Pottawattamies."[75] By early November, Kane confidently reported from Washington that he was about to obtain official sanction "with regard to the Omaha."[76]

But permission to remain among the Omaha until spring came only after great difficulty. Several members of Congress, both Whig and Democrat, caught up with the progress of the Mexican War, reacted very negatively to the Mormon course of conduct and openly suspected their designs. The fear of Indian collusion was very real. Kane "had to ward off and resist the fearful apprehension of some Western members [of Congress] that the Mormon camp intended to loiter near the Bluffs and not go over the Mountains at all." [77] He "expressed his utter astonishment at the irrational and sensitive conduct of distinguished men both politically and religiously, in opposition to our welfare." [78]

Writing confidentially to Young in early December, Kane admitted he had "found it next to impossible to do much for you before public opinion was corrected. Your permission for this winter was only obtained by personal influence . . . it became incumbent on me to manufacture public opinion as soon as possible." [79] Kane was sparring with more than a general climate of prejudice, a bewildered and increasingly suspicious Office of Indian Affairs, and a president preoccupied with the Mexican War, for he was also trying to play down other indiscretions in Texas where the war effort was most immediate. Critics charged that Lyman Wight, a disgruntled Mormon apostle settling in southern Texas, was busy interfering with the Cree Indians and "meddling" with the government's interests in the area. "His conduct was the reason of prejudice to the body of the Saints." [80] Wight's indiscretions could not have come at a worst time so far as Kane and Young were concerned, but he was beyond their influence and instruction. Nevertheless, Kane defused many of the objections and clarified some ambiguities and, after great effort, secured permission to stay on Indian lands until the spring of 1847. [81]

But Kane's reopening of negotiations in the spring by request of the Twelve for at least a one-year extension was too much for Medill. Realizing that he could not use the Battalion call any longer as a negotiating ploy, or Allen's permission, Kane argued that without the Mormons the Omaha would be annihilated by the Sioux. [82] He also argued that the present Indian agents at the Bluffs, because of prejudice and ineptitude, should be replaced by men "chosen out of their own number." [83] As early as the preceding fall, Kane had broached this subject in an unsuccessful effort to have Mormons appointed as agents among the Ponca, the Cree, the Choctaw, and several other tribes.[84] Part of Young's thinking, no doubt, was to bridle Wight down in Texas, facilitate his future settlements further west, and insure safety among his people at the Missouri while the pioneer companies found a place of refuge. His desires underlined his conviction that local agents were acting deliberately and prejudicially against the peace and safety of those at Winter Quarters.

This last request turned Medill finally and definitely against Kane. Medill had countenanced the argument that Allen had given permission that Medill never believed was his to give; he had endured Kane's end runs to the president; he had agreed to the unauthorized removal from the east to the west side; and despite all the attendant ambiguities had even consented to another winter stay among the Omaha. But he would not tolerate charges of prejudice and ineptitude against him or his agents and would not permit the appointment of Mormon substitutes among his staff organization.[85]

Countering Kane's circuitous argument (that if the president had the authority to remove white settlements from Indian lands then he could likewise allow their prolonged stay), Medill rejoined, "the Executive does not legally possess the power . . . to give any positive permission since he, like anyone else, was bound to uphold the Indian Intercourse Act." The whole "Western Country has been settled by emigration from the various states without any other aid than has been extended to the Mormons," Medill argued, "and are they more meritorious than the men who now populate the Whole West? Are they more deserving?'[86]

The commissioner believed that making exceptions to the law would undermine the statutes and their intents. Furthermore, he would do all in his power to thwart any effort by any group to assert "independence" of the agents of his department. Such a precedent would be untenable. And as to the Mormon request for agents of their own, Medill replied that it was "not so much the want of Agents . . . that is complained of as a desire to obtain such as can be made subservient to a particular interest." To him, it was an unacceptable case of "special privilege."[87] By late April, Medill once and for all denied all further government permission for the Mormons to stay another year or more at Winter Quarters, although this was later modified to extend their stay until the spring of 1848.[88]

The contention, therfore, is that Kane pushed Medill too far and created an impasse over what Medill saw as tampering and unwarranted criticism. Had Kane not argued for what Medill saw as "special privilege," the Mormons might not have had to abandon Winter Quarters and their many improvements in the spring of 1848.

On hearing the news, church leaders, recently returned from their long last trek west to the Great Basin, decided in November 1847 to abandon Winter Quarters in the following spring "as the Government was unwilling for us to remain here any longer" and settle on the east side of the river.[89] The actual removal occurred in tandem with a large exodus west, so that while some headed to the mountains, a greater number sought a new home on the bluffs of Iowa.

During the second and final year of Winter Quarters (1847–48), relations between the Omaha and the Mormons greatly improved, largely because Young's sense of diplomacy and justice replaced the impetuousness and lack of common sense among several of his overzealous lieutenants.[90] The Saints planted and harvested large corn crops, transported many Omaha shipments, and in other ways worked diligently at fostering peace.[91] Young's policy of neutrality, negotiating from strength, benevolent detachment, patience, and restraint despite constant Indian stealing and some momentary confrontations when he was away, fostered a generally healthy climate between the two peoples. Cooperation, not confrontation, was imperative. Policies with the local tribes proved so successful that they formed the basis of his later dealings with the Indians in the mountains.

To what extent Council Bluffs agents were acting prejudically against the Saints is open to debate. When in May 1848, Young cursed agent John Miller "in the name of the Lord and said his bones should rot and his soul be damned," he was convinced that Miller had persuaded both the Omaha and the Oto to get all that they could in compensation and improvements from the departing Mormons—something to which Young never believed he had consented.[92] Even the Oto, who all winter long had remained silent, were now demanding payment for living on their land, a move Miller purportedly encouraged.[93] Unquestionably the Mormons believed Miller and Mitchell were exerting undue pressures, overstepping their bounds, and causing ill will and potentially serious danger. If the agents were so concerned with the plight of the Omaha, they contended, why not buy their lands as they had done with the Pottawattami and move them to the safety of another site further south? Such a move, besides the obvious benefit of bringing in much needed federal money to the Mormons, would have extended to the Omaha the protection and long-term security they required.[94]

For his part, Medill displayed great patience in dealing with so many different spokesmen for the Mormon cause. Despite Thomas Kane's honorable intentions, he overstepped his bounds and turned a once cooperative Medill into an obstructing, offended commissioner of Indian Affairs. More than any other factor, the question of special privilege, the bending of the law for a particular people and requests for their own agents, got in the way. In retrospect, had Kane argued more intently for a government purchase of Omaha land—which even the agents had been strongly recommending—and less stridently for the appointment of Mormon Indian agents, Winter Quarters might well have lasted longer than two years.

6

"IN ONE COMMON CAUSE FOR A SEASON":
THE ECONOMIC ORDER OF WINTER QUARTERS

> Nothing in American history—not the ephemeral towns
> of mining rushes nor the hardier ones of real estate booms—
> is like Winter Quarters. An entire people had uprooted it-
> self and, on the way to the mountains, paused here and put
> down roots.[1]

One might carry Bernard De Voto's summation further and say
that perhaps there was not anything comparable in Mormon history. Never in the sixteen-year history of the church was their
physical situation more tenuous, their economy more fragile,
and their very survival more in question than in the fall of 1846.
With winter coming on, the Mormons at the Missouri and scattered across Iowa faced a raft of formidable economic problems.
Few if any crops had been planted; provisions were meager;
property sales in Nauvoo were at a standstill; the amount of
money forthcoming from the Battalion remained unknown; Indian thefts of livestock were increasing; and trading with Missouri wholesalers, farmers, and merchants was still much suspected and uncertain. They had either to band together and
support one another or to reap the inevitable consequences of
mass suffering and starvation. In the fair and equitable distribution of what little they had, individually and collectively, lay
the temporal salvation of all. Many were asked to make incredible sacrifices; some wore out with giving. The overriding concerns were community preservation and preparation for their
departure westward.

Their survival depended on a high degree of social bonding,
an economic order in which the private interests of the individual were made distinctly secondary to the welfare of the whole.
Although individuals were not asked to surrender private property into any kind of common stock enterprise, they were required to give abundantly of their time and substance for the

welfare of those around them. It was the Nauvoo Covenant in action.

At least four principles governed the Winter Quarters economy:

1. Community self-sufficiency and independence
2. Consecration of substantial wealth and sacrifice of income to the church for the benefit of all
3. Church distribution of resources in fairly equitable proportions
4. Individual stewardship, agency, and accountability

These principles represented much in Joseph Smith's "Law of Consecration and Stewardship" practiced in the very earliest days of the church in Missouri and Ohio, and adumbrated Young's later United Order in Utah. Smith's law had called for "economic equality, socialization of surplus incomes, freedom of enterprise, and group self-sufficiency." For various reasons his plan had been replaced by the less demanding law of tithes and offerings in which individuals retained their property but paid ten percent of their increase to the church.[2] Whereas the earlier law had required the surrender of private property to the bishop in exchange for privatized stewardship over land and resources, Young's Winter Quarters economy did not go quite that far. This was an economy on the move and in transition. He would wait until a more settled and favorable time to implement his finer interpretations.

Convinced that their spiritual welfare depended on their physical well-being, Young called on his followers "to unite with us in the principles of self preservation" including "all business matters pertaining to our present salvation."[3] The first order of business was to make the camp as self-sufficient as possible. In part this was inevitable, since they could expect little assistance from outside sources. But their goals were to retain as much as possible what little wealth they had in camp and, secondly, to develop small industries, keep gainfully employed, and open two-way trade with Missouri. Their poverty, sickness, uprooted condition, and removal from ample grain supplies prevented them from ever reaching economic independence—in time the Mormons were reduced almost to begging—but the attempt characterized their community.

By far their richest resource was their massive herds of livestock amounting to over ten thousand head of cattle stationed in at least four locations: in the stockyards immediately south of town where the "old beeves" were kept for slaughtering; on grazing grounds six miles north of town kept mainly for strays;[4] above the Boyer River for cattle on the Pottawattami lands; and Asahel Lathrop's large herd of church or "public" cattle over one hundred miles to the north.[5] Most families retained milch cows on their own city lots. The Municipal High Council chose beef and slaughter committees to pay herdsmen, control sales and distribution, and coordinate all livestock matters. In an agreement with the Indians, killing local game was prohibited, although this did not seem to apply to wild turkey and other fowl.

A good example of creating small industry was the manufacturing of willow baskets and related items. Though the women had started this work, the Seventy's quorums built a "basket factory," a sod hut of 20 by 14 feet.[6] At the height of production in January 1847, thirty men were employed making willow baskets, washboards, bushel and half-bushel baskets, and tables for trade in Missouri in exchange for grain and other necessities.[7]

They also tried to land additional fur-hauling contracts with Sarpy as well as with Indian agents. When it was learned that the government was about to pay $6,000 to remove the Pottawattami to the Kansas River, Young counseled his people to "take all the contracts" they could.[8]

Their most ambitious attempt at self-sufficiency was the construction of a large, expensive, water-powered flour mill in the city's north end on Turkey Creek. Since the purchase and grinding of grain was their biggest expense, Young and Alpheus Cutler recommended they build a gristmill large enough to meet their growing needs for processed flour. Ample flour was needed for both the winter and spring overland companies to the mountains. At a public meeting in August at Cutler's Park, Young proposed building the mill. The original plan was to build and use it there and later carry most of the buhrstones, gears, and other working parts westward. David Boss, Helmagh Van Wagoner, and Ira and John Eldridge put up $800 to purchase two sets of buhr millstones with all the fixtures in St. Louis and have them sent back by steamboat.[9] Pleased with the quick and favorable response to the mill proposal, Young responded, "There now we will have a mill and as for poverty, it shall not have a name in this Church."[10] Two or three horse-drawn corn mills were also established, and, when necessary, the Mormons were allowed use of

the small government mill on Mosquito Creek on the east side—
though at a high cost of fifty-six cents per bushel of meal.[11]

In late September building contracts were let out to furnish
the heavy timbers, studs, rafters, framing, and hewing for the
mill, and construction began on 5 October 1846 at a site proposed by Frederick Kesler. The High Council appointed Brigham Young, a master carpenter, to supervise all phases of construction.[12] They had expected to complete the mill before the
ground froze, but were repeatedly frustrated by a scarcity of
workhands, shipping delays, broken dams, relocating the mill-
race, and other complications. Subsequently the mill did not
begin grinding operations until the early spring, a costly postponement and a serious disappointment.[13] Once in operation it
ground ten or eleven bushels in an hour, much greater than the
average mill production of thirty to fifty bushels per day, but was
in such demand that patrons waited several hours, even days, to
use the facility.[14] Unfortunately, its benefits were never fully realized, since it was constantly plagued with problems. Though several attempts were made to sell it to the Council Bluffs Indian
agencies, the Omaha Indians laid claim to all improvements on
the campsite and stymied such sales. Eventually the mill was
largely dismantled, and the hardware ended up either in mills
on the east side of the Missouri or in the Salt Lake Valley.[15]

If one considers the building costs and the less than bounteous
return on the investment, the mill was not a financial success.
The total cost of construction, labor, and operation amounted to
almost $3,000, much of which Young apparently paid himself.[16]
In March 1847 he sold it at a loss to John Neff, one of the relatively few wealthy men left in town, for $2,600, enabling the
church to pay off debts incurred in the construction and operation of the mill.[17] But if it did not return a profit, it at least paid
the wages of 150 men for much of the winter.

As to the "consecration" of whatever wealth they still had,
Young counseled,

> We do not believe in having all things in common and on gen-
> eral principles, as some have taught, both in the Church and out,
> but we believe that it is right for every man to have his stew-
> ardship according to the ability that God hath given him; yet,
> there are cases, situations and circumstances where it is quite
> right for the brethren to unite all their energies and labors in
> one common cause for a season, as . . . we are now doing.[18]

The best documented example of cooperative economics was the Newel Whitney store, or "bishop's storehouse," which first opened its doors for business in December 1846. Based on the principle of buying in bulk at wholesale prices, the store was made possible only after Mormon Battalion families had turned over a large amount of cash to church leaders.

Early in August, Battalion members, then at Fort Leavenworth, were each paid $42 clothing money for the year—a combined total of over $20,000. Of that amount they sent back $5,835 to their families via Parley Pratt, who interrupted his journey to England to return the money to the camp. The Battalion also contributed several hundred dollars to Pratt, Orson Hyde, John Taylor, and Jesse Little for their missions to England and the east coast. The Twelve received Pratt's collection on 11 August, and though the money was sent in a packet, it was specifically directed to individual families.[19] Daniel Spencer was assigned to disburse the funds among Battalion families.[20] At a meeting of the Municipal High Council two days later Young suggested the "propriety" of sending Newel Whitney, Jonathan Wright, and John Van Cott to St. Louis "for such dry goods and groceries, hardware and provisions as they [Battalion families] most need and can be most advantageously procured. . . . We want the whole applied to wholesale purchases, so that no portion of the money shall be squandered."[21] While at St. Louis, Whitney would likewise purchase hardware for the proposed mill and provisions for the Iowa camps. After considerable arm twisting, Battalion families turned over $4,375.19 to Bishop Whitney. Young considered this money "a peculiar manifestation—of divine providence" at just the right time for the purchase of provisions and goods for the winter supply of the camp. "By the wisdom of heaven we will make every dollar sent us count as good as two or three at ordinary traffic."[22]

Whitney was delayed in returning because of low-water conditions that translated into higher overland freight costs from a point beyond St. Joseph, 140 miles south. Consequently, in early November a score of teams and wagons left the Bluffs to retrieve the sixty-ton shipment of goods and supplies.[23] Construction began on the storehouse in mid-November and it opened three weeks later even before all of the shipments had arrived. Goods purchased specifically for individuals by prior agreement were privately distributed.

The Whitney store operated until 26 March 1847 and carried

a full line of foodstuffs, textiles, household and hardware goods, various herbal medicines, and some books.[24] Many items were taken on credit or on an exchange basis, so that in time the storehouse, clearly the most popular place in town, traded in a large quantity of used items. Many crossed over to Winter Quarters from the east side of the river, some from as far away as Mt. Pisgah and Garden Grove, to shop at the store.

Essentially an ecclesiastical operation under the control of the presiding bishop, the storehouse was not a private enterprise, although every effort was made to operate it at a profit. Sales-generated income was controlled by church authorities and used to buy additional merchandise, pay back debts, provide gifts of food and other provisions to needy families, and for other financial purposes. It served as the city's financial institution and clearinghouse of obligations and performances. Eventually, after the Whitney store closed, privately owned stores flourished briefly, including one run by a non-Mormon Missouri merchant, named Estill, who had been encouraged to come and "commence a barter trade."[25] In the absence of financial, legal, and civic institutions, the governing court of law, licensing bureau, chamber of commerce, and board of trade was the Municipal High Council. When problems arose with Missouri merchants and farmers who, seeing a good opportunity, arrived in town with wagonloads of garden produce, it was the Municipal High Council that appointed a committee "to buy grain, fruit, or anything which might be brought into camp by strangers for sale."[26] By doing so, items could be bought in bulk at a cheaper cost and then sold to the citizens at prices determined by the council.[27] Likewise the council governed volume grain purchases and then supervised distribution. It even decided probate matters.[28] As to wages most labors, whether cattle ranging, blacksmithing, land clearing, clerking, or any number of other activities, were also coordinated by the council. A report of all labor performed was returned "weekly" to the council. At final settlement, every man drew his pay "in proportion to his amount of labor."[29]

These procedures did not prevent private trade and contracting between individuals in camp and the incurring of private debts. Certainly this applied to professional services such as nursing and medical care. One doctor, for his several visits relating to a maternity case, was paid "one days work, ten bushels turnips, 5½ bushels of buckwheat, one bushel beans [and] one quart whiskey."[30]

As the doctor's payment indicates, the Winter Quarters economy was built on "a general barter trade."[31] The city made no paper money (unlike the earlier Kirtland community in Latter-day Saint history) and very little coin. Payments between private parties were usually in kind and on an exchange or bartering basis. Cattle seemed to be the most popular item of exchange, but almost any needed commodity, including corn, eggs, or butter, would suffice. "I have got thousands of dollars owing me," said Young, "and I wish my debtors would offer me grain, corn, turnips, hay or even hemlock slats after harvest."[32]

With respect to the distribution of city lots and land acreages outside the city, the High Council handled them on an equal-occupancy basis. To illustrate, in the summer of 1847, while major efforts were underway to cultivate large acreages, instructions were "that one man shall not have an acre of land to his house while he has only ten cattle to take care of to the exclusion of another man who should come here with 60 head of cattle and only have 6 rods of ground."[33] Despite these provisions, land values fluctuated, with those nearer town regarded as the more valuable. Lots were given to the highest bidder, even though the council—not legally owning the land—could not transfer ownership. In effect, it could only distribute favorable locations and improvements such as fences and ploughed and cleared ground.[34] There was no private land ownership on the west banks of the Missouri River in and about Winter Quarters during the entire Mormon stay. This was not the case on the east side, where Indian claims had been surrendered to the United States.[35]

The High Council also regulated the collection of municipal taxes based on assessed personal property values. The money was used to pay herdsmen, road builders, the police, cemetery workers, the city marshal, and the camp historian.[36] The total value of all assessed property in Winter Quarters subject to taxation was $101,550.[37] In addition to taxes, the Saints were also expected to pay tithing, according to the "Lord's law of economy," a law that if lived, they believed would bring the blessings of heaven.[38] "There was a great difference," said Young, between tithing and taxation. The former was "a standing law of God for one tenth was required of every man and woman when at the head of the family," whereas taxes were levied "according to circumstances." "All have got to pay tithing," he said, even "if it's only a pound of catnup."[39]

The need to facilitate the payment and distribution of tithes and to better care for the needs of the poor in camp initiated a major change in Mormon ecclesiastical history—the call of local bishops to preside over relatively small numbers of people.[40] Shortly after the departure of the Mormon Battalion, the Pottawattamie High Council had called ninety bishops. Each was assigned to "attend to the necessities" of two or three families.[41] (Most Battalion families lived on the east bank, at Mt. Pisgah, and Garden Grove.) These "Battalion" bishops functioned in a strictly pastoral role, exercising few other ecclesiastical or administrative functions.

Winter Quarters itself was divided in October into thirteen wards with a bishop appointed over each ward.[42] Seven weeks later, at a meeting of the Winter Quarters High Council, Young proposed increasing the number of wards to twenty-two (one for each city block), since each ward was getting too large for one man to oversee.[43] Unlike their counterparts on the east side, Winter Quarters bishops were allowed two counselors and exercised both pastoral and administrative functions.[44]

The bishops' primary duty was to provide for the poor in their wards and devise means for the poor to sustain themselves "instead of calling on the rich to hand out what they have."[45] They were also expected to keep careful records of the sick and dying, report on housing needs, list the number of animals and other private properties in their wards, and to report on all spiritual and physical needs to the High Council: "Bishops ought to be able to tell what every man is doing in his Ward [and] see that every man, woman and child has something to eat."[46] When absolutely necessary, they were expected to care for the poor out of their own pockets.

Finally it devolved upon the bishops and their counselors to collect tithing from their membership and to distribute it equitably among the "poor and destitute and sick" in their own wards, for it was standard practice that tithing wealth remain in the jurisdiction from which it came, whether at Mt. Pisgah or at Winter Quarters.[47] Eventually, because "of the whining and dissatisfaction" of some people to pay tithing to their own bishops, the High Council ordered that all tithes on both sides of the river be "paid in to the presiding Bishop Newel K. Whitney and that he supply the various Bishops under his Presidency."[48] Theoretically, this approach would generate anonymous, more equitable distribution.

The placement of bishops at the block and ward level did more than encourage a higher percentage of tithe payers. It also proved successful in creating a much stronger sense of community bonding and economic cooperation than otherwise might have been the case. Wilford Woodruff, while speaking at one ward in March 1847, said,

> [I] requested the people that had means to carry something to the Bishop to the poor to carry flour meal meat coffee and sugar etc.—I promised I would do the same. . . . I carried [to] the Bishop 30 lb. flour half bushel meal, 4 lb. shugar, 2 lbs. coffee and others took him some things . . . [we] went to visit the sick.[49]

As Woodruff indicated, all were called upon to give more than tax or tithe—indeed almost everything excess they possessed. As one aptly recalled, "the spirit of gain was not among us," and poverty was everywhere. Those relatively better off—John Neff, David Boss, Helmagh Van Wagoner, and Ellis Sanders—were made poor through constant giving or providing loans that were never repaid. More than one large corn or grain contract was purchased with money borrowed from John Neff.[50] Ellis Sanders, according to Heber Kimball, "let go" an incredible $3,600 to the church.[51] Worried that such men could be ridden too long and too hard, Young confided that Sanders, "has given his all to the church, and I do not believe in pressing him down to death, he has feelings, he has given money time and again, let that money turn upon his tithing."[52]

One of the best guarantees of community survival and self-sufficiency was providing for individual initiative and performance, albeit in a very regulated social order. Though not allowed to own land, individuals were responsible for property upkeep and owned the produce, crops, and whatever other gains their labor realized. All were encouraged to plant their own private gardens. Many farmed large acreages south of town, starting in the spring of 1847 with land given out on the basis of the highest pledge of fence construction and other improvements.[53]

Those with trades and skills were encouraged to set up shop. Several small smithing establishments were in operation, as were coopers, boot and shoe makers, and tailors.[54] In the fall of 1846 a carding-machine house was erected to prepare wool and other material for clothing.[55] Trading beef and other goods with the

Indians in exchange for buffalo robes and deerskin leggings provided some with adequate winter apparel. Many women, by using their own or borrowed spinning wheels and domestic drilling purchased from Whitney's store, filled minimal family clothing requirements.

Men who were not employed about camp in trade work or at the mill or basket factory, or who were not involved in livestock and other operations, were encouraged to go to Missouri to labor as hired hands for farmers. "They have possession of one of the choicest lands in the world," said one biased laborer about the Missourians, "yet they have no spirit of enterprize no desire to make buildings which are considered convenient and comfortable for civilized and enlightened people."[56] Fence building, threshing and cleaning wheat, painting, plowing, milking, stump clearing—these and many other jobs were commonly taken.[57] And although few had little good to say about Missouri, had it not been for Missouri, its quickness to trade, and the cooperative nature of its farmers and settlers to hire on so many Latter-day Saints, albeit at minimal wages, the history of the Mormons at Winter Quarters would have been a far more tragic one.

As much as possible, families tried to meet their specific needs. But the welfare of the community at large usually demanded individual sacrifice. In so many of the community-wide projects such as exploring, hay cutting, fishing, herding, and building, the efforts of the entire community were repeatedly called upon at the expense of personal income and desires.[58] The economic freedom to do as one pleased was constrained by the necessity to use that agency for the welfare of all.

Given their desperate plight and the sacrifices they either volunteered or were called upon to make, it was inevitable that serious conflicts would arise. In the charges and complaints that were leveled can be glimpsed their precarious position and the inadequacies of even their best efforts.

Despite all their efforts and sacrifices, many people were very hungry, particularly in more isolated areas east of Mosquito Creek. One reporter, who visited the area in the fall of 1846, described the Mormons as "already on the verge of starvation," and calculated they had only enough food "with their most careful husbandry to keep soul and body together till next summer."[59] Charles C. Rich, in reporting on the worsening situation at Mt. Pisgah, admitted that "many have suffered for want of proper nourishment because it was not to be had."[60] And the remnants of the poor camp struggling at the Nishnabotona and elsewhere, without even the benefit of Mt. Pisgah's provisions, must have suffered even more. After enjoying the luxury of wild grapes, plums, walnuts, and berries that grew in abundance along the Missouri during the summer, by late fall most at Winter Quarters were confined to a scant diet of coarse flour and meal supplemented with an occasional beef. The delay in completing the mill caused other dietary problems. Willard Richards recorded that many had to grind wheat by hand. "Some ate their wheat boiled; others boiled their corn in lye."[61] Parley Pratt said his family had spent much of the winter subsisting on "a little corn meal, ground on a hand-mill with no other food."[62] Until the first large provisions arrived from Missouri and spring garden crops began to grow, hunger was their paramount concern.

While scarcity of food was one problem, distribution was another. Nancy H. Davison complained to the Winter Quarters High Council that her bishop "would not let her have anything to eat, and that she had nothing to eat, nor her children anything to wear." Just because her brother was not paying tithing was no reason for her not to receive the bishop's welfare, she contended. The council agreed.[63] Though many went without, some diarists reported comparatively richer diets that included wild turkey and baked goods. William Clayton, the store clerk, never went hungry, nor did most of the prominent families.[64] Jealousies invariably developed because of the varying degrees of family wealth that existed despite distribution efforts.

Not a few women expressed disappointment in their housing conditions. Fanny Parks Taggart, whose husband was in the Battalion and who had arrived at Winter Quarters late in the fall, recalled her disappointment.

> My husband had written to me in a letter that I received before leaving Nauvoo that there would be some provisions made for the families of those that went in the Mormon Battalion, and this had kept up my courage on the way, but the answer I received from President Young made me feel like bursting into tears.

She probably had been told that she would have to spend the winter in a sod cave or share a tent with some others. She continued: "on looking up I saw a woman standing in the door of a tent, I wiped my eyes and went to her and inquired for Asa Davis she showed me his house and I went there and was made welcome to such accommodations as they had."[65] While living in the house in the day, she slept in their wagon at night. Before the winter was over, Fanny Taggart moved to several different cabins. Others encountered similar difficulties.

Lost or stray cattle were another irritant. Those in charge of the stray herds, which included "many of the soldiers cattle," were reporting that numerous stray cattle "have not been found . . . some have swam the river from hence and crossed over on your side and we know not where they are." Other strays were reported "as low down the Missouri river as seventeen miles and other places."[66] Many were never found. After listening one night to endless complaints by John Smith and others, Hosea Stout recorded, "The thing was talked out of countenance" after which Young "moved to have the whole matter laid over till the 1st resurrection" and then "burn the papers the day before."[67]

Many flatly rejected paying their taxes, fines, and tithes.[68] There just was not enough money, they felt, to make the rounds. How could they give that which they felt they didn't have? Why keep demanding so much from so little?

Dissatisfaction reached such a level that by late December, authorities were preaching "on the subject of the insubordination of some of the people and their stubbornness, their murmurings and complaining refusing to pay tax and tithing." Warned their leader, "all those who did not intend to abide council had best flee to the gentiles again for all who are among us should both help support the poor and pay their tax whether they belonged to the church or not, or leave the camp."[69]

But the loudest criticisms, then and since, revolved around Young's handling of the Mormon Battalion funds. Some condemned him for "leeching" them for his own purposes in building a store and returning the profits. One particularly vitriolic dissenter wrote that, "all this money" was "clinched by these vultures to enable them to live in affluence and splendor."[70] Another, more recent author charges that instead of distributing the Battalion supplies Young "invested" most of it in goods that were "sold at a stiff profit." Because of Young, Battalion families received little of the money paid by the army.[71] Many claim that church leaders forced Battalion members to give up their money against their will and then used it to stock the store, selling the provisions at the cost of the health and well-being of the Saints.

Unquestionably, authorities saw the army money as an unexpected godsend. They knew also that their designs in using such funds differed from those of some in camp. When the Twelve first broached the plan to pool the money "for the benefit of the entire camp," fifty-seven people on the east side, a distinct minority, registered their dissent.[72] Most of these had already made arrangements "with the expectation of receiving funds" and were not happy at surrendering part or all of it. Their needs were reasonable. George and Linda Coulson, for instance, requested $30 of the $40 their son sent back to buy tools for a blacksmithing shop. "We have divided our litle to them that are in poorer circumstances than ourselves and continue to do so," wrote Mrs. Coulson, "but I think we soon shall want some assistance ourselves."[73] Bulah S. Clark requested $10 of the $30 sent home to purchase "a good new milch cow and the balance they can buy what they see fit."[74]

Seeing the problem, authorities convened a large outdoor meeting of Battalion families at Council Point in August 1846. Bringing with him the money recently arrived from the soldiers, Young first presented the plan of using most of it to buy materials at wholesale prices in St. Louis "so that no portion of the money shall be squandered without doing the company good."[75] He argued that they were not the only poor, indeed they were now the richer poor. Everywhere, he said, the camp was strained with poverty. All would benefit from pooled purchases, he argued, and if they did not choose to participate, the camp had little responsibility to provide for their needs, such as taking care of stray cattle. "It is not right for any person to hoard up the wealth which is earned by their friends in the army, while their brethren, who are around them in the camp are toiling from day to day to sustain them and their teams."[76] While most accepted, "there were some wonderful exceptions," and though the vote wsa overwhelmingly in favor of the proposed action, it was by no means unanimous.[77]

After the meeting, bishops were instructed to compile a list "of such things as wanted by the soldiers families" so that the most pressing needs could be met.[78] Most reasonable requests were apparently filled. Battalion families retained $1,500, or twenty-four percent, of the total sent home, and gave over the balance for large bulk grain purchases and a limited number of specific orders in their behalf.

What was most disappointing to both the families and leaders was the comparatively small amount of money the soldiers sent back. Of the approximate $22,000 paid them as clothing allowance, only slightly more than $5,000 was returned—nothing near the calculated $40,000! Perhaps some of the money had to go to buy boots, blankets, hats, and other necessities. A few men had no family back at the Bluffs. Whatever the reasons, Young was not amused. Responding to continuing sporadic complaints, he "told the Sisters that they ought not to grumble" after the Twelve for not having a sufficiency to live on, "for their dear husbands who were in the Army were . . . reserving to themselves only $17,000 for the Grog Shop, Ballroom and card Table." [79] Never one to be misunderstood, his highhandedness, bluntness, and uncompromising stance did little to dampen criticism. To obtain more money, John D. Lee and Howard Egan were secretly appointed to intersect the Mormon Battalion at Santa Fe and return with donated wages. Lee returned on 21 November with the disappointing sum of $1,277.[80] (Some wives had written letters critical of church authorities that obviously discouraged some men from sending back more.) The money was spent primarily on much-needed grain, hogs, and other provisions in Savanna, St. Joseph, and other northwest Missouri river towns in December, the most expensive time of the year.

In answer to the criticism that the Winter Quarters store "gouged" its captive customers: while it is true that Whitney had to pay more for shipping and freight during the first produce mission, it is equally true that by the fall and winter traders were paying from 60 to 90 cents for a bushel of wheat, $2 to $4 for a pound of pork, and 40 to 50 cents for a bushel of corn because of low supply.[81] But a more accurate picture of prices in the context of time and place is provided by the Winter Quarters store account book, which gives the retail prices charged to customers.

Table 2 compares known Nauvoo retail prices of May 1843 with those in Winter Quarters.[82] Price comparisons are deliberately restricted to items for which comparisons are available. Clearly prices were considerably more at Winter Quarters. Had a customer purchased the sample grocery basket presented, the total would have been $6.29 in Nauvoo compared to $9.46 in Winter Quarters three years later, an increase of almost fifty percent.

Another comparison can be made between store prices at Winter Quarters and those at Kirtland, Ohio, headquarters of the church during most of the 1830s.[83] Table 3 shows retail prices of the two country stores and offers in many ways a fairer basis for comparison, since Newel Whitney also operated the

Table 2. *Nauvoo–Winter Quarters Retail Price Comparisons*

Commodity	May 1843 Nauvoo Prices	1846–47 Winter Quarters Prices	Percent Difference
Molasses/lb.	$0.375	$1.00	270
Sugar/lb.	0.10	0.15	50
Coffee/lb.	0.12	0.15	25
Saleratus/lb.	0.07	0.167	222
Rice/lb.	0.06	0.125	52
Whiskey/gal.	0.25	1.00	400
Flour/cwt.	3.50	3.00	−16.33

Sample Purchase	Nauvoo	Winter Quarters	
2 lb. Molasses	$0.75	$2.00	
5 lb. Sugar	0.50	0.75	
5 lb. Coffee	0.60	0.75	
2 lb. Saleratus	0.14	0.335	
5 lb. Rice	0.30	0.625	
2 gal. Whiskey	0.50	2.00	
1 cwt. Flour	3.50	3.00	
Total	$6.29	$9.46	(+50%)

SOURCES: Winter Quarters Store Account Book; *Nauvoo Neighbor*, 1 May 1843.

Table 3. *Kirtland–Winter Quarters Retail Price Comparisons*

Commodity	1836–37 Kirtland Prices	1846–47 Winter Quarters Prices
Molasses/lb.	$1.00	$1.00
Sugar/lb.	0.17	0.15
Saleratus/lb.	0.19	0.17
Soap/lb.	0.13	0.13
Linsey/yd.	0.22	0.31
Tobacco/lb.	0.25	0.19
Buttons/doz.	0.08	0.13

SOURCES: "Gilbert and Whitney Store Day Book, Kirtland, Ohio, November 1836–April 1837," Library and Archives, Reorganized Church of Jesus Christ of Latter Day Saints; Winter Quarters Store Account Book.

Kirtland store, and, as at Winter Quarters, it was the only one in operation. The Winter Quarters prices averaged less than those at Kirtland ten years previously, at least with articles for which comparisons are available.

Table 4 compares the retail prices the Winter Quarters store charged its customers and the wholesale prices Mormon traders paid to get the goods.[84] The items selected are restricted to those for which wholesale and retail prices are available, thereby offering the fairest basis of comparison. The quantities approximate an average or typical order. As seen in the price lists, certain items were marked up considerably, but most only marginally so. If a person purchased large amounts of whiskey, tobacco, and soap, his costs would have been proportionately higher. Those purchasing more of the basics, such as coffee, sugar, and flour, would pay proportionately less. While the store operated for profit, an estimated 64 percent markup from wholesale to retail cannot be considered "exorbitant," especially in light of increased freight costs. A merchant of the time along any of the great rivers would have considered a markup of 50 percent as low. A 75 percent advance over the wholesale price "was more common," and many spoke of making "one per cent," meaning that what cost one dollar to buy sold for two dollars.[85]

Of the $7,906.81 spent in St. Louis and other Missouri trading centers, $1,187.46 was paid in freight, 15 percent of the total, not including the cost of sending the twenty-one pickup teams from the Bluffs to St. Joseph and back. After deducting freight charges, the Winter Quarters store was selling at 50 percent above St. Louis wholesale prices.[86]

Therefore prices were higher than at Nauvoo, but cheaper than at Kirtland nine years before. The increased costs are directly traceable to freight charges. Furthermore, the markup between wholesale and retail was well within acceptable standards and perhaps below average.

Whether Young pocketed some of the profits to repay himself for expenses incurred in constructing and operating the mill is difficult to substantiate. John D. Lee admits to some pangs of conscience for selling goods "at a heavy percent" markup in order "to liquidate the debt of building the mill."[87] He was likely referring not to the sale of the goods Whitney purchased but to the prices of hogs, teams, and wheat that he purchased out of the second installment of Battalion funds. It seems probable that some money was transferred to Young to pay back, in part, the

Table 4. *Wholesale–Retail Price Comparisons, Winter Quarters Store, 1846–47, Sample Order*

Commodity	Wholesale	Retail	Percent Difference
1 lb. Sugar	$0.125	$0.15	+ 20
1 lb. Coffee	0.125	0.15	+ 20
10 lb. Salt	0.155	0.40	+260
1 gal. Whiskey	0.40	1.00	+250
2 lb. Tobacco	0.10	0.38	+380
1 lb. Pepper	0.20	0.25	+ 25
1 lb. Saleratus	0.08	0.17	+ 52
1 Broom	0.10	0.12	+ 20
1 lb. Soap	0.035	0.13	+400
1 yd. Linsey	0.25	0.31	+ 22
1 doz. Buttons	0.10	0.13	+ 30
1 Comforter	0.50	0.38	− 22
1 Bucket	0.335	0.50	+ 50
Total	$2.50	$4.07	+ 64

SOURCES: Journal of Horace K. Whitney, 14 and 22 December 1846, and 12 January 1847; and Winter Quarters Store Account Book.

several-hundred-dollar debt he incurred in building and operating the mill.[88]

Winter Quarters provided Young the first opportunity to implement his own social and economic order. Though temporary, it was characterized by efforts to reach at least a minimal level of community self-sufficiency, by the consecration of wealth for the benefit of the whole, by the central role of the church in the collection and distribution of resources, and by individual ownerships and accountability. Though there were serious criticisms and understandable grumblings, the welfare of all prevailed over the interests of the individual.

PART TWO

"AND SHOULD WE DIE":
SICKNESS AND DEATH AT WINTER QUARTERS

And should we die before our journey's through,
Happy day! all is well!
We then are free from toil and sorrow too;
With the just we shall dwell![1]

William Clayton's memorable hymn, "Come, Come Ye Saints," written while crossing Iowa in the spring of 1846, became an instant favorite among his compatriots, a prairie-born anthem of both triumph and disaster. While predicting eventual rest in the West, it also foreshadowed the inevitable loss of life at the Missouri.

The effects of the mass exodus were bound to catch up with them sooner or later. The hasty, wintry departure from Nauvoo, the exhausting trek across Iowa, the endless spring storms, insufficient provisions and scanty diet, inadequate and improvised shelter, the subsequent forced exodus of the poor camp, and the unhealthy riverbank encampments—these were not the building blocks to good health.

By early August, it had become evident that they needed rest and recuperation at the Bluffs to "preserve their health."[2] Even before August, reports filtered in from along the trail that chills and fever were dramatically on the rise. Back at Mt. Pisgah, William Huntington reported "much sickness in camp" in the form of ague, fever, and chills.[3] Lorenzo Snow, a counselor in the Mt. Pisgah presidency, reported that July and August "witnessed a general and almost universal scene of sickness," the sick greatly outnumbering the healthy. "It was indeed a distressing scene. A great number of deaths occurred."[4]

After Huntington's own death in late August, Charles C. Rich succeeded him as president of the way-station settlement, and was to advise Young that weariness, fever, and chills would make it impossible to send many more to the Bluffs.[5] "Pisgah turned

out to be a very sickly place," one traveller reported, "the whole
family of us were sick during the fall and some of us all winter . . . we had a miserable time of it."[6] Garden Grove fared little
better. The tired and weary were suffering and dying there in
proportionate numbers.[7]

The sickness that decimated the ranks at Garden Grove, Mt.
Pisgah, and all along the Iowa trail began to paralyze the Missouri River encampments. Major A. J. Dripps, a former Indian
agent, on his way down from Fort Pierre to St. Louis in the
winter of 1846–47 passed through several Mormon encampments, describing them "as enduring great privations and suffering, many of them being entirely destitute of provisions.
These people, from all that we can learn of their position and
condition, have endured more privations during the winter than
even many of those who are suffering from famine in Europe."[8]

The accounts of sickness at Winter Quarters are plentiful.
Louisa Barnes Pratt recalled arriving at Cold Springs "half dead."
"The shaking ague," she recalled, "fastened deathless fangs
upon me," and "I shook till it appeared my very bones were pul-
verized. I wept, I prayed, I besought the Lord to have mercy on
me."[9] Heber Kimball had never before seen so much sickness as
he did in August 1846 at the Missouri.[10]

The chills and fevers of summer continued to ravish the encampments through the fall until the onset of cold weather in
late December. Special envoys travelled to St. Louis in mid-
October to purchase medicines to try to stem the spread of sickness, but to little effect. Little wonder, then, that after burying
one son and close to burying another, Wilford Woodruff lamented, "I have never seen the Latter-day Saints in any situation
where they seemed to be passing through greater tribulations or
wearing out faster than at the present time."[11]

As always, sickness played no favorites. Willard Richards was
incapacitated for weeks. Young took so sick that he claimed he
had died and visited the spirit world. Thomas Kane, himself
gravely ill at Cutler's Park, reported seeing women sitting "in the
open tents keeping the flies off their dead children" while waiting
for grave diggers to catch up with the overflowing scourge."[12]

Kane concluded that the cause of these tribulations was "a sort
of strange scorbutic disease, frequently fatal, which they named
the Black Canker."[13] Many writers have since concluded from
his account that scurvy was the chief cause of death at Winter
Quarters summer, fall, and winter.[14] However, until the onset of

winter, they suffered more from exposure than from insufficient diet, a fact they themselves recognized.

Many contemporary observers blamed their plight on the inhospitably wet Iowa spring. "The almost unparrelled rains . . . and the contamination of the atmosphere by the overflowing of the water," recalled Erastus Snow, "spread disease and death through all our camps and weakened our hands as though the Lord . . . had as in days of old given the Prince of the Power of the air especial leave to open his floodgates upon us."[15] John Pulsipher agreed with Snow's assessment. "The great exposure and fatigue in all kinds of weather since we left Nauvoo was more than my constitution could bear." He suffered from "the bilious fever" for nine months.[16] Likewise, Wilford Woodruff blamed their condition on "being exposed to the sufferings of a tedious journey of ten months in tents and waggons without houses."[17]

Eliza Lyman, who bore a son in a wagon at Cold Springs, complained that her exposure to "the scorching sun shining upon the wagon through the day and the cool air at night "was almost "too much of a change to be healthy." Stricken with fever she was reduced to "a skeleton so much so that those who have not been with me do not know me."[18] For many shelter was inadequate and offered scant protection from the elements. Attention has already been drawn to the wind-swept cabins, lean-tos, and sod caves or hovels that provided minimal protection from the elements, while some shivered in wagons all fall and winter.

Kane and several other writers, contemporary and historical, blamed the outbreak of sickness on the "singularly pestiferous" Missouri River, often described as the "Misery Bottoms." "In the beginning of August," Kane wrote,

the river diminished one-half, threaded feebly southward through the center of the valley, and the mud of its channel, baked and creased, made a wide tile pavement between the choking crowd of seeds, and sedgy grasses, and wet stalked weeds, and growths of marsh meadow flowers, the garden homes, at this tainted season, of venom-crazy snakes, and the fresher ooze by the water's edge, which stank in the sun like a naked muscle shoal.[19]

James Linn described the river as it receded in the late summer as "a quagmire of black dirt, half-buried carrion and yellow pools of what the children called frog's spawn." From out of

Table 5. *Causes of Reported Deaths at Cutler's Park, Winter Quarters, and Mt. Pisgah, 1846–48*

Chills and Fever	75
Canker	37
Consumption (Tuberculosis)	32
Scurvy	22
Measles	17
Bowel Inflammation	15
Lung Inflammation	8
Summer Complaint	8
Dropsy	8
Others	47
Not diagnosed	116
Total	385

SOURCES: Cutler's Park and Winter Quarters sexton records; Mt. Pisgah Historical Record; various private journals.

the "miasmata" of the river, great clouds of mosquitos rose almost blocking the sun. "After it became impossible to keep them from forming a crust on my horses neck," one traveller observed, "they were not content to aim at my face but stung me through my gloves and pantaloons."[20] Settlers further downstream blamed the mosquitos for repeated outbreaks of malarial fever, which likely was one of the major causes of chills, fever, consumption, and dropsy.[21]

With Cutler's Park and Winter Quarters sextons listing chills and fevers as the single largest cause of death [table 5], it may well be that in modern terminology they were dying from malaria, pneumonia, and tuberculosis throughout the summer and fall, all exposure-related diseases. Several noticed a marked, but temporary, improvement with the arrival of colder weather, further evidence that mosquitos and decomposing, bacteria-laden vegetation along the river were significant mortality factors.[22]

But the Mormons' respite was a short-lived one. Whereas the majority of deaths before the year's end were arguably exposure-related, most in the winter and early spring of 1847 resulted from protein, vitamin, and other dietary insufficiencies. Most noticeable was an outbreak of scurvy, or as they often called it, "black-leg" or "black-canker." "It commences with a sharp pain in the ankles," wrote one eyewitness, "swells and finally the leg get[s] almost black and in many cases it proves fatal. There have a great many died, within the last month."[23] Horace Whitney revealed that they knew the cause of the disease—"by the want of vegetable food and having to eat salt food"—but were nevertheless powerless to do much about it.[24]

In the late summer and early fall they supplemented their diets with wild chokecherries, melons, strawberries, grapes, and other fruits, along with various vegetables obtained from Missouri farmers.[25] But without means of refrigeration, these perishable foods were quickly consumed, reducing their diet once again to cornmeal, bacon, and some beef. Delays in commencing the mill's operation compounded their difficulties so that their winter menu was meager. Remembered Helen Whitney,

> Many of the brethren had gone down into Missouri to work or to trade for provisions, which consisted, mostly, of corn and bacon; the latter, with corn meal cakes, was our main subsistence during the winter. Vegetables, and many of the necessaries of life were not obtainable. Indian meal cake and puddings we considered very nice when used as rarities, as we were accustomed to doing in the east, but when we had little or no change, they became somewhat nauseous, particularly to the sick and delicate.[26]

Descriptions of the disease are as repulsive as they are abundant, and all accounts pointed to a dreadful time. "It is suposed to be the dregs of the ague and kanker," wrote John D. Lee, "that falls into the feet and legs and commences on the toes first with a pain, then they die away without feeling and so on continuing until the person expires."[27] "The flesh would rot and drop off some to the bones" another recalled.[28] Mary Helen Grant remembered "people dying by hundreds, principally with the scurvy." A favorite antidote seemed to be potatoes, she recalled. "We purchased one half bushel, which were used only for the sick ones, bathing their limbs in the water they were cooked in, binding the skins on to take out the black."[29]

Some, like Isaac Haight, equated scurvy with the black canker. "The black canker is beginning in her gums," Haight said referring to his daughter, "and has eaten them all off her forward teeth; nothing that we can do has yet done any good."[30] One woman, exhausted from bearing a stillborn child, fell victim to the dreaded disease.

> The scurvy laid hold of me, commencing at the tips of the fingers of my left hand, with black streaks running up the nails,

with inflammation and the most intense pain, and which increased till it had reached my shoulder. Poultices of scraped potato, the best thing it was considered to subdue the inflammation; it would turn black as soon as applied, and for all they were changed every few minutes for fresh ones, it was all to no effect.[31]

Unlike many others less fortunate, she recovered.

Just how many people were lost during the winter of 1846–47 will never be known. The standard interpretation is that some six hundred died at Winter Quarters, mostly from scurvy.[32] An heroic bronze monument at the Winter Quarters cemetery in Florence, Nebraska, lists the names of over six hundred people who supposedly died there in 1846–47. Present-day promotional literature still relies on this original estimate.

More recent scholarship, however, has restricted the period of suffering and reduced the death count. Some have argued that between mid-September 1846 and May 1848 only 359 are definitely known to have died.[33] Others have lowered the winter death toll to 200, or one in thirty.[34] One local Council Bluffs historian has argued that merely sixty-seven died at Winter Quarters in the winter of 1846–47, and of them only a handful from scurvy.[35] While it may not be possible to prove convincingly the causes of death, given mid-nineteenth-century medical diagnoses and descriptive terminology, one can arrive at a more accurate understanding of the extent of their sickness and death.

Between February and June 1846, the period between the initial Nauvoo departures and the arrival at the Missouri, comparatively few died.[36] The first rush of deaths broke out at Mt. Pisgah and Garden Grove starting in June, lasting through the summer, and climaxing in the fall. With fifty certain deaths recorded as early as 3 October 1846, it is conservatively estimated that by May 1847, at least eighty died there.[37] Garden Grove, only slightly smaller in population, suffered little less. The Mt. Pisgah coffin builder, Nelson W. Whipple, recalled "much sickness in that place in the fall and many deaths among which was Father Samuel Bent . . . Sister Lewis . . . also the wife of Samuel Williams." He concluded that "many others" died for whom he "made all the coffins and buried them."[38]

The single best starting point for mortality studies at Cutler's Park and Winter Quarters is the sexton records of both places.[39] Three hundred sixty-one people were buried in the Cutler's

Table 6. *Estimated Minimum Number of Deaths in Mormon Settlements, 1846–48*

Settlement	June 1846–May 1847	June 1847–May 1848	Total
Winter Quarters, Cutler's Park, and Cold Springs	400 (248 counted)	150 (113 counted)	550
Miller's Hollow, Trading Post, and other Iowa Settlements west of Garden Grove	150 (est.)	70 (est.)	220
Mt. Pisgah	80 (50 counted)	35 (est.)	115
Garden Grove	70 (est.)	25 (est.)	95
Ponca	23	—	23
Totals	723	280	1003

SOURCES: Cutler's Park and Winter Quarters cemetery records, Journal History, Mt. Pisgah Historical Record, various private journals.

Park burial ground and later in the nearby Winter Quarters cemetery (or cemeteries) between August 1846 and May 1848.[40] As table 6 indicates, more than twice as many people (248) died in the first year as in the succeeding year at Winter Quarters— evidence that they were better prepared, better provisioned, and better sheltered as time passed. The seventy deaths in the summer of 1847, however, may indicate a recurrence of malarial difficulties.

For several reasons, the figure of 248 deaths can be used only as a starting point, as it is the number of *known* and *recorded* deaths and not the actual total. First, if the sextons' complaints are to be believed, many died without proper records. Levi Stewart criticized the bishops who were assigned to keep mortality records "because people would go and bury in the Grave Yard unbeknowns to him and sometimes bury between the graves thus altering the number of those already reported." He confessed "that he did not know who were buried thus."[41] All through the

40
30
20
10
0
J A S O N D J F M A M J J A S O N D J F M A M J
1846   1847   1848

First Year: August 1846 - July 1847 = 248   Second Year: August 1847 - July 1848 = 113

Figure 1. Graphic representation of listed/named deaths on the west bank of the Missouri River, 1846–1848.

ensuing fall and winter the sextons were constantly nagging the bishops to provide the names of those "who had been buried and not reported." During one week alone in March 1847, another sexton complained that four or five had been buried without his knowledge.[42]

Although some of these may have been recorded eventually, the problem of nonreporting and undercounting constantly plagued officials. It is highly probable, therefore, that a large number of deceased were never officially tabulated. Some perhaps could not afford the $1.50 burial charge and the cost of coffins, ranging up to $3.50, depending on the wood used.[43] Burials in the frozen ground during the winter months were all the more difficult, and some apparently tried to take care of matters themselves.[44]

A second reason for doubting the accuracy of the sexton reports is the almost total lack of deaths reported in June, July, and August 1846. For this period only two deaths are recorded, though Kane said he saw numerous children dying all around him. Even without giving much credence to Kane's comments, it is hard to believe the official count when, during the same time, fourteen known deaths were recorded in Mt. Pisgah alone.[45] Until the Cutler's Park cemetery was laid out in late August, interments occurred at any convenient place on either side of the river. By 17 August some one hundred cases of fever were reported, and by 20 August, Heber Kimball was already aware of several deaths on both sides of the river. Said Young on 13 August, "I want this people planted in a healthy country where they may not be forever dieing."[46] Summer deaths, then, were insufficiently accounted for in the official records.

A third reason for skepticism is the undercount of scurvy-related deaths. Although cause of death was admittedly hard to explain then and is even more difficult for researchers to piece together now, certainly they recognized the disease, as earlier descriptions indicate. It is hard to reconcile the small number of only twenty-two scurvy deaths with several journal entries from eyewitnesses. John D. Lee said that "this and other pestilences have taken many to their silent tomb." Horace Whitney, a trusted diarist, wrote that "a great many" died from scurvy in February 1847 alone, while the sexton records list a mere handful of scurvy deaths for that month. John Pulsipher noted, "What the number was that died [of scurvy] I can't tell for certain, but it far exceeded anything that I ever witnessed before."[47]

Furthermore, scurvy deaths were under-reported if the Mormons used the term canker, or "kanker," synonymously with scurvy, as has been argued.[48] Although the sexton's records listed only thirty-seven deaths by canker and a combined total of fifty-nine from both canker and scurvy (sixteen less than the number expiring from chills and fever), Lee recorded that "the kanker seems to be more fatal than any other disease that has been in camp, which is certainly the dregs of colds, augues, which have been inhaled by exposures in an unhealthy atmosphere."[49]

George Bean remembered the scene he came upon when returning from a relief mission.

> Father was off in Missouri one hundred miles away seeking for bread and other provisions. Mother was sick, Casper had gone with the Mormon Battalion, his wife and child were sick, my brother James A., and sister Mary Elizabeth, aged ten years, were sick in bed, and my youngest sister had died two months before, aged seven years. . . . Nancy, the oldest, was the only one well enough to wait upon them. To make matters worse, they had nothing whatever for sick people to eat or for medicine. Dozens of neighbors had died with scurvy and blackleg because of no vegetables or decent food.[50]

The sexton records are, therefore, late starting, incomplete, and inaccurate. A more believable death total for the west side between June 1846 and May 1847 is at least four hundred—a death rate of better than one in ten. William Appleby admitted that by the late fall of 1847 well over that number had died at Winter Quarters, with "many" other deaths, as Young said, "in all places whare we have stoped."[51]

But these four hundred were only on the west side! Evidence abounds that among the estimated three thousand Latter-day Saints on the immediate east bank of the Missouri and in settlements at the Nishnabotona and west of Mt. Pisgah sickness was at least equally prevalent. Young himself said that considerably more sickness prevailed on the east than on the west side. As early as August, Wilford Woodruff reported forty or fifty wagons at Council Point containing many sick and afflicted.[52] A burial ground was finally laid out on the Pottawattami side near a bluff top not far from the Blockhouse, but unfortunately no sexton records have survived.[53] Based on the estimated east-side populations and the death rate of the west side, at least one hundred fifty died on the Iowa side during the first year. Meanwhile twenty-three died during the winter at George Miller's Ponca settlement.[54]

Therefore, as estimated in table 6, a minimum of 723 died between June 1846 and May 1847 at Winter Quarters, Cutler's Park, Cold Springs, the Ponca settlement, on the east bank, and in all the settlements as far east as Garden Grove. Based on the lower number of counted deaths at Winter Quarters the following year and with all estimates revised downward in the same ratio, at least one thousand died at the camps during the two years.

As expected, infants and young children suffered most. Of the 385 recorded deaths on the west bank, 166, or 46 percent, were infants two years and under. Over 53 percent of all recorded deaths were children nine years old and under, a proportion not unusual for the time.[55] More women than men died because roughly twice as many women lived in the camps. This can be partly explained by the absence of many men temporarily away in Missouri settlements and with the Battalion. Although only three women were reported to have died in childbed, several others likely perished from maternity complications that were diagnosed as chills or fever (table 7).

While the proportion of infant mortality was not unusual, the

Table 7. *Death Breakdown by Age (Recorded Deaths Only)*

Age	Male	Female	Combined
0–12 Months	56	34	90
1–2	38	39	77
3–9	19	19	38
10–19	14	20	34
20–29	6	27	33
30–39	8	21	29
40–49	13	10	23
50–59	8	8	16
60–69	6	8	14
70–79	2	7	9
80–90	2	4	6
Not Given	5	11	16
Total	177	208	385

SOURCES: Cutler's Park and Winter Quarters cemetery records, Mt. Pisgah Historical Record, various private journals.

overall mortality rate for that time frame was much higher than normal. On the west bank alone, the estimated four hundred deaths present an alarming 1846–47 death rate of one in ten. With an estimated 723 deaths in a population of 8,750, the Mormon settlements were perishing at a rate of one in twelve or 82.5 per thousand. In comparison, Nauvoo's estimated death rate for 1843 was a much lower 32.1 per thousand and for 1844, 24.8 per thousand.[56] In 1849 during the cholera epidemic in St. Louis an estimated 4,285 out of a population of over 50,000 died, again a ratio of one in twelve. That tragedy influenced President Zachary Taylor to proclaim a day of nationwide fasting and prayer.[57] (Cholera did not affect the Mormons until 1849, and then only sparingly.)

From the available statistics, the hard and soft counts, real and estimated, and from a careful study of contemporary accounts, disease and death were omnipresent, exacting a vicious toll on almost every family. In one family alone during October and November 1846, Henry L. Uttley (7), Jacob Uttley (9), James S. Uttley (14), Sarah E. Uttley (16), and mother Maria Uttley (34) all died victims of measles, dropsy, or canker. During a six-week period late in 1846 and early in 1847, Stillman Pond lost three daughters and one son to the chills and fevers. In May his wife, Almira, also passed away.[58]

The medical responses made to the illnesses suffered at Winter Quarters may have been as much a contributor as a deterrent to them. By modern medical standards, treatment barely fit the malady. While medical orthodoxy of the day called for bleeding and purging, the Mormons relied more on "poison doctors," the "Thompsonian" school of medical attention that specialized in herbal medicines and in abstaining from "the five deadly sins— tea, coffee, alcohol, tobacco and opium." Willard Richards was just such a doctor, and his level of medical knowledge was limited to dispensing herbal remedies. Dr. Samuel L. Sprague and a Dr. Cannon, also in camp, were likely of the same persuasion. Apparently the principle physician had departed with the Battalion, assuming he would be most needed there.[59]

Virtually every prescription for recovery was herbal in nature, since they held that God had given herbs to men to be used to treat the sick. "All wholesome herbs God hath ordained for the constitution, nature, and use of man" proclaimed one of Joseph Smith's revelations.[60] Willard Richards, in writing to the Battalion, warned them to "let surgeons medicine alone" and to rely on herbs and mild foods. When Dr. Sprague travelled to St. Louis in late October to buy medicines, he purchased mainly botanic varieties and herbal ointments such as lobelia (a wild Indian tobacco), quinine, calomel, and saleratus. Young advised a would-be storekeeper from Missouri that "in general the botanic medicines will be the most called for."[61] Some people, including "a Sister Lane a quite a notable doctoress," claimed to have discovered various herbal remedies and acted as amateur physicians.[62] Others obtained remedies from the Indians.

Joseph G. Hovey was just one of hundreds who treated a loved one with "herbs and mild foods" only to see her expire despite his best efforts. "My wife could not take any food, only a little water," he recalled. "For nine days she took but very little of anything. After considerable persuasion I got her to take an ametick of Lobelia and this helped her. She said the ice water tasted good." The following night she "took a death of cold," fell unconscious, and died.[63]

Contributing to the ineffectiveness and scarcity of their medicines were the lack of hospitals, rest centers, nursing care, and other facilities modern society expects. Though doctors made rounds and reported weekly to the High Council on the numbers of sick and dying, and bishops kept a current tabulation on the health of their ward membership, no central nursing station or accommodation was ever constructed.[64] Some women hired themselves out as nurses and midwives, but more often than not women gave their services gratuitously. Had they not been aware that a green, leafy, high-protein diet was an antidote to scurvy, the death toll would have been far greater. Knowing also that fresh fish was a good preventative, they "hauled in many loads of choice fish fresh from the water," wrote John Pulsipher, "which was a great blessing to the suffering poor—and the best medicine to cure the scurvy that we could get."[65] Leaders also counseled "those living in dugouts to get a house on the top of the ground to live during the [coming] summer, or they would be sick,"[66] for it was generally assumed that inadequate shelter during the winter had contributed to their sickly state.

Ironically, for all their suffering, leaders claimed the Winter Quarters climate healthier than Nauvoo's, maintaining that as they neared the mountains and increased in altitude, the air was purifying. "All the body of Nauvoo," said Willard Richards, "was a slough where this people have been filled with disease."[67] Ezra Taft Benson agreed, believing "the greater portion of their diseases was inhaled into their systems before they came to this place." All their colds, agues, fevers, and other afflictions were residuals of an unhealthy atmosphere at Nauvoo and elsewhere, "but I do not think this [Winter Quarters] an unhealthy location."[68] To have concluded any differently would have questioned the inspiration they were following.

Young also, at least in his public statements and letters, acted as if their health was perfectly normal. "We recommend the fresh air of [the] Missouri hills and a fresh draught of the River Water," he wrote in one letter. "It is a good preventative for constant agues."[69] In another letter to the trustees he referred to "some sickness" in camp, but "not so severe as was usual in Nauvoo."[70] By mid-fall he was reporting "the brethren in good health," that Winter Quarters was "a good place to winter" and "the health of the camp improving."[71] In a letter to Sam Brannan, Mormon leader in California, he described passing the winter of 1846–47 "as comfortable as possible" with "no more sickness than might very reasonably be expected."[72]

Why he was masking their true situation is not difficult to understand. Nothing must interfere with the gathering. He wanted all those left behind to assemble and prepare for the im-

Winter Quarters, 1846–1847. From an oil-on-canvas painting by C. C. A. Christensen. By permission of Jeanette T. Holmes and with the assistance of the Museum of Church History and Art, The Church of Jesus Christ of Latter-day Saints.

pending trek the following spring. To admit to decimating sickness was politically unwise, especially since Strang and other contenders would use their plight as an argument against the "Brighamites."

Strang indeed did try to make as much of the situation as possible. Appearing in the Strangite press were decidedly unfavorable articles on the deteriorating health of the Mormons:

> We have taken some pains to ascertain the health of the western camp, and finally succeeded in getting the sexton's account of the burials at Council Bluffs. Don't stare, reader . . . the sexton's accounts show eight hundred deaths at the Bluffs in one year from April 1847 to April 1848. We could not ascertain the number the preceding year, but those who have visited the ground say the burials cover more than twice the space, and it is universally agreed that the former year was far the most sickly.

According to Strang, one in five had died.[73] It was just this kind of information Young feared would scare off would-be immigrants both back east and in England. If, then, the anti-Mormons felt justified in exaggerating the crisis, he would do the opposite.

While minimizing publicly their setbacks, most leaders privately admitted their plight. Parley Pratt, returning in the spring of 1847 from his mission to England, found his family suffering from cold, hunger, and sickness. "One of the family was then lying very sick with the scurvy, a disease which had been very prevalent in camp during the winter, and of which many had died."[74] Writing to Joseph Stratton, leader of the St. Louis Branch, Young admitted, "There is some sickness at this place, but no more than might be anticipated in the fulfillment of the prophecy 'They shall wear out the saints of the most high' when we contemplate labors and toils of the camp the past year and the many exposures they have been subject to."[75] In a letter to Kane in December 1847, Young compared their sufferings to the recent Irish famines and urged Kane "to rouse the sympathy of the American people" to obtain donations "for the benefit of our camp" lest they "perish by cold, by sickness, and all the calamities incident to the wilderness and savage country."[76]

John D. Lee, in a journal entry in early March 1847, gave a clear indication of how pervasive and depressing the company's ill health really was. "Aggatha [Ann] is rather better of her illness but Louisa is worse and I myself am almost down. This certainly is [a] time of deep affliction and sore lamentation with this people, for daily more or less of them are consigned to the tomb."[77] It was in a letter to Orson Spencer in England, and then not until January 1848, that Young finally confessed that the "disease and sickness have been a heavy tax on the saints."[78]

The discomfort of disease, the embarrassment, the waking up to die, the unmarked graves—it all must have seemed that God was punishing the wrong people. Washington they could deal with, and Missouri they could defend against; but how do they cope with modern Israel's angel of death? "Why bring us this far only to be orphaned and abandoned on the borders of nowhere?" William Clayton may have called his block at Winter Quarters "Cape Disappointment" because of the sickness he and so many others were experiencing.[79]

Perhaps the first response made to serious illness was requesting a "priesthood blessing." Clayton, deathly sick of a fever, called upon priesthood leaders to administer to him for the restoration of his health. "The brethren all laid hands on me and rebuked my disease in the name of the Lord, President Young being mouth. I immediately felt easier and slept well all night."[80] Baptizing the sick was also practiced. Not to be confused with baptism into the church, baptism of the sick was performed to cleanse the body of illnesses of the flesh. Many at Winter Quarters, Mt. Pisgah, and in other settlements were immersed in water for the recovery of their health.[81]

Women also gave blessings of health and comfort. Louisa Barnes Pratt, having arrived at Winter Quarters in great distress, recalls how the women "thronged" about her wagon. "The sisters were moved with sympathy: they assembled at my tent, prayed, annointed me with oil, and laid hands upon me. Although I was not wholly restored, I was comforted."[82] Throughout the months ahead, many women, including Patty Sessions, "visited sick in several places annointing and laying hands" on those in need, particularly pregnant women and those suffering from female disorders.[83]

Their religion also offered several explanations for their trials, varying according to time and circumstance. A favored response was in paralleling modern with ancient Israel.[84] As God once chastened and purified the Israelites in their exodus from Egypt, even so would he reprove his people once again. If they were sick, the Lord was both punishing them for waywardness while purifying them for his purposes. As with ancient Israel, they too must become a tried and tested people.

Blaming disobedience for their discomfort, Young felt they would continue to be "subject to sickness and disease and death until they learned to be passive and let council dictate their course."[85] Suffering, then, could be as much a blessing as a punishment. "All of this pain, sorrow, death and affliction," said Young on one occasion "is for a wise purpose in God" to give them "their exaltation and glory in the Eternal world."[86]

Though death was common, spokesmen guarded against hoping for it as an easy way out. It was not something to give in to. "He gave warning against wishing ourselves dead," said one of Heber Kimball, "for the sake of getting out of trouble and . . . into heaven as we ourselves have to create our heavenly happiness by our conduct."[87] Life was a divine gift, to be lived purposefully. Taking one's own life was a cowardly, criminal way out.

Not surprisingly, they had the hardest time coping with infant mortality. In one of his few recorded funeral sermons at Winter Quarters, Young, speaking at the funeral of a two-year-old girl, gave several explanations delving into his understanding of the operations of the world of spirits and how they affected physical health. "Some times we lay hands upon the sick and they are healed instantly," he said. "Other times with all the faith and medicine they are a long time getting well; others die." Devils, though not able to destroy the spirit, were striving to obtain mortal tabernacles and were responsible, in part, for some deaths, especially among infants. "Some children are killed in this way," he said, "for the devil is making war with everything that has a tabernacle especially the saints."[88] It was an explanation seldom employed, but reflected a genuine conviction that the Indian wilderness they frequented "was the slaughter ground of the ancient Nephites and Lamanites and the spirit of Devils are hovering around it and if you are not on your guard they will enter you and lead you captive at their will."[89]

These religious responses were not always sufficient, and many refused consolation. One woman whose brother, James A. Scott, had died with the Mormon Battalion at Pueblo, New Mexico, demanded "why has he fallen, and . . . in the path of duty, under the direction of the church, fallen contrary to his faith and expectations[?] I repeat why oh why has he fallen[?]"[90] Others must have begged the same question.

The tragic story of sickness and death at Winter Quarters will always be of interest to the Latter-day Saints. It tested their faith and taxed their loyalty. Whether Latter-day Saint doctrines and practices comforted and retained them throughout their tribulation is impossible to prove convincingly. But like any other believing people, most did not easily surrender. It was part of the price they must pay for the role they had carved out for themselves, and regardless of the suffering or its causes, they were determined to turn them to their advantage. Sounded Young in characteristically unflinching terms,

> We are willing to take our full share of trouble, trials, losses and crosses, hardships and fatigues, warning and watching, for the kingdom of heaven's sake; and we feel to say; Come, calm or strife, turmoil or peace, life or death, in the name of Israel's God we mean to conquer or die trying.[91]

FROM WEST TO EAST: LOCATING A NEW ZION AND RETREATING TO IOWA

While spending the winter in their new cabin city in the wilderness, the Latter-day Saints analyzed and reanalyzed their future course of action. The wintry calm provided time to rethink plans, confer with traders, trappers, and missionaries who knew the West firsthand, obtain the most reliable maps, and formulate a more deliberate plan of action. Even so, many details of their impending march and eventual destination were not finalized until the very eve of their exodus. If Young knew precisely where he was going when he and the advanced party left in April 1847, it was the best-kept secret in camp.

Besides Peter Sarpy, who told all he knew of the prairie and mountain west, the Quorum of the Twelve conferred at length with Father Pierre-Jean De Smet, who visited the settlements on 19 November 1846.[1] "They asked me a thousand questions about the regions I had explored," De Smet later reported, "and the spot which I have just described to you [the Great Basin] pleased them greatly from the account I gave them of it."[2]

The Mormons' destination remained the same as it had a year before, that is, some secluded valley in either the Great Basin or Bear River country. In all the official correspondence coming out of Winter Quarters between August 1846 and April 1847, references to an ultimate destination were consistent but guarded. In August 1846 Kane learned that "they were intending to settle in the Great Basin or Bear River valley."[3] John D. Lee, privy to most private discussions, reported they had definitely ruled out California, "but intend setling the grater part of our people in the great Basin between the Mountains near the Bear River Valley."[4] A letter to President Polk plainly targeted "the Great Salt Lake or Bear River Valley."[5] In September, Young again spoke of Bear River, the Great Basin, or some other favorable valley.[6] And five months later, camp historian Willard Richards repeated their intent. "We have not changed our views relative to a location. . . . It must be somewhere in the Great Basin, we have no doubt."[7]

But if their target remained consistent, the complex plans for getting there evolved through at least three stages of development. Constantly debated were such matters as the time of departure, the number of men, the route, the need for another farm, regulating authority, and camp organization. Not where but how became the divisive issue.

The essentials of the first plan were to send over the mountains to the Great Basin or Bear River Valley a large number of able-bodied men, plant extensive crops, erect substantial improvements and facilities, and a year or two later return to bring on as many of the Missouri River encampments as possible. Central to the operation was completing the Winter Quarters mill well enough in advance to provide abundant seed, departing early in the spring, and gaining the full cooperation from families both to surrender their sons and husbands to the expedition and then to remain a year or two longer at the Missouri.

The proposed company was variously described as "a portion of our effective men," a "few hundred men," and "all the able bodied brethren who possibly can."[8] They were to consist of carpenters, millwrights, fence builders, and experienced farmers, who, after reaching their destination, would lay out a city, select a temple lot, sow large acreages, build permanent living quarters, erect mills, and in every possible way "prepare something tangible for our families and the Saints when they follow after."[9] The plan demanded that the advanced company winter in the West. In short, they were envisioning a large work party of several hundred men who would accomplish far more than the mere location of a site.

Critical to the plan was reaching their destination in sufficient time to plant abundant summer crops and build extensively before winter. They predicted reaching their chosen valley in a minimum of six weeks, certainly no later than 1 June 1847.[10] To make it they would have to leave "at the earliest moment," "say one month before grass grows," or as finally defined, "by the first of March."[11] Without families and excessive paraphernalia, they could "expedite their passage" and travel quickly, a lesson Iowa had taught them the hard way. Following John C. Frémont's route, they would travel up the North Platte to Fort Laramie, along the Springwater, and eventually through the South Pass.

In their absence their families would remain for "one or two years" at the Bluffs, "or up and down the river and back in Iowa" if forced to vacate Winter Quarters, and then they would come en masse in "the spring of 1848."[12] The reasoning was simple enough: to bring on large numbers of families before reaping sustaining harvests out west was potentially disastrous. Realizing the perennial objections of those left behind, Young argued that "a year's comfortable situation in any civilized community for women and children is far preferable to a year or two's risque of starvation in the wilderness."[13] Once their new settlement was secured, crops sowed, and adequate shelter provided, "then they will come to us, or we can come and bring them."[14]

Finally, in a move to lessen family fears and bolster faith in his leadership, Young called a special meeting in mid-November. Among other statements of assurance, he related a dream he had "concerning the Rocky Mountains" and promised that all "should go in safety over the mountains, notwithstanding all the opposition and obstacles government officials and others might interpose."[15]

But the "general council" or Council of Fifty had other ideas, dream or no dream. It had been instrumental earlier in the closing days before the departure from Nauvoo in planning the trek west. As an advisory arm to church leaders, its voice was important. During a series of meetings in November and December, the council, reconvening officially for the first time since Nauvoo days, met to discuss "the organization of the camp of Israel and our contemplated journey."[16] The most important meetings were held in December, with George Miller and James Emmett travelling down from the Ponca settlement on Christmas Eve day to attend. The Council of Fifty assembled the following day, Christmas, at Richards's Octagon, starting at 4 P.M. Its deliberations lasted until ten that night, from 10 A.M. until 9 P.M. the following day, and concluded late in the afternoon of Sunday, 27 December 1846.[17] Significantly, Young and Willard Richards were ill at the time and attended only intermittently. George Miller later indicated that his ideas were not "wholly overlooked in their deliberations."[18] What resulted from the meeting was a plan superseding the preliminary proposal of just a few weeks earlier.

Central to this second plan was the establishment of a large farm or way station, like Mt. Pisgah or Garden Grove, in an isolated setting in Yellowstone country north of Fort Laramie. By planting spring crops at the foot rather than over the mountains, they would choose the safer alternative rather than risk all on an over-the-mountain dash. Fewer men would be required, since few large facilities were envisioned and only planting would be required at this temporary site, but more could come on after spring. If successful at the Yellowstone, a small band might later go over the mountains, find the right valley, and at least make a tiny foothold and plant some fall crops. If successful on both counts, most of the others could be brought out in the spring of 1848 as envisioned in the original consultations. This second plan, more cautious than the first, was in part a scheduling change, a guarantee for essential wilderness crops in the summer and fall of 1847. The end result, however, should be the same. Prompting the revision was the advice some trappers were offering, the failure of the mill to begin operating in time to supply the pioneers with sufficient seed grain and flour, and a consensus that a way station further west would be a safe bet.

Much of the plan apparently stemmed from George Miller. Miller and Emmett, from their conversations with local Indians and explorations up the Niobrara River, were convinced that the spring expedition should travel west up the Niobrara rather than the more southerly route along the North Platte. Writing as early as October, Miller argued that his route was "the nearest and best rout to the pass in the mountains" and that it was "a level road all the way to Fort Larame."[19] Miller sent Emmett and Butler to explore the river and upon their return in December reported it as a "good route."[20]

Then, in late November, Justin Grosclaude and a Mr. Cardinal strongly endorsed Miller's proposed route. Grosclaude, a trader for the American Fur Company, and Cardinal, an expert hunter and trapper, claimed a knowledge of most of the Indian languages and all the best trails to and over the Rockies. They spoke favorably of at least a summer way station in the Yellowstone country near the forks of Tongue River "just five or six days above Fort Laramie," in present southeastern Montana.[21] The two men, according to Horace K. Whitney, had settled in the area of "the Salt Lakes" for sixteen years. "They narrated [and] gave an account of the climate, etc. which was quite interesting indeed."[22] They offered "to pilot the camp over the mountains" the following spring for $400. A noncommittal but interested Young listened carefully to their recommendations of establishing a summer farming station in the Tongue River area, as he himself had tentatively introduced the idea some weeks

previously. As one of the clerks recorded, "Mr. 'G.' gave an interesting account of the sources of the Yellowstone and sketched
with pencil a map of the country west of the Missouri and north
of Puncah above the Yellow Stone."²³ Because of his conversations with the two men, Young gave more serious consideration
to Miller's Niobrara–Tongue River plan. "The thought occurred
to us," he said in a letter to Miller, "that perhaps Brothers Emmett and Butler might like to explore that country [Yellowstone]
this winter to see if there was a chance for a good location or
any other speculation in that vicinity and become familiar with
routes."²⁴ Though Young was never overly enthusiastic about the
Yellowstone proposal, before long Grosclaude's suggestions had
become their concrete plan.

By mid-December, after the November round of Council of
Fifty meetings, letters were dispatched describing "the route to
our next intended location on the head waters of the Yellow
Stone River."²⁵ At a Sunday public meeting in Winter Quarters
two days after Christmas, Orson Pratt validated the way station
plan, explaining their intention to

> send out a pioneer company to get to the head waters of the
> Running Water [Niobrara] by the time grass comes or before
> and be ready to go over the Black Hills [of present-day eastern
> Wyoming] and put in a crop of corn somewhere on this side of
> the mountains near the head of the Yellow Stone. He was fol-
> lowed by Woodruff and Benson approving of his views on the
> subject.²⁶

After conferring with George Miller and others at Christmas-
time, the Council of Fifty decided to send ahead two or three
hundred men "as early as circumstances would possibly permit"
to the Yellowstone River, "perhaps at the Fork of Tongue River,"
and prepare a large summer crop for "some thousand or two
of the saints, who should follow after them as soon as grazing
would permit."²⁷ All who did not go to the Yellowstone in either
of the first two parties would "remain at this place and raise
crops preparatory for emigration the following Spring."²⁸

Despite his tentative agreement and support given the Yellowstone plan by various members of the Twelve, Young never
warmed up to it. After receiving more information and considering all the geographical and administrative matters concerned, he
tendered a revision of the original plan, only this time with the
weight of divine approval behind it. Involved were far more

than routes, rivers, and way stations. The matter had become an issue of leadership and authority.

Young developed several objections. First of all, he disagreed with the direction the Yellowstone plan would take them. He saw in it a repeat of Miller's Ponca settlement—off the main line and north by hundreds of miles from where they were intending to go. Why risk living among other potentially hostile Sioux and Mandan Indian tribes for another winter? Why chance unnecessarily an uncertain crop in an unknown area away from trading posts and settlements? In short, why delay at all? Better to take the risks of getting over the mountains than to mire in the swamps of the Yellowstone.

Young disliked what he was hearing about the Yellowstone. He gradually concluded that Grosclaude and Cardinal were influencing Miller and others the same way the Ponca Indians had done earlier and possibly for their own advantage. Joseph Holbrook, after returning from his explorations with Emmett, said that while the Niobrara was a fairly direct route, the feed along the way was "entirely eat out" by large buffalo herds. More seriously, the Sioux "expressed an unwillingness for us to pass through their country and make a large road as it would serve to drive off their Buffalo and other game." The Ponca, confided Holbrook, "expressed the same opinions as the Sioux." [29] If the warlike Sioux were concerned about a tiny exploration party, how would they react to large caravans? Besides, the Sioux were already a serious enough hazard to the settlements at the Missouri. To aggravate them further would be risking the lives of overlanders as well as weakly defended settlers back at Winter Quarters.

What Logan Fontenelle described was equally unsettling. Fontenelle, it will be remembered, was the interpreter to the Omaha Indians and a frequent visitor to Winter Quarters. A half-breed son of the mountain man Lucien B. Fontenelle, he possessed extensive knowledge of the far west. He disagreed with Grosclaude and thought the Yellowstone plan unwise. "The soil about Tongue River is red and yellow clay and you cannot raise crops on it," he advised in mid-December. "From the Ponca to the Oregon trail is a broken country—between the divides are swamps—the Creeks that run into the Running Water [Niobrara] are not miry, but it is a rough Country . . . up the Running Water you will see trouble and may break your wagons. I would not undertake to go up that River." Instead, Fontenelle strongly recommended they stick with their original plan to follow the North Platte, which he described as "a level prairie and good sound road to the Mountains." He also spoke encouragingly about the "best soil" south of the Salt Lake.[30]

Another drawback to the Yellowstone plan was the increased hardship it would place on the Mormon Battalion. Young was keenly aware that after their discharge in the summer of 1847, many of the foot-sore soldiers would be returning from the coast to their families.[31] He therefore wanted a large number of Battalion families in the proposed summer train so that as few soldiers as possible would have to travel all the way back to the Missouri.[32] They had already marched far enough at his insistence. The Yellowstone scheme would add to their march several more hundred miles than if the pioneers could reach the Great Basin directly. Enough criticisms had already been raised over the Battalion matter—why make it worse?

But most importantly, in addition to disliking the direction and the added input he was receiving about the Yellowstone plan, Young suspected the source from which it came. To his way of thinking, George Miller and his companion, James Emmett, represented a disobedient, excessively independent spirit that had manifested itself before the exodus from Nauvoo, all across Iowa, at the Missouri, and most recently at the Ponca settlement. Their goals and perspectives repeatedly varied with his and the Twelve's. Miller and others of the Council of Fifty, Young believed, like Lyman Wight, were following the shadow of the deceased Joseph Smith, not the living Quorum of the Twelve, and were really not convinced that reestablishing the church in the Great Basin was of any merit. Even during the winter, Miller had disregarded counsel by trading with Missouri without clearance and had steadfastly refused to pool his funds with Whitney's to buy at cheaper wholesale prices.

At a raucous meeting at Daniel Cahoon's cabin at Winter Quarters on 29 October, Miller railed against Young's policies and ambitions in the presence of Willard Richards. After their meeting had adjourned,

> Brigham appeared at the door and took up the subject. He had been without and heard all that was said. He handled the case very ruff. He said that Miller and Emmett had a delusive spirit and any one that would follow them would go to hell etc. that they would sacrifice this people to aggrandize themselves

From a painting of George Miller. Reproduced with permission from the Library-Archives of the Reorganized Church of Jesus Christ of Latter-Day Saints.

or to get power . . . and that he would not clean up after him any longer. He said that they would yet apostatize.[33]

Young wanted to dispel once and for all any doubt that the Quorum of the Twelve was not in command. Several in and out of camp like Peter Haws, George Miller, Lyman Wight, Lucien

The Elk Horn River ferry, from a sketch by Frederick Piercy, first printed in James Linforth, *Route from Liverpool to Great Salt Lake Valley*.

Woodward, and others were clinging to the belief that the Council of Fifty was directing the migrations west and held supreme authority at least over temporal and political matters. Miller, Haws, Emmett, and Wight all felt they were equal trailblazers to Young as fellow members of the council and would not willingly submit to his direction, particularly regarding secular affairs.

To take matters once and for all out of the hands of the Council of Fifty or any other similar group, and to scotch the already approved Yellowstone plan, would require a forceful declaration. On 11 January 1847, Young told of another dream he had the night before of Joseph Smith and his mother, Lucy Mack Smith, and reported that he and Joseph "conversed freely about the best manner of organizing companies for emigration." [34] Three days later, he presented his one and only canonized revelation to the church. Recorded today in the Doctrine and Covenants and received then as "the Word and Will of the Lord, con-

cerning the Camp of Israel in their journeyings to the West," the
document was a brilliant and well-timed statement not because
of what it said regarding the organization of companies (since
they had already had companies of hundreds, fifties, and tens all
across Iowa) but for what it declared concerning the source of
final authority. Above all, it was a lecture on apostolic supremacy.

Given first to the Twelve on 14 January, to the High Council
two days later, to the general priesthood quorums on Sunday,
17 January, and finally to the general membership on 19 January,
"the Word and Will of the Lord" said many things, but perhaps
nothing more important than this—that their journey westward,
its matter of organization, and its conduct all must be "under the
direction of the Twelve Apostles." [35]

For the first time since Joseph Smith, the faithful proclaimed,
God had once again given direction, had not left his people
alone in the wilderness, and had stated unequivocally who was in
charge.[36] Though it said nothing about their final destination or
of the feasibility of a way station, it did establish final authority.
Not the Council of Fifty, not the High Council, nor any other
group but the Twelve was in control. And those who participated
in the meetings and procedures to ratify the revelation did not
miss the issue.

Young endeavored to show that the apostles were following
the will of Joseph Smith while others were pretenders. "The
Church has been led by Revelation just as much since the death
of Joseph Smith as before," he said on 17 January. "Joseph received his apostleship from Peter, and his brethren, and the
present Apostles received their apostleship from Joseph, the first
apostle, and Oliver Cowdery, the second apostle."[37]

Hosea Stout, aware of the tensions over conflicting claims to
authority, recorded his impressions to the revelation.

> This will put to silence the wild bickering and suggestions of
> those who are ever in the way and opposing the proper council.
> They will now have to come to this standard or come out in
> open rebellion to the Will of the Lord which will plainly mani-
> fest them to the people and then they can have no influence.[38]

The revelation was delivered in person to the Ponca settlement in early February by Ezra Taft Benson, Erastus Snow, and
Orrin Porter Rockwell. They relieved Miller of his command,
told him he was wanted back at headquarters, and put the camp
under Benson's jurisdiction.[39]

Shortly after reading Young's document, even though it did not necessarily forbid the Yellowstone scheme, George Miller came out in public opposition to the plan, to the authority of the Twelve, and to Young personally. "I was greatly disgusted at the bad composition and folly of this revelation," Miller later recorded, "so disgusted that I was, from this time, determined to go with them no longer. . . . I must confess that I was broken down in spirit on account of the usurpation of those arrogant apostles and their oppresive measures."[40]

In a letter to Young on 17 March 1847, Miller stated his long-held but unexpressed objections to settling in the Great Basin, where he declared, "we would find it hard to sustain ourselves in food and raiment; and would, most likely, bring on the thoroughfare where all the slime and filth, malcontents from Missouri, Iowa, Illinois, Indiana, etc. would pass nearby us to the newly acquired Territory of California and Oregon." Better to find a location in some lonely valley in Oregon (probably the genesis of the Yellowstone plan) or, better still, in the far southwest "on the Camanshee [Comanche] lands on the eastern side of the Cordilleras Mountains so far south that we could grow cotton and even sugarcane." He argued that such a colony (very close to Lyman Wight's in southern Texas) could stand as a buffer state between warring Mexico and the United States. As a go-between, they could affect a treaty by which "we could get sea-coast on the Gulph of Mexico, where we could land emigrants from the States of England, France, Germany, Norway etc. in our own ports." He concluded with this parting, poignant testimony:

> Although I am in poverty and rags, I am not unwilling to undertake to do anything that this people persist in doing to build up this Kingdom. I have been as a beast of burthen ever since I came into the church, and have never swerved in my actions, or feelings, to do with my might all things to push forward the cause of Zion, and am, and ever have been, willing to spend and be spent for the cause. I do not say this by way of boasting, but because of the frankness of my heart.[41]

Miller and Emmett quit the church soon afterward. Miller headed south to Texas in July 1847, where he lived with Lyman Wight for a short time until he discovered that Wight was, in his words, "an intoxicated no-good."[42] In October 1847 he travelled north to Voree, Wisconsin, and later to Beaver Island, Michigan, and took up Strangism with fervor. Thrilled at having landed another former authority in Young's church, Strang gave Miller prestige and high-sounding titles such as "Prince, Privy Councellor and General Chief in the Kingdom of God," though very little real authority.[43] After Strang's death in 1856, Miller left the fragmented colony and lived his remaining years, spent and disillusioned, in Illinois. His loss was keenly felt by many in camp even if they had disagreed with him. Said Joseph Fielding, a friend of Miller's and a fellow member of the Council of Fifty, "he was dear to me in the office he held, he was indeed a fine man, and I hope to see him again in our midst."[44]

The third plan, then, the Quorum of the Twelve plan, was more than a restatement on camp organization or direction. It pronounced in unambiguous terms once and for all the supremacy of the Quorum of the Twelve over not only spiritual but also temporal and political matters. It cost the church the allegiance of some of its finest pioneers and frontiersmen, who, in the end, probably ran aground as much over personality differences as purely ecclesiastical or doctrinal concerns. Miller and Young were two powerful, domineering personalities who could not live near each other for very long.

With the matter of apostolic authority once and for all settled, the Saints could now focus on the details of preparing for their departure. Four days after announcing his revelation, Young stated confidently that "he had no more doubts nor fears of going to the mountains, and felt as much security as if he possessed the treasures of the east."[45] But at this point he had more confidence than answers. Who would go in the advance party? Was the Yellowstone still a viable option? How soon could they realistically get away, given the need to reorganize all the camps? When would all the rest come on? Many of these questions would not be answered until the eve of their journey.

Determining the makeup of the pioneer companies must be seen as part of a larger effort to organize the encampments. According to the revelation, everyone had to be accommodated within a travelling organization whether they could leave in the spring or in the fall. Young wanted to put the camps on a standby basis, ready to leave as soon as possible. The plan was to overlay the existing ecclesiastical structure of wards and branches with a travelling organization as a reminder to all that their stay was only temporary. Bishops and branch presidents, then, would become captains of travelling companies once out on the trail again. Also there was the peculiar matter of retaining "spiritually adopted" family organizations (see Chapter 10). Winter Quarters had already been so subdivided, with Young and Heber Kimball's expanded "tribal" families the largest.

Three other companies were to be organized, and from out of these the best-prepared, most able-bodied men would be selected to form the advance company. Each of the five would take an equal proportion of widows and orphans and Battalion families.[46] Wilford Woodruff and Orson Pratt were to take the remnants of Winter Quarters before incorporating everyone in Mt. Pisgah and Garden Grove.[47] George A. Smith and Amasa Lyman were ordered to organize the east bank settlements. It took these apostles five to six weeks to tour all the settlements, read the new revelations, choose captains of hundreds, fifties, and tens, and complete their preparations. Even Mt. Pisgah and Garden Grove were included. Ezra Taft Benson, meanwhile, reorganized the Ponca settlement.[48]

Evidence indicates confusion over which families to include in the anticipated departing spring companies.[49] The earliest would leave in March, followed by a second caravan once grass was up. This later company would consist of many of the Battalion families. Later companies would depart in intervals until 1 July 1847, with the rest finally vacating the Missouri the following spring.

But the matter of who would go was inextricably part of another dilemma—where to go and how to get there. By the end of January, Young had reverted back to taking the Platte route and advised his Ponca followers to convey that information on to Grosclaude and Cardinal.[50] "Say to them we have none but the best of feelings toward all good men, themselves particularly so far as we are acquainted."[51]

They did not decide on the way station possibility until the eve of their departure. By mid-February they were leaning heavily towards risking a nonstop, over-the-mountain thrust to the Great Basin with this one precaution: "should our bread stuff fail for lack of means to procure, we will then be obliged to stop a part of the camp at the foot of the mountains and plant late crops."[52] In other words, they would reverse the order and priority of the Council of Fifty plan by putting in a spring crop in the Great Basin first, and then if required, plant fall crops at the foot of the mountains.[53] As Benjamin Clapp put it, we "may as well stick the stake this year, as three or four years hence."[54]

Though early March had been their target date, Young conceded early in 1847 that it was "very uncertain whether the Pioneers will leave here before April."[55] Aggravating matters was the failure of the Winter Quarters mill, which did not operate all winter long. Obviously they could not provide large numbers of people with either adequate flour or enough seed for large midway farms.

Another complicating factor had been seen before—constant naggings from families not to be left behind among the Indians and in such a sickly place.[56] Some complained the pioneers were taking with them most available foodstuffs, leaving the rest with a scarcity of provisions until the first spring crops.[57]

In response to lingering fears and ongoing complaints, Young was characteristically blunt.

> You poor stinking curses, for you are cursed and the hand of the Lord shall be upon you and you shall go down to hell for murmuring and bickering. This people means to tie my hands continually as they did last year so that we can't go to the place of our destination. They are already coming to me saying can't you take me along? Don't leave me here, if you do I am afraid I shall die, this is such a sickly place. Well I say to them, die, who cares. If you have not faith to live here you will die over the mountains.[58]

This time he would not be hindered.

Monday, 22 March, had for some time been targeted as their departure date, but the last-minute elimination of the Yellowstone plan, delays due to organizing according to the "Word and Will of the Lord," difficulties in gathering provisions, and the time required to confront objections all forced a postponement.[59] Part of the change involved a considerable reduction in the size of the pioneer company from well over three hundred to less than half that number. A smaller company could move more quickly. Another target date, 1 April, also came and went. Finally on Saturday morning, 5 April, the first of Heber Kimball's company began rolling out. Others departed the Monday following.[60]

But the sudden arrival of Parley Pratt from his mission to England forced another week's delay. Young, Heber Kimball, Ezra Taft Benson, Orson Pratt, George A. Smith, Wilford Woodruff, and Willard Richards all returned on horseback to Winter Quarters on 12 April while the rest of the advance company was sent ahead to the Elkhorn River to cross it before heavy rains intervened.[61]

Parley Pratt met in council with his fellow apostles that eve-

ning, reported on their mission to England, the "demise" of
Reuben Hedlock's "Joint Stockism," the perils of their journey,
and Strang's successes in England, and he indicated that John
Taylor, hourly expected, was bearing the treasures of England
with him—469 gold sovereigns representing tithes from the
British Saints. He was also bringing almost $500 worth of astro-
nomical and other instruments very useful to the pioneers on
their journey.[62]

The next day John Taylor arrived by boat up the Missouri with
the money and two sextants, two barometers, two artificial hori-
zons, one circle of reflection, several thermometers, and a tele-
scope.[63] The Twelve continued their deliberations, and many
commendations and criticisms were expressed of Taylor and
Pratt's work in England. At the same time, Young urged Taylor
and Pratt to make every effort possible to join the advance party,
but the two were more anxious to rest and spend time with their
families. Young did not appreciate their refusal, and later it became a source of irritation and complaint within the Quorum.[64]

It was decided that Young should have the disposal of the
money Taylor and Pratt brought. It was also determined that
Pratt and Taylor be responsible for organizing the first "Emigration Company" along the patterns set forth by the "Word and
Will of the Lord" and that other smaller companies, if well
enough provisioned, come on in groups of no fewer than seventy-five until 1 July 1847. These later emigration companies
were to amply provide up to five hundred pounds of breadstuff
per person, enough to last eighteen months, as a precaution in
case the pioneer companies failed to reach their destination in
time to put in fall crops. After their departure, Orson Hyde, expected back later in the spring after visiting branches of the
church in the eastern states, would, as he had done in Nauvoo
the preceding spring, be in charge of the rearguard settlements.

On 14 April, all but Taylor and Pratt returned to the Elkhorn
and rejoined the pioneer company near the Platte River the following day. After organizing the company of 143 men and boys,
3 women, and 2 children (essentially amalgamating leaders from
the selected pioneers from all five companies), at 2:00 P.M. on
Friday, 16 April, after months of planning and turmoil, Young
and his pioneers headed west.[65]

The pioneer company left behind "upwards of 4,000" people
at Winter Quarters alone.[66] Their primary objective was to plant
and harvest substantial crops, gather provisions, organize them-

selves as per the proscribed pattern, and, in short, prepare for an exodus to the West as soon as possible. As they had been counseled, "all preparation and organization is for journeying and not for a permanent location at Winter Quarters."[67]

To keep the camps on a standby basis, Young had demanded that the organization stipulated by the "Word and Will of the Lord" replace that of the Winter Quarters High Council. "All the High Council that is necessary . . . will be the president and captains of emigration companies."[68] And as one emigration company left, new captains of tens, fifties, and hundreds within the various divisions would be chosen.[69] In practice, however, mainly to maintain civic functions, the Winter Quarters Municipal High Council continued with Alpheus Cutler as senior counselor. Bishops continued to be responsible to the High Council.[70]

Farming activities preoccupied everyone, for reasons already stated, and took three different forms: private, public (church), and family endeavors. Those owning property in Iowa naturally farmed their own claims. After George Miller's defection, his Ponca settlement under Titus Billings's leadership was dismantled and on 8 May 1847 crossed over to Iowa on the Winter Quarters ferry, settling as a unit seven miles north on "a good spring on Musquitoe Creek."[71] Almost everyone on the east side grew their own crops, specializing in corn, turnips, potatoes, beans, watermelons, and other market fruits and vegetables.

Meanwhile, on the west side, where federal law still prohibited homesteading, families were encouraged to plant and cultivate large gardens. Captains of hundreds and company presidents were held responsible for allotting to each family "all the ground they need, or can till, for a garden in the City of Winter Quarters, or its immediate vicinity."[72] They were also expected to regulate the larger farm acreages that extended two miles south of the city and to let out the land in lots of five and ten acres each.[73] Later in the summer many went to Missouri to assist in the wheat harvest, receiving their pay in much-needed wheat.

Most unique of all their busy agricultural pursuits were the large family farms of Brigham Young, Heber Kimball, Willard Richards, and possibly one or two other apostles. Based on the religious principle of spiritual adoption, these farms consisted of large numbers of families who had been taken into one of the leading families. In a sense they were family cooperatives and were designed at the last moment to replace the once-anticipated way stations further west.

Before leaving Young instructed those of his forty-one families not going west to farm on land he had chosen near Old Fort Calhoun, some fourteen miles north,[74] Isaac Morley was to manage the 600-acre farm, popularly called "Summer Quarters," with John D. Lee as foreman.[75] Lots were laid out early in April when work began on small buildings and fortifications.[76]

But jealousies and serious personality clashes prevented Summer Quarters from ever succeeding as anticipated. The root cause of their difficulty stemmed back to Lee's apportionment of the land. He and his company obtained seventy acres of apparently the best timbered land; George D. Grant received thirty; Isaac Morley, fifteen; and another twenty persons divided up forty-five acres. Late in April, Joseph Busby, S. A. Dunn, T. S. Johnson, and G. Arnold censored Lee and Morley for "acting partial and doing injustice in the dividend [division of produce] of the land," and they threatened "to go to Missouri sonner than bear it."[77] Eventually the Winter Quarters police came in to settle several disturbances among them.[78]

The dissension that racked Young's farm and ultimately led to John D. Lee's trial before the Winter Quarters High Council and the Twelve Apostles did not seem to work its same harmful effects on the Heber Kimball farm six or seven miles north of Winter Quarters (probably near the old Fort Lisa or Engineer cantonment locations). Daniel Davis supervised "Heber's Farm" of thirty families, who lived in homes built in a square "fort fashion," presumably like Summer Quarters. It was located only one-half mile from the river. Several hundred acres were planted and a good grist mill put in operation. Many lived at Heber's Farm through the following winter. In addition, there was a Willard Richards farm apparently located on the east bank within a mile or two of Winter Quarters.[79]

Reliable statistics are not available for the total 1847 farm acreages among the settlements. One visitor likely exaggerated when he estimated thirty thousand acres.[80] A more realistic estimate would be closer to twenty thousand. Had the family farms been more carefully prepared, the overlapping and competing levels of authority better defined, and sickness not so prevalent, their harvests would have been even more abundant. Nonetheless, the fall of 1847 found them much stronger, more prepared, and better provisioned than the year before.

Two months after Young's camp, the Emigration Company prepared to depart under the leadership of Parley Pratt and

John Taylor. They varied, however, from the organizational patterns set out in the "Word and Will of the Lord," with one president, John Smith, over spiritual matters and another, John Young (Brigham's older brother), over temporal affairs. Pratt and Taylor saw fit to make other personnel changes as required. The quarrelsome, disorganized situation at Summer Quarters had resulted in far fewer prepared to go west that summer than originally anticipated. Other problems arose between the two apostles and Hosea Stout, who was belatedly asked to come along. "I felt insulted abused and neglected," Stout recorded.[81] The apostles' authority, it seems, was not universally accepted, and whereas Young had originally envisioned several departing parties of a minimum of seventy-five men leaving intermittently until 1 July, Pratt and Taylor organized only one large company.

Young later severely castigated Pratt and Taylor for trifling with revelation and muddying the works. "When one or more of the quorum interfere with the work of the majority of the quorum they burn their fingers and do wrong."[82] Though bothered by their tampering with revelation, he was more irritated by their ineffective control over civil government and their powerlessness in curtailing Indian problems and in stemming disaffection.[83] After Pratt and Taylor's departure west, those still remaining at the Bluffs were reorganized along Young's original plan.[84]

Whatever their problems, the Pratt-Taylor Emigration Company assembled at the Elkhorn the second week of June. By 20 June, their departure date, the company consisted of 1,490 souls and 573 wagons.[85] Following the North Platte in the wake of the advanced pioneers, the Emigration Company reached the Salt Lake Valley in good time, 25 September 1847, two months after the vanguard company.[86]

Returning to Winter Quarters after identifying the site of a new headquarters near the Great Salt Lake, Young and other clusters of pioneers met the advancing Pratt-Taylor company in late August in present western Wyoming.[87] While some made it back to the Missouri as early as 3 October, the main pioneer company of 143 did not return until the end of the month, and then only after Hosea Stout had led out relief teams to meet them at Grand Island.[88] Their reentry into Winter Quarters on 31 October was one of triumph and rejoicing. Wrote Wilford Woodruff, "We drove into the city in order. The streets were lined with people to shake hands as we drove along each one drove to his own home. I drove up to my own door [and] was very rejoiced to once more behold the face of my wife and children again."[89]

Several formal meetings and informal gatherings followed soon after their return in which the pioneers sang the praises of their new home "far away in the west." Heber Kimball, telling his listeners "he was not going to flatter the country but would tell us as it is," described the large valley, the surrounding snow-capped mountains, the salt lake "so strong it would bear a person up," the scarcity of timber, and the dedicated temple plot. Then he drew the following comparison with that at the Missouri.

> It seems to me [like] a person living in a four story building in the upper room all finished off in good style and the comforts of life and then move down in a cellar where it is damp and chilly and sickly; that is the contrast between the valley there and this place here in Winter Quarters. This is as near as I can compare it.[90]

To underline their intentions to abandon Winter Quarters and to discourage a growing sentiment to stay permanently at the Missouri, and to obey the orders of an exasperated Commissioner Medill, the Twelve decided in council on 8 and 9 November, less than a fortnight after their return, to vacate Winter Quarters in the spring. The following day, they presented their decision to the Seventies, High Council, and bishops for their sustaining vote.[91] On 14 November, Young publicly declared their intentions to vacate Winter Quarters in the spring of 1848, and that those able to go west in the spring should do so, while everyone else should move back across the river.[92]

On 21 December the Twelve unveiled its "General Epistle to the Saints Throughout the World," a communiqué designed to inform the entire international church membership about the new-found Salt Lake Valley, to make a plea for contributions and donations, and to encourage everyone to emigrate to the Rockies. "We have named the Pottawattamie lands as the best place for the brethren to assemble on the route."[93]

As early as mid-March 1848 Winter Quarters residents were moving east. The transfer continued through the rest of the spring and early summer, with most settling in and about Miller's Hollow and northward near and along Pigeon Creek.[94] During the church's annual April conference held in Miller's Hollow, Orson Hyde moved that "the place hitherto known as Miller's Hollow [be] named Kanesville in honor of Colonel Thomas L. Kane, who had ever been a true friend to the saints."[95]

But whether they settled east or west of the Missouri, their ultimate destination was now confirmed. Now that they had staked out a new home in the West, no one would be justified in remaining at the Missouri. Whereas Winter Quarters had once served as headquarters of a church groping in the wilderness, Kanesville was destined to be a fitting-out station, a springboard to Zion.

MORMON SOCIETY ON THE MISSOURI FRONTIER

If the air of Winter Quarters was saddened by the moans of the sick and the sound of the grave digger's shovel, it was also brightened by the voices of happy children, choirs, dancing feet, and instrumental music. Schools in rudimentary fashion sprang up spontaneously all over town. The chopping axe, the pounding hammer, the wood saw, the rattling wagon, sleigh bells in the winter, the crackling fire, the ever-constant braying of cattle and bleating of sheep—these and a thousand other sounds gave witness to a community bristling with industry and activity.

Young people met and fell in love. Wives and mothers tended their children, cooked the meals, cleaned their humble cabins or sod homes, and cared for an almost endless list of chores. Bishop Whitney's store became a center of social intercourse, chitchat—the local rumor mill. The Council House hosted dances almost nightly. Sunday church services were well attended, the source of instruction, inspiration, the latest news, and future plans. In so many ways, Winter Quarters put on a happy face, an active appearance, and a normal demeanor.

Yet Winter Quarters was a community with a social and religious difference, for here was the place for practicing many of the peculiar doctrines of Mormonism that had been kept relatively secret in Nauvoo and that had been simmering since before the death of Joseph Smith. Here polygamy or plural marriage came more into the open, strengthening the faith of the initiated while catching many of the unindoctrinated off guard. The related Law of Adoption was preached publicly for the first time, defining circles and families of identity and social influence. Manifestations of the spiritual gifts of tongues, healings, prophesies, and visions were very much in evidence, especially among the women, who bonded together in small, influential clusters. It was a time and a place for dreams and revelations, experimentations and explanations. Temple ordinances without the temple were available for some, but not for others. It was Mormonism in the raw, and on the way to what it came to be during the latter half of the nineteenth century.

In the process, life at the Missouri proved a trial of faith and allegiance, and many, because of sickness, poverty, discouragement, or disagreement, abandoned the faith and left their friends and families.

Though enveloped by the wilderness, the Saints were not engulfed by it. A civilized people, they maintained a respectable society while struggling for survival. Makeshift schools were conducted, though less formally and regularly than at Nauvoo; music, dance, and other cultural art forms flourished; a locally appointed police force maintained law and order; and patterns of worship were regulated and localized. In various ways American society, Mormon style, thrived along the Missouri.

Although the Municipal High Council instructed bishops to operate schools in their wards, no formal standardized educational program existed either in Winter Quarters or across the river.[1] Eventually schoolhouses were built in Miller's Hollow, but in Winter Quarters classes were often held in homes or outdoors under a bower. The quality of education was uneven. Teachers were usually volunteers accepting a church assignment and were chosen according to disposition, availability, and presumably because of their ability to read and write.

The evidences of classroom instruction are few. It is known that a handful of spelling readers were purchased at Whitney's store.[2] In November 1847, the Nauvoo Library of unknown size and provenance was forwarded to the Bluffs, but how it was administered and where located are unknown.[3] No city library ever existed.

One instructor, Ellen McGary, had a bower built in front of her sod cave where she taught twenty pupils.[4] Weather permitting, classes were held outdoors until the winter, when larger homes and possibly the Council House provided shelter. Nineteen-year-old George Q. Cannon, a British convert with a comparatively good education, began his classes in late December after most cabins had been constructed.[5]

Popular with both youths and adults were the so-called singing and dancing schools. Singing and dancing had always been favorite activities. As Young's own revelation had declared, "If thou art merry, praise the Lord with singing, with music, with dancing, and with a prayer of thanksgiving."[6] As early as September

1846 the singing school had enrolled hundreds of young and old alike, who regularly held choir practices.[7] By year's end, thanks to the interest and efforts of Stephen H. Goddard, Winter Quarters could boast of a fine large choir, which began a choral tradition lasting to the present time.[8]

Dancing, their principle pastime, had been a popular and approved recreation in Nauvoo, where the Mansion House had hosted numerous balls and dancing parties. "When a Methodist," Young said, referring to his preconversion days in upstate New York, "I was not allowed to dance, would not do it for a bush[el] of apples but do it mighty quick now."[9]

Perpetuating the tradition, Hiram Gates conducted a popular dancing school for both sexes and for all ages. Begun early in February 1847 and held at the Council House, Gates's dancing school operated the first season only in the evenings with about fifty participants. The following year three to four hundred "scholars" attended, with classes running from 10 A.M. to 9 P.M. By 14 March 1848, 249 women and 191 men were enrolled.[10] His classes were the most popular attraction in town and were said to have "contributed much to the cheerfulness of the community, amid the hardships and privations to which they were exposed."[11] The dancing school was a morale builder, a safety valve, and a diversion from the tedium of frontier existence.[12]

Occasions abounded to practice the steps Gates taught them. The earliest recorded dance was held at Cold Springs, 13 July 1846, under a hastily built bower near their tents and wagons.[13] After moving to the Winter Quarters location and completing their cabins, the Saints celebrated the occasion with song and dance. Horace K. Whitney and friends "spent the evening in dancing" at Brigham Young's "house warming" and those of several others, often not retiring until the early hours of the morning.[14] Quorums, bishops, cattle and police committees, and almost everyone else scheduled dances of one kind or another for the Council House. Every notable occasion was celebrated, whether the commemoration of the "Battle of Nauvoo" or the return of the pioneers and Mormon Battalion regulars in the fall and winter of 1847–48.

The approved dances consisted of square dances, cotillions, reels and rounds, and "promiscuous universal dances," where dancers exchanged well-known partners, refrained from alcohol, and were supervised by bishops and other church leaders.[15] But the gradual development of dancing with "Gentiles" who

Mormon Battalion Ball, near Mosquito Creek, July 1846, from an oil-on-canvas painting by C. C. A. Christensen. Reproduced by permission of Nancy M. Sumison and with the assistance of the Museum of Church History and Art, The Church of Jesus Christ of Latter-day Saints.

came from the Point-aux-Poules or more distant settlements, of an improper amount of alcohol on site, and of other abuses temporarily discouraged church leaders.[16]

Alpheus Cutler did not think it appropriate "to have fidling and dancing carried on in the Camp, while others were languishing on beds of sickness."[17] The serious-minded Wilford Woodruff, for another, condemned such scenes. While there is "so much depending upon us and our prayers" he said, "should we be satisfied with the record of this city of the saints in the eternal world kept by the Angels of Heaven" if their records showed that "the Lord's anointed during the winter of 1847 and 1848 spent nine days of their time in fiddling and dancing where they did one in prayer and praise to Almighty God?"[18]

But for all the sermons, pitfalls, and improprieties, dancing remained a popular pastime, especially among the youth. Young, ever the pragmatist, knew that if they did not dance at home they would go to Point-aux-Poules and elsewhere. "If you want to dance, dance on this floor," he said, referring to the Council House. "I would not go there and dance God forbid—but I would come and dance with you."[19]

View of the old Winter Quarters site, looking east toward the Missouri River (early 1850s). From a sketch by Frederick Piercy, engraved by Charles B. Hall, New York. First printed in James Linforth, *Route from Liverpool to Great Salt Lake Valley.*

While dramatic presentations were virtually nonexistant, concerts, solo musical performances, and songfests were staged fairly frequently. Bishop Knight's twenty-second ward, for instance, sponsored a concert for the poor of his ward. "Their music is good," recalled William Appleby, "consisting of violins, horns, clarinet, tamborine, trombone, etc."[20] Occasionally visiting performers entertained the townspeople, musicians such as the enigmatic mulatto Choctaw, William McCary, who presented a flute concert at the Council House in 1847.[21] Meanwhile, Goddard's fine choir performed not only at the tabernacle on Sundays, but on various other special occasions as well.

The activity most regularly attended was the Sunday worship service, which in Winter Quarters took on two forms. The large, citywide convocation was frequently held and was the forum for general conferences. The 20 December 1846 outdoor gathering at the open bower (called the Tabernacle of the Congregation) in the center of the city was a fine example of this kind of meeting.[22] After the ringing of the Nauvoo Temple bell (recently brought into camp), several hundred crowded onto benches, sang, and prayed before listening to their leaders speak of the impending journey westward, Mormon Battalion concerns, "The Word and Will of the Lord" and other doctrinal pronouncements, Indian concerns, and a host of other topics of general interest.[23] Frequently meetings lasted several hours, depending on the weather, the number of speakers, and the nature and controversy of the topic. Bad weather often postponed such gatherings, until larger facilities were built on the east side.

The smaller, more intimate ward worship services were held every Sunday morning and evening and directed by each bishop and his two counselors, who were trained to supervise spiritual as well as temporal needs of their flocks.[24] These regular, localized services (each ward corresponded to a city block) were new in church history, the result of the city's layout, the need to satisfy the immediate needs of the people, the impossibility of congregating so many in a sufficiently commodious facility, and, most important, Young's organizational style of operating at the local levels. Sunday ward services included conducting ward business, sacrament (communion), preaching, and the performance of various ordinances, including the blessing of children.[25]

Most of the preaching was done by some local or visiting priesthood authority. Women seldom, if ever, spoke at any of the Sunday services. Topics ranged from the gathering of Israel and the impending trek to spiritual gifts and temple ordinances. On very rare occasions, various spiritual gifts were reportedly made manifest, as, for example, when Young and Heber Kimball spoke in tongues at a 29 December 1846 meeting.[26]

Women, meanwhile, had to devise more informal and spontaneous gatherings to meet their needs and provide an outlet for service, spiritual creativity, and social camaraderie. Ever since the women's Nauvoo Relief Society had been discontinued, women were even more confined to the home and family.[27] Any venturing beyond that domain was apt to be regarded negatively.

A woman's role was rigidly defined. As a mother in Zion, or a mother-to-be, her divinely appointed commission was to bear and raise children, support her husband in righteousness without unnecessary meddling or nagging, and to exemplify the womanly virtues of charity, patience, unselfishness, and godliness. "It is their duty to bear all the children they can," Young said, "and raise them up in the Name of the Lord . . . and when she has reared them up to deliver them up to their Father's instead of medling with her husband['s] business."[28]

Running the everyday household (which averaged four chil-

Table 8. *Sermon Topics and Frequency, 1848*

Topics	Frequency
Emigration	9
Gospel Obedience	9
Apostate Groups	4
Last Days/World Tribulations	3
Church Government	3
Use of Medicine	2
Repentance/Confession	2
Church History	2
Order/Reverence	2
Gospel Restoration	1
Priesthood	1
Dancing	1
Mission Work in England	1
Sacrifice/Tithing	1
Knowledge	1
Political Governments	1
	43

SOURCES: Miscellaneous Minutes, 1848, LDS Church Archives; sermons and addresses given at the Jubilee in January 1848; and the April and October Conferences, 1848.

dren) was an extremely challenging task.[29] Normal duties included housecleaning, spinning wool, dressmaking, finding stray cows, making cheese, gardening, preparing and cooking meals, conferring with friends and neighbors, visiting the sick, and, as one commentator observed, washing the family laundry.[30]

> This place [Mosquito Creek] is a poor place as to water as the spring runs very slow and gets thick very easy because of so many people and the brook is very small so that the girls have to go a mile to wash. Four of our women . . . went to go there with a wagon and stopped there the whole day to wash and did suffer much for heat and for want of wood. The water was first rate and there was also very good spring water. The women bore the burden with much patience.[31]

Not all her time, however, was spent at home. With so many men away with the Battalion, working in the Missouri settlements, on rescue missions, or herding the several fields of sheep and cattle, not surprisingly women greatly outnumbered the men at Winter Quarters.[32] It was not unusual, therefore, to see women collectively or individually involved in a variety of activities from cattle feeding to cabin building. But in the nursing, aiding, and comforting the sick, they were most obviously involved. Charitable service, with or without their Relief Society, because of the great sickness in camp, reached new heights and is abundantly confirmed by both male and female diarists.

Vilate Kimball, a wife of Heber Kimball and one of the most prominent and beloved women in all of Winter Quarters, went "from door to door ministering food and consolation to the sick, and pouring out blessings upon them, during which time she scarcely touched food herself." Her daughter said of her and those that accompanied her on her rounds, "by their united faith and works, with fasting and prayer, the sick were healed."[33]

Vilate Kimball and other women who had received endowments and anointings in company with their husbands in the Nauvoo Temple were not reluctant to lay on hands, with or without a male priesthood bearer, and pronounce blessings according to need and affliction. One man told of how he called in "all the men and women who had their endowment" to lay their hands on his infant son's head and "according to the Holy order and with the Signs of the Priesthood" anoint and bless him.[34] As more men left and sickness increased, the occasions in which women blessed and administered to the sick by the priesthood— a practice unheard of and discouraged in the church today— greatly multiplied.

After the departure in the spring of 1847 of yet another 145 men in the pioneer company, several informal "female meetings" sprang up all over town, catering to the needs of various small pockets of women drawn together by family, location, or disposition and friendship. Some meetings were held three times a week; others, like Lucy Worker's every Thursday.[35]

Patty Sessions tells of visiting with Eliza R. Snow and a "Sister Leonard" in mid-April 1847 where they "had a good time spoke in tongues, prophecied and the spirit of the Lord was with us."[36] Again at Sister Leonard's on 1 May she presided over a meeting of women got up by Eliza Snow: "They spoke in tongues. I interpreted and some prophesied."[37] Many are the references in Patty Sessions's diary to "a feast of the good things of the kingdom" and to other "great and marvellous things," where the gifts of tongues, prophecy, healing, and discernment were reportedly made manifest.

Some claimed to have received angelic visitations while others spoke of rebuking evil spirits "by the power of the priesthood which had been conferred upon us in the house of God in connection with our husbands."[38] "Frequently, without eating or drinking," Helen Whitney recalled, "we would meet in the morning, either at my mother's or some other of my father's houses, and spend the day singing, praying and prophecying." Occasionally some of the men "who could leave their work united with us and received great blessings in connection with the sisters."[39]

Several factors might account for this pentecostal display. Certainly Mormon theology provided for and encouraged it, claiming that "there are many gifts" and "to some is given one and to some is given another, that all may be profited thereby."[40] Furthermore, their failure to prevent suffering and death drove many to a heightened religious sense. What they could not do physically to prevent sickness they would try to do in faith. For many it was their last and only hope. One diarist recalls so many sick that "we thought we would have a prayer meeting, so we did." "The spirit of God did attend us," he said, as they administered and blessed one another.[41]

Fear of the hostile wilderness environment may have been another contributing factor, especially in the absence of many male defenders. Public preaching concerning evil spirits and the belief that the Bluffs region in particular was infested with them from ages past might account for the several references to evil forces. One sister tells of how at one meeting they contended with evil spirits taking hold of their small children and being "rebuked by the power of the priesthood."[42]

Loneliness and grief accentuated by isolation must also be considered. Joseph G. Hovey, a recent widower, was invited to one female meeting and given a blessing under the hands of Laura Pitkin. He later said of it,

> She laid her hands on [my] head and spoke in tongues. Sister [Emeline B.] Harris Whitney did interpret . . . that my wife did watch over me and my little ones and her heart entwined about me and loved me. . . . She was taken from me for the trial of my faith.[43]

Others who had recently lost loved ones were similarly blessed and comforted.

Besides the need for hope and faith in a brighter day, many anticipated delivery from their enemies and the wilderness. Distended and uprooted as they were, without permanent or famil-

Vilate Kimball, wife of Heber C. Kimball. Reproduced with permission from the Church Archives, The Church of Jesus Christ of Latter-day Saints.

iar surroundings, future prophecies and predictions were comforting and well received. Patty Sessions tells how "Sister Young and Whitney" laid their hands upon her head "and predicted many things that I shall be blessed with; that I should live to stand in a temple yet to be built" and "should be great." [44] Their new home in the valleys of the west would in every way be an improvement over where they now were, a fulfillment and redemption of all their faith and prayers.

Eliza R. Snow in her later years. Reproduced with permission from the Church Archives, The Church of Jesus Christ of Latter-day Saints.

They took comfort, also, in believing that as bad as things were, their trials were but divine chastisements all for their good. The less faithful and the less valiant must eventually have it much worse. Surely God would punish them.

> There were things foretold . . . that are coming swiftly upon those who have turned away and are uniting their voices and influence against that Zion which we were told should be established in [the] mountains . . . also of the wars that were right at our doors . . . that the times would be when hunger would overcome every tender feeling, and even mothers would eat their own babes. Many terrible things were so clearly portrayed to the minds of those who were present and understood as they were spoken by the gift and power of the Lord, that we felt to pray the Lord to close the vision of our minds.[45]

Finally, the all-enveloping darkness of long winter nights may have played a cruel trick or two, especially with the more sensitive or superstitious. This was a time forty years before the introduction of the electric light, and lamp posts were nonexistent in the city. Save for the light of the moon and stars and a few flickers of light from the occasional fireplace, Winter Quarters at night and in the shadow of its own cemetery was gripped in blackness. This might explain how it was that late one night

> Satan, it seems, came also, and they aver that his face and shoulders were plainly visible through the window. They not only saw him, but heard his awful footsteps as he walked around outside of the house . . . and the power was so terrible, that it was only by mighty faith and the power of the priesthood that the destroyer was rebuked from their midst.[46]

Upon hearing of such rumored visits, many men and women condemned these women's meetings saying it was "all of the devil" and out of bounds of perceived practices and norms of worship.[47]

After Young's return in the fall, as their health improved and plans solidified, and as church leaders gave stricter counsel respecting such matters, the frequency of female meetings decreased dramatically, and the operations of the gifts of the spirit declined in direct proportion.[48] Other socioreligious practices now being introduced would more than occupy their full attention. But for many the pentecostal scenes of Winter Quarters would never be forgotten.

Given, in part, to institute a "reformation" among the people, Young's "Word and Will of the Lord" said much about behavior.

Keep all your pledges one with another; and covet not that
which is thy brother's   keep yourselves from evil to take the
name of the Lord in vain. . . . Cease to contend one with another; cease to speak evil one of another. Cease drunkenness,
. . . restore that which thou hast borrowed.[49]

The Mormon code of ethics was sufficiently strict and well
enough defined that most were guilty of minor indiscretions at
one time or another. A very few, laden with economic hardships
and facing empty bread pantries, even reverted to stealing and
counterfeiting. In the absence of any other law-keeping body,
the Winter Quarters police were appointed to uphold the law
and monitor camp obedience. To every transgression and crime
a just punishment was affixed, and marshals, high councils, bishops, and especially the police busied themselves maintaining the
law of the land and of the Lord.

In a series of questions designed to test the faithfulness and
obedience of those at Garden Grove, Thomas Kington devised
the following set of questions: Do you believe in the general
church authorities? Do you believe in the High Council? Do you
believe in the law of tithing? Do you hold family prayer regularly? Do you attend public worship? And do you teach your children the principles of the gospel and forbid them to swear, lie,
or steal?[50] Kington's screening interview could have been applied
to any Mormon settlement at the Missouri, since strict obedience
was expected from everyone. Both spiritual and physical well-
being depended on it. Since Mormons had a tendency to blame
their predicaments on the community level of conformity to gospel standards, it was believed that he or she who broke the law
jeopardised everyone.

Their code of conduct is best described in two separately de-
finable though not mutually exclusive spheres—religious and
civil. As the "children of promise," there could be no room
among them for such vices as habitual drunkenness, gambling,
swearing, sabbath breaking, criticizing church leaders, lying,
nonpayment of tithes, and idleness. But in reality the offenses
existed.

Gambling, a common vice on the American frontier, found its
way among them. Whether attending Peter Sarpy's horse races
or those of his own creation, Henry W. Miller, founder of Miller's
Hollow and later the first Mormon delegate to the Iowa legis-
lature, was temporarily removed from his post as a counselor in
the Pottawattamie High Council "for betting on a horse race."[51]

Some refused to pay what they considered to be unjust bills. W. W. Phelps, for instance, on being brought before the High Council for not paying three bills for stray cattle said

> I refused to pay—and got mad and said as bad [as] I could say. When they came to ask an explanation—told them I had said so and so but I did not mean as I said. I said as bad as I could and I don't think they could tell it half as bad as I said it, but I mean to uphold the authorities and will make any satisfaction.[52]

Swearing was fairly common even though it was always preached against. Most were guilty of the occasional expletive here and there, but for one young man who had doubts about the church anyway, it was his undoing.

> Several of the council complained of Robert King for profane swearing, taking the name of God in vain. Counsellor Coulson said he saw said R. King siting on the bank of the river one evening and heard him say that he had said "by God he would never be a Mormon till the River ran up stream," but now said he "by God I'm a Mormon for the River runs upstream," but soon the current took a log that was floating upstream in an eddy and carried down stream again, now said King "I'll be Dam'd if I'll be a Mormon any longer for the River has turned down stream again."
> Council then cut R. King off from the church by unanimous vote.[53]

Usually the punishment for such indiscretions was surprisingly mild. The image of a people ready to pounce upon every transgression is inaccurate. "We should more than meet a man half way who confesses his errors," said Young. Referring to one man who had confessed his sin, Young counseled, "I know it and he knows it and when he confesses let it be dropped let it pass and go along as if nothing had happened."[54]

Moral transgressions, however, were usually dealt with more harshly. In September 1846 three young men were turned in for fornication. Said Stout, "They and the girls had been out for fifteen nights in succession untill after two o'clock and that it was his [Woodruff's] wish, and the wish of the President that I should take the matter in hand."[55] As a public example to deter further similar behavior, each man was whipped thirty-nine times.

The trafficking in liquor, especially among the Indians, was considered a grave felony. In the days before the "Word of

Wisdom" (the church's law of health) became rigidly defined, the prohibition against alcohol was loosely applied.[56] At Winter Quarters the problem was not so much in the consumption (unless in excess) as in the control of liquor. Several are the references to gay times made brighter with liquid refreshment.[57] A few enterprising individuals like John Pack bought several gallons of whiskey in Missouri and then returned with it to Winter Quarters, where he sold it at 75 cents per gallon.[58] Either fearful of indiscretions or jealous of the profits Pack and others were making, the Municipal High Council ordered in December 1846 that hereafter the sale of "ardent spirits" shall be administered only by bishops "and the net proceeds be applied to the poor."[59] The council was suspicious that some were selling clandestinely to the Indians. Anyone found guilty of such traffic would be handed over to the Indian agents "to be dealt with according to the law of the United States."[60] Peter Haws was eventually brought before the council for profiting off the Indians in just this way.[61]

More serious civil crimes did of course occur. Theft was not uncommon. For stealing a cow from his neighbor, one man was disfellowshipped for three months.[62] A more serious crime was stealing from the Missouri settlers. Alpheus Cutler told one young man who confessed to stealing from a farmer south of St. Joseph "to return the horse as soon as possible and make amends before Missouri wreaks bloodshed on the camp."[63]

Counterfeiting was a recurring problem, especially among a small ring of operators on the east side and further back at Garden Grove.[64] Garden Grove eventually earned so sordid a reputation for counterfeiting and thievery that Orson Hyde disfellowshipped the entire branch from the church, at least until local authorities pinpointed the few truly guilty parties. Brawls, disputes, and fights occurred occasionally, with reports of even one or two killings.[65]

Aware that a very small minority of his people would resort to crime, Young sanctioned the establishment of a police force under the direction of Hosea Stout. Originally little more than a security guard to protect cattle, by the fall of 1846 it had become a force of twenty-six men who received their wages from an unpopular police tax. The police were to provide protection day and night against Indian prowlers and other intruders, prevent crimes and sedition among the people, provide security for church leaders, spy out against federal attacks, and be a watchdog on camp obedience, reporting any moral or religious indiscretions to the authorities.

Hosea Stout, who seemed to glory in his role and in the unpopularity of his position, was glad of his reappointment.

It appears by the foregoing organization that the system of the "Old Police" so much feared despised and beloved in Nauvoo is now revived on precisely the same plan and mostly the same men as there was which composed the old Police in Nauvoo and with the same Captain at their head those who dreaded us because of their wickedness there may well have the same fears now. For the same men and the same organization the same leader, the same circumstances to act on will naturally produce the same results.[66]

It did not take Stout and company very long to discover seditious plots, schemes to murder the Twelve, and a host of other conspiratorial activities.[67]

Though their tactics may have been questionable, they were successful. Referring to one sting operation or "police spree" to discover who was trying to set up a gambling table, Stout said, "Several of us went into a drinking spree with some who were concerned in it. They soon got high enough to develop their plans and thus we learned all about it."[68]

Little wonder they earned a dreadful reputation and were popularly despised. When Bishops Daniel Carns and Newel Knight moved to break up a whiskey ring, it was the police who moved in and confiscated five barrels of whiskey from three illegal distributors.[69] Almost everyone, including such notables as William Clayton, Edwin D. Woolley, and Charles C. Rich, hated Stout and his police for going way beyond the mark. A police force was one thing; a morality squad quite another.

Though aware of Stout's excesses and the unpopularity of the police, Young also realized they played a valuable role in protecting the camps, in keeping people honest, and in upholding the law. With all their excesses, the police were a necessity.[70]

Thus Winter Quarters, though a temporary community, was a civilized attempt at meeting the spiritual, temporal, and emotional needs of a dynamic, industrious people. In its short history, Winter Quarters witnessed the implementation of new ways of Mormon life and culture that persist to the present day. Other practices, however, were so troublesome and so peculiar even for that time and place that they are no longer a fact of contemporary Mormonism—activities that now require the closest scrutiny.

ERRAND IN THE WILDERNESS:
THEIR SOCIAL AND RELIGIOUS LIFE

To a people firmly convinced that they were God's chosen, his modern Israel, and freshly endowed with all the powers, authorities, and doctrines requisite for both their own salvation and that of all the families of the earth, their religion was their motivation and raison d'être. Most remembered and revered Joseph Smith and now looked to Brigham Young and the Twelve to preserve the prophetic tradition and to implement the doctrines of salvation Smith introduced before his death.

Brief reference was made in Chapter 1 to the importance Latter-day Saints placed on temple ordinances. Baptisms for the dead, endowments, special anointings, marriages, sealings, and other principles and practices identified with the priesthood and the temple were of commanding significance to the believers at Nauvoo. They were no less so at Winter Quarters, where they dictated much of their residents' religious and social behavior. Mormon society cannot be understood without a knowledge of its undergirding theology.

At the heart of their faith was the doctrine of family salvation. No man or woman could be exalted to the highest "celestial" glories, the eternal presence of God, without eternal (temple) marriage. Similarly no child could be saved outside of the family unit. Through the atonement of Jesus Christ, one's resurrection, that is, immortality, was granted unconditionally irrespective of merit. But eternal life, that exalted existence with deity, was attainable only through the mercies of Christ and one's obedience to his commands, ordinances, and sacraments, the highest of which was temple, or celestial, marriage. Such a reward was attainable for all generations, present, past, and future.

Joseph Smith had taught that to obtain "an eternal weight of glory" a man must marry a wife.[1] Marriage had to be solemnized by one having divine authority or priesthood, which Mormons believed Christ, his apostles, and most of the ancient patriarchs possessed. With the proclaimed restoration of this divine authority, the "keys of the kingdom" and the necessary priesthood to officiate in the ordinances thereof were back in place. By the Melchizedek, or higher priesthood, baptisms could be performed, blessings pronounced, sacraments administered, and all other ordinances made binding both on earth and in heaven. These were the same powers that the apostle Peter purportedly held.[2]

Above all, marriages could now be performed not merely for this lifetime but "for all time and eternity." Such celestial marriages performed in the temple were often called sealings, since if the partners lived deservingly and obediently, their covenants were "sealed unto them by the Holy Spirit of promise" insuring their mutual exaltation and eternal life. "They shall pass by the angels and the gods, which are set there," Joseph Smith had proclaimed, "to their exaltation and glory in all things" and shall receive a "continuation of the seeds forever and ever"—in other words, eternal increase and progression.[3] Children of such a union were "born in the covenant" and automatically were possessions of their parents in an eternal family context. For newly converted families and young engaged couples, celestial marriage represented the ultimate achievement, the crowning ordination, something that they could do in this life to achieve a better one hereafter.

But there was more. What could be done to insure the growth of the church in the future? Like the ancient Old Testament patriarch Abraham, who received promises that "in thy seed shall all the nations of the earth be blessed," so Mormons believed that with the priesthood the ancient Abrahamic promise would be fulfilled through them. With the restoration of priesthood ordinances and covenants so long lost to mankind came the injunction to preach unto every nation and raise up a "righteous seed." In other words, to fulfill the divine destiny, two operations were required: first, the gospel must be promulgated to all the world, and second, a righteous posterity enlarged. Missionary work would accomplish the first half of the commandment; the Abrahamic pattern of marriage, the plurality of wives, would begin fulfilling the latter.

Through this expanded form of celestial marriage, the principle of a plurality of wives and a large posterity were made possible through the practice of polygyny, by which a man had more than one wife simultaneously.[4] It was popularly referred to as polygamy, while critics and opponents usually denigrated it as "spiritual wifery."

At least as early as 1831, while translating the Book of Mormon and revising passages of the Bible, Joseph Smith, believers proclaimed, was introduced to the doctrine of celestial marriage.[5] It was not proclaimed, however, until 1843 at a session of the Nauvoo High Council. Joseph married between thirty-one and forty-five wives, some for time (this life only) and others for time and eternity. It is uncertain whether any of these wives ever bore him children.[6] Plural marriage was always secretly performed. Fewer than thirty families practiced it in Nauvoo, for fear of persecution and recrimination.[7] Some who were practicing it even denied it at the pulpit, no doubt for personal-safety reasons and for the missionary cause. Despite these efforts to the contrary, polygamy was widely rumored about and condemned, especially by opponents and defectors, as religious licence for immorality. Opposition to polygamy must be regarded as a contributing factor to the deaths of Joseph and Hyrum Smith. Many of Joseph Smith's widows subsequently became the wives of Brigham Young or Heber C. Kimball.

Polygamy was likely the most peculiar and certainly the most criticized practice of early Mormonism and has received its full share of condemnation since. Yet polygamy and the vigorous missionary attempt to win new converts were puristically regarded as the means by which all mankind could obtain eternal blessings.

But what of past generations? What part did they share in the divine scheme of things? To meet their needs, the doctrine of family exaltation also extended back through all the generations of mankind. The errand of the church was to provide an opportunity for the exaltation of the entire human family since Adam. The dimensions of such a tenet were immense, taxing the faith and comprehension of even the most ardent disciples.

This doctrine was based on the belief that between death and resurrection, the spirit lives on in a "spirit world" or paradise where those who never heard the gospel while on earth would somehow, sometime, be taught that message. By accepting the gospel, and with priesthood ordinances of baptism, confirmation, endowment, and marriage done by proxy in the temple, residents of the spirit world would enjoy an equal opportunity for salvation. Said Joseph Smith of such work for the dead,

> But how are they to become saviors on Mount Zion? By building their temples, erecting their baptismal fonts, and going forth and receiving all the ordinances, and sealing pow-

ers upon their heads, in behalf of all their progenitors who are
dead, and redeem them that they may come forth in the first
resurrection.[8]

According to Joseph Smith, this is what the biblical prophet
Elijah referred to when speaking of "turning the hearts of the
fathers to the children and the heart of the children to the fathers."[9] Temple work was the "welding link" between the present
and past, the living and dead, and the key to salvation for all of
mankind.[10] This was what the apostle Paul supposedly meant
when he said "that they without us cannot be made perfect."[11]

But the blessings flowed both ways, present to past and past to
present. While the current generation could perform temple
work to save the former, past generations had extended, through
lineal descent, certain promises and blessings to the present.
Christ's earthly claim to priesthood and royal authority, Mormons believed, came through his parents' ancestry directly back
to David, Abraham, and Adam. He was an heir to the promise by
lineal (blood) descent. Another example of priesthood by descent was the ancient Israelite tribe of Levi that had been entrusted with the Levitical priesthood from generation to genera-
tion. The claim of a royal priesthood was, therefore, often based
scripturally on lineage. By reconnecting into this ancient lineage, the legal rights to the priesthood were renewed, pending
divine ratification that Joseph claimed he had received.

Yet it was confusing how such blessings could have come
through "unbelieving" fathers and grandparents (many of whom
had scorned Mormonism) and beyond them through centuries
of apostasy. The solution lay in the now obscure doctrine that
Joseph Smith, Brigham Young, and Heber Kimball were somehow directly related, by blood, to the royal lineage of the ancient
patriarchal order, and that through marriage or "adoption" into
their families, the problems caused by the apostasy were circum-
vented.[12] Consequently not only were women sealed to their husbands, husbands and their families were sealed in the temple to
other men, that is, sealed as adopted sons to prominent church
authorities who claimed right to the priesthood and its blessings
and responsibilities.[13] It was, then, to these multiple aspects of
the doctrine of family exaltation that most alluded when speaking of temple work.

To those who believed in such things, this was a glorious work.
Yet both Smith and Young had stated unequivocally that these
sacred ordinances could be performed only in temples. While it

is true that baptisms for the dead and several sealings had been performed in Nauvoo before the temple was completed, once constructed it was the only rightful place for such functions.[14]

However, leaders were pestered by incessant inquiries requesting temple ordinances in the wilderness, with or without a temple. Young responded that they must remain in temporary suspension until a later time. With reference to sealings, he said, "there will be no such thing done until we build another temple. I have understood that some of the 12 have held fourth an idea that such things would be attended to in the wilderness but I say let no man hint such things from this time fourth for we will not attend to sealing till another is built."[15]

A month ater he informed George Miller, who himself was being quizzed about the matter at the Ponca settlement, that

> the use of the Lord's house is to attend to the ordinances of the Kingdom therein; and if it were lawful and right to administer these ordinances out of doors where would be the necessity of building a house? We would recommend to the brethren to let those things you refer to, dwell in the Temple, until another house is built in which they may be transferred or continued.[16]

Even as late as January 1847, Young, who as president of the Quorum of the Twelve Apostles was the official spokesman on such matters, reminded his followers that until the construction of another temple, "let such administrations, and covenants belonging thereunto, not be named among you."[17] No doubt, one powerful reason for centralizing such ordinances in one structure was to prohibit unauthorized performances and ordinations and consequent loss of control over what authorities viewed as sacred, unifying religious ceremonies.

But what Young said publicly and what he did privately was not always synchronized. For a variety of reasons, several sources pressured for exceptions. Many in camp began realizing that some of their neighbors and associates had received more instructions, more initiations, more wives, and more blessings than themselves. Reference has already been made to the more influential positions some women enjoyed who had previously received temple endowments and anointings. A similar differentiation and sense of exclusiveness existed among the men. Several had been unable to attend the Nauvoo Temple through no fault of their own. Perhaps fearful that Young and the Twelve might meet disaster on their journey west and never return, they were demanding equal consideration.

Many who were sick and diseased sought special exemption. One man, J. W. Fox, begged Young to marry for time and eternity his dying daughter-in-law, Caroline, to his son, David.[18] Fox's request was only one of several from families in similar conditions. Men in the Battalion, such as George P. Dykes, apprehensive of their immediate future, wrote imploring letters like the following:

> I am now an orphan wandering through a wicked world without a Father of promise. Shall my days be numbered and my pilgrimage ended and I go to the silent tomb without a Father to call me forth from the deep sleep of death? or shall I enjoy in common with other citizens of the commonwealth of Israel the legal rights to adoption . . . I who have spent the prime of life in defending the truth . . . in the sacred death, or on the Battlefield shall I be forgotten in the day of choosing.[19]

Finally scores of engaged couples were requesting celestial marriage with or without a temple. It was clear to them that their delay at the Bluffs and the uncertainty of future events would postpone indefinitely the erection of another temple in the West. Joseph Smith had made exceptions; why could not Brigham Young?

Because of such pressure, Young was forced to reconsider. He was hesitant to practice in private what he had been preaching against in public. Also, he was unwilling to undermine a primary argument for moving west, namely, the building of another temple. But aware of travel delays and the painful circumstances surrounding them, compassionate to the beliefs of his people, and anxious to continue what he fervently claimed Joseph Smith had taught, if for no other reason than to prove the validity of apostolic supremacy, Young sanctioned several exceptions to his own rule. He would learn by trial and error, implementing and retracting practices as new to him as any other. Experimentation and adaptation would dictate his cautious course.

On 24 January 1847 he performed a temple sealing for Elijah Sheets and his terminally ill wife, who died only eight days later. Four months afterwards Sheets remarried once again for time and eternity. Later that year, in Willard Richards's Octagon, Rhoda Lawrence was sealed to John Loveless "for eternity" and adopted into his family. Baptisms for the dead were a rarity at Winter Quarters; however, Wilford Woodruff, with permission, performed this ordinance in the Missouri River on at least one occasion.[20]

Willard Richards as a relatively young man. Richards was later second counselor to Brigham Young. Reproduced with permission from the Church Archives, The Church of Jesus Christ of Latter-day Saints.

Such ceremonies were always conducted privately. Sealings on demand were granted at Young's discretion usually in the home of the requesting party or in Willard Richards's office. Secrecy was almost always enjoined of the participants.

Besides marriages and baptisms for the dead, adoption ceremonies formerly reserved for the temple were conducted in the wilderness. On 13 July 1846, Hosea Stout heard for the first

Heber C. Kimball, first counselor to Brigham Young. Reproduced with permission from the Church Archives, The Church of Jesus Christ of Latter-day Saints.

time a public pronouncement on the Law of Adoption from Orson Hyde. Hyde, anxious to recoup lost time for having been away in Nauvoo, invited as many of the unattached as he could to become adopted sons in his family.[21] Other apostles and leaders practicing the Law of Adoption included Willard Richards, Heber Kimball, Amasa Lyman, Wilford Woodruff, John Taylor, John Smith, Samuel Bent, Albert P. Rockwood, and Newel K. Whitney. Young alone had forty-one adopted sons, most of whom were married family men.

The practice of the Law of Adoption impacted most dramatically upon the social order of the Winter Quarters community. It dictated social spheres of influence and often one's circle of friends and associates. It even determined, as at Cutler's Park, the locale of one's tent or wagon. One's place in the family hierarchy provided some kind of social stratification, certainly an exclusiveness that the majority of people, not belonging to any particular family order, never attained. Those in Young's family lived fairly close together, as did those in Kimball's and Woodruff's. There was the expectation that in return for spiritual blessings and eternal inheritances due their spiritual father, adopted families owed him physical support. This explains the operation of the three family farms: Summer Quarters and Heber Kimball's and Willard Richards's farms. Likely there were more. It also explains why Kimball's clan lived in one part of Winter Quarters, Young's in another, and Woodruff's in a third.

Occasionally large adopted-family meetings were convened for instructional purposes. At one such meeting of Young's "tribe" (Woodruff deliberately used the term), in which all of his adopted children sat by rank according to their position in the family, Young said,

> Those that are adopted into my family . . . I will preside over them throughout all eternity and will stand at their head. Joseph [Smith] will stand at the head of this Church and will be their president, prophet and God to the people in this dispensation. When we locate I will settle my family down in the order and teach them their duties. They will then have to provide temporal blessings for me instead of my boarding from 40 to 50 persons as I do now, and will administer spiritual blessings to them.[22]

John Taylor's adopted family, consisting of at least forty-two souls, met even while he was absent on his mission to England. At least eleven families were included in Taylor's adoption, most if not all of whom had been adopted in temple ceremonies in Nauvoo.[23] Several went so far as to change their names, at least in private, to reflect their adopted status. This explains the Albert P. Rockwood-Youngs, Thomas Bullock-Richards, and Newel K. Whitney-Kimballs.[24]

Theological considerations aside, Young apparently saw in the Law of Adoption a social force for unity. "This is the principle of oneness that this people will have to go into in order to help build one another up." If it eventually spawned individual discord, it originally, and perhaps naïvely, was proposed as a means of putting all on the same footing, all brothers and sisters of one mighty family in Israel. Disparate origins and nationalities, former creeds, traditions, and ethnic differences—all ideally would be cemented together in family links where men and women would be dependent upon one another for their physical and spiritual welfare. If the unsuccessful practice of the Law of Consecration and Stewardship (see Chapter 6) had attempted to dissolve their economic differences for the benefit of all, the Law of Adoption would blend differences of culture, training, and nationality.

However, practice of the law soon spawned serious jealousies as people scrambled to gain acceptance into one or another of the greater families. Some felt that unless they were related to one of the Twelve they would lose position and influence.[25] Church leaders tried to show that it made no difference which family they were in, but their efforts had little effect in stemming what some saw as class stratification and competition for position and influence—results that were the very opposite of the social unity that Young had envisioned. This may explain, in part, why Summer Quarters, Young's farm, witnessed such controversy among adopted family members.[26]

What may have been ideally regarded was unsuccessfully practiced. Even the leaders comprehended the whole concept poorly.[27] In mid-February 1847, Young declared he had dreamed a vision of Joseph Smith, of whom he asked, "the brethren have a great anxiety to understand the law of adoption or sealing principles, and if you have a word of counsel for me, I should be glad to receive it."[28] That same day during a large indoor feast with his adopted families, Young said of the Law of Adoption, "This principle . . . is not clearly understood by many of [the] Elders in this church at the present time as it will hereafter be, and I confess that I have had only a smattering of these things, but when it is necessary I will attain to more knowledge on the subject."[29]

Adoption may have been a good doctrine, "but it failed to work as a principle of social organization."[30] In time it was discarded in favor of establishing one's personal blood lineage, which in modern Mormonism is the motivating force for the church's genealogical emphasis. Nonetheless, while practiced at Winter Quarters, the influence of the Law of Adoption on the social environment was substantial. It may have been the result of overanxiousness on the part of Young to do what he felt Joseph Smith had done or to establish means to share the Saints' meager resources more equitably. Whatever the cause, the Law of Adoption seems now to have been poorly understood and inequitably applied.

If consent for some ordinance work was gingerly given, permission for plural marriages was even more carefully guarded. Young and his fellow leaders were certainly aware that this was a stumbling block among their critics and detractors and a potentially divisive issue among followers.[31] The plan was to wait until they reached safety in isolation before outlining the doctrine in full. But concealing it until that time would be impossible; hence, wisdom dictated a go-slow approach. This may have contributed to their decision to stay on Indian lands, away from Iowa and whatever laws the new state might pass on the matter.

Plural marriage was a new practice demanding strict control and regulation, not an easy task among eleven thousand people spread over thousands of square miles. The potential for abuse and experiment was enormous and the risk of negative reactions too great to minimize. It was like gathering seeds after blowing them all over a twenty-acre field. Young knew it was a practice that could "cut" and compared it to the edge tools of the garden in the hands of the untrained.

When Helen Whitney had been given in plural marriage to Joseph Smith in Nauvoo, her mother had admitted that "these things had to be kept an inviolate secret" because "some were false to their vows and pledges of secrecy."[32] But by the time the advance company was regrouping at Sugar Creek in February 1846, several, especially the women, felt freer to discuss the matter openly. Most of those in that first company were privy to these things anyway, and that company likely carried with it the bulk of Nauvoo's plural marriage households.

Eliza R. Snow, another widow of Joseph Smith and now a wife of Brigham Young, said that despite the cold "we felt as tho' we could breath more freely and speak one with another upon those things where in God had made us free with less carefulness than we had hitherto done."[33] Referring to the same, more open climate, Zina D. Young, another of Brigham's wives, said of the Sugar Creek encampment,

> we there first saw who were the brave, the good, the self-sacrificing. Here we had now openly the first examples of noble-minded, virtuous women, bravely commencing to live in the newly-revealed order of celestial marriage. "Woman; this

is my husband's wife!" Here, at length, we could give this introduction without fear of reproach, or violation of man-made laws.[34]

At Winter Quarters the performance of celestial marriage vows and the practice of plural marriage were at first confined to the various large adopted families. Of such marriages that Young sanctioned, most were for his adopted sons, such as John D. Lee. As early as 21 December 1846, Lee received a plural wife.[35]

Public lectures and sermons on the subject were practically nonexistent. Rather, it was discussed in private, and usually behind closed family doors. For instance, on 9 February 1847 during a family meeting Heber Kimball, before leaving for the west, gathered five of his wives who had recently borne him children to give them blessings and promises.[36]

At a meeting of Young's adopted family a week later, Young and Wilford Woodruff used the occasion to expound upon the topic, giving much needed instruction. "The man is head and God of the woman," said Woodruff, "but let him act like a God in virtuous principles and God-like conversation, walk and deport-ment . . . if not found worthy they shall be hurled down to per-dition and their family and kingdom be given to another."[37]

After two years at the Bluffs, the practice of plural marriage had gone beyond specific families and become more widespread. By the spring of 1848, William Snow, a counselor in the Pot-tawattamie High Council, indicated that "it [plural marriage] had become a common thing."[38] Winter Quarters was a wilder-ness laboratory, a proving ground where leaders could evaluate the practice. Some swore by it, others swore at it, and there were enough abuses of it to make even the stouthearted wonder.

As with the Law of Adoption, the practice of plural marriage aroused several jealousies. A seemingly select few received a dis-proportionate number of companions. In a sermon designed to defuse the issue, Young also provided further justification of the practice.

> Some young Elders who never preached a sermon in their lives were afraid that he should have more blessings than they, or more wives, or something or tother. He inquired if it was any man's business how many wives the Lord gives him. Let those who are jealous go and spend as much time in the vine-yard as he had, and many women would cling to their skirts to be saved.[39]

Plural wives, then, were sometimes seen as a reward for the devoted and tested disciples.

Jealousy was certainly not only a problem among the men. Patty Sessions, aged fifty-two, had a difficult time reconciling herself to the fact that her husband had recently married Rosella, a much younger woman. "He has lain with her three nights," she confided in her diary. "She has told him many falsehoods and is trying to have him take her to Nauvoo and then to Maine and leave me for good."[40] Things worked out for Patty when Rosella soon left and returned east; however, many other marriages did not last.[41]

More discord was a logical sequitur to more plural marriages. Evidence does not exist to show that the practice was any more of a domestic success or failure than the standard monogamous situation, although the following ditty by a wife of Heber Kimball may have indicated the attitude even among leading women.

> The Lord has blessed us with another son
> Which is the seventh I have Bord
> May he be the father of many lives
> But not the Husband of many Wives.[42]

The most critical problem authorities faced was controlling the practice. Some who thought themselves authorized were acting without permission. Others abused priesthood authority by trying to take unfair advantage of a situation. No plural marriages could be performed without the permission of Young or his designee. As early as July 1846, while yet at Cold Springs, the Quorum of the Twelve "decided that no man had a right to attend to the ordinance of sealing except the president of the Church or those who are directed by him so to do."[43] As senior president of the Quorum, Young, in tandem with his fellow apostles, held the authority to administer temple blessings, including plural marriages. On rare occasions he authorized others to function in his behalf.[44] Plural marriage without such explicit permission was adultery. Community wife swapping or rotating love partners was not permissible. And presuming authorization to take another wife to satisfy one's own desires was against the rules. Such was taking unfair advantage of the practice.

A man was not at liberty to marry anyone he chose. Several factors usually had to be considered. His first marriage should be intact, and the man had to be a faithful follower and a loyal supporter of the church. Young, characteristically, was also concerned with economic needs and disparities, that poorer women, widows, and the destitute be given to someone who might provide them with a better lot than before. In practice, however, it seems the first wife had the major claim on her husband for support, and usually her permission was required for plural marriages.[45] In one case Young permitted one man to marry a young woman only if he married her widowed mother as well.

On several occasions Young roundly condemned men for "killing an innocent ignorant female," telling her she could not be saved without a man and

> that there is no harm for them to sleep together before they are sealed, then go to some clod head of an elder and get him to say their ceremony, all done without the knowledge or counsel of the authority of this church. This is not right and will not be suffered.[46]

William W. Phelps, an advisor to the Twelve and one of Young's closest friends, was himself guilty of breaking the ground rules. While returning from a mission to England, Phelps stopped off at Niagara County, New York. While there, either of his own doing or by the persuasion of two sisters anxious to migrate with the church, he instructed a local elder to perform a plural marriage if for no other reason than that he would have to spend weeks travelling in close company with the two young women. The case eventually came before the Twelve and the Council of Seventy, where Young exploded.

> It is impossible for any man to serve the second woman unless given to him by the woman [his first wife] who has the keys of the sealing powers. Then he has the privilege of taking a woman if there's nothing in the way. You are operating in the gentile world to get more wives; no, it is by the celestial law you get wives.
>
> It makes me feel [bad] when I see men in slippery places. No man is fit to hold a license who will do such things. It is like handling edge tools. A man is in danger of bleeding and I tremble and fear . . . [I] don't fear the Gentiles now, it is nothing to what I fear the Elders.[47]

Young worried that "by the strict letter of the law this people will be cut off for whoredom, a good many of them if they don't back out."[48] Phelps was excommunicated on the spot but immediately afterwards reinstated with the restoration of all his church and priesthood blessings. A legal plural marriage was then scheduled.

The abuse of sanctioning authority continued, reaching a new high in February 1848 when Henry Davis, a local leader at Mt. Pisgah, told his listeners that "it was the privilege of every Elder, Seventy, etc. to have as many wives as he could get and that he had the right to marry them."[49] Twenty months later and two hundred miles further east in Iowa City, Sidney Roberts was disfellowshipped for the unauthorized performance of "the spiritual wife doctrine and in such a way as to amount to adultery."[50] These were chilling illustrations of the Saints' greatest concerns, namely, that in their desire to practice celestial marriage, reckless enthusiasm and usurpation of authority could very easily get ahead of church leaders, who, lacking effective means of communication and speedy transportation, were often unable to exercise adequate control.

With the breakup of Winter Quarters in the spring of 1848, Young did not want any man to return to live in Iowa "who shall have more than one wife with him."[51] He also advised the two or three families "who were in the patriarchal order of marriage" at St. Louis to keep a low profile and emigrate as soon as possible.[52] Better to keep that practice to themselves, where it was causing enough of a problem, than to bring on further unnecessary external difficulties.

"I AM GOING TO GO IT, THE LORD BEING MY HELPER": THE REESTABLISHMENT OF THE FIRST PRESIDENCY

At a special conference on the afternoon of 27 December 1847, Orson Pratt introduced the matter of business everyone had crowded in to hear—the reorganization of the church and the reestablishment of the First Presidency. On a motion by William W. Major, the name of Brigham Young was presented as "first President of the Church," with Heber C. Kimball and Willard Richards as his first and second counselors. A "clear vote" by the congregation was registered for each.[1] Thus, after a period of three and one-half years, the Church of Jesus Christ of Latter-day Saints was once again organized as it had been before 27 June 1844.

During this 1,283-day interregnum, the Quorum of the Twelve Apostles, with Young as president and spokesman, had managed a bewildering array of tasks including the completion and dedication of the Nauvoo Temple, the pronouncement of endowments and anointings to a large number of believers, the exodus from Nauvoo, the call of the Mormon Battalion, the establishment of Winter Quarters, and the founding of a new headquarters in the Great Basin. Now they would make one final contribution—the reestablishment of the First Presidency.

Though destined forever to remain a point of debate, recent scholarship indicates that Joseph Smith had given the Twelve a charge to "bear off the kingdom" at least in the short run.[2] Orson Hyde, writing within three months of Smith's death, had said

> We have had a charge given us by our Prophet, and that charge we intend to honor and magnify. It was given in March last. . . . To us were committed the Keys of the Kingdom, and every gift, key and power that Joseph ever had confirmed upon our head. . . . We know the charge which the prophet gave us.[3]

Samuel W. Richards, in a letter to Franklin D. Richards, described Hyde's comments in greater detail.

He said that Joseph was preparing them for the work that
they have now got to do which is to hold the keys and build up
this kingdom in all the world. Joseph committed unto them all
the keys of the Priesthood otherwise the fulness would not have
been upon the Earth now [that] he is taken away.[4]

Wilford Woodruff, before leaving on his mission to England in
the summer of 1844, also indicated that Smith "had ordained,
anointed and appointed the Twelve to lead the Church" and that
upon "your shoulders the Kingdom of God must rest in all the
world."[5]

Nonetheless, evidence indicates that Joseph desired his son,
Joseph Smith III, to remain sufficiently loyal and faithful to his
teachings to assume eventual leadership in the church. On 17
January 1844, Joseph Smith blessed his son, then only eleven
years old, to be one of his eventual successors, "an appointment
[which] belongeth to him by blessing, and also by right."[6] Most
of the Twelve, carrying on in the absence of their former leader,
understood their apostolic charge while remembering young
Joseph's blessing. In the days to come they would debate over the
question of church leadership, for Smith had given them interim directing authority without appointing a successor. The
temporary mandate given the Twelve was one thing; reestablishing the First Presidency on a permanent basis quite another. If
the apostles understood that they had the right to direct the
church, at least temporarily, they did not immediately compre-
hend (or at least agree among themselves) that they held the authority to appoint another "first president." It was a matter more
easily, more expediently postponed than resolved, at least in the
turbulent years of 1844–47.

In the meantime, Young was acting head by right of his position as president of the Quorum. If in that tormented summer
of 1844 a leadership vacuum had developed, by late 1847, at
least in the minds of thousands at the Missiouri, that void had
been impressively filled. Young had steadily emerged as the
dominant, incontestible guiding force in the church. If Joseph
Smith had obtained his appointment by celestial mandate, Young
was proving his in the crucible of trial and failure, mud and
mountain, sickness and sixth sense, boldness and self-confidence
bordering on arrogance, tempered with compassion. The question was not who should lead, but in what capacity and in what
presiding quorum.

During these three years the Quorum of the Twelve solidified its supremacy over ecclesiastical affairs. In an October 1846 conference in England, Orson Hyde motioned "that the Twelve be acknowledged in their standing, according to the appointment of Joseph, our martyred prophet, as the 'counsellor' of the Church and 'director of all her affairs.'"[7] As noted earlier, it was the Twelve that appointed the two high councils on either side of the Missouri River, the Twelve that dispatched exploration and relief parties, and the Twelve that directed mission work to England and the east coast. And it was the plan of the Twelve Apostles that gained supremacy over the Council of Fifty plan for the final trek west. Their temporary leadership, as even George Miller admitted, "was pretty generally conceded to them, as they were the quorum next in authority and presidency of the whole Church."[8]

Young, speaking later of the role of the Twelve, said,

> Joseph told the Twelve the year before he died there is not one key or power to be bestowed on this Church to lead the people into the celestial gate, but I have given you, shewed you, and talked it over to you the kingdom is set up and you have the perfect pattern, and you can go and build up the Kingdom, and go in at the celestial gate taking your train with you.[9]

As the stock of the Quorum of the Twelve rose, so did Young's. As Quorum president since 1841, he was its mouthpiece, a leader among equals, and their presiding authority. On one occasion in December 1846 he asked the Quorum their opinion of him "when all present expressed the best of feelings and their approval of his course."[10] Hosea Stout that same month referred to him as a prophet and leader to this people.[11] Indeed Young was effectively the acting president of the church by right of his Quorum presidency in the absence of a First Presidency.

He was also popularly regarded as the sole authority to adjudicate temple sealings, the one man who held the keys or ultimate authority in the priesthood. Shortly after arriving on the west bank of the Missouri River, the Twelve held a very private meeting in which it was determined "that no man has a right to attend to the ordinance of sealing except the president of the Church or those who are directed by him to do so."[12] It was to Young that all requests for sealings, adoptions, and other temple ordinances had been directed, for as he said "if the lot is in me, I have the keys."[13] And it was to Young that most important administrative decisions were referred and appeals from lower bishop and high council courts presented.[14]

During this time Young increased in self-confidence and bold-ness. At one point in Iowa, Heber Kimball and Willard Richards had publicly contended with him over the timetable for mov-ing west (Chapter 2), but afterwards, although they may have had differences, they raised them in quiet, quorum privacy. As Young tightened control, he manifested growing confidence in his abilities and decisions, which some interpreted as arrogance and which alienated others.[15]

Objections and criticisms notwithstanding, Young was de facto leader over every aspect of Mormon life. Little wonder, then, that at the succession conference in December 1847, Orson Pratt said, "If I were to go to every man and woman to ask who is the man, they all know the man." Echoed Amasa Lyman, "He is at the head already."[16]

But if popular sentiment supported Young's leadership, sev-eral were apprehensive about forming a First Presidency. While some of their misgivings were well defined and clearly articu-lated, others were more subtle and unexpressed. Some posed constitutional arguments, some doctrinal, and others personal. While no concerted opposition ever developed, an uneasy hesi-tancy permeated Quorum deliberations.

The timing was questioned. Should Young now assume the presidency if Joseph Smith had truly desired one of his sons, Joseph or David, to inherit the post? Some supposed "that by ap-pointing a presidency it is robing [sic] some of the rising genera-tion or taking someone's rights."[17] Others wrote letters urging an indefinite postponement so as not to preempt the appointment of one of Joseph's posterity.[18] A disciple of George Miller later defended Miller's apostasy, claiming that he represented one of many who believed that "young Joseph Smith was appointed by his father to succeed him" and would not accept Young's over-tures toward the First Presidency.[19]

Others wondered why the Twelve would want to change an effective system. If they had performed so well running affairs, why change it? "If three are taken out to become a first presi-dency," complained Wilford Woodruff, "it seemed like severing a body in two. . . . I desire that it should continue on as it was."[20] Young himself had often sermonized on the enduring benefits of unity in priesthood quorums, wards, and branches, epitomized in the goodwill, love, and esteem fellow apostles held one for an-other. George A. Smith, another apostle, said, "I want to stick together as we have done. . . . We are good fellows and better in harmony. If three are picked out there may be jealousies." He concluded, "If it's the will of the Lord that their course should be taken I will twist myself to it but it's not my will."[21]

Several Quorum members seemed chary of providing Young a raised platform from which he could publicly chastise his fellows. Many had already felt Young's oral whiplashes and feared that unconstrained, he would speak his mind outside of the Quorum. Said Amasa Lyman, "It murders me to the bottom of my soul to have my name handled before the members of the Church. I have no fears about what may be said by this Quorum concerning me . . . if I do wrong I would like to be told of my faults in the presence of my friends." George A. Smith added, "If there is any chastening, let it be in the Quorum, and let me have it. . . . I should like the President to respect the feelings of his Quorum."[22]

Orson Pratt, alone among all the apostles, opposed the reestablishment with constitutional arguments. "There is no authority higher in decision than 7 of the 12," he declared, believing that a simple majority of the Twelve was "the President" or supreme power in the Church.

> I do consider the head of this Church lays in the apostleship united together. Paul says, "apostles are set in the Church," not one individual. . . . The Doctrine and Covenants points out that the First Presidency *with* the Twelve shall do so and so and there is where I consider the highest power lies in the hands of the apostles.[23]

Comparing government by the Twelve to that in Washington, Pratt argued that the Speaker of the House was but a president among equals and that "The majority of the House of Representatives decide and not the speaker."[24]

The corollary to Pratt's constitutional argument was his doubt that the Twelve held the authority to appoint three of their number to a position higher than they individually or collectively held.

> Have the other nine the right to do that, to give such power to the three? Have we a right to make the decision of three of the Twelve [i.e., a New First Presidency] higher than the Quorum of the Twelve or seven when the Book of Covenants say we have the Twelve? If they have that power there is something in the dark yet. The three men need an ordination to be appointed presidents. Who will ordain them?[25]

In other words, Pratt wondered whether the creation could be greater than the creator.

Orson Pratt, scientist, pioneer leader, and apostle. Reproduced with permission from the Church Archives, The Church of Jesus Christ of Latter-day Saints.

Echoing Pratt's concern was Wilford Woodruff's belief that a revelation would be required to reorganize the First Presidency. A quorum "like the Twelve who had been appoint[ed] by revelation, confirmed by revelation from time to time . . . would require a revelation to change the order of that quorum." [26]

Finally, despite all their accomplishments and with all respect to Brigham Young, could there really be another Joseph? Could a second First Presidency ever equal the first? The memory of Joseph Smith was still fresh and powerful, and his spiritual legacy, so firmly fostered by the Saints, loomed ever so large. Joseph Smith they eulogized as "the Prophet and Seer of the Lord, [having] done more save Jesus only for the salvation of men in this world, than any other man that ever lived in it." He claimed an almost deified image among the Saints. "He lived great, and he died great in the eyes of God and his people," declared apostle John Taylor.[27] Could anyone ever take his place?

These, then, were some of the outstanding questions and concerns in the minds of various members whether in or out of the Quorum of the Twelve. Joseph Smith may have given them a mandate for leadership, and Brigham Young may have been popularly accepted as spiritual and temporal leader, but it simply was not obvious to most that the Twelve had the power or felt the need to appoint a First Presidency.[28]

When did Young become concerned with the reestablishment? Speaking only four months after his elevation to the First Presidency, he indicated that it was "our right and privilege and was at the first conference after Joseph's death to reorganize the Church, but we were not obliged to do it. It was wisdom not to then." [29] Nor was it while crossing Iowa and establishing Winter Quarters, as there were then more pressing concerns. The first intimation may have come during the Quorum of the Twelve and Council of Fifty deliberations in the winter of 1846–47, for George Miller later intimated that he first heard of the proposal to reorganize in January 1847.[30]

In the ensuing months, Young discussed it on an individual basis, seldom if ever with a full council of even his closest advisors. Orson Pratt inferred that Young first expressed his views "on the other side of the mountains [Salt Lake Valley]," [31] and if not before, he certainly broached the topic while returning from the valley in the fall of 1847.[32]

The decision to reorganize may have been affected by concern over the real and perceived apostasies occurring at Winter Quar-

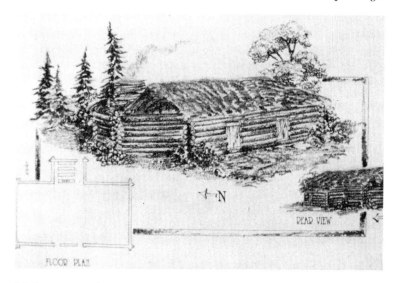

Unknown artist's conception of the Kanesville (later Council Bluffs) Log Tabernacle. Courtesy Winter Quarters Visitor Center, Omaha, Nebraska, The Church of Jesus Christ of Latter-day Saints.

ters. Reference has already been made to the fact that so many were leaving that Parley Pratt and John Taylor closed down the ferry and took other deflecting measures. If he had not suspected it earlier, Young heard of these defections firsthand from Pratt and Taylor during their prairie meeting at the Sweetwater River in early September.[33] James J. Strang, for all the scorn and derision some Mormons were heaping on him, was enjoying a measure of success. As the head of his own First Presidency, he became a rallying figure for those converted to Mormonism but disenchanted with Young.

Furthermore, there were legal considerations. Some of the property yet unsold in Nauvoo and Kirtland, including the temples, had been assigned to Joseph Smith's successors "in the First Presidency" or as his successor "as trustee for the Church."[34] Emma Smith, Joseph's widow, bitterly opposed Young, refused to go west, remarried, kept her sons with her, and laid claim to as much property in Nauvoo as she possibly could.[35] The heart of her complaint seems to have been her opposition to plural marriage, although other attendant factors—personal, financial, or otherwise—played their parts. Like a cat clutching at a carpet, Emma was fighting back, and Young would require all the ecclesiastical authority he could get.

Though he was alone in demanding a solution to the matter, Young injected a sense of urgency into November's discussions. Several times he overrode his colleagues who wanted to discuss other matters. Even church court cases turned into deliberations on succession. He was the spark, the catalyst, and driving force and, like a bull dog, persisted through until the resolution. As he said on one occasion, "I am going to go it, the Lord being my helper."[36] But before he could, he would have to confront and resolve each of the many questions and objections presented above.

To the issue of whether he was "robbing" the Smith sons of their supposed right to leadership, he said very little. The passage of time had persuaded many that neither Emma nor her sons would ever join them in the wilderness. Young may have hoped that Joseph Smith III or David would come west, as some have argued, but by late 1847 he was acting under no delusions.[37] Several attempts had been made both before and after the reorganization to bring the Smith family west but to no avail.[38]

Even after December 1847 repeated efforts were made to coax the family west, especially Joseph Smith III, for Young's presidency need not have prevented one of the sons from eventually taking a place in the Quorum of the Twelve and possibly becoming president of the church.[39] George A. Smith, a cousin of Joseph Smith III and one of the best peacemakers in the church, wrote the following to young Joseph:

> One great work accomplished by your father was the building up of the Church of Jesus Christ of Latter-day Saints. About 5000 of that body are already congregated in the mountains, who would be much pleased to see you in their midst. Consult your mother on this subject, and do as wisdom shall direct. But if you shall conclude to make the journey, I should be much pleased to enjoy your company.[40]

Emma and her sons never accepted the offer. Eleven years later, Joseph Smith III became founding President of the Reorganized Church of Jesus Christ of Latter Day Saints. Having tried unsuccessfully, yet keeping the door open to a later possible change of heart on their part, Young argued that he had done all he reasonably could.

On the matter of administration, church government had to be made more efficient. The need to employ the apostles in distant places to supervise missionary work, deflect Strang and other contenders, and manage emigration matters weighed far more heavily on Young's mind than retaining the Quorum around him. He loved his colleagues, he once declared, "as I love my eyes," but the role of the apostle as decreed in scripture was to be a "special witness" to all the world.[41] Not administration but testimony was their special responsibility. "Now is the time to take another stride," he said. "Here's the nations of the earth to be gathered. Cut your heart and things and let them expand." The apostles "ought to be in England and in Germany and in France and in Canada, every man ought to be distributed all over the world."[42] Fresh on his mind was the progress Parley Pratt, John Taylor, and Orson Hyde had recently achieved in reordering the affairs of the church in Great Britain. Nor could any of them forget their successes in 1841 when the apostles had baptized hundreds there. They belonged abroad, not at home.[43]

The logistical difficulties of apostolic presidency, furthermore, were becoming increasingly apparent. While the church had been travelling as a unit, problems were immediate and addressable. But now that part of the church was over the mountains, some of the Quorum would have to reside there while others would be needed at the Bluffs over the next several years. Others would be dispatched on missions elsewhere. How could such a disseminated Quorum preside effectively? How could even a majority be available when required? The problems already encountered between Young and John Taylor and Parley Pratt regarding their supervision at Winter Quarters were sufficient evidence that as united as they were, differences of style, philosophy, and priority very much existed and might eventually cause serious rupture. In sum, government by the Quorum was cumbersome, inefficient, and susceptible to disruption. It was possible but not preferable. Young compared it to fighting with one hand tied behind his back.

Reestablishing the First Presidency would not only reorient the Quorum of the Twelve but also provide stability and direction for the other leading quorums and councils. The First Council of the Seventy, the third most powerful quorum in the priesthood hierarchy, was to assist the Twelve in missionary work.[44] Until the Twelve functioned in that capacity, the role of the presiding Seventy was confused. "When a First Presidency [is] appointed," argued Young, "it sets the Seventy at liberty to go and do their business":

> Of necessity we must have a quorum to stay at home. Of necessity we must have a quorum to preach to the nations of the earth, ordain patriarchs, bishops. Of necessity we must have Seventy to assist. It is of necessity we have helps, governments in the Church because one quorum cannot tend everywhere.[45]

A First Presidency, concerned with both spiritual and temporal affairs, would also prevent the Council of Fifty from ever assuming temporal leadership. "If you throw the kingdom into the Quorum of Fifty they can't manage it," said Young.[46] That group of men was a "debating body" at best, George A. Smith added, an advisory group regardless of all former commissions and expectations.[47] Three of its fifty members were not even supposed to be Latter-day Saints. In Young's mind at least, government by the Council of Fifty was unthinkable,[48] and certainly the local high councils could never assume leadership over all the church, despite a few scattered arguments otherwise.[49] In short, Young argued the reestablishment of the First Presidency, like a keystone in the arch "when fitly framed together," gave order and stability to the entirety of church government.

To the widespread concern that he might overstep his bounds and publicly chastise his former colleagues, Young was unbending. As president of the Quorum for six years he already had the right and responsibility to correct them. What difference would it make if he were "lifted up a peg"? A stout defender of open communication and of his rights as president to reprove his junior officers, Young "would not be trammelled."[50] Unflinchingly, he argued

> I would rather have been shot in Carthage Jail than be under the necessity of owing to run to my brethren before I can speak before the public. Must men be eternally grumbling because my stick is the longest. . . . If my lot [as senior president of the Twelve] is to preside over the Church must I eternally be asking when should I speak? If this body is the head of the Church, I am the head of the Quorum and I am the mouthpiece and you are the belly.[51]

Having witnessed the excommunication and reinstatement of both Orson Pratt and Orson Hyde (who were posing the immediate objections), and having seen the fall of several other apostles since 1835, Young was not about to commit to silent passivity. Whoever is at the head "must be a lion."

To counter Orson Pratt's more serious contention that seven—a majority of the Twelve—were the supreme authority in the church, Young replied that that may have been possible in the absence of a First Presidency, but for logistical reasons already identified was impractical. Willard Richards countered Pratt's comparison to a republican form of government by asserting that the church was not a democracy, but a "theo-democracy, the power of God untrammeled." It was not run by popular vote but by divine mandate. As Joseph had received revelations binding on the church, he reasoned, should his true successor function with any less freedom? "There is not a set of men on earth who can say that a revelation from the Lord is wrong."[52]

Young and Richards may have detected Pratt's real uncertainty and bottom-line reservations. Did the Twelve have the right to appoint a First President? To answer this, Young relied on precedent, arguing that Joseph Smith and Oliver Cowdery had received the keys of the apostleship by revelation from the ancient apostles[53] and, in turn, had ordained each other as apostles. As the presiding apostle, Joseph Smith then had the right to assume the presidency. Though the church membership elected or sustained Joseph Smith as a prophet, seer, and revelator, Young argued "he never was ordained to that office." His apostolic ordination presupposed his claim to the First Presidency. "If there is an apostle in the Church all the keys are totally rested in him." Just as Joseph Smith had obtained the First Presidency by right of senior apostleship, so could and should it happen again. With Oliver Cowdery "gone by the board" (excommunicated in 1838) and Joseph Smith "gone to the grave," the rightful solution was once again apostolic succession.[54]

Finally, to Woodruff and Pratt's demand that such a change must come by revelation as unmistakable as Joseph Smith's, the answer may have come by degree. Heber Kimball, perhaps Young's closest supporter and confidant, told his fellow apostles that "since the organization of this Quorum Joseph organized in prison since then there has been a revelation from the Lord appointing Brother Brigham as President."[55] But Kimball's plea did not convince everyone, certainly not Orson Pratt. Young knew that in Pratt's eyes "Joseph is still the first President of the Church."[56]

A careful review of Young's public pronouncements throughout the history of Winter Quarters reveals an unmistakable pattern, an almost conscious effort at forging links between himself and Joseph. His well-known dream of 17 February 1846 was, significantly, about Joseph and further established Young as his spokesman.[57] "I want you all to remember my dream," he told the Twelve and his adopted family a few days later, "for it is a vision of God and was revealed through the Spirit of Joseph."[58] On another occasion he claimed that he and Joseph were spiritual brothers and were both heirs to the priesthood by blood from the ancient patriarchs.[59]

Perhaps the most obvious connecting line drawn between the two was "the Word and Will of the Lord" of the preceding January, which had been accepted as revelation by the various quorums, councils, and members at large. Besides establishing apostolic supremacy and giving instructions for the move west, it ended with this very important linkage.

> [Be] faithful in keeping all my words that I have given you, from the days of Adam to Abraham, from Abraham to Moses, from Moses to Jesus and his apostles, and from Jesus and his apostles to Joseph Smith, whom I did call upon by mine angels . . . and by mine own voice out of the heavens, to bring forth my work.
> Which foundation he did lay, and was faithful; and I took him to myself.
> Many have marveled because of his death; but it was needful that he should seal his testimony with his blood. . . .
> Now, therefore, hearken, O ye people of my church; and ye elders listen together, you have received my kingdom.[60]

In other words, despite Joseph Smith's death, the church was still divinely recognized and the powers still operative within the Twelve and its leader. Though no mention was made of names other than Joseph's, the connection was not missed. Three days later Young had said to a body of the priesthood "that the Church had been led by Revelation just as much since the death of Joseph Smith as before."[61] It was a theme he never relinquished in public or in private. Some may have interpreted it as aspiration, but the majority apparently viewed it with comfort and reassurance.

Only after reassuring Pratt that indeed he had received visions and revelations "as plain as he ever told Joseph and when it comes to you, you will see just as plain," was the matter finally settled. On 5 December 1847 at Orson Hyde's home near Miller's Hollow, the nine apostles assembled there sustained Brigham Young as president with Heber C. Kimball first counselor and Willard Richards second counselor.[62]

After the Twelve had approved the reestablishment of the First Presidency, it remained only to place the matter before a meeting of the general membership. Contrary to some insinuations that the succession conference was called at a time and place where few could attend, interest was so high that new and larger accommodations were required.[63] A conference began on 4 December 1847 at Miller's Hollow, but the meetinghouse was "so crowded," Wilford Woodruff complained "we could not do business." Subsequently, Young adjourned the meetings and appointed Henry W. Miller to superintend the construction, "under the direction of the Twelve," of a much larger, more commodious meetinghouse, to be completed as soon as possible.[64]

Miller immediately went to work and called upon the services of "about 200" men to assist in construction. Nelson Whipple recalled that he made the sash for the window and that nearly everyone in Miller's Hollow and surrounding areas "were cald on to do something towards it."[65] Within three weeks of hard winter labor, it was completed. Built with logs cut three miles away and carted to the site, the Kanesville Log Tabernacle, as it came to be called, was impressively large—60 feet west to east and 40 feet north to south. The walls were eight logs high and the log roof was covered with willow, straw, and dirt. A large fireplace angled outward at the west end, and two stoves were placed in the building. Also on the west end was a recess about eight by fourteen feet for the pulpit and clerk's bench. Behind the pulpit were two windows with eight lights (panes?) each. Two similar-sized windows were located on the north wall and one on the south "between the two large doors for entrance." The tabernacle was "capable of containing 1000 seated," with Norton Jacob describing it as "the biggest log cabin in the world."[66] It stood near Indian Creek four miles from Council Point.[67]

The "Jubilee" conference reconvened on Christmas Eve day in a tabernacle that was "so very new," said Thomas Bullock, that "it felt cold and somewhat unpleasant."[68] During the following four days dancing and numerous addresses and messages from high church leaders punctuated the festive spirit of the season. But their messages seemed increasingly lost in the growing suspense that a new First President was about to be appointed.

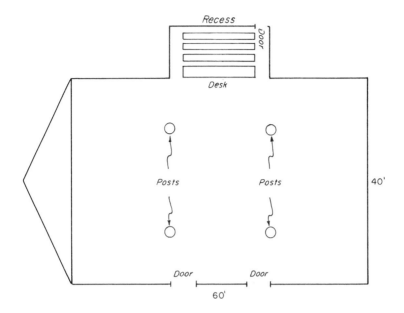

The plan of the Kanesville Log Tabernacle. Source: Journal History of the Church, 31 December 1846.

The following Monday, 27 December, broke clear and cold. Well before ten o'clock over a thousand men and women crowded into the Log Tabernacle to participate in one of the principal days in the history of the church. The marshal kept calling for people to clear the aisles, crowd the benches, free the seats at the front on the raised platform for the High Council and the Twelve, and not to crowd the fireplaces and stoves. Many kept their coats on, and several spread buffalo robes down the rows and across their laps to keep warm.

In the early afternoon after singing, "Come, Come Ye Saints" with accompaniment provided by the Winter Quarters band, Orson Pratt raised two issues of special concern. The first related to the pressing demands on the Winter Quarters mill and the need for fair use and consideration in applying for time; the second was "in relation to the full organization of the Church."

"The time has come" he said, to reestablish the First Presidency "in order to defeat the adversary." "We have been able to overcome apostates and the powers of darkness with the highest quorum taken away out of our midst. How much more shall we be able to overcome them when we have all the quorums flourishing." After three or four other speakers, the motion was made, the second tendered, and Brigham Young sustained without a dissenting vote as "the first President of the Church of Jesus Christ of Latter-day Saints." His two counselors were likewise approved and John Smith, uncle of Joseph, was lastly sustained "as patriarch to the whole Church."

In Young's acceptance remarks he claimed the presence of "the Spirit of the Lord" and said:

> this is one of the happiest days of my life. There is nothing more done this day than I knew at the death of Joseph. . . . Joseph told the Twelve there is not one principle or key to enter in the celestial Kingdom but I have given you. . . . The Kingdom is set up and you have the perfect pattern and you can lead the Kingdom in at the gate. I am going to rest.[69]

The history of the Mormons at Winter Quarters will be remembered for many things, for it was there on the banks of the Missouri that many suffered and died, proved their discipleship, or opted for a new life elsewhere. At Winter Quarters, the trek west was finalized, new doctrines made public and practiced, and a unique life-style developed. Yet it is entirely possible that the single, most important development at the Missouri was the emergence of the principle of apostolic supremacy and its logical consequence, apostolic succession. What happened in relative obscurity at the Kanesville Log Tabernacle in 1847 established a precedent that continues to dictate Latter-day Saint ecclesiastical government to this day.

At the conclusion of the conference the audience broke out in the sacred hymn used sparingly on occasions such as temple dedications: "Hosanna, Hosanna, Hosanna, to God and the Lamb, Amen, Amen, and Amen." Said George A. Smith, "Now the thing is right."

"LET YOUR HEARTS BE TOWARDS
THE SETTING SUN"

Kanesville, Iowa, so named on 8 April 1848 by Orson Hyde in honor of Thomas Kane, and forerunner of present-day Council Bluffs, Iowa, was never meant to be a permanent colony.[1] It was not church headquarters, but rather a springboard for emigration, a temporary gathering center for the Great Basin trek. Since the church was determined to pull up stakes from the Bluffs region, whatever success individual Mormons had in permanently establishing themselves in western Iowa proved counterproductive and embarrassing. Abandonment, not establishment, was the watchword.

Figuring in the decision to vacate Winter Quarters was the expectation that it would "accelerate the departure of the saints generally."[2] In reality, however, the Kanesville that grew out of Miller's Hollow on Indian and Mosquito creeks continued longer than anticipated, involving itself in Iowa politics, coping with large numbers of British Mormon immigrants, accommodating onrushing waves of California-bound gold seekers, and witnessing continued threats to church unity.

Kanesville was designed to be a fitting-out place, a layover town where those too poor, tired, discouraged, or unprepared could delay their journey, plant and sow crops, procure teams and outfits, and make other necessary preparations. And as these left for the mountains, new arrivals from the East or from overseas would take their place and repeat the preparation cycle. The whole scheme was printed and disseminated to all the branches of the church in December 1847 in the "General Epistle to the Saints Throughout the World."[3]

Realizing that much of the church's strength lay overseas, Young had sent out a gathering directive to the British Saints even before the General Epistle. "Say to the saints, Come," Young ordered Orson Spencer, then president of the church in Britain, "for all things are ready and let them flock in clouds to

New Orleans, where they will meet some one of the Elders, duly authorized to council them in reshipping to this vicinity."[4] The plan was to transport the British immigrants from New Orleans up the Mississippi to St. Louis and from there via the Missouri River to Kanesville.[5] Special care was to be taken to prevent new arrivals from falling into the hands of the Strangites.

Costs were to be minimized. Those with means were expected to give of their surplus for the less fortunate. Those who did not, Young warned, "are not worthy to be called saints, and the sooner they drop the name the greater will be the credit to the Church."[6] A direct voyage to New Orleans would nullify the need for expensive overland transportation. By carrying English converts on the same steamboats with church orders for St. Louis goods, costs could be minimized.[7] In 1849 leaders established a revolving fund out of donations of cash and property by those settlers already in the Salt Lake Valley for those anxious but too poor to come on. By chartering entire ships, handling all transportation costs and ticket sales, this church-run travel agency, called the Perpetual Emigration Fund, proved a boon to emigration, particularly in the 1850s.[8]

After a three-year delay, British Mormon emigration renewed in February 1848 when 120 set sail for American from Liverpool, with another 80 in March and 20 more in April. Marking the first direct arrival by ship of British Saints at the Bluffs, 146 arrived on board the river steamboat *Mustang* on 21 May 1848.[9] That season five ships sailed from Liverpool to New Orleans with 650 bound for Kanesville and the West. From 1849 to 1852 another 6,130 Britons arrived at the Bluffs, usually disembarking at or near Council Point four miles south of Kanesville.[10]

The evacuation of Winter Quarters, combined with the British arrivals, created a network of small satellite settlements stretching into present Mills County in the north and Fremont County to the south. As Clyde B. Aitchison has pointed out, "strictly they were not villages, or even hamlets [but] merely the collection within easy distance [of Kanesville] of a handful of farm houses in a grove on a creek, with a school or church, and perhaps a mill or trader's stock."[11]

Although small settlements had been spreading from the Bluffs east to the Nishnabotona River since the summer of 1846, the proliferation of hamlets in the area in 1848 far exceeded anything seen before. Wrote Nelson Whipple, "many gatherd up from Nauvoo and other places this summer and made heavy settlements in all directions on the good land that aboundes in the country."[12] Several of these clusters operated their own horse- or water-powered gristmills. By midsummer 1848 twenty-four branches representing small settlements were in operation. Three months later another seven were added to the list, and by year's end over forty existed (table 9).[13] A branch president managed local affairs in his area and reported directly to the Pottawattamie High Council.[14] Circuit riders, high councilmen, seventies, even apostles visited the outlying communities on a regularly assigned basis to preserve unity, encourage emigration, and assist the poor and destitute.[15]

Meanwhile Kanesville arose on the old Miller's Hollow site on Indian Creek and rapidly became the hub of all Mormon communities in the Bluffs region. During the Jubilee celebrations in January 1848, the town layout was proposed, road construction planned, and timber claims granted.[16] The Quorum of the Twelve decided that Kanesville must serve three purposes: be the commercial and religious center and temporary headquarters of the Latter-day Saints in the region, be the receiving point for incoming emigrants and outfitting post for westbound travellers, and provide settlers with an opportunity to improve the land for later sales to non-Mormon newcomers as was done at Garden Grove and Mt. Pisgah.

From the Log Tabernacle on Harmony Street just down the hill and west of the old Blockhouse, the town grew rapidly in several directions.[17] Further east, on what then was Hyde Street (now First Street), Orson Hyde built his own home. By 1849, a passing traveller described the place (often misspelled "Canesville" or "Cainsville" in contemporary sources) as "a scrubby town of 80 to 100 log cabins" situated "three miles from the river in a deep hollow." By 1850 another visitor counted 350 houses, "principally of logs." By this time the business center of town had developed on Indian Creek near the Log Tabernacle at the corner now occupied by the First Methodist Church of Council Bluffs.[18] On or near Hyde Street a large, two-story schoolhouse was erected that later served as the county's first courthouse.[19] The population of Kanesville proper, though ever in flux, reached five thousand by early 1852.[20]

As at Nauvoo and later at Winter Quarters, the Mormons organized themselves into a militia. In July 1848, Charles M. Johnson was appointed "colonel of the whole of the military among the saints in Pottawattamie County."[21] Until the formal

Table 9. *List of Mormon Branches/Communities in Western Iowa,
31 December 1848*

Name of Branch/ Community	Branch President (Where Known)	Comments
Allred's		
B.S.M's Creek		
Big Bend	Jonathan Browning	
Big Grove		
Big Pigeon	Uriah Curtis	
Big Spring	Sam Brown	
Blockhouse	Moses Clawson	In Kanesville
Burtrand		
Carterville		
Centerville	Ezekiel Lee	On Mosquito Creek
Cooley's		
Council Point	George Coulson	5 mi. south of Kanesville
D. D. Hunt's		
Farmersville		
Ferrysville	David Williams	North of Kanesville—east of Winter Quarters
Galland's Grove		
Harris Grove		20 mi. north of Kanesville
High Prairie	Ezra Bickford	
Highland's Grove	Martin Bushman	
Honey Creek		
Hydes Park		
Indian Mill		
Indian Creek	Lewis Zebuskie	At an old Indian town 9 miles from Winter Quarters
Kanesville		
Keg Creek		
Lake Branch	Benjamin F. Bird	
Long Creek	Samuel Gates (bishop)	
Macedonia	A. H. Perkins	

Table 9. (*continued*)

Name of Branch/ Community	Branch President (Where Known)	Comments
McOlney's		Also spelled McAulney's
Mill	S. G. Clark	
Mosquito Creek		8 mi. north of Kanesville
North Pigeon		
Old Agency	William B. Simmons	
Pigeon Grove		7 mi. north of Kanesville
Pleasant Grove	James D. Allen	
Pleasant Valley	Martin Bushman	
Plum Hollow		
Poney Creek		
River		
Shirts		
Silver Creek		
Springville	Henry Williams	
Unionville		
U. Keg Creek		
Welch Branch		
West Fork Boyer		North of Kanesville
Whiskey Point		

NOTE: Farther south were branches in St. Joseph, Savannah, and Western Missouri.

SOURCES: Minutes of the Pottawattamie High Council, 15 July 1848; Silas Richards to the First Presidency, 10 October 1848, Brigham Young Papers; Journal of Erastus Snow; Journal of Warren Foote; Journal of Nelson W. Whipple; *The Frontier Guardian;* Journal History.

establishment of a county and the election of recognized civic authorities, the Pottawattamie High Council under Orson Hyde's direction ruled on matters both church and state. The High Council met biweekly, first in the Log Tabernacle, later at Hyde's home, and eventually in the large Kanesville schoolhouse.

A full account of the four years of Hyde's supervision over affairs in Kanesville (he was sustained in conference as "President
of the Church east of the Rocky Mountains") is beyond the scope
of this study. But with Young and most of the authorities now in
Salt Lake Valley, it was once again left to Hyde, as had been done
earlier in Nauvoo, to complete unfinished business, settle conflicts and defections, and facilitate migrations westward.[22]

Space and time forbid a thorough historical review of Kanesville life, but three themes demand some attention: politics, economics, and apostasies. The offical directive was not to get
involved in Iowa politics and not to take sides, but "to slide between wind and water," protect their interests, and flee the state.
President Young and Heber Kimball boasted little confidence in
either political party.[23] The large numbers of Mormons then settling on Pottawattami lands were, however, a tempting target for
both Whig and Democratic candidates, especially in an election
year. In sharp contrast to their waning days in Nauvoo, Mormons in Kanesville were courted by Whigs and Democrats, especially the former who rightly sensed a Mormon sentiment
against the Democrats, the party of Thomas Ford, Lilburn W.
Boggs, Thomas H. Benton, and Martin Van Buren.[24] In a state
where party allegiance was very evenly divided, the large Mormon vote could make a substantial difference.

Both the Whigs (who controlled the state's senate) and the
Democrats (who controlled the state's lower chamber) knew the
Mormons had political demands. They were especially anxious
to establish a county organization, as well as a post office in
Kanesville, since the nearest post office was over seventy miles
away.[25] During the Jubilee celebrations of January 1848, 1,805
males signed a petition for a Kanesville post office and a similar
number for a county organization.[26] County status would not
only insure locally elected state representatives, sheriffs, justices
of the peace, and other officers but facilitate land preemptions
and the right to dispose of lands and improvements by sale at
the appropriate time. Much better to have their own county and
local leadership, they reasoned, than be a mere outpost precinct
of Monroe County under the rule of nonsympathetic "Gentiles."
Eventually, after much jostling on all sides, the Kanesville post
office was established in March 1848 with Evan M. Greene as
postmaster.[27] Pottawattamie County was organized on 24 September 1848 with William Pickett organizing sheriff. It was some
time, however, before county officers were elected.[28]

The vying between Whig and Democrat climaxed during primary runoffs in August, during which contenders for high state offices repeatedly visited Kanesville to court favor. The resulting overwhelming margin of 491 Whig votes to 32 Democrat votes was disturbing to the losing side and may have been the cause of various vote-counting irregularities that conveniently omitted the Mormon vote, thereby assuring a Democratic victory in Monroe County.[29]

The first representative from Pottawattamie County to sit in the General Assembly of Iowa was Henry W. Miller, elected in 1850, founder of Miller's Hollow and an early member of the Pottawattamie High Council. Archibald Bryant followed him in 1852.[30]

Politics aside, farming was the principle preoccupation, with a wide variety of crops and relatively bounteous harvests reported. Warren Foote fenced and cultivated six acres of corn, three acres of turnips, and a wide variety of garden crops that prospered "beyond [his] expectations."[31] Joseph Holbrook grew corn, potatoes, beans, watermelons, and turnips on his farm on Indian Creek.[32] Farmers in Galland Grove harvested several hundred acres of wheat. Produce not consumed or stored was hauled to the growing Kanesville market for local consumption or for sale to the increasing numbers of westbound travellers.

To meet the pressing needs of incoming British converts, most of whom were economically destitute, families departing for the Salt Lake Valley were urged either to give their farms away or to dispose of them at very low prices.[33] How many followed such advice is unknown, but it does indicate some measure of the seriousness of the migration problem and the poverty of the new arrivals. As Hyde admitted, "It is certainly rather a gloomy time for poor English saints that are landing here without a penny to bless themselves with."[34]

To help meet the problem of poverty, circuit riders called for donations of produce, clothing, utensils, and other goods. In January 1849 the Log Tabernacle was transformed into a "wholesale provision store" for the poor. A large community farm funded by tithing money was also established to provide employment for the emigrant poor.[35] During Kanesville's six-year history the most serious problem was providing the rapidly overturning population of poor emigrants with food, shelter, and meaningful employment without a strong industrial or manufacturing base. It was a case of too much growth with too little preparation and caused Orson Hyde to criticize his colleagues and superiors for lack of foresight and planning. Better to leave more of the emigrants at St. Louis, he argued, where they could make a decent living, than to strand them at Kanesville.[36]

But the problems of Mormon migration were soon compounded by a totally unexpected development—the discovery of gold near Sutter's Fort, California, in January 1848. Almost overnight, it seemed, Kanesville was caught up in the din and commotion the waves of goldrushers caused. The very air was filled with gold fever. In the spring of 1849 there was even talk in Kanesville of their own nearby gold discoveries. Recalled Nelson Whipple, "Some person . . . found some thing in the bluffs west of Kainsville that had the appearance of gold this raised a grate excitement of corse. Brother Hyde went over to the place with some others and saw it and dedicated it to the Lord. This was all right and in good shape but the stuff turned out to be entirely worthless and no body could tell what it was."[37]

There was no fool's gold, however, in the pockets of the California-bound travellers who besieged the city in 1849–50. Suddenly Kanesville's economy boomed, and the Mormon resident population benefitted in unprecedented terms. "We are crowded with 'Gold Diggers' as we call them," one farmer reported. "We are busy every day and night grinding and the mill is crowded full. . . . We are making money midling fast now, but it can't keep this way long."[38]

The 1849 influx was but a foretaste of what came in 1850. Walker D. Wyman in his definitive study on outfitting towns on the Missouri claims that with the construction of new ferries at Kanesville in 1849, the town attracted up to five thousand wagonloads of gold seekers the following year, with many waiting weeks to cross.[39] In the colorful words of one observer,

> The plains about Kanesville were covered with little villages of tents, generally arranged in circles with the Stars and Stripes proudly floating in the center; wagons with white covers, some at rest by the tents, others in long moving lines; vast herds of horses and oxen, mingled with shouting herdsmen, animated with teeming life the natural beauty of the same.[40]

By this time the Mormon trail west was well known and many were using William Clayton's newly published overland guide as their desert compass.

The America that the Mormons were trying to flee was rapidly catching up to them, but rather than a bane, it proved a boon to their plans and economy. Many sold homes and farms on isolated creeks and groves to buy locations nearer the river landings or along main wagon roads to maximize sales and profits. And little wonder. Prices in some instances rose ten times over. Corn increased from 20¢ to $3 a bushel. Flour at one point sold for $4 per hundred weight and hay at $25 a ton. A good set of oxen brought up to $80 per yoke and horses sold for as high as $100 each. It was, as one reported, "a fine time for making money."[41] Hyde even bought herds of cattle further downriver to sell at a profit back in Kanesville.

This unexpected infusion of money into the Kanesville economy gave to many of those previously too poor to migrate the chance to make the trip. Several schemes maximized profits, including the conversion of the tabernacle into a temporary warehouse "to store goods in for the Californians and the money which will be paid for the storeage is to be used for the benefit of the Branch."[42] Although the sudden steep increase in the cost of living proved a mixed blessing, especially to some of the new British arrivals,[43] the gold rush of 1849–51 proved far more beneficial than otherwise to the emigration cause, and in the process made Kanesville a major outfitting river town.[44]

The gold rush also enlivened Kanesville's comparatively quiet and religious nature. The clash of values between peoples with entirely different motives and objectives awaits further study. Though crime and liquor consumption obviously increased, no serious conflict developed. Rather, they eyed one another with idle curiosity at a respectable distance.

In light of the unending tribulations and disappointments, the temptations to settle in Pottawattamie County, and the growing visibility of certain unorthodox religious practices, the church suffered sizable membership losses between July 1846 and the summer of 1852. Many decided once and for all that they had had enough of Zion's glory and her peculiarities, that they had been through one too many harangues, sacrifices, and disappointments, and that their happiness lay elsewhere. Dissatisfaction and defection became a very real part of community life both at Winter Quarters and Kanesville. What constituted their grievances can be fairly well documented, although what caused the final rupture in each individual case is difficult to ascertain.

Discouragement and hunger ranked high as contributing factors. So many had lost loved ones, often several family members,

Early Kanesville, Iowa. From a sketch by Frederick Piercy. First printed in James Linforth, *Route from Liverpool to Great Salt Lake Valley*.

that the hope and enthusiasm, even the faith that once motivated them, had dissipated. Horace K. Whitney referred to one man who told Heber Kimball that he was quitting and going back east "because he [was] discouraged."[45] John D. Lee records that because of poverty and lack of food (one small meal per day) many were leaving.[46] Of these, many took up residence in the fine farming lands of western Iowa where free land was readily available. Why risk a hazardous trek in the wilderness another thousand miles away from family and civilization when the riches of the earth were at their feet? Warren Foote, writing in September 1846 said, "several have apostatized from the Church and gone down into Missouri disheartened and depressed."[47] Early in January 1847, Lorenzo Snow reported from Mt. Pisgah that "at least three families left to return to the Gentiles in the east."[48]

With the arrival of better weather late in the spring of 1847, and as the first pioneer company headed west, a large-scale defection occurred at Winter Quarters. Hosea Stout told Isaac

Higbee, the ferry operator, on the morning of 27 April "not to take anyone over who had not paid his tax for there were now great numbers going off through disafection."[49] The month following, John D. Lee reported the ferry being "thronged continually with waggons to cross, that the scattering has become so general that Brother J. Taylor and P. P. Pratt put a vetoe on any teams crossing without a certificate."[50] Early in 1848, Noah Packard, writing from Grant County, Iowa, informed Young of "a number of people" in that region that once were Latter-day Saints, "but as the saying is, they most of them lie low and keep dark, some for the sake of popularity join other denominations."[51]

For those deciding to stay in Iowa, a farm there not only would free them from the trials of an exhausting overland journey but also would lessen financial sacrifices. Making ends might come easier outside the fold. In late December 1846, Young preached against the "stubbornness" of those refusing to pay tithing and taxes. Stout believed it was the police tax that had driven so many to Missouri. At Mt. Pisgah the most serious problem in 1848 was a general refusal to pay tithing.[52] Young realized that constantly asking for money from the more affluent often led to a loss of commitment. And the voluntary giving of their means to help others "who have afterwards treated them scandalously . . . not only stumbles and shakes their faith in those persons, but they lose confidence in all their brethren and the good spirit."[53]

Orson Hyde, writing from Kanesville, intimated in a letter to Young that economics was certainly a very divisive issue.

> Others are fearful that they will be tithed too much. Some say that you require teams from them to take away people no better than themselves. Others say that women are sent over here to be supported that belong to other men . . . Bro. Stoddard says that a number are about ready to declare their independence, pay no more tithing and take no council but their own.[54]

Others left because of differences over doctrine. Some followed Miller and Emmett after they broke with Young. Later Alpheus Cutler, former president of the Winter Quarters High Council, became convinced that the Lord had a special mission for him among the Lamanites in Missouri. Gradually he and many at Keg Creek fell away from the church and espoused

"Lamanism," a contorted doctrine of redeeming Jackson County, Missouri, by inciting the local Indian population to arms. It was a wild and radical scheme that owed its beginning to a blessing Cutler claimed he had received from Joseph Smith. Said Hyde, "Indian Cutlerism, in 500 forms, would rage like wild fire through this country if the strong arm of power were not upon it all the time. I do assure you, President Young, that it requires the utmost care, diligence and watching over this people to keep their eye towards the Salt Lake Valley."[55]

Other missionaries arrived from as far away as Ohio, usually representing small dissident factions attempting to draw away converts to their cause. Local church authorities informed Young that Lyman Wight's advocates siphoned off several members who had gone south to work in Missouri.[56] "Lymanism," as it was called, declared that Wight's mission to Texas was as much ordained as was Young's to the mountains, and that being an apostle, Wight could not be excommunicated by his peers. Significantly, it was the conference of the church at Kanesville and not in Salt Lake that first refused to sustain Wight as an apostle. "You may consider that our action [is] rather hasty," wrote apostles Smith and Benson, "but we discovered that a number of the persons affected with the Texas Epidemic were busy visiting remote branches and instilling into the minds of the people the ideas that the authorities dare not interfere with Lyman in his course."[57]

Meanwhile Strangism, for all the scorn authorities were heaping on it, was still claiming converts. Although Young said repeatedly during the entire Winter Quarters/Kanesville episode that "Strangism is about wound up" and "not worthy of notice," he was engaging in rhetoric that was more wishful thinking than fact. Strangite missionaries tried with various degrees of success to fill the vacuum the Mormons left as they headed west.[58] Various Strangite apostles were proselyting among the Mormons in Cincinnati and St. Louis throughout the fall and winter of 1846. As late as October 1849 members were being cut off from the church in Kanesville because of their conversion to Strangism.[59]

The practice of plural marriage alienated others. How valid a reason it was for mass disaffection is impossible to determine. While its influence is easily exaggerated, certainly many were offended by it.[60] When John Neff, one of the wealthiest men in Winter Quarters, first became aware of polygamy during the winter of 1846–47, he almost left the church. Only after personal intervention and lengthy explanations from prominent church leaders was he persuaded to stay on.[61] If Neff had difficulties with polygamy and was reclaimed only after much attention, presumably others shared the same discovery and made a clear separation.[62]

For a variety of reasons, then, whether economic, social, doctrinal, or personal, many quit the church at the Missouri. The exact dimensions are difficult to ascertain, but certainly substantial numbers were involved—at least two thousand during the six-year period from 1846 to 1852. This does not include the approximately three thousand defectors in Nauvoo from 1844 to 1846.[63]

But while some were leaving, others returned to the fold. Of these, the most dramatic was the rebaptism of Oliver Cowdery, former scribe to Joseph Smith while translating the Book of Mormon, "second elder" in the church, and counselor in the First Presidency. "I am out of the church," Cowdery explained to an attentive Pottawattamie High Council meeting in the Log Tabernacle in the fall of 1848. "I know the door into the church and I wish to become a member thro' the door."[64] After lengthy questioning, the council unanimously voted its approval, and Orson Hyde baptized Cowdery in Indian Creek outside the tabernacle on 5 November 1848, ending his eleven-year separation.

Despite the distractions of dissidents and the attractions of rich free farmlands in western Iowa, most Latter-day Saints headed west. Between the spring of 1848 and 1852, when Orson Hyde finally pulled up stakes, approximately twelve thousand people left Kanesville for the Salt Lake Valley. Approximately half of these were British converts. (See table 10.)

Hyde's departure marked the end of the Mormon stay in Kanesville. In December 1853 the city was officially renamed Council Bluffs by a rapidly growing majority of non-Mormons intent on capturing a popular name. For years afterwards, however, Council Bluffs, Iowa, was often referred to as "Orson Hyde's former town."[65]

Across the river the tiny community of Omaha was founded just south of Winter Quarters in 1853 by William D. Brown, an entrepreneur who made a fortune as a ferry operator. It became the terminus of the Union Pacific Railroad thanks to the efforts of G. M. Dodge and Abraham Lincoln. In time, Omaha surpassed Council Bluffs as an economic, trade, and transportation center. In the late 1850s and 1860s, Florence, Nebraska, a small

Table 10. *1848–52 Emigrations West from Kanesville (Based on an Average of 3 People per Wagon)*

1848	2,400
1849	1,850
1850	2,100 (est.)
1851	1,500
1852	4,050
Total	11,900

SOURCES: Brigham Young to G. A. Smith, 13 July 1848, Brigham Young Papers; Wallace Stegner, *Gathering of Zion.*

town built on the original Winter Quarters townsite, served as a fitting-out place for later bands of Mormon pioneers.

Little remains of Winter Quarters today. The original cabins, hovels, sod houses, and buildings of that once-bustling community on the west banks of the Missouri were destroyed in a prairie fire that scorched the area in the mid-1850s. The gradual growth of Florence, Nebraska, in this century has all but obscured the original site. A modern water treatment plant now occupies the land where much of the city once stood. Only an old mill and cemetery remain as silent landmarks to what once was.

EPILOGUE

At the outset of this history, the charge was made that serious historians have too long overlooked the long-term significance of the trek era in Latter-day Saint history. Save for stirring pioneer stories, pageants, and songs glorifying the perils, hardships, and tales of faith, and except for accounts on signposts, landmarks, and trailmarkers, the consensus has been that Mormon history ended at the Mississippi in early 1846 only to begin again some few years later in the "vales of Deseret." If this study has in the least degree forced a reconsideration, perhaps even a revision, of that viewpoint and a new appreciation of what did in fact transpire of lasting substance along the way, then to that extent it is a success. The contention offered here is that the westward movement of the church can no longer be viewed in a temporary context, but rather must be seen in a transitional one. It was not only a time of transporting people, important as that was, but also a time in which the American frontier again impacted upon the culture, the government, the economy, the society, and the doctrine of the church. And in the process a new leader was tried and proven, and the vitality and faith of a people tested to the breaking point.

Despite wilderness adversities and obstacles, real or otherwise, the Latter-day Saints overcame. Though this history has not concerned itself directly with the sequel to the Winter Quarters story, namely the advance-company crossings to the Rocky Mountains, the fundamentals were all in place. The greatest sacrifices had already been made, the major decisions of which route and whereto had already been arrived at. And the reason they survived is that they chose to bond together rather than divide off separately. One of the chief characteristics of the Mormon trek experience, as best developed during the Iowa crossing and later formalized at Winter Quarters, was that there was no individual survival, no ultimate attainment, no conquest of the wilderness independent of the group. The trek was not an individualistic expression as much as it was a group effort. It was a church in exodus, and the will of the individual was sacrificed over and over again for the good of the company at large.

One might wonder what their experience says of that aspect of the Turnerian hypothesis arguing that the American frontier renewed the democratic experience and encouraged the ongoing development of individualism. Though further careful studies and analyses need to be made, preliminary observations suggest that the frontier made Mormonism an even more centralized, more theocratic institution than ever before. Conformity was essential to their survival as a people, and individual expression and independence tolerated only within the confines of obedience and discipleship. While it is true that exceptions to expected behavioral patterns did exist, and to an extent they were more tolerated than previously has been assumed, the fact remains that their success and safety was a community endeavor.

Unlike perhaps any other migration of people in American frontier history, at least any on so grand a scale, the Mormons worked together in a remarkably cohesive manner. This uniting together, doubtless caused in part by the wilderness, but more by the standards and practices of their new faith, explains such episodes as the establishment of the Nauvoo Covenant, the building of the way stations of Garden Grove and Mt. Pisgah for those coming behind, the pooling of Mormon Battalion funds despite the grumblings of some, the establishment of a strict law of economy and of the Whitney store, and, of course, the organized, compassionate role women played in the dark days of sickness and death. As Young succinctly put it, "there may be some of us who think ourselves able and prepared to go through the journey independent of the rest, but God will not suffer us to divide off and hurry away." Quite simply, no one reached the Missouri, or later the Great Basin, without the support and consent of the rest. It was all one vast interdependent army that crossed the American desert in 1846 and 1847.

In further reference to Turnerian theory, the Mormon frontier experience was not a democratic one. Many saw themselves as striving to escape the American republic in order to establish a new religious kingdom in the West. Though this was a dream not unanimously held, and which indeed was not the intention of the highest church authorities, if they did choose to remain in America, they would try to do so on their own terms. Govern-

ment, as it had been from the beginning in Latter-day Saint history, was by decree. In keeping with that tradition, the municipal
high councils at Cutler's Park, Winter Quarters, and later in Iowa,
were theocratic and not democratic expressions. With the succession of Brigham Young to the presidency in December 1847, what
democratic tendencies some members of the Quorum of the
Twelve had were eliminated. If anything, then, the trek witnessed a greater centralization and consolidation of authority.

While founded in an anxious time of learning how to survive
in a frontier wilderness, Winter Quarters also was a place of
transition, accommodation, experimentation, and implementation. The Saints were transporting their entire culture across the
void. Free as they finally were becoming from their so-called
"gentile" neighbors, they introduced into their society on a much
wider scale several new religious and cultural practices, including plural marriage and the Law of Adoption. The social and religious impact of such a large number among them having received temple endowments in Nauvoo just before the exodus
from that city was first felt in Winter Quarters. It was here, too,
that several new principles of church government were introduced, or more correctly perhaps, agreed upon, such as apostolic
supremacy and succession and the establishment of bishoprics on
a local level. Patterns of ward-level worship and organization implemented at Winter Quarters are maintained to this day.

It was also at the Missouri that the Latter-day Saints formulated a policy of peace through strength with the Indians, where
city planning took on dimensions and characteristics that set
the blueprint for towns and villages in the Mormon cordillera
throughout the Intermountain West, and where temple endowments and other practices were modified to meet their needs. It
was, in fact, a religion made practical by frontier demands.

Finally, this history provides much new primary information
pertaining to the lives and personalities of certain key individuals. More than anyone, however, Brigham Young dominated the
scene. His influence rose in direct proportion to the increasing
numbers of miles they travelled, and an accurate assessment of
the life of this religious leader, pioneer, and colonizer is impossible without an understanding of the Winter Quarters story and
his place therein. So much of what he established later in economics, urban development, ecclesiastical administration, Indian policy, and doctrine, he initiated at the Missouri.

That Young was a strong and forceful personality with shrewd political skills and determination is well known. This history has attempted to show that the crossing of Iowa demanded sound leadership and began to bring out, for all to see, whether the George Millers or the William Huntingtons among them, that Young could be uncompromising in his pursuits. Even his colleagues among the Quorum of the Twelve were sensitive and critical of his oftentimes caustic tongue and stinging rebukes.

Yet he was also a man of sensitivity and compassion. Never one to form close relationships, he seemed to care more for the people as a whole than for any one person in particular. If he were in a hurry to reach the Rockies, it was not to get away from his followers as much as to prepare for them and to save the church. And he would permit none to follow him unless they had covenanted to bring with them those who were less provisioned and less healthy but as equally willing as themselves. It is in his law of "common concern" as seen in the Nauvoo Covenant, his efforts to centralize the Battalion funds for the common good, his dispatching of rescue missions to the poor camps, his bending of the rules on temple endowments in the wilderness, and in the many "begging missions" he sent east for food and money that his concern for the public welfare may be best seen.

While it is true that he could castigate his followers with blistering, almost wilting effectiveness, he could listen as well as lecture. The unanimous sustaining vote of Young as president of the church at the Missouri was tribute to that fact. If temple ceremonies needed performing outside the temple, then he would do them. If the Law of Adoption proved a failure, then give it up. If Joseph Smith never saw the need for systematic, local priesthood government, then Young did. If sacred properties back in Nauvoo, Kirtland, and Jackson County needed to be sold for their survival, so be it. History was not their master but their servant, and Young ever contemplated the future rather than dwelling on the past. That willingness to accede to the wishes of his followers, to alter previous policy and accepted procedures, that kind of decisive, forward-looking leadership came to characterize his later administrations.

His political savvy and abundant common sense further endeared him and helps explain his success. At a time in Latter-day Saint history when several were contending to succeed Joseph Smith, Young outmaneuvered them all. He successfully throttled the Council of Fifty and its more activist-minded members, provided enough freedom to James Emmett and others like him to disgrace themselves, contended with James J. Strang by publicly ignoring him while privately sending missionaries to monitor his efforts, and contended with George Miller through open confrontation although losing in the process one of his best trailblazers. Undoubtedly, he offended many people and thereby lost the companionship of men and women that had stood by Joseph Smith but could not walk with this new leader.

He was, perhaps, even more astute in dealing with the federal government. While capitalizing on the anti-American sentiments of many of his people who blamed the U.S. government for the deaths of Joseph and Hyrum Smith, he privately negotiated for government contracts in Washington. While one hand pointed an accusing finger at America, his other lay outstretched in fellowship and reconciliation. This overture, coupled with deliberate obscuring of his destination and ultimate purposes, led to President Polk's request for the Mormon Battalion in June 1846. The president's request not only brought the Saints desperately needed funds, but in addition provided Young all the leverage he would need to winter on Indian lands despite regulations to the contrary.

No greater evidence of the allegiance of the Latter-day Saints to their pioneer leader exists than their devotion and commitment throughout the long nightmare of suffering and death in 1846 and 1847. Certainly some could fault his decision to override the advice of lieutenants and underlings who saw the perils in living so close to the river as they had done in Nauvoo. Others might even criticize him for leaving Nauvoo prematurely, thereby throwing his people into a painful and debilitating Iowa crossing. Once at the Missouri, his handling of Battalion funds unquestionably alienated many families. Though some deserted for these and other reasons, the overwhelming majority stayed on, whatever the cost. Young's star rose, almost paradoxically, in direct proportion to the perils and trials of the people. While this was as much a measure of their hopes and religious beliefs as a public acceptance of Young as leader, the fact remains that there were no rebellions against him or his colleagues. No better statement of acceptance can be made than that he was finally sustained as Joseph Smith's successor, not on the shores of the Great Salt Lake but on the banks of the Missouri River.

But giving Brigham Young too much historical prominence is inaccurate and unfair to the realities involved. This people, regardless of leadership, believed in what they were doing, that they were fulfilling prophecy, that theirs was a religious manifest destiny foretold in ancient scripture of a modern Israel in a modern wilderness fleeing a modern Egypt.

Theirs was a remarkable expression of the earliest Puritan ideal of quitting Babylon, of crossing a landlocked sea, though this time not in ships of sail but in canvas-tossed wagons, to some new land where they could build, for all to see, "a city on a hill." The theme was repeated in their sermons, their songs, their diaries, and in their religious interpretations, over and over again, leaving no doubt that many cast themselves in that prophetic role.

The story of Winter Quarters speaks to a universal theme not confined to one denomination or religious expression—the celebration of the indomitable, unconquerable spirit of man and woman against sometimes insuperable odds. Whether in the graves at Winter Quarters or the furnaces of Auschwitz, whether among the hunted Anabaptists of the sixteenth century or the condemned among the early Christian Church, the lesson remains. Given a cause to live for and believe in, human beings can and will overcome.

NOTES

CHAPTER 1

1. Brigham Young to Joseph Young, 9 March 1846, Brigham Young Papers.

2. Joseph Smith Jr., *History of The Church of Jesus Christ of Latter-day Saints*, ed. B. H. Roberts, 7:398. Hereafter cited as *History of the Church*.

3. B. H. Roberts, *A Comprehensive History of the Church of Jesus Christ of Latter-day Saints*, 2:505. Hereafter cited as *Comprehensive History*.

4. Brigham Young to Wilford Woodruff, 16 October 1845, Brigham Young Papers.

5. Irene Hascall to Ursula B. Hascall, 26 September 1845, Hascall Family Letters, 1845–54.

6. Brigham Young, *Manuscript History of Brigham Young*, comp. Elden J. Watson, 28 August 1845. Hereafter cited as *Manuscript History*.

7. Ibid., 9 September 1845.

8. William Huntington, "A History of William Huntington," 6 October 1845.

9. The "Nauvoo Covenant" reflected Young's style of leadership and his commitment to assist the poor and destitute among them. In 1839, while Joseph Smith was incarcerated at Liberty Jail in Liberty, Missouri, it was Young who drew up the "Missouri Covenant" to assist church members leaving Missouri for a new home in Illinois. Proposing that they "never desert the poor who are worthy," he persuaded more than two hundred men to sign a covenant "to stand by and assist each other to the utmost of our abilities" to find a new home in a friendlier environment. *History of the Church*, 3:250–54.

10. Huntington, "A History," 6 October 1845.

11. Irene Hascall to Ashbel G. Hascall, 8 November 1845, Hascall Family Letters.

12. A study of over forty families residing at the Missouri River in 1848 revealed an average of 5.6 members per Mormon family. Mill Branch Record Book, 1848. Arriving at a firm population count for Nauvoo is difficult. The 17,000 figure, considerably in excess of the 12,000 given in the 1843 census, probably includes many Mormons flocking into Nauvoo at the end of 1845 both to escape persecutions in

outlying areas and to participate in wagon building. Nelson Bates, whose journal gives fairly accurate accounts of populations elsewhere in Buffalo, Cleveland, Erie, and Chicago, estimates Nauvoo's January 1846 population at 17,000. A few hundred other Mormons lived near Nauvoo in surrounding towns and villages and many have been included in Bates's estimate. In contrast, Chicago's population as of 1846 was estimated at between 10,000 and 14,000. William J. A. Bradford, writing to Congress in 1846 in his *Notes on the Northwest, or Valley of the Upper Mississippi* (New York: Wiley, Putnam, 1846) said that Cook County had between "18 and 20 thousand" by 1846, but that "Chicago has now about 10,000" (p. 130).

13. Letter of Irene Hascall, 29 October 1845, Hascall Family Letters.

14. Brigham Young to David S. Hollister, 1 January 1846, Brigham Young Papers.

15. *Manuscript History*, 1 January 1846.

16. Brigham Young to David S. Fullmer, Joseph L. Heywood, and Almon W. Babbitt, Nauvoo Trustees, 11 March 1846, Brigham Young Papers.

17. *History of the Church*, 5:85.

18. Journal History of the Church, 26 April 1846. Hereafter cited as Journal History.

19. *History of the Church*, 6:222.

20. James Allen Scott, in Nauvoo in April 1846, reported on a discourse by William Smith, younger brother of Joseph Smith, who had turned sour on Young's leadership.

> "He prophesied that in six months the saints would rue going west [and] said that Joseph never said anything about moving to C[alifornia]; after he quit a man in [the] crowd asked leave to speak being granted. He mounted the stand and told the people that he was with Joseph for two or three days previous to his death—gave him the pistol in jail. Received his blessing and last instructions which were sent by him both verbal and written to the Church which were to go west to Oregon or California as the Lord should direct and affirmed that he knew that this was the council of Joseph and Hyrum. After he was done, William got up and denied it."

James Allen Scott Journal, 19 April 1846.

21. *History of the Church*, 7:398.

22. A recent article by Lewis Clark Christian argues that "Mormon leaders were formulating plans to colonize the Pacific Coast, Oregon, Vancouver Island, and other proposed sites for 'stakes of Zion' but that the center would probably be somewhere near the Great Salt Lake." Christian Lewis Clark, "Mormon Foreknowledge of the West," *Brigham Young University Studies* 21 (Fall 1980):411.

23. See John C. Frémont, *Report of the Exploring Expedition to the Rocky Mountains in the Year 1842, and to Oregon and North California in the Years 1843–44.*

24. Brigham Young to Wilford Woodruff, 17 December 1845, Brigham Young Papers.

25. Brigham Young to Orson Hyde, 2 April 1846, Brigham Young Papers.

26. *Manuscript History*, 20 January 1846.

27. Brigham Young to William Huntington, 22 June 1846, "A History of William Huntington."

28. *The Nauvoo Temple 1841–1865*, p 1. See also Nelson Bates Journal. Bates was a late worker on the Nauvoo Temple.

29. *The Doctrine and Covenants of the Church of Jesus Christ of Latter-day Saints*, Section 132. Temple work was and is at the very heart of Mormon doctrine. Specifically, the "blessings of the temple" include various ordinances, rites, key words, performances, and dramatizations, and above all, covenants and promises that the Latter-day Saints believed had been divinely restored and were essential to salvation. This package of temple rites, called the endowment, was both a symbol and conditional promise of salvation. Temple ceremonies, based on the doctrine of the eternality of the soul, included celestial or eternal marriages for the living and the dead, baptisms for the dead, and the sealing of living or deceased children to earthly families in an eternal family unit. For more on temple work as it affected this history, see chap. 10.

30. Within a few short weeks, eight thousand had received their endowments. Brigham Young to James Emmett, 26 March 1846, Brigham Young Papers.

31. See Chap. 7.

32. Certain it is that most of the apostles believed that they had been authorized "to bear off the kingdom" in Joseph Smith's absence. See Leonard J. Arrington and Ronald K. Esplin, "The Role of the Council of the Twelve During Brigham Young's Presidency of the Church of Jesus Christ of Latter-day Saints," *Task Papers in LDS History* 31, p. 11. For a more thorough review of this issue, see Chap. 11.

33. *History of the Church*, 7:223–24. One possible reason for Rigdon's failure was that Joseph had earlier tried unsuccessfully to remove him from the First Presidency. *History of the Church*, 6:47–50.

34. James Allen Scott Journal, 1 May 1846.

35. Lyman Wight, a convert since 1830 and an apostle since 1841, was not out to establish a new church but to organize a Texas settlement of the church. His purpose was to teach Indians, attract southern shareholders to the Mormon cause, raise money, and in other ways hasten and facilitate the return of the church to the believed staging site of Christ's millennial return in Independence, Missouri. Wight was not disfellowshipped until 1849. After his death in 1856, remnants of his family and followers allied themselves either with the "Utah Mormons" or with the Reorganized Church of Jesus Christ of Latter Day Saints. See Davis Bitton, "Mormons in Texas: The Ill-fated Wight Colony 1844–1858," *Arizona and the West* 2 (Spring 1969): 5–26.

36. For a good overview of Strang, his life, and teachings, see Milo

Quaife, *The Kingdom of Saint James: A Narrative of the Mormons.* A more recent work is William D. Russell, "King James Strang: Joseph Smith's Successor," in F. Mark McKiernan, Alma R. Blair, and Paul M. Edwards, eds., *The Restoration Movement: Essays in Mormon History,* 231–56.

37. William Alexander Linn, *The Story of the Mormons from the Date of Their Origin to the Year 1901,* 325. See also Jesse C. Little to Brigham Young, 6 October 1846, Brigham Young Papers.

38. James B. Allen and Glen M. Leonard, *The Story of the Latter-day Saints,* 170–71. For more on polygamy, see chap. 10.

39. James Blakeslee Journal, "My Reasons for Separating Myself from the Church at Nauvoo," typescript copy, James Blakeslee Papers.

40. Journal of Gilbert Watson, n.p., n.d., Gilbert Watson Papers.

41. Isaac Paden to Brigham Young, 26 January 1846, Brigham Young Papers.

42. Isaac Paden to James M. Adams, 27 February 1853, RLDS Library and Archives.

43. Huntington, "A History," 8 February 1846. Italics in the original.

44. Journal of Wilford Woodruff, 14–18 April 1846, Wilford Woodruff Papers, LDS Church Archives. Woodruff's own parents had to be "reclaimed" from the Strangite influence.

45. Journal History, 27 March 1846.

46. See Brigham Young to Orson Hyde, 16 March 1846, Brigham Young Papers; Journal History, 16 March 1846.

47. Young's plan of exodus was a tempting target for Strang's reporters. Appearing in the *Voree* (Wisconsin) *Herald,* (Strang's official publication) in March 1846 was the following editorial:

> "Going to Oregon or going to California we look upon as much the same thing. . . . I hope this may settle the question who is carrying out Joseph's measures and who are apostates. . . . "But did not Joseph contrive the California scheme a little before his death? No nor at any other time. He contrived a scheme for 25 men without families to take a mission among the Indians and take measures for establishing a stake among them. . . . Quite another thing from taking out thousands of women and children to perish by famine, flood and Indian war" (*Voree* [Wisconsin] *Herald*) March 1846, vol 1, no 3, p. 2.

So it must have seemed to hundreds of wavering Mormons who were as unprepared for a trek across the prairies as they were unsure of Young's claim to church leadership. Charles R. Thompson, an on-again-off-again disciple, described further Strangite missionary tactics in a letter to Brigham:

> "Soon after your departure Strangism began to be propageted with great zeal by some individuals in the city. I at first paid but little attention to it but out of idle curiosity went to hear them lecture. I considered all their arguments futile and of no weight but disliking the manner in which their arguments were treated by some out of simpa-

thy and to gratify the idle curiosity of some friends. . . . I went to hear
[John E.] Page lecture one after noon. . . . I became convinced that
Strang was the Prophet to lead the Church and the twelve were
usurpers" (Charles R. Thompson to Brigham Young, 25 December
1846, Brigham Young Papers).

48. Bernard De Voto, *The Year of Decision, 1846*, 146–47.

49. John D. Unruh, Jr., *The Plains Across—The Overland Emigrants and
the Trans-Mississippi West, 1846–60*, 119–20.

50. *History of the Church*, 3:175 and 5:67.

51. Unruh, *The Plains Across*, 332.

52. As early as July 1843 and on several occasions thereafter, delega-
tions of Pottawattami Indians had met with Joseph Smith seeking counsel and direction. Smith sympathized with them and taught them his religion, but did not preach insurrection or rebellion. *History of the Church*,
5:480, 542–49.

53. Unruh, *The Plains Across*, 332. Unruh quotes Theodore Edgar
Potter as saying, "For honesty, purity, truthfulness, trustworthiness, and
honor, between the Indian and Mormon, give us the Indian at all odds."

54. As quoted in De Voto, *The Year of Decision*, 146.

55. James Knox Polk, *The Diary of James K. Polk During His Presidency
1845 to 1849*, ed. Milo M. Quaife, 1:150–60.

56. Ibid., 1:443.

57. Brannan's ship, *Brooklyn*, arrived in San Francisco on 19 July 1846.

58. Brigham Young and the Council of the Twelve to Jesse C. Little, 6
July 1846, Brigham Young Papers.

59. Governor Thomas Ford to Sheriff William B. Bachenstos, 29 December 1845; *Manuscript History*. B. H. Roberts maintains that Ford
wrote the letter to hasten the Mormon removal, that he knew nothing
of the War Department's intent, and thus soundly condemns Ford for
his trickery and subterfuge. See *Comprehensive History*, 2: 532–35.
Ford himself admits that he wrote the letter with a scarcity of hard
facts, but it must be emphasized that Ford did not say for a certainty an
army would come. Rather, his words were that Polk "might order up a
regiment or two of the regular army, and perhaps call on me for the
militia" (italics added). After all, he did admit it was all "such guess
work," and he should not be too hastily criticized for taking any and all
possible measures to prevent what he perceived as unavoidable bloodshed if the Mormons delayed.

60. Samuel Brannan to Brigham Young, 12 January 1846, Brigham
Young Papers.

61. Manuscript of Brigham Young, 29 January 1846. The argument
that the vanguard company of Mormons may have left Nauvoo out of
fear of government interference, and not because of widespread local
insurrection, is further confirmed in a letter from Brigham Young to
James Emmett:
"When we left Nauvoo, the feelings of the people around were some-

what more favorable than they had been for sometime previous especially in the counties some distance from us, but inasmuch as the time had fully come for this church to be transplanted into a far distant country . . . we left all our homes and property to be disposed of to assist the poor to follow after us to our departed home in the west" (Brigham Young to James Emmett, 26 January 1846, Brigham Young Papers).

62. On 20 October 1845, William Huntington referred to a subtle change of the opposition's tactics from the September's crop burnings of farms near Nauvoo to troubling and harrassing "by writ, [and] lawsuit, trying to pick the brethren away one or a few at a time secretly and by imprisoning. . . . Strong guards were kept to prevent parties of the mob from taking off the brethren with their vexatious suits" ("A History of William Huntington," 20 December 1845). In late December 1845 several men from Carthage, Illinois, stormed the temple and seized a man they mistook for Brigham Young. Henry Miller had disguised himself as the Mormon leader.

63. Journal of John D. Lee, 10 January 1846, John D. Lee Papers, LDS Church Archives. For more on the Council of Fifty, see Chap. 2.

64. Joseph L. Heywood to Brigham Young, circa 15 January 1846, Brigham Young Papers.

65. Brigham Young letter, 17 December 1845, Brigham Young Papers.

66. *Manuscript History*, unpublished version, 18 January 1846, LDS Church Archives.

67. Joseph L. Heywood to Brigham Young, circa 15 January 1846, Brigham Young Papers.

68. Dale L. Morgan, *The Great Salt Lake*, 128.

69. "A History of William Huntington," 26–29 January 1846.

70. *Manuscript History*, 2 February 1846. It is significant that the first band of refugees was to have been church leaders and not the rank-and-file membership. On 1 February 1846 orders were received "for the Twelve, High Council, Trustees-in-Trust, the old Police, Presidents of Seventies with many others to be in immediate readiness." These would form the core of the first division.

CHAPTER 2

1. Reliable studies of the Iowa trek include the following: Jacob Van der Zee, "The Mormon Trails in Iowa," *Iowa Journal of History and Politics* 12 (January 1914): 3–16; Stanley B. Kimball, "The Iowa Trek of 1846," *Ensign* 2 (June 1972) 3:36–45; William J. Petersen, "The Mormon Trail of 1846," *Palimpsest* 47 (September 1966): 353–67; Roy Franklin Lawson, "The Mormons; Their Trek Across Iowa and Their Settlement in Kanesville," in Preston Nibley, *Exodus to Greatness, The Story of the Mormon Migration*, 126–64; Wallace Stegner, *The Gathering of Zion—The Story of the Mormon Trail*, 43–72; the published journal of William Clayton entitled *William Clayton's Journal—A Daily Record of the*

Journey of the Original Company of "Mormon" Pioneers from Nauvoo, Illinois, to the Valley of the Great Salt Lake; and Juanita Brooks, ed., *On the Mormon Frontier: the Diary of Hosea Stout 1844–1861* 2 volumes (hereafter cited as *The Diary of Hosea Stout*). Available unpublished journals for this epic include those of Orson Pratt, Horace K. Whitney, John D. Lee, Thomas Bullock, O. M. Allen and Eliza R. Snow.

2. Journal History, 8 March 1846.

3. Brigham Young to James Emmett and Company, 26 March 1846, Brigham Young Papers. Andrew Jenson, *Church Chronology—A Record of Important Events,* 28 February 1846, 29.

4. Eliza Maria Lyman painted a vivid picture of the icy environment when she arose and "found the ground covered with snow." It snowed all day with the wind blowing in every direction. "Our fire is out in the storm so that we cannot get warm by it. I am almost frozen so shall go into the wagon and make my bed and get into it as that is the only way I can get warm." Eliza Maria Lyman Journal, 19 February 1846, Eliza Maria Lyman Papers.

5. William Huntington said the camp was "waiting here for some brethren to come from Nauvoo—brother [Newel K.] Whitney and [William] Clayton not over." Journal of William Huntington, 17 February 1846, William Huntington Papers.

Complaining of the situation, Young said they waited at Sugar Creek three weeks "to get teams to drag out Whitney and Clayton with the public property they had in charge, such as mill irons, saws, guns, etc." Journal History, 5 May 1846.

6. Eliza Snow recalled that from 13 to 18 February "we had several snows and very freezing weather which bridged the Mississippi sufficiently for crossing heavily loaded wagons on the ice." Edward W. Tullidge, *The Women of Mormondom,* 309. See also D. E. Miller, "Westward Migration of the Mormons With Special Emphasis on the History of Nauvoo," 240. Like most studies of Nauvoo, Miller's work pays scant attention to the exodus.

7. Eliza Maria Lyman Journal, 23 February 1846.

8. Orson Pratt Journal, 18 February 1846, Orson Pratt Papers. Pratt's meteorological, topographical, and geographical observations are a reliable source of information.

9. Some have argued that not only did Joseph Smith give details about a final destination in the Rocky Mountains but that he also left instructions on the particulars of the Iowa trek. To support their claims, reference is made to the retrospective writings of Mosiah Lyman Hancock who reported an alleged visit by Joseph Smith just prior to his death. Wrote Hancock:

> "The Prophet came to our home stopped in our carpenter shop and stood by the turning table. I went and got my map for him. 'Now,' said he, 'I will show you the travels of this people.' He then showed

our travels thru Iowa, and said, 'Here you will make a place for the
winter, and here you will travel west until you come to the valley of
the Great Salt Lake.'"

"The Life Story of Mosiah Hancock" as quoted in Hyrum Andrus,
"Joseph Smith and the West," *Brigham Young University Studies* 2 (Spring–
Summer 1960): 141.

If Joseph ever made such specific statements, they are recorded no
where else. Certainly Young indicated no knowledge of them nor did
any of his advisors. In light of the many changes in travel plans made
during the Iowa journey, one cannot put credence in much of what
young Hancock remembered.

However, their plans to travel between the rivers (Des Moines and
Missouri) and presumably head toward Council Bluffs may have owed
something to Joseph Smith's attempted memorial to Congress in the
spring of 1844 in which he and Orson Hyde had proposed sending a
Mormon army of 100,000 westward to police the territories of Oregon
and California and prevent their falling into British or Mexican control.
Though the plan was considered outlandish and extreme and not even
considered by Congress, the proposed route of departure may have
played on Young's mind.

> "In case of a removal to that country, Nauvoo is the place of general
> rendezvous. Our course from thence would be westward through
> Iowa bearing a little north until we came to the Missouri River, leav-
> ing the state of Missouri on the left, thence onward until we come to
> the Platte, thence up the north fork of the Platte to the mouth of the
> Sweetwater . . . to the South Pass."

History of the Church, 6:374.

10. Journal History, 16 July 1846.

11. Clara Decker Young, "A Woman's Experience with the Pioneer
Band," *Utah State Historical Quarterly* 12 (1946): 175.

12. Discourse of Brigham Young, 14 February 1853, *Journal of Discourses*, 279.

13. Almon W. Babbitt, John S. Fullmer, and Joseph L. Heywood, Nauvoo Trustees, to Brigham Young, 27 March 1846, Brigham Young
Papers.

14. *The Latter-day Saints Millenial Star*, London, 1 (January 1841):
231–32.

15. *History of the Church*, 5:542–49.

16. James Emmett, a member of the Council of Fifty, had attended a
meeting in February 1844 during which Joseph Smith had asked for
volunteers to explore areas west of the Missouri River "to hunt out a
good location where we can remove to after the temple is completed . . .
where the devil cannot dig us out." Nothing came of the meeting because of the prophet's candidacy for the presidency of the United States
and because of the climate of hostility then developing in Nauvoo.

But three months later, Emmett, feeling little allegiance to Young, set out with 150 followers across Iowa stopping first near the "Big Woods" area (Marshalltown) on the Des Moines River. Young dispatched several couriers, including Amasa Lyman, to dissuade Emmett from his enterprise and be "regrafted into Zion." Because of his cruelties, insensitivities, and thieving propensities, many left Emmett in the winter of 1844–45 and straggled back to Nauvoo. Others, wishing to leave, were intimidated into staying for fear of their lives.

Hunted by local authorities for alleged thievery, Emmett left the Des Moines River and travelled in a northwesterly direction finally arriving at the Vermillion River in present-day South Dakota, some seven hundred miles from Nauvoo, in June 1845.

Emmett returned to Nauvoo for a reconciliation with Young since his priesthood had been renounced earlier. Young, not willing to see Emmett lead his followers out of the church or become an enemy and anxious to use Emmett's considerable skills as a woodsman, explorer, and Indian interpreter, forgave Emmett and instructed him to remain at the Vermillion and wait for instructions regarding a rendezvous with the main body of the church in the wilderness. Eventually Young sent word to have Emmett send most of his camp to the Council Bluffs region.

Emmett, as colorful a character as he was, has received very little scholarly notice. A recent but blindly sympathetic treatment is Gerald E. Jones "Some Forgotten Pioneers: The Emmett Company of 1844" in "Eighth Annual Sidney B. Sperry Symposium," (Provo: Brigham Young University, 1980), 193–209. The best manuscript sources on Emmett are "The Autobiography of Allen Russell," "A Short History of the Life of John L. Butler," and "Memorandum Recounting Experiences with James Emmett Co."

17. H. W. Mills, "De Tal Palo Tal Astilla," *Historical Society of Southern California Annual Publications,* 10:106.

18. In 1844, Van Buren County could boast a population of only 9,019. Davis County was only beginning to welcome settlers while Appanoose County to the west had just been organized. J. B. Newhall, *A Glimpse of Iowa in 1846; or the Emigrant's Guide and State Directory with a Description of the New Purchase.*

19. It is not clear what maps the Mormons used in charting their course across Iowa. Certainly they had studied John C. Frémont's maps of the tran-Missouri regions, but Frémont was sparse in his descriptions of Iowa. Most likely they used the writings and maps of Frémont's mentor, J. N. Nicollet, who in January 1845 had presented to Congress a highly detailed report on the upper Mississippi Basin with much information on Iowa's topography, biology, geology, and other physical features. J. N. Nicollet, *Report to Illustrate a Map of the Hydrographical Basin of the Upper Mississippi River.* See also "Sketch of the Public Surveys in Iowa," Executive Documents, U.S. Senate, 1st Session, 30th Congress, vol. 2.

20. *Manuscript History,* 23 February 1846.

21. Eliza Maria Lyman Journal, 3 March 1846.

22. John D. Lee Journal, 23 February 1846.

23. Journal of Jonathan Dunham, 2 March 1846.

24. See Willard Richards to Levi Richards, 9 March 1846, Levi Richards Papers; and Brigham Young to Orson Hyde, 2 April 1846, Brigham Young Papers.

25. A. w. Babbitt and Joseph L. Heywood, Nauvoo Trustees to Brigham Young, 11 March 1846, Brigham Young Papers.

26. Journal History, 27 March 1846.

27. Some argued that Young patterned the 1846 camp organization after that of "Zion's Camp," organized by Joseph Smith in 1834. That travelling army of 130 men marched from Kirtland, Ohio, to western Missouri in a vain attempt to put down Missouri persecutions. See Leonard J. Arrington, *Great Basin Kingdom—An Economic History of the Latter-day Saints 1830–1900*, 428; and Roger D. Launius, *Zion's Camp: Expedition to Missouri, 1834*.

28. John D. Lee has left a vivid account of Young's "organization speech" that he gave to the encircled crowd from atop his wagon.

"Attention! All the Camp of Israel . . . we have called you together this morning for the purpose of giving you some instructions with regard to the order and organization of the camp. . . . Many of you, I have no doubt are anxious to be traveling but not more so than I am, but we must first get ready. It takes a long time to move so large a body of people as this. It will not do to start off helter-skelter without order and decorum—if we should but few would reach the place of destination. . . . We want to count noses and under each nose I assure you there will be a mouth to feed and when we get all the camp together then we will number Israel and organize them into companies of tens, of fifties and of hundreds and place captains over them. . . . We do not intend to make a great many laws or bye laws to violate but we will have order and will not suffer men to run from one wagon to another."

Journal of John D. Lee, 17 February 1846.

29. Attempts at organization were undermined not only by the constantly changing makeup of the camp but also by both petty and serious jealousies, disagreements, and personality conflicts. Hosea Stout recorded that George Miller and John Scott "found it difficult to give prompt and unquestioning obedience to the commands of Brigham Young especially when they were issued by Albert P. Rockwood." Stout noted that "both Miller and Scott had been appointed to the Council of Fifty by Joseph Smith, so considered themselves equal in rank and authority to Brigham Young and higher than Albert P. Rockwood." *Diary of Hosea Stout*, 1:152, 15 April 1846.

Some have argued that the Council of Fifty played a key role in both the preparations for and the progression of the Mormon journey westward. See Klaus Hansen, *Quest for Empire—The Political Kingdom of God and the Council of Fifty in Mormon History*, 110. But if the Council of Fifty did exercise leadership and provide temporal direction, it is not evident. Young was centralizing command, not dispersing it. And as the camp travelled west, the Council of Fifty's influence waned in inverse proportion to Young's increasing control over the church. Michael D. Quinn, "The Council of Fifty and Its Members, 1844 to 1945," *Brigham Young University Studies* 20 (Winter 1980): 170.

   30. Journal History, 28 February 1846.

   31. Journal History, 18 February 1846.

   32. De Voto, *Year of Decision 1846*, 144. Young had stipulated precisely what would-be emigrants required in a letter to Luther C. White of Calais, Maine.

   "You will need to make provision according to the number of your family. The rule adopted by us here is as follows:

Each family of five persons should be provided with one good strong waggon well covered—the box made light, five or three wood yoke of oxen from 4 to 9 years old—two or more milk cows—some sheep, 1000 lbs. flour in stout sacks, one good musket or rifle to each male over 12 years of age, one lb. powder, four of lead, one of tea, five of coffee, 100 lbs. sugar, two lbs pepper, half a pound of mustard, ten pounds rice, cinammon, cloves, nutmets, 25 lbs. salt, five of saleratus, ten of dried apples, one bushel beans, a few lbs. dried beef, five of dried peaches, 25 lbs. seed grain, one gallon of alcohol, 20 lbs. of soap, four or five fish hooks and lines, 15 lbs of iron and steel, a few lbs wrought nails, from 25 to 100 lbs farming and mechanical tools, a bake kettle, frying pan, coffee pot, tea kettle, tin cups, tin plates, knives, forks, spoons and pans as few as will do—a good tent for each 2 families, clothing and bedding not to exceed 500 lbs. This list should be full at the moment of leaving this City."

Brigham Young to Luther C. White, 29 January 1846, Brigham Young Papers. A full stock of supplies weighed at least nineteen hundred pounds and cost up to $1,500.

   33. Journal History, 21 May 1846. The eight-hundred figure was probably an exaggeration, a technique Young used to support his arguments. Earlier, on 28 February, he recorded that one-half of the outfits were actually overloaded, and that while "a considerable number, regardless of counsel, had started in a destitute condition, and some others with only provisions for a few days," many "were provided with provisions for several months." *Manuscript History*, 28 February 1846.

   34. Noted Iowa historian Edgar Harlan observed that the Mormons "drove resistless bargains for their skill and labor with the Iowa settlers." As a result, "the spring of 1846 in the Des Moines Valley above Farmington saw more frontier cabin shanties replaced by two story dwellings

than has occurred, perhaps, in any life time and area in any western state." Edgar R. Harlan, *A Narrative History of the People of Iowa*, 1:212. Nor was all work manual labor. William Clayton frequently refers to playing in fellow pioneer William Pitts's brass band and presenting formal concerts in various Iowa communities. *William Clayton's Journal*, 5. Though time-consuming, without such means of labor and support, many would have perished. The money earned allowed many families to leave Nauvoo later in the spring.

35. See Helen Mar Kimball Whitney, "Our Travels Beyond the Mississippi." *Women's Exponent* 12 (1883–84):102; and Journal History, 26 April 1846. Many were also delayed by the need to exchange horses for oxen, which were better suited for wagon travel. Orson Pratt Journal, 20 March 1846.

36. Regulating this matter of exchanging proceeds realized from the sale of private property for outfits and equipment was one of the most frustrating economic details confronting camp leaders. Occasionally sales would be made and inaccurate records maintained by the agents resulting in harsh feelings among those who felt they had been shortchanged. Not all were as fortunate as apostle Heber Kimball who realized thirty-five yoked oxen plus other provisions from the sale of some of his Nauvoo property. Many felt the trustees were not active enough in selling properties, or favored the church authorities and the rich, criticisms that seem largely unjustified.

Young, sensing the difficulty, demanded that the trustees keep meticulous records and offered the following guidelines:

"Whenever you make sale of the property of any individual which has or may be committed to your charge for that purpose, and receive oxen horses, mules, cows, beeves, sheep, goods, cash or any other articles in payment to make a perfect entry of those identical articles, and when you shall furnish any individual with an outfit with any of those articles, or from any church funds which are or may be in your possession, that you also make a full entry with perfect description of the same and forward us a copy . . . this course strictly adhered too will cut off much occasion of difficulty and hard feeling among the Brethren hereafter."

Brigham Young to A. W. Babbitt, Joseph L. Heywood, and John S. Fullmer, Nauvoo Trustees, 12 March 1846, Brigham Young Papers.

37. Willard Richards to Levi Richards, 9 March 1846, Richards Family Papers.

38. As Willard Richards said, "a few hundred pounds may be exchanged for many hundred pounds of corn, corn meal, flour, oats, pork, etc. and thus accommodate the inhabitants on the route." Willard Richards to Levi Richards, 25 March 1846, Richards Family Papers.

39. See map of the Iowa trek.

40. Brigham Young to Parley P. Pratt, Orson Pratt, George Miller,

"and their brethren," 26 March 1846, Brigham Young Papers. Young threatened to sever Miller and the two Pratt brothers from the church unless they changed their independent attitudes. See *William Clayton's Journal*, 23 March 1846, p. 9.

41. Orson Pratt Journal, 27 March 1846. Further to reorganization, Horace Whitney records that Brigham Young, Heber Kimball, Parley Pratt, John Taylor, Peter Haws, and Bishop Miller, who had formerly been captains of companies were promoted "to the office of president," and their places filled by others. Wrote Whitney:

"In our company the vacancy of the office of captains was filled by Stephen Markham. . . . In each company there was appointed two commissaries and a clerk. In our company the leading commissary is David Yearsley. His business is to go ahead and engage grain, procure jobs for the company, etc. Our distributing commissary is Jedediah M. Grant, whose business it is to distribute corn, oats, etc. when brought into camp. Our clerk is John Pack whose business it is to record all essential matters pertaining to the company."

Helen Whitney "Our Travels Beyond the Mississippi." 118. The captains were likewise instructed to more faithfully observe the sabbath day within their companies and to exercise more spiritual direction, assuming, therefore, many of the duties of a bishop.

42. Journal History, 26 and 27 March 1846.

43. Erastus Snow provided this rationale for the course change:

"Finding it impracticable to haul grain for our teams, in the bad condition of the roads and it being far too early to sustain them upon grass we thought it expedient to deviate from the direct course which we had intended to travel [between the Fox and Des Moines rivers] and bear further south so as to keep near the border settlements where we could obtain feed for our teams."

Erastus Snow Sketch Book, No. 3, 16 March 1846, in Stanley B. Kimball, "The Mormon Trail Network in Iowa 1838–1863. A New Look," *Brigham Young University Studies* 21 (Fall 1981): 419.

44. Banks Ferry, fifty-five miles upriver from St. Joseph, Missouri, at Iowa Point near present-day Oregon, Missouri, had been established by William Banks in 1844. It was fast gaining popularity as a favorite crossing point for Oregon-bound emigrants. *History of Holt and Atchison Counties, Missouri*, 313.

45. Willard Richards to Levi Richards, 25 March 1846, Richards Family Papers. Had they adopted this plan, the Mormon trail west of the Missouri would have followed the Oregon Trail along the southern banks of the Platte River, at least at the outset.

46. Journal History, 26 March 1846.

47. Tullidge, *The Women of Mormondom*, 312.

48. Clare B. Christensen, *Before and After Mt. Pisgah*, 131. Benjamin F.

Johnson described the open prairie as a watered mud flat where "our mules feet like pegs, could find no bottom, and could go no further. So in the open treeless prairies we were compelled to stay." Benjamin F. Johnson, "My Life's Review," Benjamin F. Johnson Papers, 94.

49. It rained at least seventeen days in April. See Journal History, April 1846. William Huntington described their dilemma this way:

> "At 12 p.m. it began to rain with some 200 teams scattered over the flat prairies—roads soon became impassable—wagons constantly sticking and teams doubling and threbling—many wagons were left on the prairie overnight with families cold and without fire."

Huntington, "A History," 9 April 1846.

50. Young cautioned future travellers not to start "with old waggons, old axle trees, old tongues and old any thing and old every thing that will be breaking down every half hour and hindering the whole camp." Brigham Young to A. Babbitt, J. L. Heywood, and J. S. Fullmer, Nauvoo Trustees, 9 March 1846, Brigham Young Papers.

51. See Helen Whitney, "Our Travels Beyond the Mississippi," 126; *The Diary of Hosea Stout*, 10 April 1846; Huntington, "A History," 12 April 1846; and Journal History, 10 April 1846.

52. Their decision to move northwest and set up a farm at the headwaters of the Grand River may have been influenced by Sherwood and John S. Fullmer. Both men, during their travels to the Vermillion the year before, had stumbled upon a site that, as Fullmer said, "we thought a most desirable place for a settlement of the saints, in case a chain of settlements should be made between here [Nauvoo] and the Rocky Mountains." Located some one hundred miles west of Raccoon Barracks and a few miles north of the Council Bluff trail, not far from the Pottawattami villages, the site was reportedly well timbered, watered, and possessing good soil. Concluded Fullmer: "I don't think there is anything to compare with that place." John S. Fullmer to Brigham Young, 18 March 1846, Brigham Young Papers.

53. Brigham Young to A. W. Babbitt, John L. Heywood, and J. S. Fullmer, Nauvoo Trustees, 12 April 1846, Brigham Young Papers. Corn prices ranged from 20 cents to 26 cents per bushel back along the Des Moines River. *William Clayton's Journal*, 23 March and 8 April 1846.

Willard Richards referred to the exhorbitant prices Missourians were charging Mormon traders—from $69 to $80 for a yoke of oxen that in eastern Iowa had sold for $25 and corn as dear as 37 1/2 cents per bushel. Willard Richards to Levi Richards, 1 May 1846, Richards Family Papers.

The change in plans also owed much to the advice of settlers in that area. Commissary Sherwood had visited a Judge Miller who owned a mill on Weldon's Fork of the Grand River where, it was said, "the prospect for trade is good," work projects available, and corn 25 cents per bushel. Miller advised they travel northwest where corn prices would be cheaper. Fear of Missourians does not seem to have been a determining factor. Brigham Young to Heber C. Kimball and "all presidents and captains of the camp of Israel," 5 April 1846, Brigham Young Papers.

54. Journal of Horace K. Whitney, 12 April 1846. For a preliminary study of the Mormon farms, see Lynn Roberts Webb, "The Contributions of the Temporary Settlements Garden Grove, Mount Pisgah and Kanesville, Iowa, to Mormon Emigration, 1846–52." A definitive study of the two farms is yet to be written.

55. See Brigham Young to A. W. Babbitt, J. L. Heywood, and J. S. Fullmer, Nauvoo Trustees, 12 April 1846, Brigham Young Papers; and Journal History, 10 April 1846.

56. Journal of Horace K. Whitney, 19 April 1846.

57. Ibid., 25 April 1846.

58. Journal of Orson Pratt, 27 April 1846.

59. Said one, "We have had no meat of any kind . . . for a number of weeks, but have subsisted principally on sea biscuit, and milk porridge." Journal of Horace K. Whitney, 7 May 1846.

60. Journal of John D. Lee, 2 May 1846.

61. Wrote Helen Whitney: "I remember that day of seeing our men killing snakes in the grass, where our tents were afterwards pitched, and it was enough to give one nervous spasms to see them, and to think of sleeping in the neighborhood of such dangerous enemies." Helen Whitney, "Our Travels Beyond the Mississippi," 127.

62. Parley P. Pratt, *Autobiography of Parley Parker Pratt*, 381. Pratt's autobiography is subject to more than the occasional error and faulty remembrance. For instance, it would appear that both Orson Pratt and Henry G. Sherwood were also instrumental in locating the Mt. Pisgah site. See Journal of Orson Pratt, 15 May 1846.

63. *A Comprehensive History*, 3:55.

64. Leland H. Gentry, "The Mormon Way Stations: Garden Grove and Mt. Pisgah," *Brigham Young University Studies* 21 (Fall 1981): 456–57.

65. William Huntington was elected president with Ezra T. Benson and Charles C. Rich his counselors. Leonard J. Arrington, *Charles C. Rich—Mormon General and Western Frontiersman*, 95.

66. "Sketch of Ezra T. Benson," Journal History, 16 July 1846. Brigham Young praised the new farm in a letter to Samuel Bent back at Garden Grove.

"Good water and healthy. Some good timber but not as abundant as at your place . . . yet there is good farming land plenty. Reptiles scarce only one rattle snake and one green snake have been seen within 8 miles. The council decided this day that if there were brethren at Garden Grove who choose to come on to this place they were at liberty to do so. Should a general feeling to remove prevail we think it

would be well for a few families to tarry so as to keep possession of
our improvements for they are valuable and ought to bring something sometimes."

Brigham Young to Samuel Bent, 20 May 1846, Brigham Young Papers.
    67. A. W. Babbitt and J. L. Heywood, Nauvoo Trustees, to Brigham
Young, 11 March 1846, Brigham Young Papers.
    68. Journal of Orson Pratt, 28 April 1846. This business of temple
sales is an unexplored area in LDS history. It appears that Young may
have first broached the topic even before the exodus from Nauvoo
but was rebuffed. Now in much more stringent conditions, his colleagues were less opposed but not warmly supportive of the idea. Wrote
George A. Smith in a letter to Young,

> "We have felt much anxiety on that subject until we all agreed in
> council not to sell it last winter. But if you in your wisdom should
> think it best to sell the same to help the poor in the present emergency
> we frankly concur, notwithstanding we feel opposed to a Methodist
> congregation ever listening to a mob Priest in that holy Place, but are
> willing to sacrifice our feelings at all times for the good of the saints."

George A. Smith to Brigham Young and Council, 26 April 1846, Brigham Young Papers.
    69. Strang's arguments were based on his reading of the deeds to both
temples, which stated such properties belonged to Joseph Smith and to
his "successors in the First Presidency." Since Strang had already established his own First Presidency and Brigham Young was months away
from that development, this may have proved one of the legal barriers
to the sales. *Voree Herald*, September 1846, vol. 1, no. 9, p. 2. "All we ask
of the Brighamites, is that they will not burn the Temple down and lay it
to the mob."
    70. Journal of Orson Pratt, 29 April 1846. The initial asking price for
the Nauvoo Temple was set at $200,000, compared to a construction
cost of $600,000 to $750,000. (Robert Bruce Flanders, "Nauvoo—Kingdom of the Mississippi.") Word was sent back to the trustees and Orson
Hyde to make every effort to consummate the transactions. Young was
definitely counting on a sale of the Nauvoo Temple as several potential
buyers were reportedly interested, including Mr. W. Brunson who desired to use the temple as a literary institution (James Whitehead to
Brigham Young, 18 August 1846, Brigham Young Papers), and later, a
more serious applicant, M. Paulding of New Orleans (Joseph L. Heywood to Brigham Young, 2 October 1846, Brigham Young Papers). Apparently Young was expecting a quick sale, since he left specific instructions for the trustees to bring $25,000 of the total proceeds to the Mt.
Pisgah settlement. (See the Council of the Twelve to Orson Hyde and
Wilford Woodruff, 30 April 1846, Brigham Young Papers; and *William
Clayton's Journal*, 25.)

In light of this decision to sell, Young's determination all along to complete the temple may have owed more to economics than to prophecy. A completed structure would be most attractive to educational societies or other churches and would consequently demand a much higher price. Whether the rank-and-file temple builders or general church membership had deciphered this possibility beforehand is uncertain, but few, if any, objected once the intention was announced at Winter Quarters. In the absence of government work contracts, temple sales were essential.

Neither temple sold due in large measure to the unstable social climate in Nauvoo, legal barriers imposed by those opposed to Young, and at Kirtland by various Strangite followers.

71. Journal History, 26 April 1846.

72. Council of the Twelve to Orson Hyde and Wilford Woodruff, 30 April 1846, Brigham Young Papers.

73. Journal History, 3 May 1846.

74. Huntington, "A History," 18 April 1846. Huntington eventually received permission to accompany the Twelve if he could supply himself with the necessary provisions, but his destitute plight mirrored that of many others. "I had no team of my own wherewith to go on—no meat, no flour, no corn meal, except a few quarts of parched corn meal—had no milk and only a few crackers and how I should be provided for the Lord only knew. I did not. My soul was troubled." 27 and 28 April 1846.

75. Journal of John D. Lee, 18 April 1846.

76. Ibid., 19 April 1846.

77. See Journal History, 20 May 1846; and De Voto, *Year of Decision*, 239.

78. Journal History, 20 May 1846.

79. Journal of John D. Lee, 7 June 1846.

80. Stanley B. Kimball, *Discovering Mormon Trails New York to California 1831–1868*, 15. Roy Lawson in his thesis on the Mormon trek across Iowa agrees with another scholar of early Iowa travelers, Jacob Van der Zee, that the advance Mormon company followed a northern route crossing through the present town of Greenfield, into Cass County, arriving at an Indian village on the east Nishnabotona River, a few miles north of Griswold. They then travelled southwest into Pottawattamie County "through the townships of Wright, Woveland, Macedonia, Keg Creek, Lewis and Kane" bringing them to Indian Creek which they followed forming a camp in the form of a hollow square called Miller's Hollow on the Missouri River. Later companies apparently followed a slightly more southerly, more direct route from Mt. Pisgah to the Missouri. Lawson, "The Mormons: Their Trek Across Iowa," 45–46.

81. *Manuscript History*, 8 June 1846.

CHAPTER 3

1. William S. Muir to Brigham Young, 11 June 1846. Brigham Young Papers.

2. Their herds were estimated at between 10,000 and 30,000 head of cattle alone. The lower figure was likely closer to the truth.

3. Many who left Nauvoo in March and April, as originally planned, made the Iowa crossing in excellent time—five to eight weeks.

4. Sometimes called "Pull-Point" by the Mormons. Peter Sarpy had been in charge of the post at Trader's Point since at least 1834, but by 1846 was virtually a free agent. Coming from a long line of explorers, fur trappers, and traders, his father, Gregoire Berald Sarpy, had been the first man to navigate the Missouri River in keelboats. Peter Sarpy's brothers, Thomas and John, were clerks for the American Fur Company. He had both an Indian and a white wife living on either side of the river. Eccentric and excitable and one who loved horses and liquor, Sarpy became a wealthy man, later opening stores at St. Mary's and Decatur, Nebraska, and farming large acreages near Council Bluffs, Iowa. He died in 1865. See Charles Kelly, ed., *Journals of John D. Lee 1846–47 and 1859*, 44; Lawrence D. Clark Papers; and Hiram Martin Chittenden, *The American Fur Trade of the Far West*, 1:390.

5. The history of the Blockhouse long preceded the arrival of the Mormons. The local Pottawattami tribes, originally of Algonquin extraction from homelands near the Great Lakes, had by an 1835 treaty sold their eastern lands for a large tract of land in western Iowa roughly between the Missouri and Nishnabotona rivers.

Sensitive to Pottawattami fears of attacks and atrocities from certain marauding, war-loving bands of Sioux, the War Department dispatched Colonel Stephen Watts Kearny to the Pottawattami tract, where he supervised the construction of a small fort or blockhouse. Later, in the spring of 1848, the Jesuit priest Father Pierre Jean de Smet, a name synonymous with the Catholic Christianization of the Indians in America's northwest, established the St. Joseph's Mission among the Pottawattami. Kearny permitted the use of the Blockhouse by Father De Smet, who promptly remodeled the crudely made, windswept cabin post into a miniature churchhouse, hospital, and Catholic community center for the local Indians. D. C. Bloomer, "The Old Blockhouse in Council Bluffs," *Annals of Iowa* 2:549. The Blockhouse, bounded by Broadway, Voorhis, Union, and State streets in Council Bluffs, was torn down in 1855.

6. Heber Kimball's scribe described the view from their encampment:

"[The river] is her[e] only about 1/4 of a mile wide and the bank on this side is about 15′ high and rest up and down so that somebody had to dig out steps so as to get down to get water. The hills which incloses this great meadow are consisting of yellow clay. On the other

side the river is thick with willows and cotton trees but the higher up seemeth to be good timber."
Journal of Heber C. Kimball, 14 June 1846.

7. Journal History, 15 June 1846.

8. A conservative levy of $1 per wagon ferried would have cost the Mormons $2,000—a prohibitive sum. This might also explain, in part, why they decided against Banks' Ferry.

9. Journal of John D. Lee, 14 June 1846. Frederick Kesler was put immediately in charge of construction (Journal History, 15 June 1846). This first so-called "Mormon Ferry" was located several miles north of Sarpy's and north of Council Point at a location more convenient to their Mosquito Creek camp (Diary of Hosea Stout, 26 April 1847, 1:163–64; and the Journal of Eliza R. Snow, 28 August 1846). When completed on 29 June, it was one of the largest ferries on the river, big enough to transport three wagons simultaneously (Journal History, 28 June 1846; and Journal of Heber C. Kimball, 6 July 1846). Yet even a new ferry failed to solve the problem of the steep, almost perpendicular embankments on the west side, which one observer described as "one of the steepest hills" he had ever seen, "and at the same time very rough." Journal of Heber C. Kimball, 13 July 1846.

10. See Journal History, 15 June 1846; and Journal of Warren Foote, 10 July 1846. Pinpointing the exact location of the Mosquito Creek encampment is almost impossible because so many fanned out in all directions.

11. Brigham Young to William Huntington, 14 June 1846, Brigham Young Papers. For more on the Mormons and the Indians, see Chap. 5.

12. Lawrence G. Coates, "Brigham Young and Mormon Indian Policies: The Formative Period, 1836–1851," Brigham Young University Studies 18 (Spring 1978): 428–30. Mormon missionaries had proselyted among the Pottawattami as late as 1845.

Actually, the Pottawatami had some cause for celebration because of a recent treaty with the United States to sell their lands in western Iowa at a high price for a new home in the southwest, a fact that may have contributed to the spirit of cooperation between the two groups. The settlement also provided them with an extra measure of protection against the dreaded Sioux. The total cash settlement was $850,000. Most began moving to their new home in the summer of 1847. Leland L. Sage, A History of Iowa.

13. Journal of John D. Lee, 15 June 1846. No one was to trade, negotiate, or in any other way transact business with Indian tribes without prior permission from the federal government and its licensed appointees. When Young first met with the Indian agents at Council Bluffs, he came in contact with the capillaries of a large and complicated federal bureaucracy.

The Office of Indian Affairs (presently the Bureau of Indian Affairs) was originally established in 1824 as part of the War Department and remained a part of that agency until transferred to the Department of the Interior twenty-five years later. A commissioner of Indian affairs was first appointed in 1832 and bore responsibility for implementing government policies, programs, treaties, and other concerns with Indian tribes all over the country. The Washington headquarters supervised two types of field jurisdictions—superintendencies and agencies. Superintendencies were field headquarters responsible for Indian affairs over a vast geographic region and supervised relations among all Indian tribes within their area and between tribes and persons having business with them. Additionally, superintendents controlled all conduct and account of agents.

The jurisdiction of the St. Louis Superintendency, established in 1822, was originally very expansive, stretching from the Missouri River to the Rockies and encompassing thirty-four tribes from the Apache in the south to the Sioux in the north. By the 1840s five agents reported to St. Louis: the Upper Missouri agency among the Sioux; the Council Bluffs agency; the Fort Leavenworth agency among the Kansas, Shawnee and Delaware; the Great Nemaha subagency among the Iowa Indians; and the Osage River subagency. Thomas H. Harvey held the superintendency from 1843 to 1849 and was succeeded by David D. Mitchell.

The agents and subagents, closest government representatives to the Indians, were charged with maintaining and restoring peace, persuading tribes into ceding lands, distributing annuities and goods as required by treaty, implementing efforts at farming, and education.

The Council Bluffs agency, established in 1837 was discontinued in 1857, had oversight of the Omaha, Oto, Missouri, and Pawnee Indians in eastern Nebraska. The Council Bluffs agent originally worked out of Fort Leavenworth, but gradually spent an increasing amount of his time in Bellevue.

With the arrival of the Pottawattami at the Missouri, Edwin James was appointed Council Bluffs subagent and established himself just across the river, four miles south of the Council Bluffs agency at Bellevue. When abandoned in 1845, some of the original buildings were moved by Sarpy north five or six miles to a crossing point directly opposite Bellevue, thirty-five miles north of the Missouri line. This place became Trader's Point, or Pointe-aux-Poules, the local ferry crossing and Sarpy's new headquarters and official trading station for most of the local Indians on both sides of the river. North of Trader's Point and on the same side of the river, David Hardin, first farmer to the Council Bluffs subagency, had erected a gristmill at or near the junction of Mosquito Creek and the Missouri River, which was popularly called Council Point. It was just north of the local steamboat landing for the entire Council Bluffs region. See Edward E. Hill, *The Office of Indian Affairs, 1824–1880: Historical Sketches;* Van der Zee, "Episodes," 344; and Bloomer, "The Old Blockhouse," 549.

14. R. B. Mitchell to Thomas H. Harvey, 29 June 1846, Kane Papers, Brigham Young University Library.

15. Journal History, 21 July 1846. Affidavit of R. B. Mitchell.

16. Nor was Mitchell the only government official initially impressed with the Mormons. William E. Prince, a military officer at Fort Leavenworth, having heard rumors of Mormon antagonisms, dispatched a Lieutenant Lincoln to the Bluffs in the latter half of June to ascertain "their numbers and condition." From Lincoln's report, Prince formed a positive impression. "Their general appearance indicates poverty, they are however making every exertion, consistent with their means, for Emigration; order and quiet prevades their movements and thus for no act of theirs have given occasion for adoption of any feelings." William E. Prince to R. B. Garnett, 2 July 1846, Post Letters Sent, Post Leavenworth, National Archives, Washington, D.C., as quoted in John F. Yurtinus, "A Ram in the Thicket: The Mormon Battalion in the Mexican War," 1:41–42.

17. See Journal of John D. Lee, 18 June 1846; and Journal History, 19 June 1846.

18. Brigham Young to William Huntington, 22 June 1846, in Huntington, "A History." The year 1846 was the twilight of the great American fur trade. Since the days of Lewis and Clark in 1804, the Missouri River valley had been the main American shipping lane for furs. In succession, the Missouri Fur Company, and finally the most famous of them all, the American Fur Company, all took turns in monopolizing the American fur trade and in competing with the pervasive Hudson's Bay Company to the north. But by 1840, with a lessening demand for beaver and other furs, with the Indians ravished by disease, weakened by alcohol, and in retreat from the ever-advancing borders of civilization, the fur business was in steep decline. See Chittenden, *The American Fur Trade.*

19. Journal of John D. Lee, 18 and 19 June 1846. Emmett had been a persistent problem to everyone concerned. Until the spring of 1846, he and his company had been among the Sioux at the Vermillion River, but upon the orders of Indian agents and church leaders had moved south. Early in June, the Emmett party had reached the Bluffs, intending to merge with the main companies and set up camp approximately thirty-five miles south of Mosquito Creek, on the east bank near the Missouri state line, in order to be close to trading centers. Emmett, meanwhile, had offended his wife, alienated most of his followers, and disturbed Indian agents when it was learned he secretly had taken a squaw as another wife. He had also stolen seven Indian horses. His impolitic actions caused most of his bedraggled followers to abandon him for the main camp then nearing the Missouri River. (See *Diary of Hosea Stout,* 20 June 1846, 1:168; and Journal of John D. Lee, 11 June 1846.)

Emmett's assignment to go with Miller may have been an attempt on Young's part to put distance between Emmett and the main camp and to defuse a potentially explosive issue. Whatever the cause, he instructed Emmett and whoever wanted to go with him to accompany Miller on the fur mission to the Grand Island. The rest of Emmett's original camp was given the choice of going with Miller and Emmett or of staying where they were till further notice. (William Huntington to Brigham Young, 14 June 1846, Brigham Young Papers.)

20. Manuscript History, 25–26 June 1846.

21. Journal History, 27 June 1846.

22. Lawrence G. Coates, "Refugees Meet: The Mormons and Indians in Iowa," *Brigham Young University Studies* 21 (Fall 1981):509.

23. Manuscript History, 25–26 June 1846.

24. Frank Alfred Golder, *The March of the Mormon Battalion from Council Bluffs to California*, 96.

25. Journal History, 27 and 28 June 1846.

26. Brigham Young to William Huntington and Council at Mt. Pisgah, 28 June 1846, Brigham Young Papers.

27. Journal of Heber C. Kimball, 29 June 1846.

28. *Diary of Hosea Stout*, 30 June 1846, 1:172.

29. James Allen had been a captain in the U.S. Army since 1837. A native of Ohio, he had graduated from West Point Military Academy in 1829 in the same class as Robert E. Lee and Joseph E. Johnston. He had accompanied Henry R. Schoolcraft in his 1832 expedition to find the headwaters of the Mississippi River. In 1842 he had been assigned to Fort Atkinson in Iowa Territory to supervise the Sac and Fox Indian agency. Between 1842 and 1845 he had travelled extensively all over Iowa territory. Allen died 23 August 1846.

See C. Stanley Stevenson, "Expeditions Into Dakota," *South Dakota Historical Collections*, 9:347–49.

30. Huntington, "A History," 26 June 1846.

31. Ibid. Nearly eighty men in the Mt. Pisgah vicinity volunteered for the pioneer camp.

32. Journal of Wilford Woodruff, 26 June 1846.

33. Journal History, 30 June 1846.

34. Jesse C. Little to Brigham Young, 6 July 1846, Brigham Young Papers. See Chap. 1.

35. Journal History, 6 July 1846. Two such letters were written to George Bancroft, Secretary of the Navy, and Amos Kendall, former Postmaster General. See Golder, *March of the Mormon Battalion*, 26.

36. See Leonard J. Arrington, "'In Honorable Remembrance': Thomas L. Kane's Services to the Mormons," *Brigham Young University Studies* 21 (Fall 1981)"389–90; and Albert L. Zobell Jr., *Sentinel in the East: A Biography of Thomas L. Kane*, 3–4. Most Mormons view Kane extremely favorably, as a sympathizer and indispensable supporter and mediator of the Mormon cause. Bernard De Voto, however, without minimizing Kane's immense and timely influence for the good of the Mormon cause, has described Kane as "a romantic and neurotic young

man, sentimental humanitarian, the kind of miniature Gerrit Smith who loved all good workers and by the hundred obstructed the path of serious reformers." De Voto, *Year of Decision*, 237. A bust of Kane is on permanent display in the rotunda of the Utah state capitol building, a silent testimony to the place of honor Kane holds in Mormon and Utah history.

37. Part of Kane's letter to Mr. Dallas said,

> "He [Little] visits Washington, too, I believe, with no other object than the laudable one of desiring aid of the government for his people, who forced by persecution to found a new commonwealth in the Sacramento valley, still retain American hearts, and would not willingly sell themselves to the foreigner, or forget the old commonwealth they leave behind them."

Thomas L. Kane to the Honorable George M. Dallas, Vice-President of the United States, 18 May 1846, Thomas L. Kane Papers. It appears that Little believed the Mormons would settle in present-day California.

38. Milo Quaife, ed., *The Diary of James K. Polk, During His Presidency, 1845 to 1849*, 400 and 404. Almost every state in the union wanted representation, although the war was much more popular in the south and west than in New England. The immediate cause of the war had been the outbreak of hostilities in southern Texas over boundary disputes. Texas claimed all territory south of the Rio Grande while Mexico maintained that the border was further north at the Nueces River. Polk accepted the Texas claim and ordered General Zachary Taylor to occupy the disputed strip. Such an act of deliberate provocation enticed Mexican forces to cross the river and engage the Americans in late April. A more serious cause of the conflict was the American design to wrestle New Mexico and, more especially, California from Mexican half-hearted control before Great Britain made claim to the area. See Charles L. Dufour, *The Mexican War—A Compact History 1846–1848*; De Voto, *Year of Decision*; and David M. Pletcher, *The Diplomacy of Annexation: Texas, Oregon, and the Mexican War.*

39. Dufour, *The Mexican War*, 88.

40. Quaife, *The Diary of James K. Polk*, 436–37.

41. Ibid., 437.

42. Golder, *The March of the Mormon Battalion*, 34.

43. W. Ray Luce has argued that this was "the first recorded mention of a Mormon fighting group" and replaced the previous ideas of the Mormons building stockades or other forts along western overland trails or of shipping provisions and munitions on contract for the government. See W. Ray Luce, "The Mormon Battalion: A Historical Accident?" *Utah State Historical Quarterly* 42 (Winter 1974):33.

44. Golder, *March of the Mormon Battalion*, 83.

45. Thomas L. Kane to Elisha Kane, 29 May 1846, Kane Papers. The British communications probably were invitations to settle Vancouver

Island. Months later, Orson Hyde, Parley P. Pratt, and John Taylor presented a petition bearing 13,000 names to the British House of Commons and Her Majesty, Queen Victoria, proposing a plan for Mormon migration to Oregon on Vancouver Island. See Manuscript History, 8 February 1847. Whether the Mormons were serious, it was an effective bargaining tool.

46. Ibid. The president provided Kane with personal letters and authorized rights of passage that Kearny immediately recognized.

47. Quaife, *Diary of James K. Polk,* 444.

48. Ibid., 446.

49. Ibid. 449–50.

50. Luce, "Historical Accident?" 37.

51. Luce, "Historical Accident?" 28. Luce's argument is accepted by Yurtinus, "A Ram in the Thicket."

52. Dwight L. Clarke, *Stephen Watts Kearny—Soldier of the West,* 395.

53. Ibid., 396–97.

54. Governor J. C. Edwards to W. L. Marcy, 11 August 1846, as quoted in Golder, *March of the Mormon Battalion,* 97–98.

55. Colonel Stephen W. Kearny to Captain James Allen, 19 June 1846, as quoted in Golder, *March of the Mormon Battalion,* 101.

Ten months after Marcy's orders were dated to Kearny, Mormon leaders first heard of their exact content in a letter from William Pickett to Brigham Young. Having seen the published order in St. Louis, Pickett described them in detail taking full notice of the one-third provision. They made no reference to any statement of waiting until they arrived in California.

56. Colonel Stephen W. Kearny to Captain James Allen, 26 June 1846, as quoted in Golder, *March of the Mormon Battalion,* 101–103.

57. Journal of Heber C. Kimball, 1 July 1846.

58. Golder, *March of the Mormon Battalion,* 103.

59. Journal History, 1 July 1846.

60. Arrington, *Great Basin Kingdom,* 21.

61. Journal History, 1 July 1846.

62. It appears that most recruits thought the church would settle on the coast, a belief widely shared in the camps. Had they known they might have to march an additional 1,000 miles or more after their discharge to rejoin their families, recruiting might have been almost impossible.

63. The myth that the Mormon Battalion was the primary cause for the Mormon stay in the wilderness has persisted to the present. It also became popular, not long after the fact, to claim that the Battalion call was a sham, a bait of Mormon-haters such as Missouri's Senator Thomas Benton. As early as 1847, Young, relying on speculation from Kane, was telling his followers that their enemies in Congress believed the Mormons would be too incensed to enlist, which refusal would justify Missouri militia to attack and destroy the saints. See Golder, *March of the*

Mormon Battalion, 104; Daniel Tyler, *A Concise History of the Mormon Battalion in the Mexican War 1846–1847*, 117; and Leonard J. Arrington and Davis Bitton, *The Mormon Experience—A History of the Latter-day Saints*, 99.

If, indeed, the Battalion was but a pretext for a war against the Mormons, no concrete evidence exists to support the claim. True, there was genuine concern over Mormon collusion with the Indians and negotiations with the British, and disagreement over their ultimate destination, all of which Mormon enemies likely fomented. Nevertheless, to conclude that Polk, Marcy, and the administration were scheming for war against the Mormons, at the same time they were straining every resource and using every regiment to win a war whose outcome at that time was anything but certain, is difficult to accept. Furthermore, it would only succeed in driving the Mormons closer to the British or to the Mexicans. Though the Mormons were popularly despised, better that they should be friends than enemies.

64. Journal of Samuel H. Rogers, 5 July 1846.

65. Journal of Wilford Woodruff, 16 July 1846. This myth, too, has perpetuated through the years.

66. Yurtinus, "A Ram in the Thicket," 54.

Some have argued that one reason for the delay (much longer than Allen had stipulated in order to meet the president's time constraints) was because of the dispersion of Mormon camps between Mosquito Creek and Mt. Pisgah and Garden Grove. Though distances invariably complicated recruiting efforts and must be considered a delaying factor, the problems were less of geography and more of attitude. While some were obedient almost without question to Young's request, many others were very much opposed and, like William Huntington, required converting.

67. Regarding Independence, Jackson County, Missouri, and its surrounding regions as "Zion," the promised site of the New Jerusalem, Smith had dedicated the area as a city of refuge and gathering place for the church in August 1831. By 1833 a temple lot had been surveyed, and by year's end 1,200 Mormons had taken up residence in the frontier community. But in the summer and fall, for various political and religious reasons, they were driven out of the county and sought refuge in nearby Clay County. But the same concerns that had aggravated their Jackson County neighbors compelled those in Clay County to expel the Mormons in the summer of 1836. Differences over slavery as well as Mormon interests in the Indians were again dominant factors.

Thus from 1836 to 1838 the Mormons lived in Caldwell and Davies counties, which were purposely created for the Mormon exiles. Their most important community was at Far West, Caldwell County. Davies County, according to Joseph Smith, was sacred land where Adam called his posterity together before his death and where some day he would return. But once again persecution became intense as misunderstandings and prejudices deepened on all sides, resulting in the Haun's Mill Massacre of 1838, in which seventeen Mormons were killed, and in Governor Liburn W. Bogg's executive order to "exterminate" and drive the Mormons from the state. Smith and other leaders were incarcerated in Liberty, Missouri, while the Mormons were driven out of the state to Illinois. Repeated attempts at redress were rebuffed. When President Martin Van Buren received an appeal he replied, "Your cause is just, but I can do nothing for you." See Allen and Leonard, *Story of the Latter-day Saints,* 59–134.

68. William Hall, *Abominations of Mormonism,* 49.

69. Journal of Wilford Woodruff, 3 May 1846. No better evidence of their critical attitude exists than their response to the outbreak of the Mexican War. "I confess that I was glad to learn of war against the United States," said Hosea Stout, "and was in hopes that it might never end untill they were entirely destroyed for they had driven us into the wilderness and was now laughing at our calamities." *Diary of Hosea Stout,* 27 May 1846, 1:163–64.

70. Lucius N. Scovil to Brigham Young, 14 April 1846, Brigham Young Papers.

71. *The Diary of Hosea Stout,* 28 June 1846, 1:172.

72. Journal History, 5 July 1846.

73. Such sentiments were concisely expressed by William Hyde who later became a sergeant in the Battalion.

> "The thoughts of leaving my family at this critical time are inde-scribable. They were far from the land of their nativity, situated upon a lonely prairie with no dwelling but a wagon, the scorching sun beat-ing upon them, with the prospect of cold winds of December finding them in the same bleak, dreary place. My family consisted of a wife and two small children who were left in company with an aged father and mother and a brother. . . . When we were to meet with them again, God only knew."

The Journal of William Hyde as quoted in Tyler, *Concise History of the Mormon Battalion,* 128.

74. Journal History, 13 July 1846.

75. Journal of Wilford Woodruff, 17 July 1846. It was Young's intent that most wages be pooled and administered centrally for the coopera-tive benefit of all. See Chap. 6 for a fuller treatment of this issue.

76. Journal History, 17 July 1846.

77. Ibid., 21 July 1846.

78. *Diary of Hosea Stout,* 5 July 1846, 1:178.

79. Said Helen Whitney of Kane: "This young man looked a mere stripling, being delicate in form as well as features. But we soon learned who he was . . . as it were, like an angel of mercy . . . one whom the Lord, no doubt, raised up to act as a mediator." Whitney, "Our Travels Beyond the Mississippi," 50.

80. Journal of Wilford Woodruff, 11 July 1846. Hosea Stout, one of the more hardened antagonists of the Battalion plan, proved how much Kane's influence assisted recruiting efforts. Having learned of Kane and Little's work in Washington, of the lengthy negotiations, and of Kane's bringing special dispatches to Colonel Kearny, Stout admitted, "This made the matter plain and I was well satisfied for I found that there was no trick in it." *The Diary of Hosea Stout*, 13 July 1846, 1:178.

81. Journal History, 17 July 1846. Thirty-three wives and numerous children accompanied the Battalion. Beside laundresses, most officers took their wives and families. See Kate B. Carter, *The Mormon Battalion*, 14–15.

82. The "Liberty Pole," located approximately two miles south of Redemption Hill or Mosquito Creek encampment, was probably on the west banks of the west Mosquito Creek. Cut and raised by W. Johnston and Samuel N. Rogers on 12 July, it consisted of a white sheet with an American flag underneath. The pole was both the rallying point for the Battalion and a landmark. Another liberty pole was raised at the Elkhorn River, and a third possibly directly across the river from the eventual Winter Quarters encampment.
See Journal of Samuel H. Rogers, 13 July 1846; and George Whitaker, "Life of George Whitaker—A Utah Pioneer," 21.

83. Thomas L. Kane, "'*The Mormons.' A Discourse Delivered Before the Historical Society of Pennsylvania March 26, 1850*," 31. It seems that Kane's recounting of this episode is slightly overdramatic, something Kane was prone to be when drumming up sympathy for the Mormon cause. Helen Whitney says that this song was called "Jewish Maid" and had been introduced in Nauvoo by the popular singer and writer, John Kay. According to Whitney, the chorus was changed by Kay so that after singing "By the rivers of Babylon we sat down and wept, we wept when we remembered Zion," the words were deliberately altered from "No more shall the children of Judah sing" to "Again shall the children of Judah sing the lays of happy time." Concluded Whitney: "this was sung according to the faith of the Saints, who did not weep when they 're-membered Zion' for Zion they had brought with them." Whitney, "Our Travels," 10.

84. Clarke, *Kearny*, 113.

85. Journal History, 5 April 1848.

86. Journal History, 2 July 1846. R. B. Mitchell, Indian subagent, also signed the treaty concluding "I willingly certify that it is for the apparent good of both parties, and that there is no prospects [sic] of evil arising therefrom." For Allen's permission, see Journal History, 10 July 1846.

87. Said Allen: "The Mormon people now in rout [sic] to California are hereby authorized to pass through the Indian country on their rout, and they may make stopping places at such points in the Indian country as may be necessary to facilitate the emigration of their whole people to California, and for each time as may reasonably be required for this purpose." Journal History, 18 July 1846.

88. John Charles Frémont, *The Expeditions of John Charles Fremont, Travels from 1838 to 1844*, 1:182.

89. See Huntington, "A History," 22 June 1846; and Journal History, 7 July 1846.

90. R. B. Mitchell to Thomas H. Harvey, 29 June 1846, Kane Papers.

91. Journal History, 7 July 1846.

92. Ibid.

93. Journal History, 20 July 1846.

94. The English difficulties were not entirely unknown. Woodruff had complained of these matters as early as the previous October. "It has caused me tears and sorrow," Woodruff then wrote from England, and "I have grown old under it." Elders Hedlock, Ward, and Clark of the Joint Stock Company, the agency established to coordinate emigration affairs, prevented Woodruff from examining the emigration office minute books and account ledgers. Although he at one time called for their dismissal for mismanaging funds, Woodruff later concluded matters had improved and were well under control. See Wilford Woodruff to Brigham Young, 1 October and 24 October 1845, Brigham Young Papers.

But by the time Woodruff had reported back in person, matters had so deteriorated that the three other apostles were dispatched, and they arrived in England 3 October 1846. Learning that £1500 of hard-earned immigration contributions—money that would have financed chartering ships for passage of English Mormons to America—had been "squandered" and that debts were being incurred at the rate of £300 per year, they took stern action. Wrote Hyde and Taylor: "Every department was run into debt just as far as possible" as Hedlock and company had embezzled funds for their own private purposes. Hedlock was excommunicated, and Ward disfellowshipped on 17 October 1846. Hyde was highly critical of Woodruff's failure to "clean house" earlier. See Orson Hyde and John Taylor to Brigham Young, 22 October 1846, Brigham Young Papers; Manuscript History, 17 October 1846.

95. Journal of Horace K. Whitney, 21 July 1846.

96. Journal History, 29 June 1846.

97. Journal of Heber C. Kimball, 27 July 1846.

98. Journal History, 27 July 1846. George Miller had also learned firsthand that the Pawnee would not willingly permit a Mormon stay. The Pawnee were off hunting when Miller arrived at their village, but visiting Ponca Indians informed Miller "that it would not do at all; that our big captain knew nothing about Indian customs, that the Pawnees wintered their horses at Grand Island, and that our immense herd would eat up all the feed before winter would be half gone, and when the Pawnees came in from their summer hunt they would kill all our cattle and drive us away." The plan, at least in the eyes of the Ponca, "was wholly impracticable." Mills, "De Tal Palo," 107.

99. *Diary of Hosea Stout*, 31 July 1846.

100. See Journal of John D. Lee, 1 August 1846; and Journal of Horace K. Whitney, 17 July 1846.
101. See Journal of Heber C. Kimball, 20 July 1846; and Journal History, 20 July 1846.
102. Journal of John D. Lee, 7 August 1846.

CHAPTER 4

1. The precise location of the Cold Springs encampment is uncertain. Some contemporary writers said it was thirteen miles from Mosquito Creek while others claimed it was only four miles from Council Point. See Heber C. Kimball Journal, 13 July 1846; and Journal of Horace K. Whitney, 21 October 1846. A consensus estimate would place it four miles from the west bank landing in present Omaha, Nebraska. Gail Holmes contends it was on the Little Papio Creek just north of Interstate 80 and near the corner of 61st and Patterson streets in Omaha. See Gail George Holmes, "Winter Quarters Revisited—Untold Stories of the Seven-Year Stay of Mormons in the Missouri Valley 1846–53," 19–20; and Holmes's leaflet "Historic Mormon Sites to Visit in Greater Omaha–Council Bluffs."

2. The history of whites in the area begins with Lewis and Clark, who in the summer of 1804 disembarked just north of present Omaha on the west side and named the spot Council Bluffs, later called Ft. Calhoun. In 1811, Manuel Lisa, early developer of the Missouri Fur Company, established Fort Lisa in the same region. Eight years later in 1819, Colonel Henry Atkinson established a military post and engineer encampment just one-half mile north of Fort Lisa and five miles below the original Council Bluffs. Initially named Camp Missouri, it was successively called Cantonment Missouri, Cantonment Council Bluffs, and finally in 1820, Fort Atkinson, at which time it was removed to the old Council Bluffs site. Fort Atkinson was abandoned in 1827. See Van der Zee, "Episodes in the Early History of the Western Iowa Country," 331; Chittenden, *The American Fur Trade* 1:114; and Mattes, *The Great Platte River Road,* 104–22.

3. Journal of Heber C. Kimball, 20 July 1846.

4. See Brigham Young to Captain Jefferson Hunt and all members of the Mormon Battalion, 19 August 1846, Brigham Young Papers; and Journal of Heber C. Kimball, 7 August 1846.

5. The exact site of Cutler's Park probably corresponds to where Springville school now stands at the corner of 60th and Girard streets in Omaha. Other local historians have suggested the boundaries as 48th, 60th, State streets and Hartman Avenue, which includes the west half of Forest Lawn Cemetery. The author, who has visited the site on several different occasions, believes it was situated on either side of Mormon Bridge Road west of Forest Lawn Cemetery and included Potter Field, now an old cemetery lot.

6. See *Diary of Hosea Stout*, 7 August 1846, 1:184; and Kane, "The Mormon," 84.

7. See *Diary of Hosea Stout*, August 1846, 1:184; and Manuscript History of Cutler's Park, 9 August 1846. The organization of a High Council was nothing new in church history. Such had served as the local seat of church government at Kirtland, Far West, and at Nauvoo. What apparently was different here was the name "Municipal" High Council and its secular functions in the absence of a mayor and other elected civic officials.

8. Constituting the Municipal High Council were Alpheus Cutler as president, Reynolds Cahoon, Cornelius P. Lott, Albert P. Rockwood, Ezra Chase, Daniel Russell, Alanson Eldredge, Thomas Grover, Jedediah M. Grant, Samuel Russell, Winslow Farr, and Benjamin L. Clapp. Manuscript History of Cutler's Park, 7 August 1846.

9. Journal History, 9 September 1846.

10. See Journal of John D. Lee, 9 August 1846; and Journal History, 9 August 1846.

11. *Diary of Hosea Stout*, 12 August 1846, 1:186.

12. See Journal of Willard Richards, 12 August 1846; and Winter Quarters High Council Minutes, 13 August 1846. The 1st Division also included 359 wagons, 1,051 oxen, 142 horses, and 588 cows.

13. Winter Quarters High Council Minutes, 4 September 1846. These divisions were in part family units, since many leaders of the various subdivisions had been "spiritually" adopted into either Brigham Young's or Heber C. Kimball's families in the Nauvoo Temple. Those daily arriving who were not yet "adopted" or attached were assigned to one or the other at least temporarily. A third division was organized September 9th in order to accommodate the ever-swelling population. Winter Quarters High Council, 17 August 1846. For more on adoption see Chap. 10.

14. Journal of Horace K. Whitney, 3 October 1846.

15. Winter Quarters High Council Minutes, 28 August 1846.

16. Ibid. See also Journal History, 28 August 1846.

17. Winter Quarters High Council Minutes, 28 August 1846.

18. The treaty, officially signed 31 August 1846, read as follows:

"We the undersigned chiefs and braves representative of the Omaha nation of Indians, do hereby grant to the Mormon people the privilege of tarrying upon our lands for two years or more, or as long as may suit their convenience, for the purpose of making the necessary preparations to prosecute their journey west of the Rocky Mountains, provided that our great father, the president of the United States, shall not counsel us to the contrary.

"And we also do grant unto them the privilege of using all the wood and timber that they shall require.

"And we furthermore agree that we will not molest their cattle, horses, sheep, or any other property.

                    Big Elk   Standing Elk   Little Chief"

Journal History, 3 September 1846. Significantly nothing was included about Indian ownership of improvements.

19. Journal History, 9 September 1846.

20. Helen Whitney, "Scenes and Incidents at Winter Quarters," *Woman's Exponent* 13 (1884–85):91.

21. Journal History, 5 September 1846. That the wells at Cutler's Park were not yielding sufficient water was another factor.

The new or "upper" ferry was in fact the first one moved north approximately twenty miles. It was designed to provide a much more direct course between Miller's Hollow on the east side near the Blockhouse and Winter Quarters on the west side, thereby eliminating the long and hazardous journey up steep bluffs that had always characterized the original or "lower" ferry. Sarpy, who had been promised eventual use of the Mormon ferry, willingly agreed to the move.

22. Journal History, 8 September 1846.

23. Journal of Wilford Woodruff, 18 September 1846.

24. Manuscript History of Cutler's Park, 10 and 11 September 1846.

25. Journal of Wilford Woodruff, 23 September 1846.

26. *Diary of Hosea Stout,* 24 September 1846, 1:201.

27. Thomas H. Harvey to William Medill, Commissioner of Indian Affairs, 3 December 1846 as quoted in Oscar G. Winther, ed., *The Private Papers and Diary of Thomas L. Kane,* 25–29.

28. Many remembered all too well the sickness and death suffered by the inhabitants of the swampy, low-lying, riverfront areas of Nauvoo.

29. Journal of Eliza R. Snow, 22 September 1846.

30. Winter Quarters High Council Minutes, 16 September 1846. Heber C. Kimball, who professed to know something about "philosophy" and the workings of chemistry, observed "that the best mettals was always the heaviest and when melted would settle at the bottom and the bad [impure air contaminants] or useless dross arise and run off and he believed the principle was true and would carry out on any or all subjects."

31. See Journal History, 23 September 1846; and Whitney, "Scenes and Incidents," 13:115. In Nauvoo, each block contained four one-acre lots.

32. The number of lots later increased to 820 as the city expanded. See Journal History, 26 February 1847.

33. Most wells were thirty-five feet deep and built with stones readily available from the riverbed. Journal of Horace K. Whitney, 31 December 1846.

34. Winter Quarters High Council Minutes, 22 September 1846.

35. Wilford Woodruff records that on his block two families were as-

signed per lot, or forty families to the block. Journal of Wilford Woodruff, 23 September 1846.

36. Journal of Norton Jacob, 24–26 September 1846; and Journal
History, 29 September 1846.

37. See Journal of Horace K. Whitney, 23 September 1846; and Journal of Wilford Woodruff, 23 September 1846.

38. Journal History, 24 February 1847. Later the vacated land was
used for planting garden crops.

39. Account book of Gilbert Belnap, 21 September 1846.

40. See Journal History, 22 September 1846; and Journal of Norton
Jacob, 22 September 1846.

41. A Methodist minister who lived near Winter Quarters as early as
1848 has commented on the scarcity of timber in the region:

"In the uplands the trees were more scattering and shorter, requir-
ing, according to the idiom of the country, two trees in order to get a
log long enough to make a fence post. Indeed, timber was so scarce in
the bluffs that we did not expect to see the prairie between the Missouri and the Nishnabotona all settled up in our lifetime."

Reverend John Todd, *Early Settlement and Growth of Western Iowa*, 64.

42. Wrote R. B. Mitchell, Indian subagent, concerning woodcutting
on Pottawattami lands: "It becomes my duty to suffer no useless waste
of timber within the limits of the sub-agency. I hope that you will charge
strictly those that have settled within my sub-agency to use the timber
only so far as may be necessary for conveniences and comfort." Journal
History, 12 September 1846.

43. See Journal of Horace K. Whitney, 13 October 1846; and Journal
of Joseph G. Hovey, Fall 1846.

44. Journal of Horace K. Whitney, 10 December 1846.

45. See Whitney, 13:139; and Journal History, 11 December 1846.

46. Whitney, "Scenes and Incidents," 13:139.

47. Journal of Horace K. Whitney, 10 November 1846; and Journal
History, 19 December 1846.

48. See Manuscript History of Winter Quarters, 3 December 1846;
Journal of Wilford Woodruff, 3 December 1846; and *Diary of Hosea
Stout:* 2 January 1847, 1,222–28. Richards, a native of upstate New
York, whose octagon house construction flourished in the 1840s and
1850s, very likely had previously seen and studied the relative econom-
ics of octagon clay-building construction.

49. Little is known of the Brigham Young home other than that it was
on Main Street six rods west of Willard Richards's Octagon and close to
the Council House. This would have put it on the southern end of the
city. It had a brick chimney but no windows and was probably similar in
design to Kimball's (Journal History, 8 November 1846 and 7 January
1847). For many years some Florence, Nebraska, area residents believed
that the old James C. Mitchell home on State Street overlooking Flor-

ence Park was the original Young home, but this is not so. See Scrapbook of Lawrence D. Clark.

50. See Journal History, 13 and 22 December 1846; Ray F. Lawson, "The Mormons; Their Trek Across Iowa," 57; and Winter Quarters High Council Minutes, 19 September 1846. It is, unfortunately, impossible to pinpoint the exact location of most buildings in Winter Quarters, since little, if anything, now remains and no plat with house locations has yet been found. An educated guess would place the Council House in block twenty-two not far from Brigham Young's home, which was probably on a corner lot in block twenty-five (Winter Quarters High Council Minutes, 19 September 1846).

Other public buildings included a store, a carding-machine house, a hostel for visitors, and possibly a few small schoolhouses. Winter Quarters High Council Minutes, 16 September 1846.

51. See Record Book of Bathsheba W. Smith, 14; and Journal History, 31 December 1846.

52. *Diary of Hosea Stout*, 24 November 1846, 1:213.

53. Tullidge, *Women of Mormondom*, 316–17.

54. *Diary of Hosea Stout*, 8 July 1847, 1:265.

55. Stegner, *Gathering of Zion*, 107.

56. Whitney, "Scenes and Incidents," 13:134.

57. Tyler, *A Concise History of the Mormon Battalion*, 130. It is a mistake to conclude that Mormon Battalion families possessed inferior housing to the rest; generally, the opposite was true. Latecomers were almost invariably consigned to sod houses or caves. Journal History, 7 August 1847.

If the Mormons were not the first to build sod houses, they were certainly among the first. They may have learned of this style of prairie construction from new settlers in western Iowa Territory.

58. Winter Quarters High Council Minutes, 28 February 1847; and Journal History, 15 February 1847.

59. Journal of Eliza Maria Lyman, May 1847.

60. See Brigham Young to the Nauvoo Trustees, 14 November 1846, Brigham Young Papers; and Journal of Joseph G. Hovey, Fall 1846. As one old settler said, "for twelve years he had not seen such a moderate season."

61. Journal of Thomas Bullock, 28 November 1846.

62. Manuscript History of Winter Quarters, 19 December 1846; and Journal History, 1 April 1848.

63. Journal History, 26 February 1847.

64. Thomas Gregg, *History of Hancock County, Illinois*, 346–47; and James Whitehead to Brigham Young, 18 August 1846, Brigham Young Papers.

65. Elizabeth Gilbert to Brigham Young, 13 August 1846. Brigham Young Papers.

66. Journal History, 25 August 1846.

67. Ibid., 6 October 1846.

68. This first relief mission consisted of Orville M. Allen, Samuel Smith, Amos Tubbs, Pliny Fisher, William H. Kimball, Amasa Russell, John Y. Greene, James McFale, Joseph Knight Jr., Samuel Savoy, Charles Decker, W. G. Steritt, Clement Evans, Peter Van Orden, and one or two others. See Winter Quarters High Council Minutes, 8 September 1846; and Journal History, 9 and 14 September 1846.

69. *Comprehensive History*, 3:1–24.

70. Nauvoo Trustees to Brigham Young, 31 August 1846, Research Card 1400, Nauvoo Restoration Corporation research files of James L. Kimball.

71. The terms of the treaty were: (1) the surrender of all Nauvoo arms, to be returned to the Mormons once across the river; (2) guaranteed safety of all those surrendering; (3) ten men, including the trustees and clerks, to remain in Nauvoo to hasten evacuation and complete business transactions; and (4) a speedy evacuation. *Comprehensive History*, 3:15.

72. Thomas L. Kane, "The Mormons," 9–10. Kane confided to Jesse C. Little, once back in Washington, that he would propagandize "the murderous treatment at Nauvoo" as further ammunition in his efforts to persuade the Polk administration to sympathize with the Mormon plight and permit settlements on both Pottawattami and Omaha lands. "You may depend upon it," Little wrote, "the Colonel [Kane] has done us good." Journal History, 6 October 1846.

This is a good example of the Mormon aptitude for capitalizing on real and perceived injustices. They did it with the Haun's Mill Massacre, with the Mormon Battalion, now with the poor camp, and later with Mt. Pisgah's and Garden Grove's difficulties. If they were to suffer, they would make it pay a dividend in one form or another.

73. Journal History, 7 October 1846.

74. Journal of Thomas Bullock, Fall 1846.

75. Journal History, 27 September 1846.

76. Ibid., 28 September 1846.

77. Bishop Newel K. Whitney, who had already returned to the Mississippi to arrange for the purchase and delivery of the most essential provisions, had reported that a maximum of fifty wagons would be sufficient to remove all the camp. Allen had returned with twenty or more, so that Murdock and Taylor required only an added twenty-five or thirty (Journal History, 6 October 1846). The precise number in the poor camp is difficult to estimate. As late as 31 August trustees estimated 750 adults in Nauvoo and 175 in Leè County, most of whom were barely subsisting and "very destitute of clothing." Research Card 1400, Nauvoo Restoration Corporation research files of James L. Kimball. But by October many had already left. It is estimated from the 151 souls listed in O. M. Allen's return company roster that the total poor camp, including those in Murdock's rescue company, approximated 350 to 400.

78. Journal History, 28 September 1846.
79. Minutes of the Pottawattamie High Council, 2 October 1846.
80. While assisting Allen in organizing the first rescue company in sight of Nauvoo across the river, Thomas Bullock, company clerk, recorded what must have seemed at the time a miraculous occurrence and is even now regarded as a stroke of incredible fortune. On 9 October, at a time when food supplies were in shortest supply, several large flocks of quails flew into camp, some falling on the wagons, some under, some even on the bare breakfast tables. Wrote Bullock:

"The boys caught about 20 alive . . . every man and woman and child had quails to eat for their dinner—after dinner the flocks increased in size. Capton Allen ordd the bren [sic] not to kill, when they had eaten and were satisfied . . . not a gun was afterwards fired and the quails flew round the camp, many a lighted in it . . . this was repeated more than half a dozen times."

To the suffering faithful it was a miraculous sign of providential mercy (Journal of Thomas Bullock, 9 October 1846). Few other accounts of this famous "Mormon miracle" exist. Orville M. Allen's journal at the time was kept by Bullock, and the two accounts are almost verbatim. Kane's report of the incident is likely secondhand, since he probably was not an eyewitness.

81. Kane also began the myth that several children were born while the poor camp languished on the Mississippi's west side. One recent article contends that the pioneer story of nine babies being born in one night did not occur at Sugar Creek as Eliza R. Snow intimated, but in the poor camp. See Carol Lynn Pearson, "'Nine Children Were Born': A Historical Problem from the Sugar Creek Episode," *Brigham Young University Studies* 21 (Fall 1981): 443–44. Pearson relies heavily on the reminiscences of Jane Johnston as dictated orally almost forty years after the fact.

The truth of the matter is that nine children were not born during the entire poor-camp sojourn of over a month near Montrose. Bullock's census of the largest contingent of refugees lists names, birthdates, and birthplaces. Only one child was listed as having been born within the month, and that one at Nauvoo. See Journal of Thomas Bullock, 7 October 1846. The chances of nine children being born within a month's time are minute; nine born the same night beyond belief. More likely the old references are to nine births while Young's first company crossed from Sugar Creek in the east to Mosquito Creek in the west of Iowa.

82. Journal of Thomas Bullock, 15 November 1846. Their sickened state is well remembered. Wrote Bullock: "My wife, washing, although so very sick that she had to leave the wash tub to vomit and when spreading her clothes on the ground to dry, had to lie full length on the prairie." Journal of Thomas Bullock, 25 October 1846.

83. Journal of Thomas Bullock, 22 and 24 November 1846.

84. Record book of Bathsheba Smith, 17.

85. Journal History, 1 February 1847.

86. See George Miller to Brigham Young and the Twelve, 1 August 1846, Brigham Young Papers; and Autobiography of Anson Call, 22 July 1846.

87. Russell Rich, *Ensign to the Nations—A History of the Church from 1846 to the Present*, 83. The Miller camp High Council consisted of George Miller, Newell Knight, Joseph Holbrook, Anson Call, Erastus Bingham, John Mikesell, Thomas Gates, Titus Billings, David Lewis, Hyrum Clark, A. W. Bartholemew, and Charles Chrisman. Autobiography of Anson Call, 22 July 1846.

88. See George Miller to Brigham Young, 13 August 1846, Brigham Young Papers; and Mills, "De Tal Palo," 107.

89. See Journal History, 15 September 1846; Winter Quarters High Council Minutes, 12 December 1847; and Orson Spencer to Brigham Young, 20 October 1846, Brigham Young Papers.

90. Jacob Gates to Brigham Young, 2 September 1846, Brigham Young Papers.

91. Journal History, 9 September 1846.

92. Ibid., 20 August 1846.

93. See *Diary of Hosea Stout*, 15 September 1846, 1:193; Journal History, 9 September 1846; and Journal of Horace K. Whitney, 10 October 1846.

94. Mills, "De Tal Palo," 111.

95. Remembered Anson Call, a member of the Ponca High Council: "They sought to lead the Company into the wilderness, upon their own responsibility independent of the Council of the Twelve. Every member of the council opposed them." Autobiography of Anson Call, Fall 1846. For more on the split, see Chap. 8.

96. Brigham Young to George Miller, 20 September 1846, Brigham Young Papers.

97. Journal History, 1 February 1847; and Autobiography of Joseph Holbrook, 23 August–1 September 1846, p. 47.

98. Autobiography of Joseph Holbrook, 8 September 1846.

99. See Hiram Clark to Brigham Young, 9 September 1846, and Brigham Young to Orson Spencer, 20 October 1846, Brigham Young Papers.

100. Brigham Young to George Miller, 20 September 1846, Brigham Young Papers.

101. Autobiography of Joseph Holbrook, 26 December 1846–31 January 1847. The loss of Newell Knight particularly was mourned among the Mormons, for he had played a prominent role in the very early days of the church in upstate New York.

102. Counting heads has often been an inexact science. An historical count is even more treacherous. Most accounts have inflated estimates of the Latter-day Saint population. The long-assumed number, first presented by John Taylor and later accepted by B. H. Roberts, is 15,000

at the Missouri at the end of 1846. (See *Comprehensive History* 3:52; and *The Latter-day Saints Millenial Star* 8 [November 15, 1846: 114].) J. Sterling Morton, one of Nebraska's finest turn-of-the-century historians, relied on Heman C. Smith, former historian of the Reorganized Church of Jesus Christ of Latter Day Saints, in concluding that 16,000 Mormons crossed the Mississippi with 12,000 of them at the Missouri River by the fall of 1846. (J. Sterling Morton, *Illustrated History of Nebraska*, 134–35). Similarly, William Alexander Linn estimated a very large host, at least 15,000, contending that practically the entire Nauvoo population crossed the Mississippi (Linn, *Story of the Mormons*, 365 and 369). Perhaps both men relied on Kane, who estimated 5,000 scattered over Iowa in the late fall of 1846 and another 11,000 at Winter Quarters and across the river (Winther, *Diary of Thomas L. Kane*, 30–34).

Significantly, the more contemporary the manuscript the more conservative the figures. Thomas H. Harvey, an on-site visitor to Winter Quarters in November 1846, hazarded a guess of 10,000 (Winther, *Diary of Thomas L. Kane*, 25–29). His Council Bluffs Indian agent, R. B. Mitchell, who was a far more frequent visitor to the Mormon communities, estimated a lesser number of between 5,000 and 8,000 (R. B. Mitchell to Thomas H. Harvey, 29 June 1846, Kane Collection).

103. See Journal History, 31 December 1846; and *Diary of Hosea Stout,* 24 December 1846, 1:219. The same study accounted for 814 wagons, 145 horses, 388 1/2 yoke of oxen, and 463 cows.

104. Brigham Young to Sam Brannan, 6 June 1847, Brigham Young Papers.

105. See Journal History, 31 December 1846; and Minutes of the Blockhouse Branch 1846–49, 27 December 1846.

106. The 2,500 figure is based upon the following: (1) membership statistics of two branches that are on record; (2) the fact that several other bishops reported to the Pottawattamie High Council whose jurisdictions were small but nearby; and (3) that only fifty-three of the over five hundred in the Mormon Battalion came from Winter Quarters, the rest coming from the east side and the farms. See Pottawattamie High Council Minutes, 24 July 1846; Journal History, 31 December 1846; and Minutes of Blockhouse Branch.

107. Stanley B. Kimball, "The Saints and St. Louis, 1831–1857: An Oasis of Tolerance and Security," *Brigham Young University Studies* 13 (Summer 1973):507. Kimball argues that in late 1845 only 400 Mormons lived in St. Louis, but by 31 January 1847 the number had more than tripled to 1,478.

108. Journal of Lorenzo Snow, Winter 1846–47; and Journal History, 12 February 1847. This figure is based on five members per family.

109. By using clerk records kept by the poor camp and sexton records at Winter Quarters and Cutler's Park, a preliminary overview of national origins is possible. Based on a sample of 312 people, native Americans constituted 76 percent of the Mormon population; Britains

21 percent; Canadians (Upper and Lower Canada) 2 percent. The five states of New York, Pennsylvania, Illinois, Ohio, and Massachusetts combined to claim 48 percent of the total with New York the largest source of converts. Only 11 percent claimed origin in one of the southern states.

110. The totals given in the text are independently borne out by a non-Mormon observer, Mr. S. Chamberlain, who, heading east from Council Bluffs on 26 June 1846, passed through the many Mormon wagon companies at that time spread clear across Iowa Territory. In a report to the *Hancock Eagle* later carried by the St. Louis *Daily Missouri Republican*, Chamberlain gave the following tabulation:

> "The whole number of teams attached to the Mormon expedition, is about three thousand seven hundred, and it is estimated that each team will average at least three persons, and perhaps four. The whole number of souls now on the road may be set down in round numbers at twelve thousand. From two to three thousand have disappeared from Nauvoo in various directions. Many have left for Council Bluffs by the way of the Mississippi and Missouri rivers—others have dispersed to parts unknown; and about eight thousand or less still remain in Illinois. This comprises the entire Mormon population that once flourished in Hancock county. In their palmy days they probably numbered between fifteen and sixteen thousand souls, most of whom are now scattered upon the prairies, bound for the Pacific slope of the American continent."

Taken from the (St. Louis) *Daily Missouri Republican*, 15 July 1846, p. 2, as found in the Cecil Snider Newsclipping Collection, "Attitudes toward Mormonism in Illinois as Recorded by the Press."

CHAPTER 5

1. The Book of Mormon, Alma 9:16−17.
2. Doctrine and Covenants, 49:24.
3. Journal of Wilford Woodruff, 31 December 1846.
4. Helen Whitney, "Scenes and Incidents," 14:82.
5. Hosea Stout blamed the intrusion on Bishop George Miller for allying himself with the Ponca against the Sioux. Charles Kelly, ed, *Journals of John D. Lee to 1846−47 and 1859*, 12 February 1847, p. 72. However, it is more likely that the Sioux, in their war of extermination against the Omaha, stumbled upon Lathrop's herds without any particular inducement.
6. Journal History, 13 February 1847.
7. Winter Quarters High Council Minutes, 27−28 August 1846.
8. Journal History, 1 August 1846.
9. Ibid., 7 August 1846. "The Omaha frequently deposited their dead in the branches of trees, wrapped in buffalo robes and blankets

leaving with them arrows, pipes and other trinkets, which they considered sacred and they should not remove them."

10. Some writers have argued that Young taught and encouraged interracial marriages. See James S. Brown, *Giant of the Land: Life of a Pioneer*, 320; and Hall, *Abominations of Mormonism Exposed*, 59. But if he ever did consent to it before or after, Young was resolutely opposed to it at the Missouri.

11. Winter Quarters High Council Minutes, 7 August 1846.

12. See Journal History, 26 March 1847; and *Diary of Hosea Stout*, 18 October 1846, 1:205.

13. Journal History, 18 October 1846.

14. Ibid., 25 March 1847.

15. Ibid., 9 December 1846.

16. *Diary of Hosea Stout*, 9 December 1846, 1:216.

17. Ibid., 12 December 1846, 1:217.

18. Journal History, 28 August 1846.

19. Ibid., 7 January 1847. The initial report was of forty deaths but the number increased as more information trickled into camp. See Journal History, 12 December 1846 and 4 January 1847.

20. Diary of Appleton Milo Harmon, Winter 1846−47, p. 10.

21. See Journal History, 12 December 1846; and Journal of Horace K. Whitney, 14 December 1846. Fighting between the Sioux and the Omaha eventually drove the Omaha and Oto into an alliance. William W. Major to Brigham Young, 10 June 1847, Brigham Young Papers.

22. Diary of Appleton Milo Harmon, 10.

23. Journal of Horace K. Whitney, 13 October 1846.

24. Journal History, 15 October 1846.

25. Ibid., 18 October 1846.

26. Brigham Young to Logan Fontenelle, 17 October 1846, Brigham Young Papers.

27. Journal of Heber C. Kimball, 25 October 1846. It was Big Elk's suggestion that a picket fence be raised on the southern line of Winter Quarters.

28. See Journal History, 18 and 24 October 1846; and Journal of Horace K. Whitney, 18 October 1846. Alpheus Cutler thought it best for the people "to live close together in small groups inclosed by a strong fence."

29. *Diary of Hosea Stout*, 18 October 1846, 1:205.

30. Logan Fontenelle to Brigham Young, 12 November and 28 December 1846, Brigham Young Papers. In December these included a tent, two poles, a kettle, and a dress.

31. Journal History, 24 October 1846.

32. *Diary of Hosea Stout*, 18 April 1847, 1:250.

33. See Journal History, 8 May 1847; and Winter Quarters High Council Minutes, 19 April 1847.

34. Winter Quarters High Council Minutes, 19 April 1847; and Journal History, 25 March 1847.

35. *Journal History*, 8 January, 1 and 7 February, and 25 March 1847.
36. Winter Quarters High Council Minutes, 19 April 1847.
37. *Diary of Hosea Stout*, 25 May 1847, 1:256–57.
38. Ibid., 5 June 1847, 1:259. The history of the Danites is as clouded by the lack of firm evidence as it is by the polemical literature bent on proving they were "a Mormon Ku Klux Klan." Begun by Sampson Avard in the summer of 1838 during the Missouri persecutions, this secret society, first called "the Brothers of Gideon," then the "Daughters of Zion," and finally "the Sons of Dan," was established initially to intimidate dissenters and prevent apostates from inciting Missouri retaliations. Later it became a vehicle of aggression to punish non-Mormon troublemakers. Joseph Smith was apparently not a partner in the creation of the band, although Sidney Rigdon, his counselor, apparently played a founding role. Eventually the Danites "went beyond the bounds of legality or propriety and began retaliation against those who had committed crimes against the Saints." See Allen and Leonard, *Story of the Latter-day Saints*, 121.

Apparently such a pirate band continued on in Nauvoo under the names Danites and "Destroying Angels." Bill Hickman and Tom Brown are two names associated with this group. See J. M. Reid, *Sketches and Anecdotes of the Old Settlers, and New Comers, The Mormon Bandits and Danite Band*, 34–36.

For more on the topic of the Danites, see Paul Bailey, *The Armies of God;* Leland H. Gentry, "The Danite Band of 1838," *Brigham Young University Studies* 14 (Summer 1974): 421–50; and Rebecca Foster Cornwall and Leonard J. Arrington, "Perpetuation of a Myth: Mormon Danites in Five Western Novels, 1840–90," *Brigham Young University Studies* 23 (Spring 1983): 147–65.

See also Chap. 9 for a discussion of police at Winter Quarters.
39. *Journal History*, 19 June 1847; and Orson Hyde to Nathaniel H. Felt, 21 June 1847, Brigham Young Papers.
40. See *Diary of Hosea Stout*, 22 June 1847, 1:262; and Manuscript History of Winter Quarters, 24 June 1847.
41. Orson Hyde to Nathaniel H. Felt, 21 June 1847, Brigham Young Papers.
42. *Diary of Hosea Stout*, 24 June 1847, 1:262.
43. Kelly, *Journals of John D. Lee*, 25 June 1847, p. 180.
44. *Diary of Hosea Stout*, 24 June 1847, 1:262.
45. Winter Quarters High Council Minutes, 1 November 1846. Whether Mitchell was such has not been determined.
46. Willard Richards to Thomas L. Kane, 16 November 1846, *Journal History*. According to Richards, Harvey dismissed Case from his employment without pay and ordered him to cross the river.
47. *Journal History*, 6 November 1846.
48. Winter Quarters High Council Minutes, 19 April 1847.
49. Thomas L. Kane to William Medill, Commissioner of Indian Affairs, 21 April 1847, Thomas L. Kane Papers.

50. Robert A. Trennert Jr., "The Mormons and the Office of Indian Affairs: The Conflict Over Winter Quarters, 1846–1848" *Nebraska History* 53 (Fall 1972): 382. Trennert's fine article is somewhat critical of the Mormons and generally defends the actions of the government.

51. Journal History, 24 December 1846. Peter Haws, for one, was found guilty by the High Council for selling liquor to the Indians.

52. Journal of Warren Foote, 16 June 1846.

53. Golder, *March of the Mormon Battalion*, 98–99.

54. Orson Spencer to Brigham Young, 26 November 1846, Brigham Young Papers.

55. See *St. Louis Weekly Union* 30 March 1847; and Journal History, 30 March 1847.

56. L. Frank Marshall to President James K. Polk, 4 July 1846 as quoted in Golder, *March of the Mormon Battalion*, 96.

57. Journal History, 31 August 1846.

58. At another occasion Willard Richards, writing for the Twelve, made it clear that allying with the Indians was never part of their thinking:

"To the oft repeated and unqualified declaration that the 'Mormons' are forming alliances with the Indians and preparing to come down upon the U.S., we offer but one proof; all the tribes we have passed through or located amongst, or are surrounded with that we have any knowledge of, have killed our cattle without number and stolen all our horses they could lay their hands on, and if stealing and death does not assure an alliance, we cannot prove it."

Journal History, 24 February 1847.

59. Journal History, 20 July 1846.

60. William Medill to Thomas H. Harvey, 27 July 1846. Letters sent by the Office of Indian Affairs 1824–82. A follow-up letter of 22 August confirmed this understanding, stressing that while his department would not "violate any principles of hospitality or employ hardship towards people in apparent difficulty and distress, no encouragement must be given to the Mormons to remain in the Indian country a moment beyond a suitable time for them to continue their journey." William Medill to Thomas H. Harvey, 22 August 1846, Letters of the Office of Indian Affairs (OIA).

61. William Medill to Judge J. K. Kane, 3 September 1846, Letters of the OIA. Until his son was returned home to Philadelphia, Judge Kane presented documents and arguments before the president on his son's behalf.

62. William Medill to Thomas H. Harvey, 2 September 1846, Letters of the OIA.

63. Ibid., 16 November 1846.

64. Thomas H. Harvey to William Medill, 3 December 1846 as quoted in Winther, ed., *Diary of Thomas Leiper Kane*, 25–29.

65. Affidavit of James Allen, Journal History, 18 July 1846.

66. Harvey to Medill, 3 December 1846, as quoted in Winther, *Diary of Thomas Leiper Kane*, 25–29.

67. Ibid.

68. Winter Quarters High Council Minutes, 1 November 1846.

69. Journal History, 15 November 1846.

70. Harvey to Medill, 3 December 1846, as quoted in Winther, *Diary of Thomas Leiper Kane*, 25–29.

71. Journal History, 9 August 1846.

72. Ibid., 20 August 1846.

73. See Jesse C. Little to Brigham Young, 6 October 1846, Brigham Young Papers; and Journal History, 7 September 1846.

74. Jesse C. Little to Brigham Young, 6 October 1846, Brigham Young Papers.

75. Thomas L. Kane to Brigham Young, 26 October 1846, Journal History, 5 December 1846.

76. Thomas L. Kane to Brigham Young, 5 November 1846, Brigham Young Papers.

77. Orson Spencer to Brigham Young, 26 November 1846, Brigham Young Papers.

78. Ibid. Reported Spencer:

"two thirds of the Trustees of the General Assembly of the Presbyterian Chh had visited him and Dort Robert Breckenridge of Baltimore Chief among the Chief Priests had come from that city solely to expostulate with him. Dort B said to him: what in the name of God are you doing! Do you mean to uphold the Mormon religion?"

Little wonder Young could say to Kane, "God be with you always to protect and cheery you, my boy, in your pilgrimage of mercy." Journal History, 4 September 1846.

79. Thomas L. Kane to Brigham Young, 2 December 1846, Brigham Young Papers.

80. Orson Spencer to Brigham Young, 26 November 1846, Brigham Young Papers. For more on Wight, see Chap. 2.

81. William Medill to Thomas H. Harvey, 24 April 1847 as quoted in Winther, *Diary of Thomas Leiper Kane*, 40. Trennert overlooks the fact that permission to stay among the Omaha was indeed given until the spring of 1847. See Trennert, "The Mormons and the Office of Indian Affairs," 393.

The official document of permission, however, had not reached the Bluffs before spring, if ever. "We would like to see the permit," asked Willard Richards of Kane, "and hope the hard earned paper may not be lost so as to weary our friend over again." Journal History, 15 February 1847.

82. Thomas L. Kane to William Medill, 21 April 1847, Thomas L. Kane Papers.

83. Thomas L. Kane apparently to President James K. Polk, approxi-

mately 20 March 1847, as quoted in Winther, *Diary of Thomas Leiper Kane,* 35–36.

84. Letter of Orson Spencer to Brigham Young, 26 November 1846, Brigham Young Papers; and Journal History, 31 December 1846.

85. Superintendent Thomas H. Harvey, in response to Mormon charges of religious prejudice on the part of Indian agents, had said earlier,

> "Your party, being Mormons, does not constitute the objection, but the fact of your being there without authority of the Government; in the execution of my duty I know no sects of parties, and I am sure that the Government at Washington acts upon the same principle."

Thomas H. Harvey to Alpheus Cutler, 5 November 1846, Journal History, 6 November 1846.

As to the quality of his agents, Trennert argues that John Miller "was one of the better men in the Indian service and was devoted to protecting the tribes in his charge from frontiersmen and the ineptitude of the government." Trennert, "The Mormons and the Office of Indian Affairs," 384.

86. William Medill to Thomas H. Harvey, 24 April 1847, as quoted in Winther, *Diary of Thomas Leiper Kane,* 42.

87. Ibid.

88. Winter Quarters High Council Minutes, 10 October 1847. A few months later, Charles R. Dana who was in Washington on a relief mission, called on various government officers, including Medill, "who found a good deal of fault with Colonel Kane and his treatment to them." Dana further recorded,

> "[He] told me also that the Colonel wanted them to appoint some of the Mormons to act as agents for the Indians and this they refused to do, some of the colonel's requests he says they could not grant because it was contrary to the law which he read also read several letters from agents complaining of our people trading with the Indians and cutting timber and making permanent settlements etc."

Journal of Charles R. Dana, volume 2, 14 October 1847.

Dana, himself an Indian, went on to say of Medill's objection, "that was the time I wanted to laugh. And that was the time that I saw the revelation being fulfilled that says in my own due time will I (the Lord) vex this Nation and if the heads of the Nation are not vexed then I am no judge of such matters."

Despite his own predictions, Dana recorded that a week later, in a subsequent meeting, Medill said "he would do all in his power to aid our people . . . provided that they will officially through the head of the church make known their request." President Polk and James Buchanan each gave Dana "$10 in support of the Mormon encampments." Journal of Charles R. Dana, 18 and 20–21 October 1847.

89. *Diary of Hosea Stout,* 9 November 1847, 1:287.

90. Journal History, 23 January 1848.

91. G. D. Grant to Brigham Young, 17 April 1847, Brigham Young Papers. In light of the generally positive climate between the two peoples, Young's benign policies toward them, and effective protection of a small tribe which the Sioux in all likelihood would have destroyed, it is difficult to agree with the contention that "if the Mormon encampment was not positively harmful to the Indians, it did them little good." Trennert, "The Mormons and the Office of Indian Affairs," 396.

92. Journal History, 8 May 1848.

93. *Diary of Hosea Stout,* 7 May 1848, 1:303.

94. Record Book of Bathsheba W. Smith, 18. Significantly, even Commissioner Medill had suggested to Harvey this same solution to the entire problem. Such land, if purchased, would have become federal property and no longer governed by the stipulations of the Indian Intercourse acts.

CHAPTER 6

1. De Voto, *Year of Decision,* 435.

2. Leonard J. Arrington, Feramorz Y. Fox, and Dean L. May, *Building the City of God,* 15. Joseph's Law of Consecration and Stewardship was abandoned in 1834, and in 1838 the so-called "lesser-law" of tithing was introduced. See Doctrine and Covenants, 119.

3. Journal History, 23 August 1846.

4. This herd was driven into town every Saturday when all hands turned out to select their lost cattle. *Diary of Hosea Stout,* 3 October 1846, 1:203.

5. Asahel Lathrop, formerly with George Miller's Ponca camp, became disenchanted with Miller's leadership, and left the Niobrara settlement with ten other families to come to Winter Quarters. Having travelled the west banks of the Missouri for 200 miles, he recommended his tiny settlement as an ideal grazing ground for the almost 1,200 head of church cattle at a spot roughly equidistant between Winter Quarters and the Niobrara River. The prairie grass, rush bottoms, and peavines were particularly abundant at the Lathrop settlement. Journal of Horace K. Whitney, 6–13 February 1847.

The rush bottoms along the Missouri above Winter Quarters were covered with a growth of rushes or "jointed grass" that stayed green most of the winter. Such growth is now almost extinct. Lathrop's herd was probably located just east of Tekamah, Nebraska. Kelly, *Journals of John D. Lee,* editor's note, 23.

6. Seventy is a proselyting office in the higher Melchizedek priesthood of the church. Two other Melchizedek priesthood offices are elder and high priest.

7. See Journal History, 8 November 1846; Kelly, *Journals of John D.*

Lee, 14 December 1846, p. 37; and *Diary of Hosea Stout,* 2 January 1847, 1:222–23.

8. Kelly, *Journals of John D. Lee,* 2 February 1847, p. 64. It was public knowledge that the Senate had ratified the Pottawattami treaty in the summer of 1846 and had agreed to pay the Pottawattami $850,000 over several years. Transportation costs would be paid out of an initial $50,000 payment.

9. See Winter Quarters High Council Minutes, 16–17 and 20 August 1846; and Journal History, 30 August 1846. By contemporary standards, the Winter Quarters mill was a large affair. The average capital outlay for most mills of the time in the state of Missouri was only $500. See Priscilla Ann Evans, "Merchant Gristmills and Communities, 1820–1880: An Economic Relationship," *Missouri Historical Review* 68 (April 1974):323.

10. Winter Quarters High Council Minutes, 16 August 1846.

11. Kelly, *Journals of John D. Lee,* 14 December 1846, p. 38. On the east side Jacob Meyers had erected a much smaller mill in Miller's Hollow.

12. Winter Quarters High Council Minutes, 20 September and 8 November 1846.

13. Journal History, 19 March 1847. Efforts to accelerate the mill's operation were repeatedly made. By late November residents were urged to volunteer three days out of every nine to complete the mill race. George Miller's expertise was also utilized in the late winter after he left his Ponca settlement. Winter Quarters High Council Minutes, 28 February 1847.

14. See Thomas Bullock, Historical Department Journals, 20 March 1847; and Journal of Wilford Woodruff, 16 February 1848. Compare with Evans, "Merchant Gristmills," 323.

15. Some local historians contend that the mill stood for many years at the corner of 9124 North 30th Street in Florence, Nebraska. See Gail G. Holmes, "Reflections on Winter Quarters," an undated, unpublished paper, Utah State Historical Society, 4; and Papers of Lawrence D. Clark. The mill now standing in Florence and marked as the old Mormon mill corresponds to the original location but contains little, if any, of the original materials.

16. See Winter Quarters High Council Minutes, 28 February 1847; and letter of Brigham Young to Thomas J. Thurston, 27 December 1846, Brigham Young Papers.

17. Winter Quarters High Council Minutes, 25 March 1847. The sale, approved by the High Council, was one of convenience and expediency. Neff agreed to purchase the mill and allow Young the right to manage it "as he sees proper." In return Neff agreed to take only 20 percent of grinding tolls the first year.

Early in 1848, Indian Agent John Miller, on behalf of the government, offered to buy the mill for the Indians, but the sale was never consummated, apparently because of objections from the Omaha, who believed they owned all improvements. Journal History, 11 January 1848.

18. Journal History, 7 August 1847.

19. Orson Hyde to Brigham Young, 7 August 1846, Brigham Young Papers. Hyde said this clothing money payment was "unexpected." According to Willard Richards, the amount returned was $5,860. Journal of Willard Richards, 11 August 1846.

20. Journal History, 12 August 1846.

21. Ibid., 13 and 14 August 1846.

22. Ibid., 21 August 1846. The Battalion money amounted to almost half of the $7,906.81 Whitney and company took with them in early September. The balance came from other families and general church funds (Winter Quarters Store Account Book, 76, Brigham Young Papers). Although some of the soldiers' money was set aside to purchase personal items specially requested, most was earmarked for the bulk buying of wheat, flour, and other edibles. Of the total sent, $982.75 was used to buy wheat alone. Journal History, 6 September 1846.

23. See Journal History, 1 November 1846; and Journal of Horace K. Whitney, 12 November 1846.

24. Winter Quarters Store Account Book. William Clayton was one of the principle clerks and adjusters.

25. Estill was allowed to use the Council House as his base of operations. See Journal History, 25 March and 16 June 1847. William E. Clifford and a Mr. Hathaway opened a small store at the home of Albert P. Rockwood in early February 1847. Whether it operated in competition with the main store, or operated after Whitney's store closed, is unknown. Journal History, 8 February 1847. Said Young to Mr. Estill: "The church store house will not probably be of the size and height to suit your taste and convenience, but you can doubtless get some place on your arrival that will accomodate you while you can build or purchase, if you choose. Should you wish to build our people can accomodate you on short notice."

26. See Journal History, 22 September 1846; and Journal of Willard Richards, 4 October 1846. Notwithstanding this regulation, persons were at liberty to purchase materials at Sarpy's trading post although they were generally discouraged from doing so.

27. Cattle, sheep, and hog prices were set by High Council–appointed committees for payment at times of exchange on sale for slaughter. Journal History, 27 August 1846.

28. Ibid., 11 November 1846. "If a man apostatizes," declared Young, "his property need not apostatize—if any brother sees his neighbor giving away and leaving his family on this people who has property he can go to Brother Higbee and tell him the case and I'll warrant you he won't cross him." Winter Quarters High Council Minutes, 7 November 1847.

29. Brigham Young to George Miller, 20 September 1846, Brigham Young Papers. Young continued: "Every one will preserve his individual

interest and receive his just dues, even if he does nothing for it these be publicly known that he is an idler and he will have the privilege of retiring among the gentiles and eating the fruit of his own labors." Slavery, even among those from the South in camp, was barely noticeable. Some slaves may have been in camp with their southern owners, but likely there were few. At one point, Young said he did not want slaves. See Brigham Young to Joseph Herring, 13 September 1846, Brigham Young Papers. The official policy was to hold neither with slavery nor abolitionism as "our creed teaches us more the principle of holding men, either white, red or black by moral power than by any legal ties." Meeting of the Twelve, June 1849, Brigham Young Papers.

30. Autobiography of Joseph Holbrook, 5 February 1848.

31. Journal History, 7 August 1847.

32. Winter Quarters High Council Minutes, 7 November 1847.

33. Ibid., 25 July 1847.

34. *Diary of Hosea Stout*, 29 April 1847, 1:253.

35. Mormon occupants on the east side acquired valuable preemption rights up and down the river for over fifty miles north and south and thirty to forty miles inland. B. H. Roberts, *The Mormon Battalion*, 24.

36. The rate of tax assessment was set at 0.75 percent.

37. *Diary of Hosea Stout*, 24 December 1846, 1:220. Assessed property included cabins, wagons, furniture, domestic animals, and all improvements. An additional tax of 37 1/2 cents was assessed in November on every man who did not volunteer to work periodically on road building and repair (Winter Quarters High Council Minutes, 8 November 1846). Another tax of time was levied that same month in which "every able-bodied man" reserved each tenth day for wood collecting. *Diary of Hosea Stout*, 25 November 1846, 1:213.

38. Doctrine and Covenants, 119:4. "Those who have thus been tithed shall pay one-tenth of all their interest annually; and this shall be a standing law unto them forever."

39. Journal of Wilford Woodruff, 17 December 1847. Despite such comprehensive declarations, some of the most destitute and some Battalion families not producing income were exempt from paying on the donations of goods and services they received. Also some of the rich who had given so very much to others, if not exempted, had their contributions figured as tithing. Winter Quarters High Council Minutes, 19 December 1847.

40. This transaction was very much in accord with the then-current interpretation of the office of bishop. Church doctrine expressly taught that in an ideal economic order all substance imparted to the poor "shall be laid before the bishop of my church and its counsellors . . . to administer to those who have not, from time to time, that every man who has need may be amply suppled and receive according to his wants." Doctrine and Covenants, 42:31, 33. More administrative duties were later assigned bishops.

41. Journal of Wilford Woodruff, 17 July 1846; and Pottawattamie High Council Minutes, 3 August 1846. Initially, families chose their own bishops.

42. Journal History, 4 October 1846.

43. *Diary of Hosea Stout,* November 1846, 1:214. The Winter Quarters High Council divided the city into twenty-two wards and nominated bishops. Those not already high priests would be ordained to that office. See city drawing, Chap. 4. Bishops appointed were Edward Hunter, William Fossett, David Fairbanks, Daniel Spencer, Levi Riter, George W. Harris, Joseph Matthews, Luman H. Calkins, Dr. Lang, Isaac Davis, Abraham Hogland, Ephraim Badger, David Yearsley, John Benbow, Benjamin Brown, Brother Lutts, John Vance, John Higbee, Joseph B. Noble, A. Everett, and Willard Snow. A twenty-third ward with Joseph Knight Jr., bishop, comprised clusters of settlements about Miller's Hollow near the Blockhouse on the Iowa side. Journal History, 26 November 1846.

44. Winter Quarters High Council Minutes, 25 November 1846. For more on bishops, see Chap. 9.

45. Journal History, 23 November 1846.

46. Journal of Thomas Bullock, 13 December 1846. During the winter the bishops not only acted individually but collectively. In mid-February a series of feasts and picnics was arranged for the 117 poorest adults and their families at Winter Quarters. The first eight wards staged the first day's spread, and the next eight the spread on the following day, and the third eight the spread on the third day. At the conclusion of the affair, twenty-two bushels of provisions remained "untouched" and twelve baskets of fragments remained. Journal History, 16 and 27 February 1847.

47. Ibid., 15 November 1846. Some of the collected tithing was used to pay the partial support of members of the Quorum of the Twelve. See Minutes of a meeting of the Twelve and others, 17 November 1847, Brigham Young Papers. Compare with Journal of Joseph Fielding, 127.

48. Winter Quarters High Council Minutes, 26 September 1847. Exactly how tithes were collected under this revised method is not given.

49. Journal of Wilford Woodruff, 7 March 1847. Picnics, dances, and parties for the poor were also arranged by some of the more ambitious bishops.

50. Journal History, 8 November 1846.

51. Minutes of the meeting of the Twelve and others, 18 December 1847, Brigham Young Papers. The original figure was $36,000, but it is presumed the true figure was $3,600. Extra zeroes were often carelessly added.

52. Winter Quarters High Council Minutes, 19 December 1847.

53. Ibid., 26 September 1847.

54. After two years twenty boot and shoe makers were in operation on both sides of the river. Winter Quarters High Council Minutes, 21 January 1848.

55. John Pack returned from Missouri on 1 October 1846 with a carding machine purchased at a cost of forty dollars, money likely provided from church funds. See Winter Quarters High Council Minutes, 2 October 1846; and Journal of Willard Richards, 2 October 1846.

56. The Diary of John Pulsipher, 12.

57. Kelly, *Journals of John D. Lee*, 14 December 1846, p. 38.

58. A good example of the individual's good being sacrificed for the group's welfare occurred while they were settling in at Cutler's Park when some critics received this bit of advice:

> "There has been some faultfinding by those who recently arrived in camp, because they want to cut their own hay and put in their own turnip patch, but we must be one and feel a genuine interest for the whole, and when anyone is told by the foreman to pick up a basket of chips and tumble them out again, then pick them up again and find no fault."

Journal History, 16 August 1846.

59. Ibid., 20 November 1846.

60. Charles C. Rich to Brigham Young, 3 October 1846, Brigham Young Papers.

61. Journal History, 31 December 1846.

62. *Autobiography of Parley P. Pratt*, 357.

63. Winter Quarters High Council Minutes, 28 November 1847.

64. *William Clayton's Journal*, 26–27 and 31 January 1847, pp. 71–72.

65. Autobiography of Fanny Parks Taggart, late fall 1846.

66. Pottawattamie High Council Minutes, 31 October 1846.

67. *Diary of Hosea Stout*, 4 February 1847, 1:235.

68. Winter Quarters High Council Minutes, 28 November 1847.

69. *Diary of Hosea Stout*, 15 December 1846, 1:218. Only a handful in Winter Quarters were non-Mormons.

70. Hall, *Abominations of Mormonism Exposed*, 107.

71. Kelly, *Journals of John D Lee*, editor's note, 34 and 55. Another critic of more recent times argues the Twelve took "about forty thousand dollars" sent by the Battalion and was the cause of starving innocent women and children. Stanley P. Hirshson, *The Lion of the Lord—A Biography of Brigham Young*, 78.

72. Pottawattamie High Council Minutes, 18 August 1846.

73. George and Linda Coulson to Brigham Young, 18 August 1846, Brigham Young Papers.

74. Bulah S. Clark to Brigham Young, 19 August 1846, Brigham Young Papers.

75. Journal History, 14 August 1846.

76. Ibid.

77. See Pottawattamie High Council Minutes, 23 August 1846; and Journal History, 26 August 1846. As to the "arm twisting," Young warned those that kept all their money that "such a course of conduct will release us from all obligations that we are under to see that they are

provided for and taken care of . . . for it is not right for any person to hoard up wealth which is earned by their friends in the army, while their brethren, who are around them in the camp are toiling hard from day to day to sustain them and their teams." Journal History, 14 August 1846.

78. Pottawattamie High Council Minutes, 23 August 1846.

79. Journal of Thomas Bullock, 13 December 1846.

80. See Journal History, 21 November 1846; and Kelly, *Journals of John D. Lee,* 21 November 1846, p. 21. The mission was kept secret not because authorities were unwilling to tell Battalion families, but to prevent possible "robbery and murder." Lee was paid $160 for making the perilous journey. Journal History, 29 August 1846.

81. See Eldridge Tufts to Brigham Young, 10 February 1847, Brigham Young Papers; and *Diary of Hosea Stout,* 2 January 1847, 1:222.

82. Nauvoo retail prices are taken from *The Mormon Neighbor,* 1 May 1843, vol. 2, no. 1, p. 3. What few 1846 Nauvoo prices are known indicate a slight decrease in retail prices. See *Hancock Eagle,* 8 May 1846, vol. 1, no. 6, p. 3. Winter Quarters prices are derived from the Winter Quarters Store Account Book, Brigham Young Papers. The sample amounts approximate any of the several hundred individual purchases made at the store.

83. See Gilbert and Whitney Day Book, Kirtland, Ohio, November 1836–April 1837; and Winter Quarters Store Account Book.

84. The basis for the wholesale price list is the prices charged Mormon traders at St. Joseph, Savannah, and Oregon, Missouri, in December 1846 by Smith and Donnell, Nave and McCord, Middleton and Berry, and Mr. Tootle and Company. See Journal of Horace K. Whitney, 14 and 22 December 1846 and 12 January 1847. Though not the same as the St. Louis prices Whitney paid, they probably were not much more. River towns tried to be competitive.

The retail prices are taken from the Winter Quarters Store Account Book, Brigham Young Papers. There is no difference in price between December 1846 and March 1847.

85. Gerald Carson, *The Old Country Store,* 93–94.

86. A full comparison of prices charged at Sarpy's Trading Post with those at Winter Quarters is impossible. However, a handful of items can be compared:

Items	Sarpy's (1846–47)	W.Q. (1846–47)	Ft. Laramie (1849)	Ft. Kearny (1849)
Molasses/gal.	$0.75	$1.00	—	—
Sugar/lb.	0.13	0.15	0.10–0.40	0.25–0.64
Coffee/lb.	0.12 1/2	0.15	0.02–0.40	0.19
Liquor/gal.	—	$1.00	$6.00	$1.68
Flour/cwt.	—	$3.00	$6.00	$2.00

Whereas it may be argued that Sarpy was able to undersell certain items, other trading posts charged much higher prices comparatively.

See Unruh, *The Plains Across*, 265; Kelly, *Journals of John D. Lee*, 15 December 1846, p. 39; and Winter Quarters Store Account Book.
    87. Kelly, *Journals of John D. Lee*, 27 January 1847, p. 60.
    88. Ibid., 27 January 1847, pp. 60 and 61, and 27 February 1847, p. 102. As late as November 1847, Young still owed money to Battalion families.

CHAPTER 7

    1. *Hymns—The Church of Jesus Christ of Latter-day Saints*, Hymn 13. For an adequate summary of the history of this popular song see Paul E. Dahl, "'All is Well . . .': The Story of the Hymn That Went Around the World." *Brigham Young University Studies* 21 (Fall 1981): 491–514.
    2. Journal History, 3 August 1846.
    3. Huntington, "A History," 26 July 1846. Ague was defined loosely as an acute or violent malarial fever characterized by fits or paroxysms consisting of a burning fever followed by severe cold and shivering.
    4. Journal of Lorenzo Snow, Summer 1846.
    5. Charles C. Rich to Brigham Young, 11 August 1846, Brigham Young Papers.
    6. Journal of Charles R. Dana, vol. 3, Fall 1846. Incomplete death records kept at Mt. Pisgah give the names of seventeen people who died between 31 May and 17 September alone. It is obviously incomplete, not even including William Huntington, but provides an incontestible basis for estimating the degree of suffering at the upper farm. Mt. Pisgah Historical Record.
    7. Journal of Nelson W. Whipple, Summer 1846.
    8. Journal History, 29 March 1847.
    9. Kate B. Carter, gen. ed., *Heart Throbs of the West*, "Journal of Louisa Barnes Pratt," 8:241.
    10. Journal of Heber C. Kimball, 12 August 1846.
    11. Journal of Wilford Woodruff, 17–21 November 1846. Appleton Milo Harmon echoed the sentiments of both Kimball and Woodruff.

> "The past winter in fact the past twelve months has been as trieing a scene for the Saints as they ever had to pass through. Sickness death loss of cattle and teams poverty in all most every shape. Exiles in a Christian land."

Diary of Appleton Milo Harmon, Winter 1846–47, p. 11.
    12. Kane, "The Mormons," 94.
    13. Ibid., 92. Since the first recorded death by scurvy was not reported until February, one wonders if Kane, who left the preceding fall, really did see such scenes on the scale he indicated.
    14. See Lesley Goates, "The Tragedy of Winter Quarters'" and Clyde B. Aitchison, "The Mormon Settlements," 281.
    15. Journal of Erastus Snow, April–May 1846.
    16. Diary of John Pulsipher, approximately January 1847, p. 15.

17. Journal of Wilford Woodruff, 17–21 November 1846.
18. Journal of Eliza Maria Lyman, 14 July 1846.
19. Kane, "The Mormons," 92–94.
20. Linn, *The Story of the Mormons*, 376; John Todd, *Early Settlement and Growth of Western Iowa or Reminiscences*, 98; and Winther, *Diary of Thomas Leiper Kane*, 13.
21. Todd, *Early Settlement and Growth of Western Iowa*, 95. Norma Kidd Green, a student of frontier river settlements, has written the following:

> "Malaria was ever present along the westward moving frontier where settlements were always on the water front. Heavy rains and flooding brought stagnant ponds and produced swampy land, perfect breeding places for mosquitoes. That ubiquitous insect was not just suspected of a connection with the 'shakes' or 'ague,' but this illness had become associated with low lying ground."

Norma Kidd Green, "The Presbyterian Mission to the Omaha Indian Tribe," *Nebraska History* 48 (Autumn 1967):270.
22. See Journal of Horace K. Whitney, 7 October 1846; and Brigham Young to Charles C. Rich, 7 January 1847, Brigham Young Papers. Deaths in the following year, though one-third of the 1846–47 count, were again much more common in the summer than in the winter, another possible proof that malaria and other similar communicable diseases and disorders were greater summer killers than all other causes.

To what extent bad drinking water and crude sanitation efforts contributed to the general malaise is difficult to determine. Although the Missouri River was notoriously muddy, it was not polluted with raw sewage and other contaminants. Probably much of the Saints' drinking water came from the two nearby creeks of cleaner, clearer water. Most outhouses were positioned away from the river, producing minimal seepage. Only three fatal cases of typhus fever and three of diarrhea/cholera were reported between 1846 and 1848.
23. Journal of Horace K. Whitney, 18 March 1847.
24. Ibid. See also Journal History, 18 March 1847.
25. See Journal History, 24 August 1846; *Diary of Hosea Stout*, 24 and 30 July 1846, 1:181; Journal of Heber C. Kimball, 18 June 1846; and Journal of Wilford Woodruff, 5–7 October 1846.
26. Whitney, "Scenes and Incidents," 13:139.
27. Kelly, *Journals of John D. Lee*, 28 February 1847, pp. 104–105.
28. Diary of John Pulsipher, 13.
29. "Incidents in the Life of Mary Helen Grant," *Journal of History* 10 (April 1917): 177.
30. Journal of Isaac Haight, 16 September 1846.
31. Whitney, "Scenes and Incidents,: 14:78.
32. *Comprehensive History*, 3:151. Linn accepted Kane's estimate although he argued that malaria, not scurvy, was the greatest killer. J. Sterling Morton and Clyde A. Aitchison also accepted Kane's figures.

See Linn, *Story of the Mormons*, 376; Morton, *History of Nebraska*, 127; and Aitchison, "Mormon Settlements," 281. Aitchison blamed scurvy for destroying one-ninth of the local Indian populations the year before, a conclusion not borne out by correspondence from the local Indian agents.

33. Allen and Leonard, *Story of the Latter-day Saints*, 236.

34. Arrington and Bitton, *The Mormon Experience*, 98.

35. Holmes, "Reflections on Winter Quarters," 3.

36. This estimate is derived from most of the camp journals, the Journal History, and correspondence of the time. See Journal of Patty Sessions, 17 and 18 March, 3 and 9 May 1847; and Journal of Horace K. Whitney.

37. Charles C. Rich to Brigham Young, 3 October 1846, Brigham Young Papers.

38. Journal of Nelson W. Whipple, Summer 1846.

39. See Andrew Jenson's compilation, Manuscript History of Cutler's Park and of Winter Quarters. There were at least four sextons, Levi Stewart, William Huntington, a Brother Wallace, and Benjamin R. Laub. Winter Quarters High Council Minutes, 8 November 1846, 16 January, and 25 April 1847.

40. The Mormons had at least two, possibly three, burial grounds on the west side of the Missouri. Their first was "the mound," or Cutler's Park cemetery, two and one half miles west of Winter Quarters (likely near the present-day Potter Field). The second was the Winter Quarters cemetery "east of the Mound" and "on the hill west of Winter Quarters." Burials began in the Winter Quarters cemetery on 15 September, a week before people began moving onto the site. See Journal History, 15 September 1846; and Winter Quarters High Council Minutes, 15 September 1846.

The action taken in mid-November "to lay out a new burying ground on the second bluff west of Winter Quarters" seems to indicate that they moved the first Winter Quarters cemetery higher up the bluff. See Journal History, 16 November 1846. Two contemporary observers pinpointed the cemetery "just back of Winter Quarters," southwest of the city, "on the right hand side of the road going to Cutler's Park." See Diary of Appleton Milo Harmon, Winter 1846–47, p. 9; and Journal of Joseph G. Hovey, 21 June 1847, p. 40.

This sexton's record is amplified by the author's inclusion of almost thirty deaths listed in various private journals but not recorded in the sexton's reports.

41. Winter Quarters High Council Minutes, 8 November 1846.

42. Ibid., 21 March 1847.

43. Ibid., 16 January 1847. Basswood or walnut were the popular choices.

44. Appleton Milo Harmon, however, records that both his mother and sister died in January 1847 and were buried in the Winter Quarters

cemetery even though the ground was frozen three feet deep. Diary of Appleton Milo Harmon, Winter 1846–47, p. 9.

45. Mt. Pisgah Historical Record.

46. See Journal History, 17 August 1846; Journal of Heber C. Kimball, 20 August 1846; and Winter Quarters High Council Minutes, 13 August 1846.

47. Kelly, *Journals of John D. Lee,* 28 February 1847, pp. 104–105; Journal of Horace K. Whitney, 18 March 1847; and Diary of John Pulsipher, 13.

48. See Ernest Widtsoe Shumway, "History of Winter Quarters, Nebraska, 1846–1848," 36; and Journal of Isaac Haight, 16 September 1846. Haight, a contemporary observer, equated black canker with scurvy.

49. Kelly, *Journals of John D. Lee,* 6 March 1847, p. 110.

50. F. D. B. Horne, ed., *Autobiography of George W. Bean,* 30–31.

51. See Journal of William S. Appleby, 9 December 1847; and Journal of Wilford Woodruff, 23 February 1848.

52. See Journal of Wilford Woodruff, 22 and 24 August 1846; Journal of Warren Foote, 2 and 10 November 1846 and 26 March 1847; and Journal History, 1 August 1846.

53. Journal of Warren Foote, April 1849. This may have been on or near the present site of Fairview Cemetery in Council Bluffs. Others who died on the east side may have been buried near settlers' homes or on recently acquired private property. See Journal of Nelson W. Whipple, Spring of 1848.

54. Rich, *Ensign to the Nations,* 83. These 23 deaths, out of a population of 396, occurred within a nine-month period.

55. Matthew Thomas, "Disease in a Mormon Community," 32. Back in Nauvoo, children under ten had accounted for 59 percent of all deaths in 1843 and 52 percent in 1844.

56. Ibid. These are conservative estimates. The Nauvoo death ratios were probably based on the calendar year, whereas the figure determined at the Missouri was from June until May.

57. Patrick E. McLear, "The St. Louis Cholera Epidemic of 1849," *Missouri Historical Review* 63 (January 1969):171–81.

58. Jenson, "List of Burials," Manuscript History of Cutler's Park.

59. Winther, *Diary of Thomas Leiper Kane,* 22.

60. Doctrine and Covenants, 89:10. As early as 1834 members were taught that roots and herbs should be "applied to the sick in order that they may receive health." Donald Q. Cannon and Lyndon W. Cook, eds., *Far West Record—Minutes of The Church of Jesus Christ of Latter-day Saints, 1830–1844,* 96–97.

61. Journal History, 19 August and 21 October 1846 and 25 March 1847.

62. Journal of Warren Foote, 24 February 1847.

63. Journal of Joseph G. Hovey, 14–15 September 1846.

64. Journal History, 14 August 1846 and 12 January 1847.

65. Diary of John Pulsipher, Summer 1847, p. 13. The best fishing holes were in small lakes several miles north of Winter Quarters. Ice fishing was little practiced, if at all.

66. Journal History, 26 March 1847. Apparently few lived in the dugouts the following winter, and fewer still in exposed wagons.

67. Minutes of a Meeting of some of the Twelve, 6 March 1847, Brigham Young Papers.

68. Kelly, *Journals of John D. Lee*, 6 March 1847, pp. 109–10.

69. Brigham Young to W. W. Phelps, 7 September 1846, Brigham Young Papers.

70. Journal History, 25 August 1846.

71. Brigham Young to the Nauvoo Trustees, 27 September 1846.

72. Journal History, 6 June 1847.

73. *The Gospel Herald*, 29 June 1848, p. 2.

74. Pratt, *Autobiography*, 357.

75. Journal History, 6 February 1847.

76. Ibid., 6 December 1847. Though Young was dramatizing slightly in order to create sympathy, he had every reason to paint a less than rosy scene.

77. Kelly, *Journals of John D. Lee*, 8 March 1847, p. 113.

78. Journal History, 23 January 1848.

79. *William Clayton's Journal*, 27 October 1846, p. 67.

80. Ibid., 22 August 1846, p. 62.

81. Journal of Leonora Cannon, 17 September 1846. One wonders how wise it was to perform such a rite on those suffering with chills, fever, and pneumonia. The practice is no longer current in the church.

82. Carter, *Heart Throbs of the West*, 8:241.

83. Journal of Patty Sessions, 9 and 18 May 1847. Occasionally both husband and wife administered together. See Sessions, 1 April 1847. For more on women and their activities, see Chap. 9.

84. Doctrine and Covenants, 136:22.

85. Journal of Wilford Woodruff, 21 March 1847.

86. Ibid., 23 February 1848. "The sectarian world," Young said, "with the knowledge they have would if it was in their power sweep the fall of man, death, pain, sorrow and affliction with all their attendant evils into oblivion and caused man to have lived externally as he was before the fall . . . but such a cause would in the end have been the greatest curse that could have been heaped upon man."

87. Journal of Heber C. Kimball, 9 August 1846.

88. Journal of Wilford Woodruff, 23 February 1848. It would be a mistake, however, to conclude that they saw the devil as the root cause of all illness and death. Disease was a natural part of living, and death was ultimately in the hands of Providence. Cannon and Cook, *Far West Record*, 97.

89. Journal of Wilford Woodruff, 15 December 1846. Nephites and

Lamanites were ancient American peoples in Book of Mormon history who continually warred against each other. Ultimately the Lamanites exterminated their foes and, according to belief, became the ancestors of the American Indian.

90. Margaret Scott to Brigham Young, 17 September 1848, Brigham Young Papers.

91. Journal History, 16 April 1847.

CHAPTER 8

1. Dale L. Morgan, *The Great Salt Lake*, 186.

2. Hiram Martin Chittenden and Alfred Talbot Richardson, *Life, Letters and Travels of Father Pierre-Jean De Smet, S.J. 1801–1873*, 1:56. Lewis Clark Christian, in a recent dissertation on the factors contributing to the choice of the Salt Lake Valley as the eventual destination, questions De Smet's influence and how accurate and firsthand his knowledge really was. See Lewis Clark Christian, "A Study of the Mormon Westward Migration Between February 1846 and July 1847 with Emphasis on and Evaluation of the Factors that Led to the Mormon Choice of Salt Lake Valley as the Site of Their Initial Colony."

De Smet later served as chaplain in the infamous "Johnson's army" of 1858. At that time De Smet described the Latter-day Saints as "that terrible sect of modern fanatics, flying from civilization . . . [who] never ceased to defy the Government." Chittenden and Richardson, *Life, Letters and Travels of De Smet*, 1:717–18. His tone in 1846 was apparently more conciliatory. For more on De Smet, see Chap. 2.

3. Journal History, 7 August 1846.

4. Journal of John D. Lee, 7 August 1846. There is some indication that their destination was private information, now known by most in camp and revealed only to Kane after he had won the confidence and trust of Mormon leaders. Young had his reasons for confidentiality. First, Mormon Battalion enlistees might not look favorably at a march inland over 1,000 miles from their eventual coastal destination; second, he wished to keep the federal government guessing; and third, if the valley did not turn out as expected, changes could easily be made.

Eliza Lyman expressed the popular sentiment while watching the departing pioneer wagons in early April: "They are going west to look for a location for the Latter-day Saints and have no idea where that is but trust that the Lord will lead them to the place." Journal of Eliza Maria Lyman, 8 April 1847.

5. Journal History, 9 August 1846.

6. See Brigham Young to the Nauvoo Trustees, 11 September 1846; and Brigham Young to Joseph A. Strattan, 12 September 1846, Brigham Young Papers. Christian contends that the Bear River Valley mentioned referred to the one in present Wyoming rather than its counterpart in present northern Utah. See Christian, "A Study of the Mormon West-

ward Migration," 223 and 238. However, most of the trappers spoke highly of the Cache Valley area of Utah, and it may be that Young had the more northerly area in mind.

7. Journal History, 15 February 1847. The only modification of their destination plans was abandoning any further consideration of locating a portion of the British Saints at Vancouver Island. While as late as August 1846 lip service was still being given to the idea of British converts reaching the area by water rather than by the more costly overland crossing, it was probably never more than a political, half-baked economic alternative, and it lost all further meaning after the signing of the Oregon treaty in June 1846. Considering the need for consolidating their resources once in their mountain retreat, maintaining close communication and unity, and protecting themselves from all potential offenders, it is hard to believe the references to the scheme were anything but a smoke screen to gain any possible British and American concessions. Journal of John D. Lee, 7 August 1846.

In February 1847, Orson Hyde, Parley Pratt, and John Taylor presented a petition bearing 13,000 names to Queen Victoria and to Parliament "proposing a plan for emigration to Oregon or Vancouver's Island." Years later, during the federal government's efforts to disenfranchise the church because of polygamy, John Taylor, then president, quietly commissioned studies into the possibility of relocating the church to Vancouver Island, British Columbia.

8. Brigham Young to Joseph A. Strattan, 12 September 1846, Brigham Young Papers; Journal History, 28 September 1846; and Brigham Young to the Nauvoo Trustees, 27 September 1846, Brigham Young Papers.

9. Journal History, 15 November 1846.

10. Minutes of the Winter Quarters High Council, 8 September 1846.

11. Brigham Young to the Nauvoo Trustees, 11 and 27, September and 14 November 1846, Brigham Young Papers; and Journal History, 15 November 1846.

12. See Diary of Hosea Stout, 9 September 1846, 1:192; and Journal History, 28 September and 15 November 1846.

13. Brigham Young to the Nauvoo Trustees, 11 September 1846, Brigham Young Papers.

14. Brigham Young to Joseph Herring, 13 September 1846, Brigham Young Papers.

15. Journal History, 8 and 12 November 1846. The nature and details of this dream are not specified, but it did seem to provide him with a certain amount of assurance and confidence.

16. Journal History, 29 December 1846.

17. See Journal of Willard Richards, 24–27 December; and Journal History, 27 December 1846.

18. Northern Islander, 20 September 1855.

19. Diary of Hosea Stout, 25 October 1846, 1:207.

20. See Manuscript History, 17 December 1846; and Joseph Holbrook to Brigham Young, 7 December 1846, Brigham Young Papers.

21. Brigham Young to George Miller, 25 November 1846, Brigham Young Papers.

22. Journal of Horace K. Whitney, 24 November 1846.

23. Journal History, 24 November 1846. The valleys of the Tongue and Powder rivers were favorite wintering grounds for trappers on account of the abundance of game and pasture located there. Chittenden, *American Fur Trade*, 2:766.

24. Brigham Young to George Miller and Council, 25 November 1846, Brigham Young Papers.

25. Journal of Thomas Bullock, 10 December 1846. He continued: "the Buffalo grass is fine and plenty on the head waters of the Yellowstone—a stream strikes above the two forks on Tongue River—the winter sets in there about the 1st Novr and lasts till last of March."

26. *Diary of Hosea Stout*, 27 December 1846, 1:221. Mary Richards, who also attended the meeting, noted that it was similarly contemplated that, time and energies permitting, they would send out from the proposed Yellowstone winter base "a company across the mountains" to the Basin or Bear River Valley "to put in a crop of wheat in the fall." Journal of Mary H. P. Richards, 27 December 1846.

27. Journal History, 7 January 1847.

28. Brigham Young to Hannah Stailey, 8 January 1847, Brigham Young Papers.

29. Joseph Holbrook to Brigham Young, 7 December 1846, Brigham Young Papers.

30. See Journal of Thomas Bullock, 12 December 1846, Brigham Young Papers; and Journal History, 12 December 1846. Fontenelle also suggested that before departing they build a leather boat or "revenue cutter" to aid in fording swollen streams and rivers.

31. A detachment of the Battalion, incapacitated by illness and weakened conditions, along with most of the women and children, had been sent north to Pueblo, New Mexico. This contingent also wanted to rejoin their families at the earliest moment.

32. Journal History, 25 January 1847.

33. *Diary of Hosea Stout*, 29 October 1846, 1:208.

34. Manuscript History, 11 January 1847.

35. Doctrine and Covenants, 136:3.

36. Almost everyone at Winter Quarters accepted the revelation without reservation. The Municipal High Council's response was typical.

"Reynolds Cahoon moved that the communication be received as the Word and Will of God, seconded by Isaac Morley. Alanson Eldredge approved of the same; it was plain to his understanding. Reynolds Cahoon said it was the voice of righteousness. Winslow Farr said it reminded him of the first reading of the Book of Mormon; he was perfectly satisfied and knew it was from the Lord. Cornelius P.

Lott was perfectly satisfied. George W. Harris was so well satisfied that he wanted all to say Amen at once. Thomas Grover felt that it was the voice of the Spirit.

The vote passed unanimously. . . . Hosea Stout said if there is anything in Mormonism that is the voice of the Lord to the people so is the word and will of the Lord."

Later in the day, the presiding council of Seventies similarly voted unanimously in support of it. Journal History, 14 January 1847.

37. Ibid., 17 January 1847.

38. *Diary of Hosea Stout,* 14 January 1847, 1:227–29.

39. Journal History, 25 and 29 January 1847.

40. Mills, "De Tal Palo," 111–12.

41. George Miller to Brigham Young, 17 March 1847, Brigham Young Papers.

42. Mills, "De Tal Palo," 143.

43. Unbound minute book of Strangite conferences held between July and October 1850, J. J. Strang Papers. As late as 1854, Miller was urging Wight to abandon Texas and join Strang. "The more I reflect on the subject the more I an convinced that it would be to the best you could do under all the sircumstances, both in a spiritual and temperal point of view." George Miller to Lyman Wight, 19 January 1854. Wight refused.

44. Journal of Joseph Fielding, Spring 1847, Book 5, p. 126.

45. Journal History, 18 January 1847.

46. Journal History, 18 and 25 January 1847.

47. See Journal of Wilford Woodruff, 15 and 18 February 1847; and Journal of Erastus Snow, early February 1847.

48. Journal History, 12 and 15 February 1847.

49. See Twelve apostles to Titus Billings, 25 March 1847, Brigham Young Papers; and Journal History, 25 March 1847.

50. Journal History, 29 January 1847.

51. Ibid. He went on to say he would "be pleased to have them accompany us." They never did.

52. Journal History, 15 February 1847.

53. Arguing against the way-station plan, Isaac Morley said it would dilute their efforts. "If there is a company here, a company at the mountains and a company across the mountains it is weakening our hands—the building [of] another city is [full] of trouble and expense." Willard Richards, at the same meeting and of the same mind as Morley, argued that "if we go 5 or 600 miles to put in a crop this spring, we are too late—we have to be particular in picking our location so as to irrigate the farm. You can plant two acres here to one there." He concluded,

"Will it not be better to leave the families here this season where they have houses to shelter them from the storms and other necessaries prepared and let the pioneers go over the mountains and prepare the place, then return and bring the families over next season in perfect safety to the place of gathering without having to make and leave another stopping place for the devil."

See Minutes of a meeting of the Twelve and others, 6 March 1847, Brigham Young Papers; and Kelly, *Journals of John D. Lee*, 6 March 1847, pp. 109–11.

54. Minutes of the Twelve and many of the High Council, 6 March 1847, Brigham Young Papers.

55. Brigham Young to Joseph A. Strattan, 22 January 1847, Brigham Young Papers.

56. Kelly, *Journals of John D. Lee*, 6 March 1847, pp. 108–10.

57. Patty Sessions referred to the "scarcity of provisions at Winter Quarters and how hard it was even to get a little corn-meal" (Manuscript History of Winter Quarters, 15 April 1847). Camp leaders were aware of the problem. To minimize demands on camp supplies, Young recommended they take with them only 100 pounds of provisions per pioneer. As he had done back in Iowa, Joseph Young objected to the foolhardiness of the scheme and strongly suggested more ample supplies. The final company took with them closer to 300 pounds of provisions per person. Manuscript History of Brigham Young, 3 March 1847.

58. Kelly, *Journals of John D. Lee*, 21 March 1847, p. 129.

59. Journal of Horace K. Whitney, 22 and 23 March 1847.

60. Ibid., 8 April 1847. On 8 April, Whitney and most camp leaders set out for the main rendezvous point out at the Elkhorn ferry fifteen miles west.

61. Ibid., 12 April 1847; see also Journal History, 12 April 1847; and Journal of Wilford Woodruff, 12–13 April 1847.

62. Journal of Erastus Snow, 7 and 8 April 1847. One wonders if Young had not been delaying purposely their departure until Pratt and Taylor's return. He must have known the funds and instruments were on their way.

63. Journal History, 13 April 1847. Besides these instruments, they had recently obtained several maps of Texas, Oregon, and California including Frémont's, Mitchell's, and a most recent map from General Atchison. Journal of Erastus Snow, 18 February, 27 March, and 4 April 1847.

64. Said Young months later: "I told Bro. Parley if you go with us you will never be sorry for it but if you don't you will always be sorry for it. I tell you, they will lose more ground than they ever gained." Young wanted all the Twelve not only to find Zion but also to discuss the creation of a First Presidency. He may also have been suspicious of how Taylor and Pratt would manage affairs at Winter Quarters and with the following immigration companies. See Minutes of Miscellaneous Trustees Minutes, 17 November 1847, Brigham Young Papers; and *Diary of Hosea Stout*, 26 November 1847, 1:289.

65. Journal History, 16 April 1847. See Journal of Horace K. Whitney,

16 April 1847; and Journal of Erastus Snow, 16 April 1847. The above two journals disagree on the total number constituting the camp. Whitney says only two women joined them; Snow says three.

66. See Manuscript History of Winter Quarters, 16 April 1847; and Journal History, 2 June 1847.

67. Journal History, 16 April 1847.

68. Ibid.

69. See Minutes of the Winter Quarters High Council, 10 July 1847; and *Diary of Hosea Stout,* 10 July 1847, 1:266.

70. Some slight evidence indicates that the continuation of the High Council and others of Hyde's policies were criticized after the rest of the Twelve returned in the fall. *Diary of Hosea Stout,* 9 November 1847, 1:287.

71. Autobiography of Joseph Holbrook, 10 May 1847, p. 57. The Ponca camp initially received a very cool reception from their east bank neighbors who "looked down" upon them "as cold apostate Mormons." John L. Butler said they "threw out insinuations about us, and said, oh, they are not worth our notice, they belong to Emmett's Company and they are thieves." Young later demanded they "quit their talk" and accept them readily and without prejudice. John Lowe Butler, "A Short History of the Life of John Lowe Butler," 53.

72. Journal History, 16 April 1847.

73. *Diary of Hosea Stout,* 29 April 1847, 1:253.

74. The land about Old Fort Calhoun had once been cultivated, perhaps by soldiers of an earlier time.

75. *Diary of Hosea Stout,* 23 March 1847, 1:242 and 23 August 1847, 1:270. Young wanted two thousand acres under cultivation eventually.

76. Kelly, *Journals of John D. Lee,* 30 March 1847, p. 140. Kelly, in editing the Lee journals, relied heavily on a Mr. E. G. Connely of Omaha who located and described the site:

> "Summer Quarters is about thirteen miles (by present highway) north of old Winter Quarters. The land lies between two streams, is perfectly flat, with good, friable soil . . . and was the largest and best tract within easy reach of Winter Quarters."

Ibid., 1 April 1847, p. 141.

77. Ibid., 16 April 1847, p. 150 and 20 April 1847, p. 153.

78. Hosea Stout, visiting the area in August, penned this negative report.

> "It is in a low hemed in place and it looks most desolate, sickly and gloomy. I found a majority of the place sick and in the most suffering condition. Some whole families not able to help each other and worse than all they were quarreling and contending with each other in a most disgraceful manner. . . . They had fine and extensive crops of corn beans cabbage melons etc. and had they been at peace with each other, would have been in a fair way to do well."

Diary of Hosea Stout, 25 August 1847, 1:270.

The month before, the Summer Quarters camp had set off a burial ground on a bluff above the farm. Seventeen died during the summer and were buried there.

79. Journal of Joseph G. Hovey, 27 April 1847, p. 39; Christeen G. Kimball to her mother, 7 May 1847, Correspondence of Christeen G. Kimball; Journal of James H. Flanagan, 13 December 1847; and Journal History, 24 March 1847.

80. Journal History, 6 September 1847.

81. *Diary of Hosea Stout,* 12 June 1847, 1:260.

82. Journal of Wilford Woodruff, 4 September 1847.

83. *Diary of Hosea Stout,* 26 November 1847, 1:289. See also Minutes of Miscellaneous Trustees Minutes, 17 November 1847, Brigham Young Papers. Some personal matters were also divisive.

84. Winter Quarters High Council Minutes, 10 July 1847.

85. Journal History, 15, 17–18, and 21 June 1847. By September the number of wagons had been reduced to 566. Ibid., 25 November 1847.

86. Ibid., 25 September 1847.

87. Most of the wagons with oxen returning from Salt Lake to the Missouri left the valley on 16 August. More than half of the original pioneers returned, including all of the Twelve but Taylor and Pratt. Journal History, 16–17 August 1847.

88. Having encountered bad weather and Pawnee Indian harassment, their situation up until Stout's arrival was desperate. "The President said it was more joy more satisfaction to meet us than a company of angels," Stout recalled. For their rescue efforts, Young "treated" them to some whiskey. "It came welcome to the pioneers." *Diary of Hosea Stout,* 18 October 1847, 1:283.

89. Journal of Wilford Woodruff, 31 October 1847. An unidentified observer described the scene thus:

"The company then drove into the town of Winter Quarters in order, arriving there about an hour before sunset. The streets were crowded with people who had come out to shake hands with the Pioneers as they passed through the lines, and the weary travelers truly rejoiced to once more behold their wives, children and friends after an absence of over six months, in which time they had traveled over 2000 miles, sought out a location where the Saints could dwell in peace, and accomplished one of the most interesting and important missions of this dispensation."

Journal History, 30 October 1847.

90. Journal of Joseph G. Hovey, 28 October 1847, p. 47.

91. Minutes of a Meeting of the Twelve, Seventies, High Council, and Bishops, 10 November 1847, Brigham Young Papers.

92. Journal History, 14 November 1847.

93. Ibid., 21 December 1846. It may well be that this was the first printing of any kind in Nebraska history.

94. See Journal History, 15 and 20 March 1848; and *Diary of Hosea Stout*, 1 April 1848, 1:307.

95. Journal History, 8 April 1848.

CHAPTER 9

1. Journal of Thomas Bullock, 13 December 1846.
2. Winter Quarters Store Account Book, Brigham Young Papers.
3. Journal History, 11 November 1847.
4. Ida Mae Jones Marshall, "History of Ellen Sophronia Pratt McGary."
5. Journal of Leonora Cannon, 30 December 1846.
6. Doctrine and Covenants, 136:28.
7. Journal History, 13 September 1846.
8. Journal of Mary H. P. Richards, 27 December 1846. Andrew Jenson, *Latter-day Saint Biographical Encyclopedia*, 4:704–5. This was the genesis of the future Mormon Tabernacle Choir, as Goddard, soon after his arrival in the Salt Lake Valley, became leader of the Tabernacle Choir when it sang in the Old Tabernacle.
9. See Karl E. Wesson, "Dance in the Church of Jesus Christ of Latter-day Saints 1830–1940," 25; and Miscellaneous Minutes, 17 January 1848.
10. Journal History, 5 February 1847 and 12 January and 14 March 1848.
11. Ibid., 1 February 1848.
12. Kenneth W. Godfrey, "Winter Quarters: Glimmering Glimpses Into Mormon Religious and Social Life," 157.
13. Leonora Cannon Journal, 13 July 1846.
14. Journal of Horace K. Whitney, 12 November 1846.
15. Wesson, "Dance in the Church," 32.
16. *Diary of Hosea Stout*, 14 November and 21 December 1847, 1:288 and 291.
17. Journal of John D. Lee, 23 August 1846.
18. Journal of Wilford Woodruff, 13 February 1848.
19. Minutes of a meeting of the Twelve and other leaders, 23 December 1847, Brigham Young Papers. Not so much the kind of dance but its location concerned church leaders. Rather than go to public halls and expose themselves to base elements, the Mormons favored "the right environment—their own." Leona Holbrook, "Dancing as an Aspect of Early Mormon (Church of Jesus Christ of Latter-day Saints) and Utah Culture," 8.
20. Journal of William Appleby, 14 December 1847.
21. Journal of Horace K. Whitney, 16 February and 29 March 1847. McCary did more than merely entertain. A magician, one-man band,

travelling sideshow, and musician all in one, this charlatan and his wife claimed much more. He called himself "Adam, the Ancient of Days returned," and even convinced some men and women that he was a modern prophet. Before they caught up with him, he had taught his own brand of celestial marriage, violating the chastity of several women over on the east side. He was eventually ridden out of town.

22. Kane, "The Mormons," 101.

23. Journal of Mary H. P. Richards, 20 December 1846.

24. Winter Quarters High Council Minutes, 13 December 1846. On the east side "presidents" supervised "branches" and were also instructed to hold weekly meetings.

25. See Journal History, 25 October 1846; and Minutes of the Blockhouse Branch, 10 June 1849. The Blockhouse Branch minute book lists over 100 names of children blessed.

26. Journal of Wilford Woodruff, 29 December 1846.

27. The last meetings of the Nauvoo Relief Society were held in March 1844. The organization was later revived in the Salt Lake Valley. Allen and Leonard, *Story of the Latter-day Saints,* 161.

28. Journal of John D. Lee, 7 June 1846.

29. The average of four children per family is derived from Thomas Bullock's census of the poor-camp families. Of seventeen families with parents between thirty and fifty years of age, the average family size was 5.9 (Journal of Thomas Bullock, October 1846). A study of over forty families in the Mill Branch on the east side revealed a 5.6 average (Mill Branch Record Book, 1848).

30. Journal of Eliza Maria Lyman, May 1847.

31. Journal of Heber C. Kimball, 17 June 1846.

32. The bishops' census report, Journal History, 31 December 1846, indicates that at Winter Quarters the number of women exceeded that of men at a ratio of 2.5 to 1.

33. Helen Whitney, "Scenes and Incidents," 14:98.

34. *Diary of Hosea Stout,* 25 June 1846, 1:170.

35. Helen Whitney, "Scenes and Incidents," 14:98; and Journal of Joseph G. Hovey, 4 July 1847, p. 41.

36. Journal of Patty Sessions, 13 April 1847. For a corraborative testimony, see Journal of Eliza R. Snow, 1 January and 14 March 1847.

37. Journal of Eliza R. Snow, 1 May 1847.

38. Helen Whitney, "Scenes and Incidents," 14:106.

39. Ibid., 98.

40. Doctrine and Covenants, 46:11–12. Joseph Smith, however, had cautioned against excesses, especially the gift of tongues.

41. Journal of Joseph G. Hovey, 4 July 1847, p. 41.

42. Helen Whitney, "Scenes and Incidents," 14:106.

43. Journal of Joseph G. Hovey, 4 July 1847, p. 41.

44. Journal of Patty Sessions, 29 May 1847.

45. Helen Whitney, "Scenes and Incidents," 14:98.

46. Ibid., 118.

47. Ibid.

48. Kenneth Godfrey argues that only "a very, very few of the Mormon women" were involved in the exercising of spiritual gifts. See his "Winter Quarters: Glimmering Glimpses," 160. However, in light of the documentation available, this does not seem to be the case. In the sources quoted above, at least twenty-two women were referred to by name and several references are made to meetings in which over fifteen people were in attendance. Certain it is that many did not participate, but equally sure is the relative popularity of the female meeting. To what extent similar activities were happening on the east side is not presently known.

49. Doctrine and Covenants, 136:20–21, 23–25.

50. Journal History, 7 March 1848.

51. Pottawattamie High Council Minutes, 9 October 1847.

52. Winter Quarters High Council Minutes, 28 November 1847.

53. Pottawattamie High Council Minutes, 24 July 1847.

54. Winter Quarters High Council Minutes, 28 November 1847.

55. *Diary of Hosea Stout*, 4 and 5 September 1846, 1:190–91.

56. See Doctrine and Covenants, 89; and Paul Henry Peterson, "A Historical Analysis of the Word of Wisdom."

57. Wine and whiskey were occasionally used even by the leaders. See *Diary of Hosea Stout*, 3 June 1847, 1:259; and Minutes of a Meeting of the Twelve, Brigham Young Papers, 5 December 1847. Moderation rather than total abstention was the ruling guideline.

58. Journal of Horace K. Whitney, 3 October 1846.

59. Winter Quarters High Council Minutes, 24 December 1846.

60. Journal History, 17 and 24 December 1846.

61. Pottawattamie High Council Minutes, 6 January 1849.

62. Pottawattamie High Council Minutes, 15 March 1847. Disfellowshipment was a reprimand given to a member by which he or she was deprived of the opportunities to participate in religious meetings, temple ordinances, and other church blessings. Membership was retained.

Excommunication, on the other hand, was the strongest religious punishment. It meant the loss of one's membership, including the priesthood and all other ecclesiastical positions and responsibilities.

63. Winter Quarters High Council Minutes, 1 April 1847. Another, less penitent horse thief, after having been found guilty by two bishops, was sentenced to the standard maximum penalty for serious crimes of thirty-nine whiplashes on his bare back, which the marshal inflicted. In addition, he was instructed to restore fourfold what he had taken and pay all costs. See Journal History, 17 and 25 January 1848; and Winter Quarters High Council Minutes, 17 January 1848.

64. See Journal History, 11 August 1846; and Journal of Nelson W. Whipple, "1846," pp. 63–64.

65. Journal History, 19 July and 8 August 1846; and Journal of Wilford Woodruff, 14 April 1848.

66. *Diary of Hosea Stout*, 19 November 1846, 1:212.

67. Ibid., 21–24 January 1848, 1:299. See Journal of Isaac Haight, 1 February 1847; and *Diary of Hosea Stout*, 8 January 1847, 1:224.
68. *Diary of Hosea Stout*, 1 January 1848, 1:293–94.
69. Ibid., 4 January 1848, 1:294.
70. Compliments, such as the following from Joseph Fielding, were rare:

> It is plain that nothing but the strictest laws enforced with what some call vigor altogether considered by many in the Camp oppressive and has been a source of much evil and feeling, yet if we had not had laws a great part of our Corn would have been destroyed. Some of the Police would at times give way to passion, and would seem like black-guards. . . . I have heard them call their Brethren . . . damned infernal liars. The office of Policeman is no desirable one [for] if there be any rough ones, they have to deal with them.

Journal of Joseph Fielding, Winter 1874–75.

CHAPTER 10

1. Doctrine and Covenants, 132:16.
2. Matthew 16:16–19.
3. Doctrine and Covenants, 132:19.
4. In the early days of the church, the term "celestial marriage" usually implied plural marriage. Danel W. Bachman, "A Study of the Mormon Practice of Plural Marriage Before the Death of Joseph Smith," 19. Bachman's study may herald further research into one of the most poorly understood, hotly debated topics in Mormonism.
5. Bachman, "Plural Marriage," 64–68. Bachman infers that Joseph Smith may have understood the doctrine even earlier than 1831. Bachman clearly implies that the doctrine "emerged from a primarily religious context" rather than "rationalizations for his own moral indiscretions." In this view, he stands very much at odds with Fawn M. Brodie, prominent biographer of Joseph Smith, who sees the Mormon prophet as an imaginative, creative genius, a megalomaniac driven by lust and the quest for economic gain. See her *No Man Knows My History: The Life of Joseph Smith, the Mormon Prophet* and Smith, *History of the Church,* V:xxxiii.
6. Bachman, "Plural History," 112–15.
7. Ibid., 176 and 189.
8. *History of the Church,* 6:184.
9. Malachi 4:5–6.
10. Doctrine and Covenants, 128:17–18.
11. Young taught that even the resurrection was not possible until temple proxy work was completed in behalf of the dead. "As saviours on Mt. Zion," the saints were "to save our fathers and Israel clear back to Father Adam who are still lying in their graves and waiting for the re-

demption of their bodies through your instrumentality." Journal of Wilford Woodruff, 15 December 1846.

12. For a good introductory overview of the Law of Adoption, see Gordon Irving, "The Law of Adoption: One Phase of the Development of the Mormon Concept of Salvation, 1830–1900." *Brigham Young University Studies* 14 (Spring 1974): 291–314. A disappointingly small amount of research has been done on this phase of Mormon thought and practice and who originated it. Young taught at Winter Quarters that Joseph Smith knew of the doctrine and had "had a vision and saw and traced back our bloods to the royal family." See Kelly, *Journals of John D. Lee*, 17 February 1847, p. 91; *Diary of Hosea Stout*, 28 February 1847, 1:238; and Doctrine and Covenants, 86:8–10. Young took pains to convince his listeners that the doctrine was Joseph Smith's, not his. "Joseph showed me the pattern." Journal History, 16 February 1847.

13. Irving argues that 74 percent of all those adopted were linked to Willard Richards, Heber C. Kimball, John Taylor, or Brigham Young. Irving, "Law of Adoption," 245.

14. *Comprehensive History*, 2:66.

15. Journal of John D. Lee, 9 August 1846.

16. Brigham Young to George Miller, 20 September 1846, Brigham Young Papers.

17. Journal History, 6 and 29 January 1847.

18. J. W. Fox to Brigham Young, 23 March 1847, Brigham Young Papers.

19. George P. Dykes to Brigham Young, 17 August 1846, Brigham Young Papers.

20. Journal of Elijah F. Sheets, 24 January and 6 April 1847; Trustees Minutes, Brigham Young Papers, 21 November 1847; and Journal of Wilford Woodruff, 4 April 1848.

21. *Diary of Hosea Stout*, 13 July 1846, 1:178.

22. Kelly, *Journals of John D. Lee*, 16 February 1847, p. 83. One of Young's first sermons in the Salt Lake Valley was on the adoption doctrine. See Journal of Horace K. Whitney, 15 August 1847.

23. Journal of Leonora Cannon, 2 January 1847.

24. *Diary of Hosea Stout*, 13 July 1846, 1:178, editor's note.

25. Diary of Heber C. Kimball, 31 January 1847.

26. This is the contention of Juanita Brooks. See *Diary of Hosea Stout*, 9 December 1847, 1:290, editor's note.

27. Decades later it remained a tenet of mystery and debate. In 1887 several church leaders said that "even among the members of the Twelve Apostles there seems to be little known about the laws of Adoption. . . . President George Q. Cannon said he did not understand the matter." Daily Journal of John M. Whitaker, 16 November 1887 as quoted in Bachman, "Plural Marriage," 150–51.

28. Journal History, 16 February 1847. The overriding conviction many held that they were true descendants of the ancient patriarchs

may well have contributed to the pentecostal fervor of the times. Bishop Newel K. Whitney, one of Kimball's senior adopted sons, said during a Kimball family assembly, "don't marvel if you should see many great things in your midst yet while you live that you now not have the least idea of; I should not even wonder if some of our old holy fathers should visit us in the flesh whilst we live" (Journal of Heber C. Kimball, 14 February 1847). Little wonder, then, that Whitney later tolerated the many women's gatherings, prayer meetings, and blessing sessions in Winter Quarters during the summer of 1847.

    29. Kelly, *Journals of John D. Lee,* 16 February 1847, p. 86.

    30. Irving, "Law of Adoption," 303.

    31. Said Henry Jacobs, a recently returned missionary from upstate New York,

> "No, I did not teach the doctrine. I defy any person to say I ever taught a man to have more wives than one, but I had to contend with it. It is in every man's mouth, every child in the east knows it. I've been so close-pinched as to tell a lie."

Minutes of a Meeting of the Twelve and Seventy, 30 November 1847, Brigham Young Papers.

    32. Tullidge, *Women of Mormondom,* 369.

    33. Journal of Eliza R. Snow, February 1846.

    34. Tullidge, *Women of Mormondom,* 327.

    35. "About 6 eve. Pres. B. Young by permission, not according to law, as the sealing ordinances were stopped when the Endowment stopped in the Temple for that ordinance belongs to the Temple alone, solemnized the right of matrimony between Emeline and myself. [He] charged the family to lock these things up in our breast and there let them remain."

Kelly, *Journals of John D. Lee,* 21 December 1846, p. 43. Several of Lee's at least fourteen wives were sealed to him at Winter Quarters. Ibid., 27 February 1847, p. 103.

    36. Helen Whitney, "Scenes and Incidents," 14:11. Two of these five wives, Sarah Ann Whitney and Lucy Walker, were former wives of Joseph Smith who Kimball then remarried "for time only."

    37. Kelly, *Journals of John D. Lee,* 16 February 1847, p. 81.

    38. Pottawattamie High Council Minutes, 18 March 1848. Snow was condemning the practice of men taking wives and then not supporting them adequately.

    39. Journal History, 13 September 1846.

    40. Journal of Patty Sessions, 4 November 1846.

    41. Minutes of the Pottawattamie High Council, 18 March 1848.

    42. Journal of Mary H. P. Richards, 10 February 1847. This was written on the occasion of the birth of her son, Solomon.

    43. Journal of Wilford Woodruff, 24 July 1846.

44. Patriarch John Smith, for one, who remained back in the Salt Lake Valley during the first year of that settlement, was authorized "to seal Sister Mercy Thompson widow of Robert Thompson to any good man holding the Priesthood that she may choose." Brigham Young to John Smith, 1 September 1847, Brigham Young Papers.

45. There is some confusion on this matter. Polygamy, without the assent of the first wife, was akin to bigamy. It therefore was customary for the husband to remember the "Law of Sarah" and ask the first wife for permission for a later marriage, although this was not rigorously enjoined. If it had not been strictly required in Nauvoo (see Bachman, "Plural Marriage," 165–66), at Winter Quarters it was demanded of almost all men. See Minutes of a Meeting of the Twelve and Seventy, 30 November 1847, Brigham Young Papers.

46. Kelly, *Journals of John D. Lee*, 16 February 1847, p. 80.

47. Minutes of a Meeting of the Twelve and Seventy, 30 November 1847, Brigham Young Papers. Phelps's case points out that women may often have compounded the problem by requesting, even demanding, a plural marriage. Certainly, women were not passively sitting by.

48. Ibid.

49. Journal History, 11 February 1848.

50. Pottawattamie High Council Minutes, 6 October 1849.

51. Meeting of the Twelve Apostles, 13 November 1847, Brigham Young Papers.

52. Ibid.

CHAPTER 11

1. Minutes of the Conference in the Log Tabernacle, 27 December, Brigham Young Papers. See also Journal of Norton Jacob, 24–27 December 1847.

2. The Reorganized Church of Jesus Christ of Latter Day Saints (RLDS) has always claimed succession by lineal descent. The president's chair should properly belong to Joseph Smith's descendants. The first president of the RLDS Church was Joseph Smith III, and succeeding presidents have come from the expanded-family descendants of Joseph and Emma Smith. For a review of the RLDS position, see Russell F. Ralston, *Succession in Presidency and Authority;* and W. Grant McMurray, "True Son of a True Father: Joseph Smith III and the Succession Question," *Restoration Studies, I, Sesquicentennial Edition*, ed. Maurice L. Draper and Clare D. Vlahos, 131–41.

In contrast, the position of the Church of Jesus Christ of Latter-day Saints (LDS) has been that of apostolic succession. This tenet calls for the elevation to the First Presidency, the highest ecclesiastical office in the church, of a member of the second-ranking quorum, the Twelve Apostles, traditionally the president of that quorum. For a detailed discussion of the LDS viewpoint, see B. H. Roberts, *Succession in the Presidency of the Church of Jesus Christ of Latter-day Saints;* and Joseph Fielding Smith's similarly entitled work *Succession in the Presidency of the Church of Jesus Christ of Latter-day Saints.*

3. Orson Hyde to E. Robinson, 19 September 1844, as quoted in Leonard Arrington and Ronald Esplin, "The Role of the Council of the Twelve," 11.

4. Samuel W. Richards to Franklin D. Richards, 23–26 August 1844, as quoted in Andrew F. Ehat, "Joseph Smith's Introduction to Temple Ordinances and the 1844 Mormon Succession Question," 209. Ehat credits Ron Esplin for assistance in finding the source. Esplin's article, "Joseph, Brigham and the Twelve: A Succession of Continuity," *Brigham Young University Studies* 21 (Summer 1981): 301–41 is a well-documented, thoroughly pro–Brigham Young review of the succession crisis.

Ehat argues that those succeeding Joseph Smith had to have the highest ordinances, endowments, and second anointings of the temple, i.e., "their calling and election made sure." Quoting Samuel Richards still further, Ehat continues: "He [Joseph] also took them through all the ordinances which is necessary for the Salvation of Man, that they having experienced them all, by passing through them, might be prepared to lead the People in the path which they had trod when he had finished his work ordained and anointed the Twelve to lead this people."

5. Journal of Wilford Woodruff, 25 August 1844, as quoted in Ehat, "Temple Ordinances," 208. A copy of the actual "charge" has not yet been located.

6. Ehat, "Temple Ordinances," 137. Recent developments and charges of forged documents may alter the wording of such a blessing but not necessarily the intent. Ehat argues that Joseph Smith III and his younger brother, David Hyrum, were the only children born of Joseph and Emma Smith after they had received temple sealings and endowments. Hence they were "born under the covenant" and were heirs to eternal blessings. Esplin contends that David, born after his father's death, was even more favored. See Esplin, "Joseph, Brigham and the Twelve," 318. Clearly Joseph wanted to see his sons eventually carry on in the work he had begun if they remained faithful to his teachings.

7. Manuscript History, 17 October 1846.

8. Mills, "De Tal Palo," 135.

9. Brigham Young to Orson Spencer, 23 January 1848, Brigham Young Papers.

10. Journal History, 19 December 1846.

11. *Diary of Hosea Stout,* 30 December 1846, 1:221.

12. Journal of Wilford Woodruff, 24 July 1846.

13. Miscellaneous Trustees Minutes, 17 November 1847, Brigham Young Papers.

14. See Sorensen, "Civil and Criminal Jurisdiction" for an overview of Young's place in court action. Time and again, Young single-handedly

ruled on criminal, doctrinal, ethical, and moral matters. See Minutes of Meeting of the Twelve and Seventy, 30 November 1847.

15. For example, while determining a matter of tax assessments, Young lectured members of the Winter Quarters High Council:

> "that when the authorities devise a plan do not find fault with it and if you find a man that knows more than you follow him. A man who stands as a counsellor to this people sees as in open vision . . . a thousand things that others do not and if he's always right do not be afraid to follow him. We would have been far from here [Winter Quarters] now had it not been for want of confidence in him."

Winter Quarters High Council Minutes, 20 December 1846.

16. Minutes of the Conferences in the Log Tabernacle, 27 December 1847.

17. Journal of Wilford Woodruff, 6 April 1848.

18. Minutes of the Conferences in the Log Tabernacle, 6 April 1848.

19. Wingfield Watson, "An Open Letter to B. H. Roberts, Salt Lake City, Utah," 18–21.

20. Minutes of a Meeting of the Twelve Apostles at Orson Hyde's Home, 5 December 1847, Brigham Young Papers.

21. Ibid.

22. Orson Pratt, who originally raised this issue perhaps more as a request of Young than an objection, contended that

> "The President is the mouthpiece but he has no right to chastise him [a fellow apostle] behind his back. I do not believe Pres. Young has it in his heart to prejudice the minds of the people against anyone of the Quorum. But still it has that effect and I consider it materially wrong. . . .
>
> "There is no man in this Quorum who I respect more than Brother Young, and no man that I would wish sooner to be at the head than Brother Young . . . and although I consider I have seen errors in him, I feel that I could lay down my life for him, yet I feel for the rights of my brethren."

Pratt may have had in mind the severe chastisements that Young levelled against Parley Pratt (his brother) and John Taylor when Young's eastbound returning party met with the Pratt-Taylor westbound emigration train on the Sweetwater River in early September 1847. Pratt himself had been thoroughly scolded on various occasions.

23. Miscellaneous Trustees Minutes, 17 November 1847, Brigham Young Papers.

24. Minutes of a Meeting of the Twelve, 5 December 1847. See Doctrine and Covenants, 107:24, for Pratt's contention that if the Twelve were equal to a First Presidency, why choose one.

25. Minutes of a Meeting of the Twelve and Seventy, 30 November 1847.

26. Journal of Wilford Woodruff, 12 October 1847.

27. Doctrine and Covenants, 135.

28. Said Joseph Young, Brigham's brother and president of the Council of Seventy, "Brigham Young has suggested a new thought to me that the Church has the authority and can make a Presidency." Minutes of a Meeting of the Twelve and Seventy, 30 November 1847.

29. Minutes of the Conferences in the Log Tabernacle, 6 April 1848. There are several other references to this apparently purposeful postponement.

30. Mills, "De Tal Palo," 111.

31. Minutes of a Meeting of the Twelve at Willard Richards' Home, 15 November 1847, Brigham Young Papers. It may be that Young viewed the overland journey west as an ideal time to discuss the issue privately with each of the Twelve. This may partly explain his serious displeasure with John Taylor and Parley Pratt, who refused to go in Young's advance company. He later expressed dissatisfaction with other activities of Pratt and Taylor, especially their bringing back with them unauthorized plural wives. He also opposed their alterations to the authorized style and makeup of emigration parties. See Journal of Wilford Woodruff, 4–7 September 1847; and Miscellaneous Trustees Minutes, 17 November 1847.

32. Wilford Woodruff said that on 12 October 1847, during the return journey to Winter Quarters, he "had a question put to me [by] President Brigham Young what my opinion was concerning one of the Twelve apostles being appointed as the President of the Church" (Journal of Wilford Woodruff, 12 October 1847). Said Young, "From Great Salt Lake City till now 'the tappings of the Spirit to me is the Church ought to be now organized'" (Arrington and Esplin, "The Role of the Council of the Twelve," 21.). Once back at the Missouri, the matter was discussed intently throughout November.

33. Levi Graybill's decision to leave the church is evidence that some were defecting because no president had been sustained: "I think that it was in the spring of 1847," he recalled years later, "that Bishop Miller came . . . and stated to us that we had no church, for the church could not exist without a head, and that we were without a prophet in the flesh." "Testimony of Elder Levi Graybill," Journal of History 4 (January 1911): 109.

34. Minutes of a General Council Meeting, 22 January 1848, Winter Quarters, Brigham Young Papers.

35. Lawyer Almon W. Babbitt, one of the Nauvoo Trustees, described Emma's activities in a letter received just after the reorganization.

"She has made a deed of the whole White purchase to four lawyers . . . the intent is to brake up the title to the Church, holding the action that a religious corporation cannot hold more than ten acres of land . . . this conveyance operates as a compleet estopel of our selling lands in the city. . . .

Emma has joined the Methodist Church . . . they [the Methodists] are laying plans to get in possession of the temple and other proper- ties through Emma . . . the effect of Emma's operation will operate strongly against the Trustees closing out the business."

36. Miscellaneous Trustees Minutes, 17 November 1847.

37. See Ehat, "Temple Ordinances," 143; and Esplin, "Joseph, Brig- ham and the Twelve," 333–36.

38. In April 1847, in a letter to Lucy Mack Smith, aging mother of the Prophet, Young pled with her not to remain with her daughter-in-law, Emma Smith.

"Be assured of this that our faith and prayers have been and are and will be for your welfare; we will rejoice in your prosperity, and as we have hitherto done so will we continue to bless you by all the earthly means in our power . . . and if our dear Mother Smith should at any time wish to come where the Saints are escorted and she will make it manifest unto us, there is no sacrifice we will count too great to bring her forward and we ever have been, now are and shall con- tinue to be ready to divide with her the last loaf."

Brigham Young and the Twelve to Lucy Mack Smith, 4 April 1847, Brigham Young Papers. See also Nathaniel Felt to Orson Hyde, 1 June 1847, Brigham Young Papers.

39. One of Hyrum's sons, Joseph F. Smith, was so appointed and in- deed did become president of the church from 1901 to 1918. In turn, his son, Joseph Fielding Smith, Joseph Smith's grandnephew, was an apostle for over sixty years and served as president from 1970 to 1972.

40. George A. Smith to Joseph Smith III, 13 March 1847, RLDS Li- brary and Archives.

41. Doctrine and Covenants, 107:23–24, 33, and 35.

42. Minutes of Meeting of the Twelve, 5 December 1847.

43. Amasa Lyman seconded Young's proposal. "The intersts of Zion are to be watched over in the Valley, States, Europe and all other parts of the world. The quorum has to be spread abroad," while the president is required at headquarters. "Somebody has to preside. I presume three will go to the Valley, there they will . . . watch over the interests of Zion. They may send me," Lyman concluded, "to preside over the Gentiles." Ibid.

44. Minutes of a Meeting of the Twelve and Seventy, 30 November 1847. During the Winter Quarters period there were approximately thirty-six quorums of seventy in addition to the First Quorum of Sev- enty. A full quorum consisted of seventy men.

45. Ibid.

46. Minutes of a Meeting of the Twelve, 5 December 1847.

47. Pottawattamie High Council Minutes, 6 January 1849.

48. Ehat, "Temple Ordinances," 192.

49. An on-going debate during these years was whether a "high

priest" held greater authority than a "seventy." If so, members of a High Council such as at Winter Quarters and across the river should have more say in the shaping of church policy than seventies. Joseph Young, president of the First Council of Seventies, even believed that if the Twelve were ever annihilated "some of the High Council would be for leading the Church." Such a philosophy may have motivated Alpheus Cutler, one-time senior president of the Winter Quarters High Council, later to quit the church and organize his own in western Iowa. See Pottawattamie High Council Minutes, 18 November 1848; and "History of the Cutlerite Faction of the Latter-day Saints," *Journal of History* 13 (October 1920): 454-57.

It is significant that neither Winter Quarters nor Kanesville were ever "stakes" of the church. Such an organization (comparable to a diocese or parish) represented permanency, whereas Young wanted their stay at the Bluffs to be only temporary. The two high councils at the Missouri, therefore, were "travelling" and not "standing" seats of government and not permanent. "We are only travelling and have stayed all night," said Young to the Winter Quarters High Council about their stay at the Missouri, "and the Council is only to regulate things for the morning— anything done here is not a precedent." Winter Quarters High Council Minutes, 19 December 1847.

50. Defending his point he said, "Joseph's instructions were if one of the Twelve were to go into wrong, just go and get him home and smother it up. But I talk to men because I want them to live . . . not . . . to die. . . . The only way to save . . . men is to talk as I do . . . I believe I am able to classify what is right and what is wrong." Miscellaneous Trustees Minutes, 17 November 1847.

51. Ibid. Young did not hestitate to criticize in public or in private when he saw the need. Years later, after word had been received in Salt Lake that many in the Martin handcart companies had perished from exposure and starvation on account of leaving the Missouri too late in the season, Young came down so hard on Franklin D. Richards and Daniel Spencer during an open conference of the church "that it was years before Richards was ever again of much consequence in the councils of the Church." Stegner, *Gathering of Zion*, 258.

52. Miscellaneous Trustees Minutes, 17 November 1847.

53. Doctrine and Covenants, 27:12 and 128:21. Young argued that Peter, James, and John were a First Presidency. "Joseph said so many a time." Peter was the president. Minutes of a Meeting of the Twelve and Seventy, 30 November 1847.

54. Minutes of a Meeting of the Twelve and Seventy, 30 November 1847. Young's convincing argument was that an election or an appointment of any other potential candidate could not preempt what was rightfully now his by ordination. "You can't make me President because I am President you can't give me power because I have it." Minutes of a Meeting of the Twelve, 5 December 1847. What he sought was the unanimous approval and support of the Quorum of the Twelve.

55. Miscellaneous Trustees Minutes, 17 November 1847.
56. Minutes of a Meeting of the Twelve, 5 December 1847.

57. "Joseph stepped toward me and, looking very earnestly, yet pleasantly, said 'Tell the people to be humble and faithful, and be sure to keep the spirit of the Lord and it will lead them right. . . . Tell the brethren to keep their hearts open to conviction, so that when the Holy Ghost comes to them, their hearts will be ready to receive it."
Journal History, 16 February 1847.
58. *Diary of Hosea Stout*, 28 February 1847, 1:238.
59. Kelly, *Journals of John D. Lee*, 17 February 1847, p. 91.
60. Doctrine and Covenants, 136:37–41.
61. Manuscript History, 17 January 1846.
62. Journal History, 5 December 1847; and Minutes of a Meeting of the Twelve, 5 December 1847. The three missing apostles were Parley Pratt and John Taylor, then in Salt Lake Valley, and the wayward Lyman Wight in Texas.
63. "Testimony of Elder Levi Graybill," 109.
64. See Journal of William I. Appleby, 4 December 1847; and Journal of Wilford Woodruff, 4 December 1847.
65. Journal of Nelson W. Whipple, Winter of 1847–48.
66. Thomas Bullock, Historical Department Journals, 22 December 1847; and Journal of Norton Jacob, 24 December 1847.
67. Lawrence D. Clark concluded that the Log Tabernacle was built near or on the location of Harmony, Benton, and Frank streets in present Council Bluffs (Papers of Lawrence D. Clark). Gail Holmes, another local historian, has placed it between Baughn and Logan, north of Harmony Street. The Log Tabernacle is not to be confused with the Pigeon Creek Tabernacle built in 1849 and located six miles north. See George A. Smith to Brigham Young, 7 May 1849, Brigham Young Papers.
After the succession conference the Log Tabernacle was used extensively for church conferences, balls, and dances, and as a meetinghouse for the Blockhouse Branch. For several months the Pottawattamie High Council convened in it. But the damaging spring runoffs of 1848 and 1849 inflicted irreparable damage on the structure, seriously weakening its foundation and supports. Some efforts were made to raise the floor and repair the building, but with little success. It apparently was dismantled in the fall of 1849 and many of the logs reused in building the Pigeon Creek Tabernacle. See Pottawattamie High Council Minutes, 26 August 1849.
The Log Tabernacle was built on the Iowa side rather than at Winter Quarters because of the recent decision to abandon Winter Quarters the coming spring.
68. Conference minutes, 24 December 1847, Brigham Young Papers.
69. Minutes of the Conferences in the Log Tabernacle, 27 December 1847.

CHAPTER 12

1. Journal History, 8 April 1848.

2. Ibid., 25 November 1847.

3. Among other things, the epistle contained the following:

"Gather yourselves together speedily, near to this place, on the east side of the Missouri River, and, if possible, be ready to start from hence by the first of May next. . . . Let the Saints who have been driven and scattered from Nauvoo . . . gather immediately to the east bank of the river . . . and when here, let all who can, go directly over the mountains; those who cannot, let them go immediately to work at making improvements, raising grain and stock. . . .

"To the Saints in England, Scotland, Ireland, Wales, and adjacent islands and countries, we say emigrate as speedily as possible to this vicinity."

Journal History, 21 December 1847.

4. Journal History, 25 November 1847.

5. Nathaniel Felt was assigned clearing agent for the church in St. Louis and Lucius N. Scovil in New Orleans.

6. Journal History, 25 November 1847.

7. Ibid., 7 February 1848.

8. Allen and Leonard, *Story of the Latter-day Saints*, 282–84.

9. See Journal History, 9 March and 21 May 1848; and Nathaniel Felt to Brigham Young, 28 March 1848, Brigham Young Papers.

10. Emigration compilations and records in the reading room of the LDS Church Archives. Mormon voyagers were no more immune to the hazards of river transportation than their fellow travellers. By far the most dramatic and serious loss of life was the fatal explosion of the steamboat *Saluda* in April 1852, in which scores were killed.

11. Clyde B. Aitchison, "Mormon Settlements in the Missouri Valley," 288.

12. Journal of Nelson W. Whipple, Spring and Summer 1848.

13. Pottawattamie High Council Minutes, 15 July 1848; and Silas Richards to the First Presidency, 10 October 1848, Brigham Young Papers.

14. The High Council adjudicated both civic and religious matters in the absence of established civic government. Pottawattamie High Council Minutes, 8 January 1848.

15. Journal History, 8 April 1848. Said William Snow: "We have now in this county about 40 branches of the church organized . . . and some fifty elders selected to preach they generally go two together giving each Branch a preach once in about two weeks" (William Snow to Brigham Young, 2 October 1848, Brigham Young Papers). A few branches had both a bishop and a branch president. See table 9.

16. Pottawattamie High Council Minutes, 8 January 1848.

17. See D. C. Bloomer, "The Mormons in Iowa," *Annals of Iowa*, 596; and Roy Franklin Lawson, "The Mormons: Their Trek Across Iowa and Their Settlement in Kanesville," 78.

18. Merrill J. Mattes, *The Great Platte River Road*, 123.

19. See Bloomer, "Mormons in Iowa," 597; and Lawson, "The Mormons," 78.

20. Morton, *History of Nebraska*, 131. Bloomer's more exaggerated figure of 7,828 in 1850 likely included satellite communities.

21. Pottawattamie High Council Minutes, 10 June 1848.

22. It was enough for Hyde, in his sometimes self-congratulatory manner, to proclaim "I have sometimes thought that no other man in this Kingdom ever took such responsibility and performed so much labor for nothing and then work with his own hands to earn bread before he eat it." Orson Hyde to Brigham Young, 25 April 1850, Brigham Young Papers.

23. Journal History, 24 March 1848.

24. Said Reverend Sidney Roberts, Whig delegate dispatched to Kanesville in March 1848,

"From whence comes [your] affliction? Although individuals of every party and creed may have participated in bringing about this result, may it not with great safety be affirmed, that the Loco Focos as a party have been mainly instrumental in confirming the ruin of those who have too willingly and credulously supported that party? . . . Were they not the leaders of the same Loco Focos party who had driven you from your homes in Missouri? Did not the same Governor whom you had been instrumental in electing stand by and permit Joseph and Hyrum Smith to be murdered before your eyes? . . . You now have it in your power to vindicate yourselves."

Ibid., 1 March 1848.

25. Journal of William I. Appleby, 28 November 1848.

26. See Journal of Thomas Bullock, 9 February 1848; and Journal History, 16 January 1848.

27. It appears that Thomas Kane, who received a copy of the petitions, was highly influential in persuading the postmaster general to grant the post office with Evan M. Greene as postmaster. Brigham Young to Thomas L. Kane, 9 February 1848, Brigham Young Papers. Apparently the county organization made in September 1848 was spearheaded by the Democrats, including Babbitt and William Pickett. But it became an organization without representation, especially when it became clear the Mormons would vote the Whig ticket. Consequently, only two precincts, one at Kanesville and the other at Mt. Pisgah, were organized, and both of them were placed under the judicial review of Monroe County commissioners. The argument made for postponing the county organization was that Indian claims had not been extinct six

months. George Albert Smith and Joseph Young to the First Presidency and the Twelve, 2 October 1848, Brigham Young Papers.

28. See Bloomer, "The Mormons in Iowa," 596; and William Snow to Brigham Young, Brigham Young Papers, 8 October 1848.

29. Apostle George A. Smith wrote that James Sloan was appointed to return the polling books to the county clerk at Albia, county seat of Monroe County. "The clerk," he said, "at first refused to receive them, but afterwards did so, and reported they were stolen and made no returning of them to the Secretary of State. The result was that Miller, the Jack Mormon [i.e., a sympathetic non-Mormon] candidate for Congress was beaten." George Albert Smith and Joseph Young to the First Presidency and the Twelve, 2 October 1848, Brigham Young Papers.

30. Bloomer, "The Mormons in Iowa," 598–99.

31. Journal of Warren E. Foote, 3 June 1847.

32. Autobiography of Joseph Holbrook, 58.

33. See Orson Hyde, Ezra Taft Benson, and George A. Smith to Brigham Young, 5 April 1849, Brigham Young Papers; and Journal of Wilford Woodruff, 19 May 1849.

34. Orson Hyde to Brigham Young, 25 April 1850, Brigham Young Papers.

35. Pottawattamie High Council Minutes, 25 May 1850.

36. Journal of Wilford Woodruff, 18 May 1850.

37. Journal of Nelson W. Whipple, Spring of 1849.

38. Journal of Warren E. Foote, 15 May 1849.

39. Walker D. Wyman, "The Missouri River Towns in the Westward Movement," 85.

40. Joseph Shafer, ed., *Across the Plains in 1850 by John Steele,* 26–27.

41. Orson Hyde to Brigham Young, 27 April 1851, Brigham Young Papers; Orson Hyde to Brigham Young, 25 April 1850, Brigham Young Papers; and Journal of Warren E. Foote, 1 April 1850.

42. Private journal not yet to be identified, 25 April 1852, LDS Church Archives.

43. Wilford Woodruff once complained of there being only one yoke of oxen per seventeen families because of yielding to pressures to sell out at such high prices. One sale of oxen at $50 to $70 could buy three homesteads at the Bluffs. Journal of Wilford Woodruff, 15 May 1850.

44. By 1852, Kanesville contained sixteen mercantile establishments, two drugstores, five hotels, four groceries, two jewelers, one harness maker, eight wagon shops, two tinsmiths, two livery stables, two cabinet shops, five boot and shoe makers, two daguerrotype rooms, five physicians, nine lawyers, one gunsmith, one cooper, three barbershops, four bakers, one mill, and seven blacksmith shops. Walker D. Wyman, "Council Bluffs and the Westward Movement," *Iowa Journal of History* 47 (April 1949): 103.

45. Journal of Horace K. Whitney, 29 January 1847.

46. Kelly, *Journals of John D. Lee,* 7 May 1847, p. 162.

47. Journal of Warren E. Foote, 29 September 1846 and 10 July 1847.
48. Journal of Lorenzo Snow, Winter 1846–47.
49. *Diary of Hosea Stout*, 27 April 1847, 1:252–53.
50. Kelly, *Journals of John D. Lee*, 7 May 1847, p. 162. Many were abandoning Summer Quarters over land disputes and other concerns that plagued that particular endeavor.
51. Noah Packard to Brigham Young, 6 December 1848, Brigham Young Papers.
52. *Diary of Hosea Stout*, 20 December 1846, 1:219 and 2 January 1847, 1:222–23; and Journal History, 4 April 1848.
53. Journal History, 5 April 1848.
54. Orson Hyde to Brigham Young, 22 April 1848, Brigham Young Papers. An embittered James Stephens Brown, who forsook the Mormons at the Missouri, tried to persuade his son to quit the church.

"I was like you. I followed up the tide met with poverty, death and many other things while I was in Winter Quarters while I found if I kept other man's council instead of my own, I could not support my family and all the blessings was by giving some considerable to others that I did not think worthy of it, and on the other hand cirses were pronounced if you did not get along nor prosper, but I thank God I have been blessed and prospered abundantly."

Daniel Brown to James Brown, 16 April 1854, Papers of James Stephens Brown.
55. Orson Hyde to Brigham Young, 27 April 1850, Brigham Young Papers.
56. Report of George Albert Smith, Ezra Taft Benson, and Joseph Young to the First Presidency and the Twelve, 2 October 1848, Brigham Young Papers.
57. George A. Smith to Brigham Young, 7 October 1848, Brigham Young Papers.
58. In November 1846, Ezra Taft Benson, then back on the east coast, reported that Strang and his counselor, George H. Adams, were in Pittsburgh, and that "The apostates and whoremongers are ralleying around Strang's standard." Kelly, *Journals of John D. Lee*, 29 November 1846, p. 28.
59. J. A. Stratton to Brigham Young, 27 December 1846, Brigham Young Papers; and Pottawattamie High Council Minutes, 13 October 1849.
60. One writer of the Reorganized Church of Jesus Christ of Latter Day Saints claims dissatisfaction over polygamy was a primary cause of wide-scale alienations, but this is difficult to substantiate statistically. James L. Doty Jr., "The Beginnings of the Reorganization of the Omaha-Council Bluffs Area," *Restoration Trail Forum* 7 (February 1981): 1, 4, and 6.
Ten years later, William W. Blair and E. C. Briggs, leaders in the Re-

organization movement, organized several branches in Pottawattamie and Decatur counties. In their "revival of pure and undefiled religion," their success came "among the old [LDS] members" who had decided to stay behind. "Conference Minutes of the Church of Jesus Christ of Latter-day Saints 1859 and 1860."

61. *Diary of Hosea Stout*, 1 April 1847, 1:243, editor's note.

62. Ironically, the most serious doctrinal dissension did not immediately result from polygamy or the Law of Adoption, but from a difference of opinion over the doctrine of the resurrection. Although documentation is sporadic, it appears that many had been persuaded to believe in a form of reincarnation, a resurrection "by birth or through the womb," that "some had been teaching." See Journal of Wilford Woodruff, 21 November 1847. The provenance and promulgators of such a viewpoint are not yet known, but it did attract the attention and sermonizing of many church authorities. This might explain Young's address during the succession conference in December 1847 in which he discussed the matter in depth. Only Adam, he said, held the keys of resurrection. See Chap. 11.

63. Arriving at a number for those who left the church at the Missouri is difficult. The chart below is a rough approximation based upon three estimates: calculations of the numbers of Latter-day Saints on the Missouri and Mississippi rivers in December 1846; the numbers of British emigrants who began arriving at the Bluffs from 1848 to 1852 and who crossed the plains; and the estimated Mormon population in Utah as of 1852. Data for the British emigration was derived from in-house emigration books and calculations in the search room of the LDS Church Archives.

The 14,500 population figure for Utah in 1852 was taken from a proposed official publication compiled by Earl Olson and others summarizing church membership through the years. The approximate death rate is in line with the regular Nauvoo death rates and the reduced death rate at the Missouri in 1848.

Estimated Mormon population on the Missouri and Mississippi rivers, December 1846 (see Chap. 4)	11,800
Total British emigrants, 1848–52	6,992
Arrivals from California (est.)	200
Total potential number who could have crossed to Utah up until December 1852	18,992
Estimated 1852 Utah Population	14,500
Number who did not go west	4,492
Less average mortality loss at	

40 deaths per thousand per year over 5 years—based 11,800 pop.	2,360
Estimated total who did not go west	2,132
Estimated percent of those at the Bluffs who did not go west (not counting Nauvoo disaffections)	11.2

64. Pottawattamie High Council Minutes, 4–5 November 1848.
65. Wyman, "Missouri River Towns," 106.

BIBLIOGRAPHY

ESSAY

The historiography on the topic of this book makes for relatively short and skimpy reading. Save for Conrey Bryson's recent short overview, *Winter Quarters* (Salt Lake City: Deseret Books, 1986), no single volume hitherto existed detailing the history of Winter Quarters, and most of the several Brigham Young biographies skip over this area. As indicated in the Introduction, I have relied most heavily on the primary sources to fill the vacuum—diaries, letters, minutes, and biographies.

Nonetheless, several printed sources were consulted and found very helpful. By far the most useful are published manuscripts of the following contemporary journals: *William Clayton's Journal—A Daily Record of the Journey of the Original Company of "Mormon" Pioneers from Nauvoo, Illinois, to the Valley of the Great Salt Lake* (Salt Lake City: Deseret News, 1921); Charles Kelly, ed., *Journals of John D. Lee 1846–47 and 1859)* (Salt Lake City: Western Printing Company, 1938); Elden J. Watson, comp., *Manuscript History of Brigham Young 1846–1847* (Salt Lake City, 1971); and most helpful of all, Juanita Brooks, ed., *On the Mormon Frontier—The Diary of Hosea Stout 1844–1861*, 2 vols. (Salt Lake City: University of Utah Press, 1964).

Only two theses address themselves directly to the history of the Mormons in the Council Bluffs region. Ernest Widtsoe Shumway's "History of Winter Quarters, Nebraska 1846–1848" (M.A. thesis, Brigham Young University, 1953) is a good beginning, but only that. Shumway relied almost exclusively on secondary references and either was not allowed access or consciously chose not to use the manuscript sources in the Historical Department of the Church of Jesus Christ of Latter-day Saints in Salt Lake City. Consequently, his work is incomplete, omitting many of the relevant issues and concerns. Another thesis suffering from the same difficulty is Lynn Robert Webb's "The Contributions of the Temporary Settlements Garden Grove, Mount Pisgah, and Kanesville, Iowa to Mormon Emigration, 1846–1852" (M.A. thesis, Brigham Young University,

1954). Clyde B. Aitchison's article "The Mormon Settlements in the Missouri Valley," *Quarterly of the Oregon Historical Society* (1907): 276–289, was only marginally informative.

Few general survey histories devote so much as a chapter to Winter Quarters, and of these most rely uncritically on the observations of Thomas L. Kane in his published lecture *"The Mormons." A Disclosure Delivered Before the Historical Society of Pennsylvania, March 16, 1850* (Philadelphia: King and Baird Printers, 1850). Mormon historian Brigham H. Roberts's still useful though dated six-volume study, *A Comprehensive History of the Church of Jesus Christ of Latter-day Saints* (Salt Lake City: Deseret News Press, 1930), provides a sympathetic overview. Bernard De Voto's *Year of Decision, 1846* (Boston: Little, Brown and Company, 1943) is still a superbly written interweaving of main currents in American history for that eventful year, and it provides excellent insights into the Mormon exodus as a part of the much larger American scene, including the Mexican War. A noninterpretive study commemorating the centennial of the trek, using primary sources, is Preston Nibley's *Exodus to Greatness: The Story of the Mormon Migration* (Salt Lake City: Deseret News Press, 1947). No less readable through more sarcastic in tone than De Voto's is the recent work by Wallace Stegner, *The Gathering of Zion— The Story of the Mormon Trail* (Salt Lake City: Westwater Press, 1981). Written in a journalistic, flowing style and from a non-Mormon vantage point, Stegner's book devotes one chapter to Winter Quarters and provides color and human interest, but fails to offer any new facts on the subject. Dale L. Morgan's *The Great Salt Lake* (Indianapolis: Bobbs Merrill Company, 1947) devotes even less time to Winter Quarters, but is factual and informative.

Other general published histories that are only marginally informative but invaluable in providing Mormon context and the modern Mormon historical approach are Leonard J. Arrington's *Great Basin Kingdom—An Economic History of the Latter-day Saints 1830– 1900* (Cambridge: Harvard University Press, 1958), by far the best study of Mormon economics in the nineteenth century; *The Mormon Experience—A History of the Latter-day Saints* (New York: Vantage Books, 1980), by Leonard J. Arrington and Davis Bitton; James Allen and Glenn Leonard's *The Story of the Latter-day Saints* (Salt Lake City: Deseret Book Company, 1976); and *The City of God* (Salt Lake City: Deseret Book Company, 1976), by Leonard J. Arrington, Feramorz Y. Fox, and Dean L. May.

The single best background study for understanding trail migrations in America in the mid-nineteenth century is John D. Unruh Jr.'s *The Plains Across—The Overland Immigrants and the Trans-Mississippi West 1840–60* (Urbana: University of Illinois Press, 1979). Perhaps the most significant, scholarly work on Oregon, California, and

Mormon trail movements west, Unruh's book provides indispensable statistical overviews and trends in a flowing narrative rich with flavor and human interest. Another valuable insight into the Oregon and Mormon trails is Merrill J. Mattes's *The Great Platte River Road: The Covered Wagon Main Line via Fort Kearny to Fort Laramie* (Lincoln: Nebraska State Historical Society, 1969). An unpublished work helpful in understanding Missouri River towns is "The Missouri River Towns in the Westward Movement" (Ph.D. dissertation, Iowa State University, 1935), by Walker D. Wyman.

By far the most reliable starting point in studying Mormon plans for the trek west and their eventual destination is Lewis Clark Christian's "A Study of the Mormon Westward Migration Between February 1846 and July 1847 with Emphasis on and Evaluation of the Factors that led to the Mormon Choice of Salt Lake Valley as the Site of Their Initial Colony" (Ph.D. dissertation, Brigham Young University, 1976). A good distillation of Christian's work was recently published as "Mormon Foreknowledge of the West," *Brigham Young University Studies* 21 (Fall 1981): 403–15.

The story of the Mormon crossing of Iowa has been left largely untold although two authors have given much attention to the question of "where" they went. Stanley Kimball has written extensively on the subject, including *Discovering Mormon Trails, New York to California 1831–1868* (Salt Lake City: Deseret Book Company, 1979), perhaps the best single map study of Mormon trails, and his most recent "The Mormon Trail Network in Iowa 1838–1863: A New Look," *Brigham Young University Studies* 21 (Fall 1981): 417–30. Before Kimball, Jacob Van der Zee's "The Mormon Trails in Iowa," *Iowa Journal of History and Politics* 12 (January 1914): 3–16, was probably the authority, and it must still be consulted, especially for the trail in western Iowa. Another outdated but still valuable contribution to the Iowa crossing is Roy Franklin Lawson's "The Mormons: Their Trek Across Iowa and Their Settlement in Kanesville" (M.A. thesis, Creighton University, 1937). Edgar Ruby Harlan's *A Narrative History of the People of Iowa* (Chicago: American Historical Society, Inc., 1931) also provides some assistance, although Harlan relied heavily on Van der Zee.

Several publications were helpful in providing a necessary understanding of the upper Missouri River country prior to the Mormon arrival, particularly with respect to the Indians and the fur trade. "Annual Reports of the U.S. Office of Indian Affairs" and other related Senate and House documents provided indispensable information. Of no less value were Hiram Martin Chittenden's *The American Fur Trade of the Far West*, 2 vols. (Stanford: Academic Reprints, 1954), also Hiram Martin Chittenden and Alfred Talbot Richardson's

Life, Letters and Travels of Father Pierre-Jean De Smet, S.J. 1801–1873, 4 vols. (New York: Francis P. Harper, 1905). Of specific value in understanding the local Indian tribes were Ray H. Mattison's "The Indian Frontier on the Upper Missouri to 1865," *Nebraska History* 39 (September 1958) 241–66; Margaret E. Hansen's "Removal of the Indians from Nebraska" (M.A. thesis, Colorado State College of Education, 1949); and most recently, Robert A. Trennert Jr.'s "The Mormons and the Office of Indian Affairs: The Conflict Over Winter Quarters, 1846–1848" *Nebraska History* 53 (Fall 1972): 381–400.

On the role and history of the Mormon Battalion the most enduring standard study is Daniel Tyler's *A Concise History of the Mormon Battalion in the Mexican War 1846–47* (1881; reprint, Chicago: Rio Grande Press, 1969). Frank A. Golder's *The March of the Mormon Battalion from Council Bluffs to California* (New York: Century Co., 1928) was also helpful. Recently John F. Yurtinus has completed the definitive scholarly study on the subject in his "A Ram in the Thicket: The Mormon Battalion in the Mexican War" (Ph.D. dissertation, Brigham Young University, 1975), now being published. Until all the papers of President James K. Polk are edited and published by Vanderbilt University, the only reliable manuscript source on Polk and his administration for the Battalion era remains Milo Quaife's *The Diary of James K. Polk During His Presidency, 1845 to 1849* (Chicago: A.C. McClurg and Company, 1910).

Next to nothing has been written on the social and cultural life of the Mormons at Winter Quarters, and what little has been said is still unpublished. Maureen Ursenbach Beecher has written extensively on Mormon women and has willingly shared with me many of her findings supportive of her recent Mormon History Association paper on the topic given in May 1983 and published as "Women at Winter Quarters," *Sunstone* 8 (July 8 and August 1983) 4:11–19. Beecher's work is sorely needed and updates and corrects so much in Edward W. Tullidge's *The Women of Mormondom* (New York: 1877). Kenneth W. Godfrey's similarly unpublished paper "Winter Quarters: Glimmering Glimpses Into Mormon Religious and Social Life" also proved helpful. The only work remotely helpful on sickness and death among the Mormons, a grossly neglected topic, is Matthew Anthony Thomas's "Disease in a Mormon Community, Nauvoo, Illinois: 1839–1846" (B.A. thesis, Harvard University, 1977).

Virtually nothing has yet appeared on church theology and practife for the period under study. Several very recent works, however, while focusing on Nauvoo, provide indispensable background information on specific beliefs and practices. For understanding the doctrine of plural marriage, Danel W. Bachman has written a sympathetic yet scholarly treatise "A Study of the Mormon Practice of

Plural Marriage Before the Death of Joseph Smith" (M.A. thesis, Purdue University, 1975). Andrew F. Ehat's "Joseph Smith's Introduction to Temple Ordinances and the 1844 Mormon Succession Question" (M.A. thesis, Brigham Young University, 1982) is a provocative reexamination of temple work and its importance in Nauvoo. Finally, for the poorly understood Law of Adoption, the best single study is Gordon Irving's "The Law of Adoption: One Phase of the Development of the Mormon Concept of Salvation, 1830–1900," *Brigham Young University Studies* 14 (Spring 1974): 291–314. All three of the above point to a refreshing change in Mormon historiography, a courageous willingness to tackle debatable topics heretofore considered off limits.

Several works are now coming forth on church government during the post–Joseph Smith era. Ronald K. Esplin, especially, has made truly valuable, albeit sympathetic, studies of the role of the Twelve Apostles in the following three works: "Joseph, Brigham and the Twelve: A Succession of Continuity" *Brigham Young University Studies* 21 (Summer 1981): 301–41; "Brigham Young and the Power of the Apostleship: Defending the Kingdom Through Prayer, 1844–45" (Sidney B. Sperry Symposium Sesquicentennial Look at Church History, January 16, 1980); and his and Leonard J. Arrington's "The Role of the Council of the Twelve During Brigham Young's Presidency of the Church of Jesus Christ of Latter-day Saints," *Task Papers in LDS History* 31 (Salt Lake City: Historical Department of the Church of Jesus Christ of Latter-day Saints, 1979). For two clashing opinions on the ill-defined Council of Fifty, contrast Klaus Hansen's *Quest for Empire—The Political Kingdom of God and the Council of Fifty in Mormon History* (Lansing: Michigan State University Press, 1967) with Michael D. Quinn's "The Council of Fifty and Its Members, 1844 to 1945," *Brigham Young University Studies* 20 (Winter 1980) 2:163–197. While much has been written on James J. Strang and his claim to succession, I have relied on Strang's official publication, *The Voree Herald,* and William D. Russell's "King James Strang: Joseph Smith's Successor?" in *The Restoration Movement in Mormon History* (Lawrence, Kansas: Coronado Press, 1973), edited by F. Mark McKiernan, Alma R. Blair, and Paul M. Edwards, pp. 231–56.

The best source available for a study of Kanesville history is the town newspaper, *The Frontier Guardian,* which began publication in 1849 and continued until 1852. Orson Hyde served as editor and took pains to cover church practices and theology, plus Whig party politics, in fascinating detail.

Those sources listed below are the works cited in this study. Many other studies were consulted, however.

PRIMARY SOURCES

Archives, Libraries, and Other Depositories

The Historical Department of The Church of Jesus Christ of Latter-day Saints. Salt Lake City. Hereafter referred to as the LDS Church Archives.

Library and Archives, Reorganized Church of Jesus Christ of Latter Day Saints. The Auditorium, Independence. Hereafter referred to as RLDS Library and Archives.

The Marriott Library. Salt Lake City. University of Utah.

The Nauvoo Restoration Corporation. Salt Lake City.

The New York Public Library. New York City.

Special Collections, Harold B. Lee Library, Provo, Utah. Brigham Young University. Hereafter referred to as BYU Library.

The Utah State Historical Society. Salt Lake City.

Unpublished Journals and Diaries

Allen, Orville M. Journal. LDS Church Archives.
Appleby, William S. Journal. LDS Church Archives.
Bates, Nelson. Journal. RLDS Library and Archives.
Black, Joseph Smith. Diary. Typescript. BYU Library.
Blakeslee, James. Journal. Typescript. RLDS Library and Archives.
Bullock, Thomas. Journal. LDS Church Archives.
———. Historical Department Journals. LDS Church Archives.
Cannon, Leonora. Journal. LDS Church Archives.
Dana, Charles R. Journal. LDS Church Archives.
Dunham, Jonathan. Journal. LDS Church Archives.
Fielding, Joseph. Journal. LDS Church Archives.
Flanagan, James H. Journal. LDS Church Archives.
Foote, Warren E. Journal. LDS Church Archives.
Glines, James Henry. Journal. LDS Church Archives.
Haight, Isaac. Journal. Typescript. Bancroft Collection of Mormon Papers, Library of Congress. Microfilm at Marriott Library, University of Utah.
Harmon, Appleton Milo. Diary. Typescript. Bancroft Collection of Mormon Papers, Library of Congress. Microfilm at Marriott Library, University of Utah.
Hovey, Joseph G. Journal. LDS Church Archives.
Huntington, William. Journal. BYU Library.
Jacob, Norton. Journal. LDS Church Archives.
Kimball, Heber C. Journal. LDS Church Archives.
Lee, John D. Journal. LDS Church Archives.
Lyman, Eliza Maria. Journal. Typescript. BYU Library.

Pratt, Orson. Journal. LDS Church Archives.
Pulsipher, John. Diary. LDS Church Archives.
Richards, Mary H. P. Journal. LDS Church Archives.
Richards, Willard. Journal. LDS Church Archives.
Rogers, Samuel H. Journal. BYU Library.
Scott, James Allen. Journal. Typescript. LDS Church Archives.
Sessions, Patty. Journal. LDS Church Archives.
Sheets, Elijah F. Journal. LDS Church Archives.
Snow, Eliza R. Journal. LDS Church Archives.
Snow, Erastus. Journal. LDS Church Archives.
Snow, Lorenzo. Journal. LDS Church Archives.
Stout, Hosea. Journal. LDS Church Archives.
Watson, Gilbert. Journal. RLDS Library and Archives.
Whipple, Nelson W. Journal. LDS Church Archives.
Whitney, Horace K. Journal. LDS Church Archives.
Woodruff, Wilford. Journal. LDS Church Archives.

Unpublished Histories, Reminiscences, and Autobiographies

Blakeslee, James. "My Reasons for Separating Myself from the Church at Nauvoo." James Blakeslee Papers. RLDS Library and Archives.
Butler, John Lowe. "A Short History of the Life of John Lowe Butler," Autobiography. LDS Church Archives.
Call, Anson. Autobiography. LDS Church Archives.
Holbrook, Joseph. Autobiography. LDS Church Archives.
Huntington, William. "A History of William Huntington." BYU Library.
Johnson, Benjamin F. "My Life's Review." Microfilm copy. Benjamin F. Johnson Papers. LDS Church Archives.
McArthur, Daniel D. Autobiography. LDS Church Archives.
Marshall, Ida Mae Jones. "History of Ellen Sophronia Pratt McGary." LDS Church Archives.
Miller, D. E. "Westward Migration of the Mormons With Special Emphasis on the History of Nauvoo." Salt Lake City: Nauvoo Restoration Corporation, 1963.
Smith, Bathsheba W. "Record Book of Bathsheba W. Smith." BYU Library.
Taggart, Fanny Parks. Autobiography. LDS Church Archives.
Whitaker, George. "Life of George Whitaker—A Utah Pioneer." Typescript. Utah State Historical Society.
Young, Brigham. "Manuscript History of Brigham Young." LDS Church Archives.

Correspondence Files

Brown, Daniel, to Brown, James. 16 April 1854. James Stephens Brown Papers. Utah State Historical Society.

Hascall Family Letters, 1845–54. RLDS Library and Archives.

Kane, Thomas L., to Dallas, George M. Letter of 18 May 1846. Kane Papers. BYU Library.

Kane, Thomas L., to Kane, Elisha. Letter of 29 May 1846. Kane Papers. BYU Library.

Kane, Thomas L., to Medill, William. Letter of 21 April 1846. Thomas L. Kane Papers, Yale University. Microfilm copy in LDS Church Archives.

Kimball, Christeen G., to her mother. Letter of 7 May 1847. Correspondence of Christeen G. Kimball. LDS Church Archives.

Miller, George, to Wight, Lyman. Letter of 19 January 1854. RLDS Library and Archives.

Mitchell, R. B., to Harvey, Thomas H. Letter of 29 June 1846. Kane Papers. BYU Library.

Office of Indian Affairs, Letters sent by, 1824–82. Microfilm. National Archives, Washington, D.C.

Paden, Isaac, to Adams, James M. Letter of 27 February 1853. RLDS Library and Archives.

Richards, Willard, to Richards, Levi. Letter of 9 March 1846. Richards Family Papers. RLDS Library and Archives.

Smith, George A., to Smith, Joseph, III. Letter of 13 March 1847. RLDS Library and Archives.

Watson, Wingfield. "An Open Letter to B. H. Roberts, Salt Lake City, Utah." 13 November 1894. Unbound pamphlet. RLDS Library and Archives.

Young, Brigham. Incoming and outgoing correspondence in the Brigham Young Papers, 1845–1850. LDS Church Archives. (The majority of letters cited in this work are derived from the Brigham Young Papers. For space considerations, they are not listed here.)

Ecclesiastical and Institutional Archives and Minutes of Special Meetings

"Conference Minutes of the Church of Jesus Christ of Latter-day Saints 1859 and 1860." Record Book. RLDS Library and Archives.

Mill Branch Record Book, 1848. LDS Church Archives.

Minutes of the Blockhouse Branch, 1846–49. LDS Church Archives.

Minutes of the Conferences in the Log Tabernacle, 24 and 27 December 1847; 6 April 1848. Brigham Young Papers.

Minutes of a General Council Meeting. 22 January 1848. Brigham Young Papers.

Minutes of a Meeting of the Twelve, Seventies, High Council, and
    Bishops. 10 November 1847. Brigham Young Papers.
Minutes of a Meeting of the Twelve and Seventy. 30 November
    1847. Brigham Young Papers.
Minutes of a Meeting of the Twelve. 13 November; 15 November, 5
    December 1847. Brigham Young Papers.
Minutes of Miscellaneous Trustees Minutes. 15, 17, and 21 Novem-
    ber 1847. Brigham Young Papers. LDS Church Archives.
Mt. Pisgah Historical Record. LDS Church Archives.
Pottawattamie High Council Minutes, 1846–1852. LDS Church
    Archives.
Unbound conference minute book, July and October 1850. J. J.
    Strang Papers. RLDS Library and Archives.
Winter Quarters High Council Minutes, 1846–1848. LDS Church
    Archives.
Winter Quarters Store Account Book. 1846–47. Brigham Young
    Papers.

Financial Records

Belnap, Gilbert. Account Book. LDS Church Archives.
Kirtland, Ohio. Gilbert and Whitney Day Book, November 1836–
    April 1837. RLDS Library and Archives.
Winter Quarters. Store Account Book. LDS Church Archives.

Special Vertical Files and Historical Compilations

Clark, Lawrence, Scrapbook. Lawrence Clark Collection. LDS
    Church Archives.
Journal History of the Church. A chronological collection of news-
    papers and other items related to The Church of Jesus Christ of
    Latter-day Saints as compiled by Andrew Jenson. LDS Church
    Archives.
Manuscript History of Cutler's Park. LDS Church Archives.
Manuscript History of Winter Quarters. LDS Church Archives.
Research card collection. Nauvoo Restoration Corporation.
Snider, Cecil. Newsclipping Collection on Mormon History. New
    York Public Library.

PUBLISHED WORKS

Books

Allen, James B., and Leonard, Glen M. *The Story of the Latter-day
    Saints.* Salt Lake City: Deseret Book Company, 1976.
Arrington, Leonard J. *Charles C. Rich—Mormon General and Western*

Frontiersman. Provo, Utah: Brigham Young University Press, 1974.

——. *Great Basin Kingdom—An Economic History of the Latter-day Saints 1830–1900.* Cambridge: Harvard University Press, 1958.

——. and Bitton, Davis. *The Mormon Experience—A History of the Latter-day Saints.* New York: Vintage Books, 1980.

—— Fox, Feramorz Y.; and May, Dean L. *Building the City of God.* Salt Lake City: Deseret Book Company, 1976.

Bailey, Paul. *The Armies of God.* Garden City, New York: Doubleday and Company, Inc., 1968.

Barron, Howard H. *Orson Hyde-Missionary-Apostle-Colonizer.* Bountiful, Utah: Horizon Publishers, 1977.

The Book of Mormon. Translated by Joseph Smith Jr. Salt Lake City: The Church of Jesus Christ of Latter-day Saints, 1959.

Bradford, William J. A. *Notes on the Northwest, or Valley of the Upper Mississippi.* New York: Wiley, Putnam, 1846.

Brodie, Fawn M. *No Man Knows My History: The Life of Joseph Smith, the Mormon Prophet.* 2nd ed., rev. New York: Alfred A. Knopf, 1971.

Brooks, Juanita, ed. *On the Mormon Frontier—The Diary of Hosea Stout 1844–1861.* 2 vols. Salt Lake City: University of Utah Press, 1964.

Brown, James S. *Giant of the Land: Life of a Pioneer.* Salt Lake City: Bookcraft, Inc., 1960.

Cannon, Donald Q., and Cook, Lyndon W., eds. *Far West Record—Minutes of the Church of Jesus Christ of Latter-day Saints, 1830–1844.* Salt Lake City, Deseret Book Company, 1983.

Carson, Gerald. *The Old Country Store.* New York: E. P. Dulton and Co., Inc., 1965.

Carter, Kate B., gen. ed. *Heart Throbs of the West.* 12 vols. Salt Lake City: Daughters of the Utah Pioneers, 1947. Vol. 8: "Journal of Louisa Barnes Pratt."

——. *The Mormon Battalion.* Salt Lake City: Daughters of the Utah Pioneers, 1956.

Chittenden, Hiram Martin. *The American Fur Trade of the Far West.* 2 vols. Stanford: Academic Reprints, 1954.

——. and Richardson, Alfred Talbot. *Life, Letters and Travels of Father Pierre-Jean De Smet, S.J. 1801–1873* 4 vols. New York: Francis P. Harper, 1905.

Christensen, Clare B. *Before and After Mt. Pisgah.* Salt Lake City: Clare B. Christensen, 1979.

Clarke, Dwight L. *Stephen Watts Kearny—Soldier of the West.* Norman: University of Oklahoma Press, 1961.

Clayton, William. *William Clayton's Journal—A Daily Record of the Journey of the Original Company of "Mormon" Pioneers from Nauvoo, Illinois, to the Valley of the Great Salt Lake.* Salt Lake City: Deseret News, 1921.

De Voto, Bernard. *The Year of Decision, 1846.* Boston: Little, Brown and Company, 1943.

The Doctrine and Covenants of The Church of Jesus Christ of Latter-day Saints. Salt Lake City: Deseret Book Company, 1967.

Dufour, Charles L. *The Mexican War—A Compact History 1846–1848.* New York: Hawthorn Books, Inc., 1968.

Flanders, Robert Bruce. *Nauvoo—Kingdom on the Mississippi.* Urbana: University of Illinois Press, 1965.

Frémont, John C. *Report of the Exploring Expedition to the Rocky Mountains in the Year 1842, and to Oregon and North California in the Years 1843–44.* Washington: Blair and Rivers, 1845.

Golder, Frank Alfred. *The March of the Mormon Battalion from Council Bluffs to California.* New York: The Century Co., 1928.

Gregg, Thomas. *History of Hancock County, Illinois.* Chicago: Charles C. Chapman & Co., 1880.

Hall, William. *The Abominations of Mormonism Exposed Containing Many Facts and Doctrines Concerning That Singular People During Seven Years' Membership With Them from 1840 to 1847.* Cincinnati: I. Hart and Company, 1851.

Hansen, Klaus. *Quest for Empire—The Political Kingdom of God and the Council of Fifty in Mormon History.* Lansing: Michigan State University Press, 1967.

Harlan, Edgar Ruby. *A Narrative History of the People of Iowa.* Chicago: The American Historical Society, Inc., 1931.

Hill, Edward E. *The Office of Indian Affairs, 1824–1880: Historical Sketches.* New York: Clearwater Publishing Company, Inc. 1974.

Hirshson, Stanley P. *The Lion of the Lord—A Biography of Brigham Young.* New York: Alfred A. Knopf, 1969.

History of Holt and Atchison Counties, Missouri. N.a., n.p., 1882.

History of Pottawattamie County Iowa. Chicago: O. L. Baskin & Co., Historical Publications, 1883.

Horne, F. D. B. ed. *Autobiography of George W. Bean.* Salt Lake City: Utah Printing Company, 1945.

Hymns—The Church of Jesus Christ of Latter-day Saints. Salt Lake City: Deseret Book Company, 1973.

Jackson, Donald, and Spence, Mary Lee, eds. *The Expeditions of John Charles Fremont, Travels from 1838 to 1844.* Urbana: University of Illinois Press, 1970.

Jenson, Andrew. *Church Chronology—A Record of Important Events.* Salt Lake City: Deseret News, 1914.

———. *Latter-day Saint Biographical Encyclopedia.* 4 vols. Salt Lake City: Andrew Jenson Memorial Association, 1936.

Journal of Discourses. 26 vols. 1854–86. Lithographic Reprint. Salt Lake City, 1966.

Kane, Thomas L. *"The Mormons." A Discourse Delivered Before the Historical Society of Pennsylvania, March 16, 1850.* Philadelphia: King and Baird Printers, 1850.

Kelly, Charles, ed. *Journals of John D. Lee 1846–47 and 1859.* Salt Lake City: Western Printing Company, 1938.

Kimball, Stanley B. *Discovering Mormon Trails New York to California 1831–1868.* Salt Lake City: Deseret Book Company, 1979.

Launius, Roger D. *Zion's Camp: Expedition to Missouri, 1834.* Independence, Mo.: Herald Publishing House, 1984.

Linforth, James. *Route from Liverpool to Great Salt Lake Valley.* Liverpool, England: Franklin O. Richards, 1855.

Linn, William Alexander. *The Story of the Mormons from the Date of Their Origin to the Year 1901.* New York City: The Macmillan Company, 1923.

Mattes, Merrill J. *The Great Platte River Road: The Covered Wagon Main Line Via Fort Kearny to Fort Laramie.* The Nebraska State Historical Society History Series. Vol. 25. Lincoln: Nebraska State Historical Society, 1969.

Morgan, Dale L. *The Great Salt Lake.* American Lake Series, edited by Milo M. Quaife. Indianapolis: The Bobbs Merrill Company, 1947.

Morton, J. Sterling. *Illustrated History of Nebraska.* Lincoln: Jacob North and Company, 1906.

The Nauvoo Temple 1841–1865. Nauvoo Restoration Corporation, 1977.

Newhall, J. B. *A Glimpse of Iowa in 1846; or the Emigrant's Guide and State Directory with a Description of the New Purchase.* Burlington, Iowa: W. D. Skillman, Publisher, 1846.

Nibley, Preston. *Exodus to Greatness: The Story of the Mormon Migration.* Salt Lake City: Deseret News, 1947.

Pletcher, David M. *The Diplomacy of Annexation: Texas, Oregon, and the Mexican War.* Columbia: University of Missouri Press, 1973.

Polk, James Knox. *The Diary of James K. Polk During His Presidency, 1845 to 1849.* Edited by Milo M. Quaife, 2 vols. Chicago: A. C. McClurg and Company, 1910.

Pratt, Parley P. *Autobiography of Parley Parker Pratt.* Late edition. Salt Lake City: Deseret Book Co., 1980.

Quaife, Milo. *The Kingdom of Saint James: A Narrative of the Mormons.* Newham, Connecticut: Yale University Press, 1930.

Ralston, Russell F. *Succession in Presidency and Authority.* Independence: Herald Publishing House, 1958.

Reid, J. M. *Sketches and Anecdotes of the Old Settlers, and New Comers, The Mormon Bandits and Danite Band.* Keokuk, Iowa: R. B. Ogden, Publisher, 1876.

Rich, Russell R. *Ensign to the Nations—A History of the Church from 1846 to the Present.* Provo, Utah: Brigham Young University Press, 1972.

Roberts, Brigham Henry. *A Comprehensive History of The Church of Jesus Christ of Latter-day Saints.* 6 vols. Salt Lake City: Deseret News Press, 1930.

———. *The Mormon Battalion: Its History and Achievements.* Salt Lake City: Deseret News Press, 1919.

———. *Succession in the Presidency of the Church of Jesus Christ of Latter-day Saints.* Salt Lake City: George Q. Cannon and Sons, 1900.

Sage, Leland L. *A History of Iowa.* Ames: Iowa State University Press, 1974.

Shafer, Joseph, ed. *Across the Plains in 1850 by John Steele.* Chicago, 1930.

Smith, Joseph, Jr. *History of the Church of Jesus Christ of Latter-day Saints.* Edited by Brigham Henry Roberts. 7 vols. Salt Lake City: Deseret Book Company, 1973.

Smith, Joseph Fielding. *Succession in the Presidency of the Church of Jesus Christ of Latter-day Saints.* Salt Lake City, 1964.

Spitz, Lewis. *The Renaissance and Reformation Movements.* Chicago: Rand McNally Co., 1971.

Stegner, Wallace. *The Gathering of Zion—The Story of the Mormon Trail.* New York: McGraw-Hill Book Company, 1964.

Stenhouse, T. B. H. *The Rocky Mountain Saints: A Full and Complete History of the Mormons.* New York: D. Appleton & Co., 1873.

Sunder, John E. *Joshua Pilcher—Fur Trader and Indian Agent.* Norman: University of Oklahoma Press, 1968.

Todd, Rev. John. *Early Settlement and Growth of Western Iowa or Reminiscences.* Des Moines: The Historical Department of Iowa, 1906.

Tullidge, Edward W. *The Women of Mormondom.* New York City, 1877; Lithograph Reprint, 1957.

Tyler, Daniel. *A Concise History of the Mormon Battalion in the Mexican War 1846–1847.* Glorieta, N.M.: The Rio Grande Press, Inc., 1969.

Unruh, John D., Jr. *The Plains Across—The Overland Emigrants and the Trans-Mississippi West 1840–60.* Urbana: University of Illinois Press, 1979.

Winther, Oscar G., ed. *The Private Papers and Diary of Thomas Leiper Kane A Friend of the Mormons.* San Francisco: Gelber-Lilienthal, Inc., 1937.

Young, Brigham. *Manuscript History of Brigham Young.* Compiled by Elden J. Watson. Salt Lake City: Elden J. Watson, 1971.

Zobell, Albert L., Jr. *Sentinel in the East: A Biography of Thomas L. Kane.* Salt Lake City: Nicholas G. Morgan Sr., 1965.

Articles and Task Papers

Aitchison, Clyde B. "The Mormon Settlements in the Missouri Valley." *The Quarterly of the Oregon Historical Society* 8 (1907): 276–89.

Andrus, Hyrum. "Joseph Smith and the West." *Brigham Young University Studies* 2 (Summer 1960): 129–47.

Arrington, Leonard J. "'In Honorable Remembrance': Thomas L. Kane's Services to the Mormons." *Brigham Young University Studies* 21 (Fall 1981): 389–402.

———. and Esplin, Ronald K. "The Role of the Council of the Twelve During Brigham Young's Presidency of the Church of Jesus Christ of Latter-day Saints." *Task Papers in LDS History* 31. Salt Lake City: Historical Department of The Church of Jesus Christ of Latter-day Saints, 1979.

Beecher, Mary Ursenbach. "Women at Winter Quarters." *Sunstone* 8 (July and August 1983): 11–19.

Bitton, Davis. "Mormons in Texas: The Ill-fated Wight Colony 1844–1858." *Arizona and the West* 2 (Spring 1969): 5–26.

Bloomer, D. C. "The Mormons in Iowa." *Annals of Iowa* 2 (January 1897): 586–602.

———. "The Old Blockhouse in Council Bluffs." *Annals of Iowa* 2 (October 1896): 549–52.

Christian, Lewis Clark. "Mormon Foreknowledge of the West." *Brigham Young University Studies* 21 (Fall 1981): 403–15.

Coates, Lawrence G. "Brigham Young and Mormon Indian Policies: The Formative Period, 1836–1851." *Brigham Young University Studies* 18 (Spring 1978): 428–52.

Cornwall, Rebecca Foster, and Arrington, Leonard J. "Perpetuation of a Myth: Mormon Danites in Five Western Novels, 1840–90." *Brigham Young University Studies* 23 (Spring 1983): 147–65.

Dahl, Paul E. "'All Is Well . . .': The Story of the Hymn That Went Around the World." *Brigham Young University Studies* 21 (Fall 1981): 515–27.

Doty, James L., Jr. "The Beginnings of the Reorganization of the Omaha-Council Bluffs Area." *Restoration Trail Forum* 7 (February 1981): 1, 4, and 6.

Esplin, Ronald K. "Joseph, Brigham and the Twelve: A Succession of Continuity." *Brigham Young University Studies* 21 (Summer 1981): 301–334.

———. "Brigham Young and the Power of Apostleship: Defending the Kingdom Through Prayer, 1844–1845." Sidney B. Sperry Symposium Sesquicentennial Look at Church History, January 16, 1980.

Evans, Priscilla Ann. "Merchant Gristmills and Communities, 1820–1880: An Economic Relationship." *Missouri Historical Review* 68 (April 1974): 317–26.

Gentry, Leland H. "The Danite Band of 1838." *Brigham Young University Studies* 14 (Summer 1974): 421–50.

———. "The Mormon Way Stations: Garden Grove and Mt. Pisgah." *Brigham Young University Studies* 21 (Fall 1981): 445–61.

Goates, Lesley. "Tragedy of Winter Quarters." 1967. Unpaginated. On file at the LDS Church Archives.

Godfrey, Kenneth W. "Winter Quarters: Glimmering Glimpses Into Mormon Religious and Social Life." An unpublished paper given at the Mormon History Association and in the author's possession.

Grant, Mary Helen. "Incidents in the Life of Mary Helen Grant." *Journal of History* 10 (April 1917) 2: 168–202.

Green, Norma Kidd. "The Presbyterian Mission to the Omaha Indian Tribe." *Nebraska History* 48 (Autumn 1967).

"History of the Cutlerite Faction of the Latter-day Saints." *Journal of History* 13 (October 1920): 454–57.

Holbrook, Leona. "Dancing As An Aspect of Early Mormon (Church of Jesus Christ of Latter-day Saints) and Utah Culture," in "Papers Delivered at the Third Canadian Symposium on History of Sport and Physical Education, 19 August 1974."

Holmes, Gail George. "Historic Mormon Sites to Visit in Greater Omaha-Council Bluffs." Leaflet, n.d.

———. "Reflections on Winter Quarters." Unpublished paper, n.d. Utah State Historical Society.

———. "Winter Quarters Revisited—Untold Stories of the Seven-Year Story of Mormons in the Missouri Valley 1846–53." Omaha, n.d.

"Incidents in the Life of Mary Helen Grant." *Journal of History* 10 (April 1917): 77.

Irving, Gordon. "The Law of Adoption: One Phase of the Development of the Mormon Concept of Salvation, 1830–1900." *Brigham Young University Studies* 14 (Spring 1974): 291–314.

Jones, Gerald E. "An Early Mormon Settlement in South Dakota." *South Dakota History* 1 (Spring 1971): 119–31.

———. "Some Forgotten Pioneers: The Emmett Company of 1844."

Eighth Annual Sidney B. Sperry Symposium (1980), pp. 193–209.
Kimball, Stanley B. "The Iowa Trek of 1846." *Ensign* 2 (June 1972): 36–45.
———. "The Mormon Trail Network in Iowa 1838–1863: A New Look." *Brigham Young University Studies* 21 (Fall 1981): 417–30.
———. "The Saints and St. Louis, 1831–1857: An Oasis of Tolerance and Security." *Brigham Young University Studies* 13 (Summer 1973): 489–519.
Luce, W. Ray. "The Mormon Battalion: A Historical Accident?" *Utah State Historical Quarterly* 42 (Winter 1974): 27–38.
McLear, Patrick E. "The St. Louis Cholera Epidemic of 1849." *Missouri Historical Review* 63 (January 1969): 171–81.
McMurray, W. Grant. "True Son of a True Father: Joseph Smith III and the Succession Question." In *Restoration Studies, I, Sesquicentennial Edition,* 131–41. Edited by Maurice L. Draper and Clare D. Vlahos. Independence: Temple School, the Auditorium, 1980.
Mattes, Merrill J. "The Jumping Off Places on the Overland Trail." In *The Frontier Re-examined,* edited by John Francis McDermott. Urbana: University of Illinois Press, 1967.
Mattison, Ray H. "The Indian Frontier on the Upper Missouri to 1865." *Nebraska History* 39 (September 1958): 241–66.
———. "The Upper Missouri Fur Trade: Its Methods of Operation." *Nebraska History* 42 (March 1961): 1–28.
Mills, H. W. "De Tal Palo Tal Astilla." In *Historical Society of Southern California Annual Publications* 10:86–173. Los Angeles: Historical Society of Southern California, 1917.
The Nauvoo Temple 1841–1865. Nauvoo Restoration Corporation, 1977.
Pearson, Carol Lynn. "'Nine Children Were Born.': A Historical Problem from the Sugar Creek Episode." *Brigham Young University Studies* 21 (Fall 1981): 441–44.
Petersen, William J. "The Mormon Trail of 1846." *Palimpsest* 47 (September 1966): 353–67.
Quinn, Michael D. "The Council of Fifty and Its Members, 1844 to 1945." *Brigham Young University Studies* 20 (Winter 1980): 163–97.
Russell, William D. "King James Strang: Joseph Smith's Successor?" In *The Restoration Movement: Essays in Mormon History,* 231–56. Edited by F. Mark McKiernan, Alma R. Blair, and Paul M. Edwards. Lawrence, Kansas: Coronado Press, 1973.
Sorensen, Stephen J. "Civil and Criminal Jurisdiction of Latter-day Saint Bishops and High Council Courts, 1847–52." *Task Paper in LDS History* 17. Salt Lake City: Historical Department of the Church of Jesus Christ of Latter-day Saints, 1977.

Stevenson, C. Stanley. "Expeditions Into Dakota." In *South Dakota Historical Collections* 9:347–49. Compiled by the State Department of History. Pierre: Hipple Printing Co., 1918.

"Testimony of Elder Levi Graybill." *Journal of History* 4 (January 1911): 109.

Trennert, Robert A., Jr. "The Mormons and the Office of Indian Affairs: The Conflict Over Winter Quarters, 1846–1848." *Nebraska History* 53 (Fall 1972): 381–400.

Van der Zee, Jacob. "Episodes in the Early History of the Western Iowa Country." *Iowa Journal of History and Politics* 11 (July 1913): 323–63.

———. "The Mormon Trails in Iowa." *The Iowa Journal of History and Politics* 12 (January 1914): 3–16.

Watson, Wingfield. "An Open Letter to B. H. Roberts, Salt Lake City, Utah," dated 13 November 1894. A 30-page unbound pamphlet in the RLDS Library and Archives. Also includes a few pages entitled "A Word to George Q. Cannon," 1896.

Whitney, Helen Mar Kimball. "Our Travels Beyond the Mississippi." *Woman's Exponent* 12 (1883–84) and 13 (1884–85).

———. "Scenes and Incidents at Winter Quarters." *Woman's Exponent* 13 (1884–85), 14 (1885–86), and 15 (1886–87).

Wyman, Walker D. "Council Bluffs and the Westward Movement." *Iowa Journal of History* 47 (April 1949): 99–118.

Young, Clara Decker. "A Woman's Experience with the Pioneer Band." *Utah State Historical Quarterly* 12 (1946).

Government Publications

U.S. Congress. House. *Report of the Commissioner of Indian Affairs.* 30th Cong., 2d Sess., 1848.

U.S. Congress. Senate. *Annual Report of the Commissioner of Indian Affairs.* 27th Cong., 3d Sess., 1842.

U.S. Congress. Senate. *Report of the Commissioner of Indian Affairs.* 28th Cong., 1st Sess., 1843.

U.S. Congress. Senate. *Report of the Commissioner of Indian Affairs.* 29th Cong., 1st Sess., 1845.

U.S. Congress. Senate. *Annual Report of the Commissioner of Indian Affairs.* 30th Cong., 1st Sess., 1847.

U.S. Congress. Senate. *Report to Illustrate a Map of the Hydrographical Basin of the Upper Mississippi River* by J. N. Nicollet. Executive Document. 30th Cong., 1st Sess., 1847.

NEWSPAPERS

Daily Missouri Republican (St. Louis), 15 July 1846.
The Frontier Guardian (Kanesville), 7 March 1849.
The Gospel Herald, 29 June 1848.
Hancock Eagle, (Nauvoo) 8 May 1846.
The Latter-day Saints Millenial Star, (England) Vol. 8, Chapter 5.
The Mormon Neighbor (Nauvoo), 1 May 1843.
Northern Islander (Beaver Island, Michigan), 20 September 1855.
St. Louis Weekly Union, 30 March 1847.
The Voree Herald, March 1846; April 1846.

THESES AND DISSERTATIONS

Bachman, Danel W. "A Study of the Mormon Practice of Plural Marriage Before the Death of Joseph Smith." (Master's thesis; Purdue University, 1975)

Bennett, Richard E. "A Study of the Church of Jesus Christ of Latter-day Saints in Upper Canada, 1830–1850" (Master's thesis; Brigham Young University, 1975)

Christian, Lewis Clark. "A Study of the Mormon Westward Migration Between February 1846 and July 1847 with Emphasis on and Evaluation of the Factors that Led to the Mormon Choice of Salt Lake Valley as the Site of Their Initial Colony" (Dissertation; Brigham Young University, 1976)

Ehat, Andrew F. "Joseph Smith's Introduction to Temple Ordinances and the 1844 Mormon Succession Question" (Master's thesis; Brigham Young University, 1982)

Flanders, Robert Bruce. "Nauvoo—Kingdom of the Mississippi" (Dissertation; University of Wisconsin, 1964)

Hansen, Margaret E. "Removal of the Indians from Nebraska" (Master's thesis; Colorado State College of Education, 1949)

Hill, Marvin S. "An Historical Study of the Life of Orson Hyde, Early Mormon Missionary and Apostle From 1805–1852" (Master's thesis; Brigham Young University, 1955)

Lawson, Roy Franklin. "The Mormons: Their Trek Across Iowa and Their Settlement in Kanesville" (Master's thesis; Creighton University, 1937)

Peterson, Paul Henry. "A Historical Analysis of the Word of Wisdom" (Master's thesis; Brigham Young University, 1972)

Shumway, Ernest Widtsoe. "History of Winter Quarters, Nebraska, 1846–1848" (Master's thesis; Brigham Young University, 1953)

Thomas, Matthew Anthony. "Disease in a Mormon Community,

Nauvoo, Illinois: 1839–1846" (B.A. thesis; Harvard University, 1977)

Webb, Lynn Robert. "The Contributions of the Temporary Settlements Garden Grove, Mount Pisgah and Kanesville, Iowa, to Mormon Emigration, 1846–52" (Master's thesis; Brigham Young University, 1954)

Wesson, Karl E. "Dance in the Church of Jesus Christ of Latter-day Saints 1830–1940" (Master's thesis; Brigham Young University, 1975)

Wyman, Walker D. "The Missouri River Towns in the Westward Movement" (Dissertation; Iowa State University, 1935)

Yurtinus, John F. "A Ram in the Thicket: The Mormon Battalion in the Mexican War" (Dissertation; Brigham Young University, 1975)

INDEX